The Art of Ceramics

European Ceramic Design 1500–1830

The Art of Ceramics

European Ceramic Design
1500–1830

HOWARD COUTTS

PUBLISHED FOR

THE BARD GRADUATE CENTER FOR STUDIES IN THE DECORATIVE ARTS, NEW YORK

by Yale University Press • New Haven and London

Designed by Beatrix McIntyre
Set in Bembo by Best-set Typesetter Ltd., Hong Kong
Printed in Italy

Library of Congress Cataloging-in-Publication Data
Coutts, Howard.
        The art of ceramics: European ceramic design 1500–1830/Howard Coutts.
            p. cm.
        Includes bibliographical references and index.
        ISBN 0-300-08387-4 (cloth:alk.paper)
            1. Pottery, European. 2. Design—Europe—History. 3. Art and society—Europe—History.
NK4083.C68 2001
738/.094/0903 21
[B]   00-054077

Preface

Ceramics are a long-standing love of mine, fostered by my mother and grandmother. When I began work as a curatorial assistant at the Victoria and Albert Museum in 1978, first in the Library and then in the Department of Prints and Drawings, I was able to see how they fitted into the history of European art and design, and patterns of luxury spending among the very rich.

The chance to write this study came in 1987 with a three-year Research Fellowship in the Art History Department of the University of St Andrews, sponsored by the Leverhulme Trust, held in conjunction with the Royal Museum of Scotland, Edinburgh. This gave me the opportunity to work with their extensive collections of European ceramics, and in particular to use their library resources, built up by Revel Oddy in the 1970s. For their help and assistance I am deeply grateful, and also to Elizabeth Conran and my colleagues at The Bowes Museum for the encouragement to finish it.

Many specialists have answered queries, or commented on individual chapters of this work; it is perhaps invidious to mention names, but I am particular grateful to John Mallet, Timothy Wilson, Maureen Mellor, David Gaimster, the late T.H. Clarke, Godfrey Evans, Oliver Impey, J. D. Van Dam, Charlotte Jacob-Hanson, Hilary Young, Aileen Dawson and Ivan Day. It is perhaps a truism to say that any mistakes that remain are my own, but it is especially true in this case.

The title of Chapter 7, 'The Ascendancy of Sèvres' is taken from Gerald Reitlinger's *The Economics of Taste*, vol. 2, 'The Rise and Fall of objets d'art prices since 1750', a volume that did so much to stimulate my interest in decorative arts during my student days, and take them as seriously as the fine arts. My final thanks are to John Nicoll and Beatrix McIntyre at Yale University Press, who have seen this project through to publication.

Contents

Detail of fig. 1. Diego Velazquez (1599–1660), *Old Woman Cooking Eggs*, Oil on canvas, 100.5 × 119.5 cm. National Gallery of Scotland, Edinburgh.

Introduction

The regular progress of cultivated life is from necessaries to accommodations, from accommodations to ornaments
Sir Joshua Reynolds, dedication to *Seven Discourses*, 1778[1]

There have been many books on European ceramics in the period covered by this study, 1500–1830; the subject has been avidly researched since the mid-nineteenth century at least, when the systematic collecting of European ceramics first began.[2] The literature is enormous and often remarkably detailed; we often know where items were made, how they were manufactured, and the range of wares made by the different centres of manufacture. However, until recently, less attention has been paid to the quality of their visual impact, or their place within early modern European society. The purpose of this study is to analyse ceramics in visual and historical terms, and place them within the history of European design.

Ceramics – objects made of baked clay – are one of the most enduring of human artefacts. They do not, and did not, exist in isolation, but form part of a broader pattern of the productivity and economic activity of past cultures and can be used to reconstruct and interpret aspects of those cultures. Being of baked clay, they are highly durable and, even when broken, can provide information about the society that produced them. Their value is thus proportionally greater to the historian who lacks written records, most obviously the archaeologist, who may well find that ceramics – albeit in broken form – form the largest product of his or her excavations.[3]

Ceramics have a multitude of uses, and their existence can be found at virtually all levels of society. Since the means of their creation subjects ceramics to extreme temperatures, the medium is especially useful for items that need to be heat- or weather-resistant, such as pots for cooking, bricks for building, tiles for covering roofs, pipes for water and waste disposal, and, most recently, items for electrical insulation. If covered in a thin layer of glass – a 'glaze' – they become non-porous and thus especially useful for domestic items for eating and drinking. The variety of uses has increased through the years as the materials have been refined and methods and techniques of manufacture grown more sophisticated.[4]

This study focuses on ceramics made for domestic use, but only those which show a degree of elaboration of form or decoration that places them beyond ordinary 'utilitarian' items. We may take as our starting point Velazquez's *Old Woman Cooking Eggs* in the National Gallery of Scotland in Edinburgh (fig. 1).[5] It was painted in Seville, in about 1618, and shows an old woman cooking in her home, surrounded by a few simple utilitarian vessels of domestic use. In the foreground the artist has carefully portrayed a variety of simple ceramic items, such as two jugs, a dish, and a cooking bowl on a heater, of a type that were manufactured in Europe for everyday use right into the nineteenth century. The decoration on them is relatively slight, it probably did not contribute greatly to their cost, and they would have had little function as symbols of wealth or taste in seventeenth-century Spain. It is decoration

Detail of fig. 125. Chamber pot (*bourdalou*). Courtesy of Brian Haughton Antiques, London.

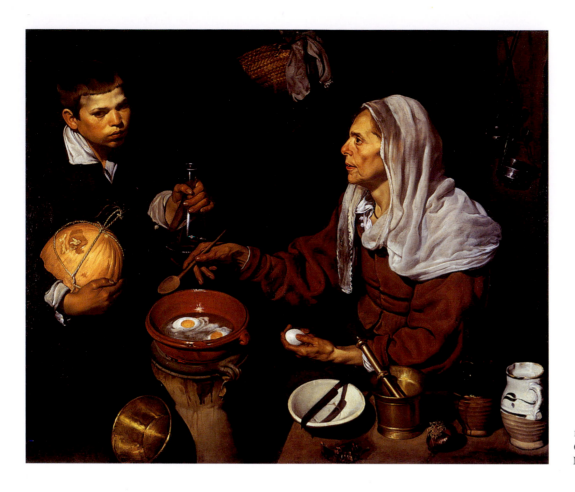

1 Diego Velazquez (1599–1660), *Old Woman Cooking Eggs*, Oil on canvas, 100.5 × 119.5 cm. National Gallery of Scotland, Edinburgh.

and shapes beyond the purely functional that will form the focus of this study.

For this purpose, I shall take as a basic ceramic item the simple round pot made on the potter's wheel – though this technique in itself may be taken as an example of economic and industrial sophistication – which, with the application of a glaze, is suitable for most forms of domestic use. Any moulded, applied, or coloured decoration added to this basic pot implies an element of show or display. This 'extra' or visual use of an object would have been recognised from a very early stage in the manufacturing process as something requiring special consideration, as when the rock-crystal carver, Jacopo da Trezzo, wrote to Duke Cosimo de'Medici in Florence in 1550 to enquire whether the cup he had commissioned was 'to drink from or only to look well'.[6] Similarly the director of the Sèvres porcelain factory, the comte d'Angiviller, writing of some elaborately decorated cups and saucers, noted that 'porcelain with some enamelling is often more an object of decoration than everyday usage'.[7] This element of display naturally reached its peak in objects made for kings and other heads of state,[8] as objects in royal use represented the wealth and power of the state, and were intended to impress both subjects and emissaries from foreign countries. Celia Fiennes, on her travels through England in 1698, noted acutely that the elaborate throne and canopy at Windsor Castle were 'newly made to give audience to the French Embassadour [sic] to shew the grandeur and magnificence of the British Monarch – some of these foolerys are requisite sometimes to create admiration and regard to keep up the state of a Kingdom and nation'.[9]

The capacity of objects to mean something beyond their ostensible 'useful' function and to tell us about the lives and status of their first owners has long been recognised, and forms the basis of most modern 'material-culture studies' (fig. 2).[10] This approach to artefacts analyses them in terms of their social function and meaning; it has its origins in Karl Marx's division of objects into 'use' value and 'exchange' value, that is, the difference between the ostensible usefulness of things, and their values as 'commodities' – goods with a socially recognised value, such as gold and silver, which can be bought and sold. This interpretation was developed by the great economist Thorstein Bunde Veblen (1857–1929) who, at the end of the nineteenth century, began to discuss man-made artefacts from the point of view of a surplus of production, used by what he termed a 'leisure class' which indulged in extravagant spending or 'conspicuous consumption'.[11] He went on to discuss basic human behaviour such as eating, drinking and the wearing of clothes in terms of social display, which could show degrees of 'differentiation within the class'.[12] Veblen's approach has been further developed by later theorists, who tend to stress the seamless link between basic functional artefacts and items of decoration and display, since they both represent what has been called 'abstract social labour', that is, the quantity of workmanship put into an object, which can represent the spending power or social standing of its owner. Some writers, such as Baudrillard, maintain that there is often no real distinction between the two, since frequently what we deem 'useful' in our society would be considered a luxury in other societies.[13]

Nowhere is this truer than in the development of the European rituals of eating and drinking, in which increasingly elaborate foods were served in specialised utensils in a specific order, in a manner that went beyond the mere satiation of appetite. This reached a peak in the development of formal dining in the seventeenth and eighteenth centuries, as the habit of serving a variety of foods in courses, all in particular types of container, led to a vast new range of ceramic types, and forms a major theme of this study, although for the wealthiest classes items of gold or silver still tended to be preferred. The importance of formal dining in the early modern period was recognised

2 Tapestry of a housewife on a mule, with the inscription *ICH HET HUSRAT G[E]NUG WER ICH SUS IMAS FUOG* (*I have household articles enough, otherwise I would not be so important and have such authority*) Swiss, *c.*1465. The Burrell Collection, Glasgow.

by writers of the time: its purpose was seldom the simple satiation of the appetites of the hungry, so much as to entertain one's friends and superiors and confirm one's place within a hierarchical social grouping, as described by writers such as Sydney Smith (1771–1845).[14] Often a certain amount of political discussion and activity would have taken place, especially in eighteenth-century Britain, to which luxury foods and ceramic items formed a suitable background. This trend reached its apogee in England in the early nineteenth century, when fashionable novelists such as Theodore Hook allowed much of their plot to revolve around the dinner party, the setting for political and social intrigue.[15]

Elaborate dinner parties required fine utensils appropriate to both the food that was served and the diners who ate it. In this respect ceramics can take on a further meaning, as indicators of negative differences in class and culture, especially when a mistake in correct usage has been made. The aforementioned Hook gleefully commented on the *nouveau riche's* inability to decode the right way of holding a dinner party, even with the aid of a vast quantity of rich plate.[16] It is not that food or drink in general tastes any different in variously shaped containers, but that the correct ordering of artefacts was regarded as essential to a well-run dinner party, and misunderstanding of this order revealed ignorance of tacit social codes. Bertrand Russell recounted how, as a youth of seventeen, he was left alone after dinner with the puzzled Prime Minister William Gladstone, who said to him 'This is very good port they've given me, but why have they given me it in a claret glass?'.[17] Gladstone was not complaining that the wine tasted any different in a claret glass, but that his sense of decorum relating to the organisation of a well-run dinner party had been breached.

Sometimes changes in diet could in themselves lead to new forms of ceramics. The spread of tea, chocolate and coffee drinking among the rich in the seventeenth century required a whole new range of drinking vessels designed to withstand hot liquids.[18] Such new drinks were at first perceived as products primarily for the rich and affluent, but their consumption soon spread throughout society, reaching the middle and working classes in the eighteenth century.[19] This in turn was seen as a threat to the good ordering of society, and contemporary commentators such as Josiah Hanway, in his *Essay on Tea* (1757), railed against 'beggars' and 'common labourers' who could be seen in public drinking tea out of porcelain bowls instead of their traditional beverages.[20]

A further stimulus to the creation of elaborately decorated ceramics is the concept of ever-changing fashion, whereby usable items were discarded, not simply when they were broken or worn out, but when they no longer represented the latest taste or fashion, something essential in display pieces for the rich. In this respect, the history of European ceramics is to some extent the history of style. Central to this idea is the concept of 'taste', a knowledgeable appreciation of form and style held only by the wealthier classes, who could afford both education and the paraphernalia of wealthy living.[21] This is particularly true of ceramics designed for room decoration, and the seventeenth century saw the development of the 'china cabinet', a room full of expensive ceramics, usually Oriental, which in turn was supplanted in the eighteenth century, when the 'vase madness' of the 1760s saw the replacement of Eastern porcelain vases with those of European manufacture in the neo-classical style. The object-type remained the same or similar, but its style and decoration altered, creating a 'market opportunity' for enterprising ceramic manufacturers: Josiah Wedgwood wrote to his business partner Thomas Bentley in 1767 that 'Novelty is a great matter in *slight* matters of taste'.[22] In this respect one would like to see more studies of shopping as a leisure activity;[23] the records of such London merchants as Thomas Bentley, the partner of Josiah Wedgwood, and William Duesbury of the Derby factory, make clear the tremendous effort that was put into cajoling a possibly reluctant but fashionable clien-

3 Earthenware toy cradle, decorated with slips, Staffordshire, *c.*1800, and porcelain vase decorated in *pâte-sur-pâte* by Léon-Marc-Emmanuel Solon, Minton, *c.*1870. The Bowes Museum, Barnard Castle, Co. Durham.

tèle into purchasing wares in the latest taste, when they probably already had more than enough for everyday use.[24]

One by-product of the idea of rapidly changing styles and fashions is the concept of nostalgia for a certain period in the past, which could be recalled with the aid of objects from that period. It is perhaps significant that the fashion for collecting antiques (in the modern sense of good-quality objects from the relatively recent past) developed in the nineteenth century, when sudden changes in society and technology led to an interest in objects that had belonged to the wealthier classes of the preceding century. In the field of ceramics this interest began with a renewed appreciation of the finer and more elaborate productions from Meissen, Sèvres, and other major European porcelain factories of the mid-eighteenth century, but soon came to embrace the cruder pottery made in Staffordshire and elsewhere in Europe for people of lesser wealth. This latter interest was encouraged by the emphasis placed on the hand-made, skilled craftsmanship and 'truth to materials' (i.e. making objects in which the technique of construction is thought to be sympathetic to the materials used) by exponents of the Arts and Crafts Movement. By the end of nineteenth century the concept of 'the art of the potter' had developed, in which ceramics began to be discussed and appraised in terms of what one man – a skilled craftsman – could make on his own with simple clays, without recourse to separate workshops for enamelling, gilding and firing. This approach to ceramics was pioneered by Louis-Marc-Emmanuel Solon (1835–1913), who in *The Art of the Old English Potter* of 1883 was the first to analyse a whole range of 'simple' English country pottery, apparently quite at variance with the elaborate *pâte-sur-pâte* porcelain that Solon himself had carried out for Minton's (fig. 3).[25] The point was that he felt he had something in common with the potters of the past, in that they were both exercising their skill in manipulating materials for the benefit of humanity, and he is correspondingly scathing of the work of the unskilled. In his great book *The Ancient Art of Stoneware in the Low Countries and Germany* of 1892 he contrasted the 'coarse' labourer who made simple pots with the 'elegant vase' or 'graceful ewer' made by an 'ingenious and skilful craftsman',[26] although he did not underestimate the debt that the latter owed to the former.[27]

This approach inspired a number of books on ceramics that interpreted ceramics aesthetically in terms of what one man could make using 'natural' materials and simple technology, usually little more than clay, a potter's wheel and a kiln.[28] It was about this time that simple handmade pottery came to replace lavishly decorated and moulded porcelain in the affections of collectors and the general public, and the highest praise was given to objects that were relatively simple in form. The emphasis was on artefacts that could be appreciated through handling rather than simply looked at and admired, although the simple and pure shapes of early Chinese porcelain were especially esteemed. Though this approach has many virtues – most notably in its understanding of the technical processes whereby pieces are made, and how the materials are used – it does tend to neglect the great mass of ceramics that we are familiar with today. They are usually the product of not just one man but a whole industrial production line, starting with a design or designer who may live many miles away from the actual site of production, or may even have lived in a different period. Most European ceramics of 1500–1830 were not made by single potters working happily with their materials and producing wares for a public that regarded pots as individual works of art. Excavations at sites such as the delftware works at London reveal piles of fused plates (wasters), clearly not made individually, but made in masses, and probably painted by women and children working on pittance rates. Pottery was one of the first businesses to become industrialised, leading to specialisation of labour and the employment of women and children at subsistence rates for the simpler work. The truth is that the work of the potter was, until the later nineteenth century, one of the most unpleasant of industrial occupations, leading to a wide variety of diseases, caused by the dangerous materials with which he worked.[29]

This study aims to open up the field of European ceramics by discussing them as marketable commodities made within a consumer society for its wealthier members at a certain moment in time. It discusses their design in terms of the major stylistic trends – Renaissance, Baroque, rococo and neo-classical – that dominated European design at any given time, and identifies their use as artefacts within the home at a particular period. Such an approach will, I hope, lead to a greater understanding of their technical and visual qualities, and place them within the context of other good-quality artefacts, such as paintings or buildings, made for the wealthy classes, which have long been recognised as subjects for serious academic study. The distinction between the 'fine' and 'decorative' arts is a relatively recent one, and it is not always generally realised that they were all evaluated by the same standards of taste by people of fashion. The Earl of Shaftesbury, the great eighteenth-century philosopher of aesthetics, wrote in his essay on taste entitled *Characteristicks* (1711, revised 1714) that:

> Nothing which is found charming or delightful in the polite world, nothing which is adopted as pleasure, or entertainment, of whatever kind, can any way be accounted for, supported, or established, without the pre-establishment or supposition of a certain taste . . . by one of these tastes, he [a gentleman] understands how to lay out his garden, model his house, fancy his equipage, appoint his table.[30]

The first two of these tastes – garden design and architecture – have long been the subject of academic study, and, while the turnout of a gentleman's carriage remains neglected, the process whereby a gentleman might 'appoint his table', and use other ceramics in his house, form the subject matter of this book.

CHAPTER I

Pottery-Making in Medieval Europe

Pottery has been made in Europe in every locality possessing sufficient quantities of clay, and adequate human resources and demand to make it worthwhile. The materials needed for its production are relatively simple: clay and water, with a plentiful amount of fuel (wood or coal) to fire the clay, and people to manage the production. These requirements tend to localise large-scale pottery production to a few distinct areas, although sites for lesser production, such as family concerns or small workshops, can be found all over Europe.[1] The clay itself originates in the ground, or in river banks, and is composed of particles of decomposed rocks, mostly granitic and feldspathic, broken down by the action of water, frost, and carbonic acid, which is produced by the decay of vegetation. The finest clays are composed of the smallest particles. It is most easily dug from open pits; in medieval times and later, there were complaints about the damage that potters did to roads and other localities (hence our term today 'pot-holes'). It would appear that clay was extracted from the area within which a potter could easily travel in a day, with the result that it was generally sourced from an area of four or five kilometers in circumference.[2]

However, clay is not normally in a fit state to be worked directly when it is first dug from the ground. It usually has to be sieved or otherwise treated to get rid of impurities, and then fillers, such as sand, rock fragments, or ground-up pottery, called *grog*, may be added to reduce the risk of shrinking and cracking in heat of the kiln.[3] The quality of the clay can also be improved by compacting the particles in order to remove the air between them, the clay being compressed (kneaded or 'wedged') or 'trampled' by foot. It may also be left damp for a time, so that the water breaks down the particles still further. Another technique involved excavating the clay before winter and leaving it outside in the cold, in order to allow the effects of snow and ice to break it down further.[4]

A pot can be made in many ways, but the most common form of manufacture consists of shaping the clay by hand, sometimes by winding up coils of clay to form a coil pot, or else, more usually, by 'throwing' (forming the clay by hand) on a moving horizontal wheel that utilises centrifugal force, a technique used by the Ancient Greeks.[5] We know relatively little about the history of the potter's wheel in medieval Europe, since the earliest depiction does not appear until the thirteenth century. It seems, however, to have comprised two types: firstly, a raised surface above a cartwheel, which was turned with a stick until sufficient momentum has been gathered; and secondly, a smaller wheel supporting another circle of wood linked by wooden struts which was moved by action of the feet, leaving the hands free to form the pot (a 'kick-wheel').[6]

The use of the potter's wheel both speeded up production and led to the standardisation of product that we are familiar with today. Most obviously, the pot produced thus is uniformly round in its girth, though a skilled potter can produce variations in its width to produce a concave or convex outline. Further alterations can be made when the pot is still damp, such as pulling out a part of the neck of the pot to make the lip of a jug.

Once the pot is formed, it must be left to dry until it is leather-hard, preparatory to firing. A final, sharp, profile can be achieved through 'turning', that is, cutting back the clay surface of the pot on the wheel with a sharp tool. A handle or other pieces can be added with liquid clay ('luting'). Just before firing, some applied decoration can be added, either by impressing the pot with a mould, or incising decoration with a tool, be it of bone, wood or metal. Decoration can also be applied in the form of coloured liquid-clays of finer quality ('slips'), often white or brown. The pot is then ready to be covered with a mixture of minerals and water called a 'glaze', that is, an outer covering, which, when heated, turns to glass, making the pot impervious to liquids. In Medieval Europe, the glaze was nearly always a lead-glaze, formed by the reaction of lead oxide and silica. Glazes could have other minerals added to produce different colours, such as copper to produce a green colour, or iron to produce a reddish-brown or brown colour. The particles of the glaze in powder form (iron filings or natural lead sulphide ['galena']) could be sprinkled onto a pot damped with flour and water, but were often suspended in water, into which the pot was dipped, to gain a more even overall effect.[7]

The pot was now ready to be fired in a large oven on the ground called a 'kiln'. This could range from something akin to a huge bonfire, built up with masses of wood and sticks, through to a properly constructed brick oven, with a domed top or chimney outlet, which allowed some degree of temperature control.[8] The pots have to be fired slowly at first, to allow the water to escape; then to a point between 450–700°C to drive out the water of crystallisation, at which point the clay becomes hard and water-resistant, the clay particles begin to melt and coalesce and it is no longer capable of reverting back to its malleable state. Clay at this stage is the rather brittle product we know as 'earthenware'; if the clay is of suitable quality and the temperature is increased to 1,200°C, it becomes a tough impervious form of pottery, no longer in need of a glaze, called 'stoneware'.

During the firing the pot may undergo a change of colour, depending on its mineral content, its glaze, and the gases that are present in the kiln. Where there is an atmosphere rich in oxygen (an 'oxidising' atmosphere), clays with a high iron content turn red, producing the colour so familiar in pottery, whereas those low in iron turn white. When the clay is fired in an atmosphere with little oxygen (a 'reducing' atmosphere) the clay rich in iron will turn black or grey. The glazes are similarly affected by the difference in the amount of oxygen in the chamber; a lead-glaze on an oxidized surface will vary from pale yellow to amber or brown, whereas a glaze fired in a reduced atmosphere will turn pale yellow-green to dark olive green.[9]

The result of such processes will be a comparatively simple pot which has a variety of uses. Pots were in general domestic use in Europe in the Middle Ages (generally regarded as the period up to 1500 AD), although not nearly as extensively as one might first suppose. The range of domestic artefacts had increased to serve the aristocracy that came with the rise of feudalism,[10] but it would appear that in general pottery was regarded as a low-status material throughout the period, used mostly for kitchen wares and storage in unglazed form, although some of the finer glazed and decorated wares were presumably used at the dining table.[11] Little is known of the status of potters, and there is hardly any mention of guild status for them until the fifteenth century at least.[12] It is often thought that most pottery was made on a seasonal basis by families otherwise engaged in farming.[13] The variety of workshops might range from a house-

4   Master of Mary of Magdalene, *c.*1500. *The Marriage at Cana*. Oil on panel. 113 × 37.2 cm. The National Gallery of Victoria, Melbourne.

hold-style production, producing goods as necessary for the household or related households, through to a kind of 'mass-production' that can be assumed for some of the commoner types found.

Some idea of the uses of pottery vessels can be gauged from the picture by the Master of Mary Magdalene (*c.*1500), (fig. 4) depicting *The Marriage at Cana* – when Christ performed the miracle of turning water into wine – in the form of a fashionable fifteenth-century feast. The diners use metal utensils on the table, and pottery is only used for the large, undecorated storage jars of water or wine seen in the centre of the picture.[14] While the rich ate off silver, gold or pewter, the poorer classes frequently made do with plates, cups and bowls made out of wood, which were tougher and more durable than those of ceramic.[15]

Most Medieval European pottery is, to some extent, of a type, in that it never strays very far from its obviously handmade origins. In particular, most items made in the earlier period appear to have been jugs and pitchers, or storage jars and cooking pots, which were made in regional centres across Europe. It is, however, possible to detect certain regional variations across the Continent. The technique of glazing appeared in Italy and southern France from Byzantium sometime around the ninth century. In France the most common items made after the fall of the Roman Empire were kitchen wares, globular cooking pots, and short-necked pitchers and jugs, which were made in whitish clay and either glazed or decorated very simply with vertical parallel lines in red ochre.[16] In northern France unglazed 'blackwares' were made, with simple stamped or rouletted decoration.[17] Glazed wares only became common in France in the twelfth century. A green or green-speckled glaze was developed, and a new shape of pitcher, with a tall, cylindrical neck, and a handle running from the shoulder to the lip, appeared. Such wares, some of which have been excavated from the defenses of Paris, appear in uniform sizes and may represent standard measures. Polychrome wares, with green and brown vertical stripes appeared in the thirteenth century, and applied or rouletted ornament became more common, especially for tablewares.[18] Many were made in the region of Gascony, specifically Saintonge wares, made in La-Chapelle-des-Pots, five kilometres north-east of Saintes.[19] These wares comprise jugs painted in green and yellow, the design being outlined in brown or black, or scrolls with green leaves in yellow shields, or large green birds with yellow shields. Such wares were exported to England and elsewhere.[20]

Distinctive pottery was also made in other parts of Europe, especially those with good trading connections, particularly Germany and the Netherlands. In Denmark a range of lead-glazed jugs, some with faces impressed in them, pipkins and low-fired 'Jutish' pots were made (fig. 5).[21] Round pots (*Kügeltöpfe*) developed from the eighth century onwards in Lower Saxony and elsewhere, and, with the addition of legs, became the cooking skillet or *Grapen*.[22] At Badorf and Pingsdorf in the Rhineland simple red-painted earthenware, decorated in dots, circles or wavy lines, was made, which was exported all the round the Baltic.[23] However, the technique of glazing was less in evidence, and potters concentrated on producing an intrinsically hard and durable body, which was to culminate in the production of stonewares in the fifteenth and sixteenth centuries. Where suitable clays were lacking, as in the Danube region, graphite was added to the body or the surface, to produce a dark ware with an iron-like structure (*Eisentonware*). A dark sheen on the body of the 'smoked' wares was produced by throwing green twigs into the kiln during firing and blocking up the ventilation shafts, producing a smoky atmosphere. Some of these can be associated with Bruges area of the Netherlands.[24]

England lagged slightly behind countries on the Continent both in terms of wealth and technological development. The fast wheel and the kiln were introduced to

5. Dutch redware tripod pipkin. The British Museum, London.

6   Groups of slip-decorated and polychrome jugs found in South-East England: late thirteenth-century slip-decorated Rouen jug; early thirteenth-century slip-decorated London jug; late twelfth-century slip-decorated London tripod pitcher; mid thirteenth-century Kingston zoomorphic polychrome decorated jug. The British Museum, London.

England in late Saxon times, and the technique of glazing appeared only in the tenth century, at Stamford in Lincolnshire and Winchester in the South-West.[25] Pots made here were coloured by naturally occuring iron oxides, producing a pale yellow or orange in an oxidising atmosphere, or green under reducing conditions. Simple decoration was applied, consisting of rouletting, incising, stamping and applied strips, mostly on pitchers with pinched spouts and a single handle, but also on the more rarely encountered tripod pitcher with a tubular spout. In southern England a number of potteries supplied London with light-bodied white-firing wares, including tall jugs and pitchers, some with glazed decoration, the most distinctive being the so-called 'Tudor green', which had appeared by the sixteenth century (fig. 6).[26] The shape and capacity of cooking pots changed from tall and upright to a wide, squat shape, presumably on account of changes in cooking technique, while the tripod cooking pot was common across the Midlands and southern England.

As on the Continent, most specialised drinking and eating vessels for ordinary people seem to have been made of wood.[27] The number of types and shapes of ceramic wares increased in the fifteenth century to include vessels for drinking from directly, with a corresponding increase in the fineness of the body of the ware.[28] Sixty-five pottery vessel forms have been identified in Britain from the late Saxon to the Tudor period, which can be classed according to three main types: the cooking or storage pot, the bowl/pan/dish, and the jug or pitcher.[29] The largest seem to have been cooking pots, with a capacity of three to five pints, which, from the evidence of soot on their bases, seem to have been left directly in the fire itself. Other types, such as the earlier Cornish 'bar-lug' pots, were suspended over the fire. The later Middle Ages in Britain saw a shift to the use of metal cauldrons, in which a pottery pot might be boiled with its contents, and in turn British cooking pots became reduced in size and began to imitate the smaller three-footed skillets from the Low Countries, with one or two loop handles. There seem also to have been large pans for the frying of food, or to catch the dripping from roasting meat. Jugs and pitchers of various forms are also known, including the complex 'puzzle' jugs, in which the drinker had to stop up a number of concealed holes in the body of the jug in order to prevent the fluid spurting out. A characteristic English type was the tall jug or pitcher, whose height was roughly three-times its diameter. Often jugs have a slight convexity at the base – the so-called 'Baluster' type – where they have been pulled off the wheel, and sometimes the potter has thumb-printed the base to facilitate steadiness.

It was these jugs in particular that were decorated with slip decoration or coloured glazes from the late twelfth century onwards, perhaps inspired by French examples imported through London and other ports. A jug excavated in London, now in the British Museum, is decorated with red and white slips, clearly imitating the geometric and spotted decoration of examples made at Rouen. The kiln at Kingston-on-Thames in Surrey made green and yellow-glazed examples with zoomorphic decoration following northern French examples.[30] In general, decoration on British pottery seems to be fairly closely associated with dining wares, in that ordinary cooking pots were unlikely to receive much ornamentation.[31] The most ambitious products were some remarkable jugs in the shape of animals, or riders on horses, called 'aquamaniles', copied from metalwork prototypes (fig. 7). The most famous examples of wares with animal-type decoration are the jugs with a grotesque face at the neck, occasionally with human hands at the side.[32] Sometimes decoration resembled strips or pellets that were a feature of ironwork decoration on doors or furniture; sometimes it took the form of heraldic decoration, as with York White Ware seal jugs which have applied seals that appear to be based on the coat-of-arms of the Quincy family.[33] Other decoration may be symbolic, relating to charms against witchcraft, or simply unidentified, as in the fish, shields, ships and jousting scenes that appear on pottery from Rye.[34]

7   Bronze acquamanile from Hexham, height 33 cm, and pottery acquamanile from Norfolk, height 21.3 cm. The British Museum, London.

8 A wall tile from Tring parish church, showing scenes from the apocryphal account of Christ's childhood. Lead-glazed earthenware with 'encaustic' decoration. English, early fourteenth century. Victoria & Albert Museum, London.

One of the major questions concerning medieval pottery is the extent to which it was seen as an important product in itself, to be exported to other countries, or simply as a local product to provide containers for storage and cooking. There is relatively little evidence in the form of written documents, until the sixteenth century at least.[35] However, there seems to have been a certain amount of export of the pottery in medieval Europe, both between localities and countries, though nearly always of the finer types, since simple pottery could have been made and bought locally.[36] Excavations in England and elsewhere reveal a wide variety of pottery and other goods with links from outside the area of excavation, including green-glazed and otherwise decorated jugs imported from Rouen and Saintonge in France, or greywares or slip-wares from the Low Countries.[37] Customs records reveal evidence of a trade with Netherlandish ports in pots as such, but the imports were of little value relative to that of wool or wine.[38] Some types of imported pottery may simply have come as containers for imported goods, adjuncts to the wine or the salt trade.[39]

The pottery so far described could not rival metalwork or even glassware in decorative effect and thus has no high place in the history of the decorative arts. In Britain there was no guild for potters, although tile-makers successfully petitioned for guild status in 1468, and an Act of Parliament of 1477 laid down regulations for their manufacture. This contrasts with countries which made more sophisticated pottery such as the Netherlands, where the fifteenth-century records of the Guild of Potters of Bergen op Zoom gives precise instructions on the making of pots.[40]

However, one form of ceramic was artistically ambitious and reflects advanced taste of the time – the coloured floor-tiles which are found in the great churches and palaces, each comprising a different shape or colour, which were laid together to form patterns in the manner of a mosaic. The origins of this kind of patterning may lie in the Roman pavements made from coloured marbles of the thirteenth century, known as *Opus Alexandrinum*. This kind of tile paving was soon developed into a technique whereby the patterning was obtained not simply by laying differently coloured or shaped tiles together, but by inlaying the red clay of the individual tile with clays or a slip of another colour, the most frequently encountered being that of white in red. Once fired, the whole was then glazed with a clear or yellowish lead-glaze and fired again.

The technique seems to have been perfected in France in about the thirteenth century. Heraldic motifs were a common form of decoration, although figures of animals, people, biblical scenes or knights jousting are also known. Complex patterns could be formed by laying tiles with segmental patterns alongside one another in order to produce a complete image, mostly obviously in the case of four tiles each featuring an arc of a circle which together create the patterned effect resembling a rose window in a large Gothic church. The technique spread to England, and commercial tileries, serving many different patrons, had been developed there by the later thirteenth century (fig. 8).[41] Shaped tiles could be used to remarkable effect, as in the scene of Adam and Eve seizing the apple from the snake in the Garden of Paradise, in Prior Crauden's chapel at Ely of about 1324, the figure tiles here being painted with a white slip.[42] Patterned tiles on the French model have been found at Byland, Rievaulx, Fountains and Melrose Abbeys, and seem to be linked to the Cistercian Order.[43] These were glazed and fired only once to reduce the risk of warping that could affect flat surfaces.[44] The most spectacular tiles are in the Chapter House at Westminster Abbey of 1253–9, featuring royal portraits, 'rose windows', heraldic beasts and hunting scenes, and may have been made at Chertsey Abbey on the River Wey, which seems to have been a major centre for such tile production.

Overleaf, detail of fig. 15. Plate painted with a scene of a maiolica painter at work.

CHAPTER 2

The Spread of Tin-glazed Earthenware: Italian Maiolica

The pottery we have discussed so far was mostly lead-glazed to make it non-porous. In spite of the existence of regional types, it all bears a family resemblance in so far as it never strays very far from the simple type of pottery that can be made by hand or with the help of a potter's wheel. It seems to have been made throughout Europe, and was clearly sufficient for everyday use, but would not have provided items for display or decoration, or to demonstrate wealth.

However, finer types of pottery were known in medieval Europe, originating from the Middle East. Certain parts of Europe began to import pottery decorated with 'tin-glaze', a technique that had arisen in Mesopotamia (present-day Iraq) early in the ninth century. The technique consisted of dipping the once-fired ware into a lead-glaze of which the main ingredients were potash, sand, and oxides of lead and tin; the tin oxide remained suspended in the glaze and, on firing, gave the vessel a whitish appearance, so that it resembled porcelain, which was known from imports from China. This tin-glazed ware was liable to chip easily, but had the advantage that the glaze did not run, as was often the case in a lead-glaze. This meant that over this glaze other minerals could be applied which, when fired, produced decoration of different colours.

By the middle of the century a blue overglaze was produced by cobalt oxide, which resembled the underglaze blue of Chinese porcelain, and in the tenth century copper and manganese oxide were added to produce the colours of green, purple or brown-black. The manufacture and use of these wares spread along the coast of northern Africa in the wake of Islamic conquests and up into southern Spain. They were imitated in southern Italy and Sicily, since the latter area had a considerable Muslim population, and may even have employed Muslim craftsmen from Tunisia.[1] The wares they produced were relatively simple, comprising mostly tall jars and bowls. Cobalt and manganese wares from Maghreb were imported into Italy at the end of the twelfth century, whilst in the southern Italian regions of Apulia and Sicily polychrome decoration was being produced, using pigments derived from copper, manganese, iron, antimony, yellow and cobalt. This was the origin of the elaborately coloured Italian tin-glazed earthenware that is so famous today.[2]

Tin-glazed earthenware seems to have been made in many places in Italy. It must have been expensive as the tin had to be imported from Devon or Cornwall in England.[3] The earliest types seem to bear some relation to Arabic pottery, including tall drug-jars (*albarelli*) and a type of small bowl with a wide flat rim (*tondino*), as well as the *tagliere*, a flat-based dish with steep, shallow sides. However, other shapes seem specifically Italian, such as the pear-shaped jug, and a small broad footless jug with a large applied spout (*pannata*), which was made in Umbria and Lazio. The handles of Italian jugs are different from those on the rest of the Continent, in that they are generally raised slightly above the rim of the vessels and descend almost vertically to the shoulder. There was also a special type of drug-jar which resembled a baluster pot with two handles protruding from the middle. In the fifteenth century this was refined with a pedestal-foot and a lid to produce an elegant kind of vase.[4]

The earliest tin-glaze wares of northern Italy are known as 'archaic' and are often decorated in the naturalistic Gothic style using the colours of manganese-purple and green, or purple alone, the motifs being objects such as stylised leaves, birds, heads and simple geometric forms (fig. 9). Their manufacture seems to have commenced in the thirteenth century.[5] The background is frequently cross-hatched in order to make the main motifs more prominent. This type is associated with finds at Siena, Orvieto, Faenza and elsewhere. It should be emphasised that tin-glaze wares were expensive and most pottery made in Italy was still simple lead-glazed ware, although finer forms existed, often in the form of incised slipwares, with the pattern cut through the white slip to reveal the red clay below, sometimes with the addition of green and brown in the glaze.[6]

Italian tin-glazed earthenware is today called 'maiolica': the word is derived from the name of the Spanish island of Majorca, where much Moorish tin-glazed earthenware made at Valencia and Malaga was transhipped in the fifteenth century. In the fifteenth and sixteenth centuries the term apparently referred to pottery made there and decorated additionally with metallic oxides (lustreware),[7] which was made, first, at Malaga in Granada, then also at Manises in Valencia.[8] This comprised a painted decoration of silver, copper or sulphur oxides, which was painted onto the glaze and 'reduced' to a metallic golden colour by a second or third firing in a low-oxygen kiln. Large vases and plates were commonly made, and exported throughout Europe. This kind of pottery was certainly known in fifteenth-century Europe, most famously perhaps in Filippino Lippi's *Annunciation* of 1483–4 at San Gimignano, or Hugo van der Goes's *Adoration of the Shepherds* painted for the Florentine Tomaso Portinari and given to Santa Maria Novella in about 1475. Some Spanish lustreware even bears the arms of noble Italian families, such as the magnificent tall vases with handles in the British Museum which bear the coat-of-arms of the Florentine Giuliano Gondi (1421–1501) or Piero de' Medici (after 1465) (fig. 11).[9] Other lustrewares are decorated with Christian symbols, such as the IHS emblem, and are thus clearly made for export.

The major pottery-centres of fifteenth-century Italy appear to have been Pesaro and Faenza, which developed certain local styles of decoration, such as a broad-leaf type decoration of Gothic foliage. However, the most innovative centre in the fifteenth century seems to have been in Tuscany, in the area around Florence, including Montelupo and Bacchereto, where potters copied motifs derived from Hispano-Moresque lustreware, such as the flower design and the leaf pattern, but in simple colours as they could not then get the effect of lustreware.[10] They also copied the spiky *mudéjar* leaf-patterns of Valencia, but rather than being painted in solid colour, they were outlined and filled with graded tones of pigment.[11] For the period 1420–40 there exist a number of large dishes painted with heraldic animals, with an obvious debt to Hispano-Moresque prototypes, and with a rich background devised of small leaves and flowers.

Florence is best known for the remarkable series of 'oak-leaf' drug-jars (*albarelli*) in which the motif is painted in cobalt-blue against a background of serrated leaves and stalks – the 'oak-leaves' of the name (fig. 10).[12] A large number are known with a crutch painted under the handles, which could be from the series of over 1,000 made by Giunta di Tugio for the Hospital of Santa Maria Nuova in 1430–1.[13] The type appears to have been imitated at a number of other pottery centres including Siena, Faenza and Viterbo.

By the 1470 and 80s maiolica painters had advanced beyond the basic colours of cobalt-blue, copper-green and manganese-brown to include several shades of yellow

9 Jug painted with a bird. Tin-glazed earthenware. Height 25 cm. Probably Tuscany, early fifteenth century. The J. Paul Getty Museum, Los Angeles.

10 Below. Drug jar. Tin-glazed earthenware, painted in manganese purple and copper green. Height 25 cm. Florence (possibly workshop of Giunta di Tugio), *c.*1430. The J. Paul Getty Museum, Los Angeles.

11 Right. Jar bearing the *stemma* (coat-of-arms) of Piero de' Medici (d.1469). Tin-glazed earthenware, painted in blue, yellow, purple and gold lustre. Probably Manises, Valencia, after 1465. Height 57 cm. The British Museum, London.

and orange from mixtures of antimony and iron, olive greens from copper and antimony, a turquoise-blue from copper and soda, a mauve-purple from cobalt and manganese, which created a range of colours with which Italian maiolica painters could explore styles and methods of decoration which went far beyond Hispano-Moresque ware.[14] New types of decoration appeared, including 'Persian palmettes' or decoration in polychrome colours based on peacock feathers (fig. 12), and the 'bryony-flower' style of decoration which was copied in orange rather than lustre.[15]

The great advance in ceramic decoration and design came not so much from the development of new colours and pigments, as from developments in the fields of printing and paper-making, which greatly increased the range of figurative and decorative motifs. Imagery had of course been drawn from religious images, or stained glass, coats-of-arms, or pattern books drawn on vellum (sheepskin).[16] However, the most obvious motifs were, as we have seen, naturalistic ones which could be copied from nature or transcribed in simple patterns, often as decoration on objects. Figurative images which suggest the transmission of the motifs via paper first occur on Italian pottery from the mid-fifteenth century onwards. From Florence come twelve maiolica roundels painted with men at work representing the months, from the workshop of Luca della Robbia (1400–82), now in the Victoria and Albert Museum. Della Robbia habitually used the maiolica technique of tin-glaze for his sculptures; they may date from 1450–6, but do not seem to have led to a trend in pictorial maiolica.[17] As an alternative to the tin-glazed tradition, we have a whole series of large plates from north-east Italy decorated with figures in court dress in the International Gothic style, which are made in the so-called *sgraffiato* ware. The body of the plate was covered with a liquid slip which was scraped away to reveal the design, the whole being covered in a transparent lead-glaze. The design was often heightened with colours which had a tendency to run into the glaze, producing an uneven effect.[18] The main centres of production seem to have been the great cities of north-eastern Italy, Venice, Padua, Ferrara and Bologna, cities which are particularly

12 Dish with decoration in imitation of peacock feathers. Tin-glazed earthenware. Diameter 39 cm. Probably Faenza, 1470–1500. The J. Paul Getty Museum, Los Angeles.

13 Dish, reddish earthenware, transparent glaze, coated in slip with an incised design. Probably Ferrara, *c.*1480–1510. Diameter 40 cm. British Museum, London.

14 Dish. Tin-glazed earthenware, painted in colours. Diameter 28.8 cm. Possibly Castel Durante, Italy. Victoria & Albert Museum, London.

associated with the Gothic court style of Gentile da Fabriano (*c.*1385–1427) and Pisanello (*c.*1395–1455) (fig. 13).

Such figurative developments led to a style of maiolica that is predominantly pictorial, where the surface of the ware is used as a basis for a single composition. The increasingly pictorial style has been christened in Italy *stile bello* (beautiful style), featuring human portraits, as well as animal and other motifs, and to this extent the design and decoration of maiolica become at this point an aspect of the art of the Renaissance, whereby the styles and ideals of classical art were imitated and surpassed. The most-often quoted examples are the hexagonal tiles in the church of San Petronio, Bologna, which bear the date '1487', but may be later.[19] Each tile bears a central device surrounded by an elaborate border, comprising masks, trophies, shields, badges and religious symbols, often painted to imply relief, with the suggestion of architecture. Similarly, the service made for Matthias Corvinus of Hungary in Pesaro between 1476 and 1490 bears figurative decoration in the central medallions.[20] It is not clear from where many of these figures derive, but a series of profile portraits on a series of tall *albarelli* (drug-jars) has recently been attributed to Naples, as they appear to reflect portraits of the royal family which had appeared on bronze medals.[21]

The great impetus to this development of Italian maiolica seems to have been the evolution of print-making in Italy in the fifteenth century, first with *niello* engravings, produced from engraved silver plates filled with a black substance called 'nigellum', succeeded by engravings on a copper plate, from which a 'pull' or engraving could be taken.[22] The dissemination of visual ideas was also helped by the use of woodcuts as book illustrations: the first recorded use of woodcuts in a book is the *Meditationes* of Cardinal Torquemada, published in Rome in 1467. Their use soon spread to the great printing centres of Florence and Venice.[23]

It was not long before pottery painters began to use details from prints in their designs, adapting them with much intelligence and skill. Some early plates attributed to Deruta are decorated with animals derived from *niello* prints by Maso Finiguerra.[24] Three other plates attributed to Deruta bear versions of the *Labours of Hercules* taken, presumably via engravings, from Antonio Pollaiuolo (*c.*1432–98).[25] Other sources that could be used include medals and plaquettes.[26] Some maiolica painters may have produced their own designs, as in the case of a plate attributed to Castel Durante, which is painted with a central panel of nymphs bathing overlooked by a satyr. It is dated on the back 17 November 1503; this is one of the earliest-known dates for a plate showing a narrative scene (fig. 14).[27]

The possible status of the maiolica painter can be gauged by a dish in the Victoria and Albert Museum of about 1510, which shows him seated with his bowls of colours in front of a fashionably dressed couple, the woman possibly having her portrait painted (fig. 15). It is clear that the painter regarded himself as equal to his fashionably dressed clients, having his own skills and abilities which were worthy of respect.[28]

Thus at the turn of the century, some kinds of maiolica were becoming a product for the wealthy, individually designed and painted, and reflecting developments in painting and sculpture. Even as great a collector as Lorenzo de' Medici politely compared a gift of tin-glazed earthenware to the work of silversmiths or jewellers.[29] It was Medici influence which led to the first pottery workshop to have consistently produced artistically ambitious pottery, when in 1498 a maiolica workshop was set up in the Medici villa at Cafaggiolo by two potters from Montelupo, Stefano and Piero di Filippo. This workshop produced some of the finest maiolica of the early Renaissance, creating pieces that reflect developments made in painting and sculpture in Florence itself. For instance, a round plate in the Victoria and Albert Museum is painted with a representation of Donatello's *St George*; he stands before a carefully painted background of rocks and trees, with a lake behind, and may be a representation of Donatello's statue when it still held a lance in hand. An even more beautiful dish is

15   Plate painted with a scene of a maiolica painter at work. Tin-glazed earthenware, painted in colours. Mark: *SP* in circles. Diameter 23.5 cm. Cafaggiolo, *c*.1510. Victoria & Albert Museum, London.

16   Plate painted with a scene of *Diana and Endymion*. Tin-glazed earthenware, painted in colours. Mark: *SP* in circles. Diameter 26 cm. Cafaggiolo, *c*.1510. The Calouste Gulbenkian Foundation, Lisbon.

17   Plate bearing the coat-of-arms of Pandolfo Petrucci (d.1512). Tin-glazed earthenware, painted in colours. Siena, *c*.1510. The British Museum, London.

18 Drawing after a fresco by Girolamo Genga, attributed to Jacopo Ripanda. 14.3 × 16.5 cm. Musée des Beaux-Arts, Lille.

19 Dish. Tin-glazed earthenware, painted in colours. Faenza, possibly Casa Pirota, c.1520–5. British Museum, London.

painted with *Diana and Endymion*, in a style very close to that of Botticelli or his pupil Filippino Lippi (fig. 16).[30]

Another centre of fine maiolica was the Tuscan town of Siena. Here the best maiolica seems to centre around an order from the tyrant Pandolfo Petrucci, who in about 1509 commissioned a group of distinguished Renaissance artists, including Luca Signorelli (1441(?)–1523), Pintoricchio (c.1481–1513) and Girolamo Genga (c.1476–1551), to decorate a room in his palace with frescoes depicting scenes from classical history, which were complemented by a floor of maiolica tiles in the 'grotesque' taste. This was a style of decoration developed by Pintoricchio,[31] and was named after the decoration found in the underground excavations (grottos) of the Golden House of Nero in Rome. It was a fanciful style which showed a variety of motifs, men and mythological creatures intertwined amid foliage in vertical format, without any attempt to give any suggestion of depth or solid support for the subjects, a style of decoration much criticised by the Roman architectural-theorist Vitruvius.[32] Such grotesque decoration appears on the rim of a magnificent dish in the British Museum which bears a central scene of Pan playing his pipes with the arms of Pandolfo, who died in 1512 (fig. 17).[33]

It would appear also that the figurative decoration of the Petrucci room had a strong influence on the design of Italian maiolica, centred on the great pottery-producing town of Faenza. The designs of Girolamo Genga in the Petrucci Palace were copied in circular format in an album dated 1516 now in Lille Museum (fig. 18), suggesting their use for plates, and indeed a dish attributed to Faenza in the British Museum (fig. 19)[34] is painted with such a scene from classical history. Faenza was also the origin of an important decorative technique, the famous 'white-on-white' (*bianco sopra bianco*); in fact, white on a bluish-tinted background, which appeared about 1520, and was much used for border decoration.

Painters at Faenza also used prints by German artists such as Martin Schongauer (c.1445–91) and Albrecht Dürer (1471–1528). Dürer published his great woodcut of the *Apocalypse* in 1498, to be followed by the woodcuts of the *Large Passion*, the *Small Passion*, and the *Life of the Virgin* in 1511.[35] These prints came to be used by maiolica painters south of the Alps,[36] and a plate in the British Museum bears a scene copied from Martin Schongauer's *Death of the Virgin* as engraved by Israel Van Meckenem.[37] Similarly a beautiful Cafaggiolo dish in the British Museum is composed of two Dürer prints, the figures from the *Satyr Family* and the landscape background from *Hercules at the Crossroads*, but the whole is bound together in a way which commands respect for the painter as an artist in his own right.[38]

The other great centre of pottery production in Italy was the aforementioned Deruta, close to Perugia, which had been listed as a pottery centre as early as 1358, when large quantities of pottery were supplied to the Convent of St Francis of Assisi.[39] Here the artistic style was heavily influenced by local religious symbols and artists, such as the Umbrian painter Pietro Perugino (before 1469–1523). A dish in the British Museum records a version of the Nativity which often occurs in the work of Perugino. Other types feature a central panel of a saint, the Virgin or an angel set in segmental panels, or a portrait of the classical profile of a beautiful young woman (fig. 20). The painting is often surrounded by blue, with the pattern design in yellow lustreware. This can be of leafy palmettes or scale pattern, which the great ceramic historian Bernard Rackham saw as derivative of designs from Siena.[40] Many of these wares are 'lustred', in the style popularised by Spanish earthenware.[41]

However, the whole history of maiolica painting was soon to be affected by artistic events in Rome. In the period 1510–20 the great painter Raphael (1483–1520) was at work on his great cycle of frescoes in the Vatican, in which the classicising style reached its fullest development. Many of Raphael's designs were propagated through the means of prints, and he was the first artist to use printmaking as a way of spreading his ideas and even produced compositions, such as *The Massacre of the Innocents*, specifically for engraving. His chief engraver was the Venetian Marcantonio Raimondi, whose prints were a major factor in the propagation of Raphael's style throughout the world.[42]

The dissemination of prints after Raphael seems to have led to the development of the *istoriato* (storytelling) style in maiolica. Here, the whole plate (or virtually the whole plate) was treated as a canvas, with the central panel depicting a religious or classical scene adapted from a print source, often with the name of the scene inscribed on the reverse of the plate. The main centre of production seems to have been the court of the Dukes of Urbino and the neighbouring pottery town of Castel Durante. This town was not unknown to the makers of fine maiolica; attractive plates with grotesque border decoration on a dark ground had been made in Castel Durante as early as 1508 by 'Zouamaria Vro', who was probably the documented potter Giovanni Maria di Mariano, and a major workshop for the making of maiolica had been set up in Urbino by Guido Durantino before 1520.[43] It would appear that the period around 1520 was crucial for the development of Italian maiolica; certainly a series of well-painted dishes featuring large static figures[44] suggest that at this point the painters could have aimed at grand, monumental effects rather than the small-scale, delicate figure painting showing a particular moment in the narrative that became typical.

The chief exponent of *istoriato* maiolica painting seems to have been a painter called Nicola da Urbino. The known facts relating to him are very few.[45] He is probably the Nicola di Gabriele Sbraga recorded in Urbino from 1520 who died in 1537/38.[46] He was described as a fully fledged painter or *maestro* in 1520, and links are recorded with Guido Durantino, head of a maiolica workshop. His first works known to us are based on stylistic attribution alone: a series of seventeen plates, clearly intended as part of a service, in the Correr Museum, Venice. The scenes depicted include subjects from Ovid's *Metamorphoses*, the legends of King Solomon, the Four Seasons and the Italian novella *Ottinello and Giulia*. The general tonality of the works is blue, similar to works attributed to Faenza, but the level of painterly skill is much higher. Certain plates, such as *Solomon Adoring an Idol* or *Solomon, the Young Man and the Harlot* show a knowledge of Renaissance architecture as embodied in the works of Raphael's friend and mentor, Bramante. However, the series as a whole looks back to the fifteenth century and in particular to the woodcuts in the Venice edition of Ovid's *Metamorphoses* of 1497.[47] For instance, the scenes of *Orpheus and the Beasts* and *The Death of Orpheus* are closely based on compositions of the woodcuts in this particular edition, republished in Venice in 1508.[48]

Shortly after painting this series, Nicola's style began a broadening which brought him right up to date and in touch with developments in Renaissance painting. In particular, he adopted a richer palette of colours, and began to depict figures naked or in classical dress, rather than the dress of the early sixteenth century, which appears in the Correr plates. The series of plates in the 'Flag and Ladder' series, probably painted for the Calini family of Brescia (fig. 21), again include subjects from classical and Christian sources, including the *Metamorphoses* and St George and the Dragon, but this time the figures are wholly classical in garb, if not actually naked. Much of this change seems to be due to the influence of Raphael; for instance, the fleeing princess in the plate of *St George and the Dragon* is clearly derived from the figure in Raphael's painting of 1505 in the Louvre, and even the architecture, with its circular temples, shows knowledge of Bramante's *Tempietto* in Rome.[49]

In about 1524–5 he is thought to have painted a service intended as gift from the Duchess of Urbino to her mother Isabella d'Este, who had already shown an interest in fine maiolica, as indicated by a recorded order for a series of plates via Alfonso Trotti of Ferrara of 1518.[50] Twenty-one plates and dishes painted by Nicola survive,

20   Dish with a profile portrait of a woman. Tin-glazed earthenware painted in greyish-blue and gold lustre. Diameter 38.9 cm. Deruta, *c.*1500–25. The Wallace Collection, London.

21 Right. Dish painted with the *Apollo and Marsyas* and the coat-of-arms of the Calini family. Tin-glazed earthenware, painted in colours. Diameter 41.4 cm. Urbino, workshop of Nicola da Urbino, *c.*1525. The J. Paul Getty Museum, Los Angeles.

22 Plate painted with a scene of *Apollo and Marsyas* and the coat-of-arms of the D'Este family. Tin-glazed earthenware, painted in colours. Urbino, workshop of Nicola da Urbino, *c.*1525. Courtesy of the Trustees of the Wernher Collection, London.

23 Illustration from the 1497 edition of Ovid's *Metamorphoses.*

bearing Isabella's coat-of-arms and a selection of her personal devices or *imprese*. The range of subjects again include classical and biblical scenes, including some subjects from Ovid, which also occur on the other two services, such as *Peleus and Thetis*, *Apollo and Marsyas* (fig. 22), and *Apollo, Pan and Midas*. Again Nicola seems to have used the Venice Ovid of 1497 as a source for compositions, as in the scene of *Apollo and Marsyas*, but with the clothed figures of the book illustration changed to nudes in the plate (fig. 23).[51] Some of Nicola' scenes may derive directly from Raphael's greatest pupil, Giulio Romano, who worked at Mantua from 1524 onwards,[52] and is recorded as providing designs for maiolica tiles in 1528. It is possible that Nicola even had first-hand knowledge of Raphael's studio, as he seems to have been familiar with at least one of Raphael's drawings.[53]

In 1528 Nicola signed a dish now in the Bargello, Florence, painted with the *Martyrdom of St Cecilia* copied from a print after Raphael.[54] This can be seen as part of a trend whereby maiolica became less inventive, and more directly dependent on printed sources. It is one of a number of plates inscribed *In Botega di Maestro Guido Durantino* (In the workshop of Maestro Guido Durantino); Guido Durantino appears to have run one of the leading maiolica workshops in Urbino in the sixteenth century. Pieces so inscribed date from 1528 to 1542, and include two important services

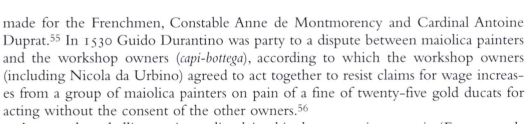

made for the Frenchmen, Constable Anne de Montmorency and Cardinal Antoine Duprat.[55] In 1530 Guido Durantino was party to a dispute between maiolica painters and the workshop owners (*capi-bottega*), according to which the workshop owners (including Nicola da Urbino) agreed to act together to resist claims for wage increases from a group of maiolica painters on pain of a fine of twenty-five gold ducats for acting without the consent of the other owners.[56]

Among the rebellious painters listed in this document is a certain 'Francesco da Rovigo'. This would appear to be none other than the painter Francesco Xanto Avelli da Rovigo, who began to sign his work after this date, possibly to assert his individual status as a maiolica painter. His origins are unclear; he could be the painter who signed his work 'FR' or 'FLR' in the 1520s, or inscribed the title of pieces with a peculiar diagonal stroke resembling a 'y'.[57] He was clearly a painter of some pretensions, who wrote poetry in praise of Francesco Maria I, Duke of Urbino, which allude to events dating from 1509 to 1538.[58] He often shows knowledge of poetry; for a service painted for the Pucci family he draws on Virgil's *Aeneid*, Ariosto's *Orlando furioso*, Ovid's *Metamorphoses* and *Heroides*, Petrarch's *Rime*, Pliny's *Historia naturalis*, Valerius Maximus's *I fatti e detti*, and Justin's epitome of Trogus Pompeius's *Historiae philippicae*.[59] He often added complicated inscriptions explaining the subject of his work on the back of his plates, and one of them even depicts one of his own poems.[60]

24 Left. Plate painted with *The Triumph of Alcyone*. Tin-glazed earthenware, painted in colours. Urbino, by Francesco Xanto Avelli da Rovigo, dated 1533. Diameter 48 cm. The Wallace Collection, London.

25 Left. Engraving of *Venus Rising from the Sea* by Marco Dente da Ravenna after Raphael.

26 Left. Engraving of *The Slaying of Cerebus* by Gian Jacopo Caraglio after Rosso.

27 Above. *The Massacre of the Innocents* engraved by Marco Dente da Ravenna after Baccio Bandinelli (1493– 1560).

28 Dish, lustred and signed by Maestro Giorgio Andreoli and dated 1524 on the base. Tin-glazed earthenware. Diameter 39.9 cm. The J. Paul Getty Museum, Los Angeles.

Xanto's technique of composition is quite different from Nicola's (and the quality of painting less good), in that he seems to have been almost totally dependent on prints as sources for his figures. However, his technique was not always to simply copy the whole engraving, but to select certain figures from a print and combine them with others. It is not clear how he did this, but the scale of the figures on the plates is that of the prints themselves, and it may be that he had cut-outs, or tracings of the figures in the prints, which he then distributed on the plate surface and pricked or traced around preparatory to painting. The same figures recur time and time again on plates, with attempts to disguise their origin by adding drapery, or rotating them through 90 degrees. A favourite source of prints was Giulio Romano's erotic engravings, *I Modi*, which depict figures in contorted poses of love-making; they can often be traced in his designs, often clothed and completely divorced from their salacious origin.

A good idea of Xanto's range and skills can be gained from one of his most ambitious plates, the great *Triumph of Alcyone* plate in the Wallace Collection in London (fig. 24). It is inscribed and signed and dated on the back 'M.D.XXXIII/ Triumpha quì Nettu nelle salse onde/Su le qual gode lamorosa Stella/ Ignuda frà suoi figli, e, uaga, e, bella/Vien coronata de fioretti, e, fronde/ Fra: Xanto, A./da Rovigo ì/ Urbino' (Neptune triumphs here in the salt waves on which the amorous, naked Star rejoices between her sons and, fair and lovely, comes crowned with flowers and leaves).[61] At least ten different prints were used in its production, including *Venus Rising from the Sea* by Marco Dente da Ravenna after Raphael (fig. 25), *The Slaying of Cerebus* by Gian Jacopo Caraglio after Rosso (fig. 26), and a figure in reverse on the right of *The Massacre of the Innocents* by Marco Dente da Ravenna after Bandinelli (fig. 27). The differences in scale of the figures in the prints account for the differences in scale in the plates, suggesting that Francesco used the images with little adaptation; the general impression of the plates is of a skilful, but slightly overripe, performance.

Other painters who practised the *istoriato* style with success include the putative Andrea da Negroponte, Baldassare Manara and Virgiliotto Calamelli in Faenza. The majority of such plates are attributed to the workshops of Urbino, though it would appear that *istoriato* maiolica was made to some degree all over Italy. In general their work is less striking and inventive than that of Nicola da Urbino or Fra Xanto, and relied on simple adaptations of prints, with perhaps some attempt to hide their origin.[62]

One of the major figures of the time was Maestro Giorgio of Gubbio, probably Maestro Giorgio Andreoli, who worked at the little town of Gubbio, and in 1498 was granted citizenship of the town and exemption from taxes. Much of his work seems to have taken the form of adding highlights in red or gold lustre to already painted maiolica, including that of Xanto, though some works, such as those by Francesco Urbini, seem to have been painted in Gubbio itself (fig. 28). His work is often signed in lustre on the base 'MoGo' and the earliest dated piece is of 1515.[63] To our eyes these additions are not necessarily an advantage, especially as the quality of painting of many of the *istoriato* pieces was rather poor, although he was praised in a brief of 1519 by no less a person than Pope Leo X.[64]

From the 1540s a number of services are known which were designed by Renaissance artists rather than maiolica painters. This development seems to have started in Urbino, where well-developed maiolica workshops, allied with a high level of court culture, led to the creation of great services intended as diplomatic gifts from one ruler to another. Our first documented case of an artist supplying designs for maiolica, where the pieces can still be identified, is the great service sent by Duke Guidobaldo II of Urbino to the Emperor Charles V (1500–58) and his brother-in-law Cardinal Alessandro Farnese (1520–89) painted with scenes from *The History of Troy*. The service is presumed to date from the later 1540s, and may possibly be connected with Guidobaldo's marriage to Vittoria Farnese in 1548. The designs were created by the

minor Venetian painter Battista Franco (*c*.1510–1561), who had a certain facility for drawing, but had just completed an unsuccessful fresco of *The Coronation of the Virgin* on the vault of the tribuna of Urbino Cathedral, and so was moved to maiolica decoration. His designs fill the space admirably, but are representative of the rather stiff classicism that pervaded Italian art after the death of Raphael (figs 29 and 30).[65]

Franco's service was clearly judged a success, for in 1560 the duke turned to another artist, Taddeo Zuccaro (1529–66), to provide more designs for maiolica. Zuccaro had been called to Urbino to paint the portrait of the duke's daughter on her marriage to Federico Borromeo in 1560, and, before he left, provided designs for a service painted with scenes from the life of Julius Caesar.[66] Again a large number of drawings by Zuccaro and related plates have come down to us, but they are quite different in character from Franco's. The depiction of the scenes is more pictorial, more architectural, with a greater suggestion of depth and painterly quality. In some ways, they are less suited to maiolica than Franco's rather flat designs, as much of the subtlety was lost when painted onto the plates. But they represent an extremely culturally ambitious art form of the later sixteenth century (figs 31 and 32).

At this stage our knowledge of the making of maiolica and the practices of the workshops receives a boost from a remarkable contemporary guide to the whole sub-

29 Design for Dish with *The Reception of a Warrior by King Priam*. Pen and wash. Battista Franco (1510–61). Diameter 27 cm. Victoria & Albert Museum, London.

30 Dish painted with *The Reception of Helen by King Priam* after Battista Franco. Tin-glazed earthenware, painted in colours. Urbino, workshop of the Fontana, *c*.1545–51. Diameter 41 cm. Victoria & Albert Museum, London.

31. Interior of wine-cooler painted after Taddeo Zuccaro (1529–66). Width 62 cm. The Wallace Collection, London.

32 After Taddeo Zuccaro (1529–66) *The Capture of Tunis*. Pen and brown wash. Diameter 34.2 cm. The Royal Library, Windsor.

33 Depiction of maiolica potters at work, from the manuscript of Piccolpasso's *Three Books of the Potter's Art*.

34 Drawing of different types of ceramic design, from Piccolpasso's *Three Books of the Potter's Art*.

ject: the manuscript of *I tre libri dell'arte del vasaio* (The Three Books of the Potter's Art) by the Durantine Cipriano Piccolpasso (*c.*1523/4–1579). Piccolpasso was a military engineer who undertook his book for the benefit of Cardinal François de Tournon, Bishop of Lyon, who died in 1562. Its function was to act as a manual on the manufacture of maiolica, presumably so that it could be emulated elsewhere. Piccolpasso describes in great detail the collecting and the washing of the clays, the functioning of the kilns and the application of colours. He also includes some intriguing depictions of the potters at work (fig. 33), showing them with prints or drawings pinned up as patterns behind them, as well as illustrations of different types of standard design (fig. 34).[67]

Urbino was not the only centre of fine maiolica in sixteenth-century Italy. Another great hub of maiolica production appears to have been Venice, though few documentary examples survive to record its productions. Certainly in 1520 Alfonso I d'Este of Ferrara was ordering a set of eleven drug-jars from Venice through no less a person than the artist Titian, who was at work on paintings for Alfonso's 'Camera'; Alfonso confessed himself well-pleased with the result. The main production of the town seems to have been incised slipwares of the kind that were made in the fifteenth century, and maiolica painted in blue and white with a blue-tinted glaze. A certain amount of 'figurative' painting was also done; the main workshop seems to have been that of Domenico da Veneziana (active 1547–68) who is believed to have been responsible for a whole series of drug-jars painted with heads of pretty women.[68]

By the second half of the sixteenth century, the use of prints for the decoration of Italian maiolica had become rather tired and lacking in invention, with most painters simply adapting an oblong print to a round dish. More interesting was the origin of what today is called the *stile compendario*, where most of the vessel is left white with a central design painted in blue or other colours. The centre of production for this type is thought to have been Faenza. Such pottery drew respect from the whole of Europe, on account of its whiteness and lightness,[69] and was the prized possession of kings and princes.[70] The white wares were also made in the workshops of Virgiliotto Calamelli and Leonardo Battisi at Faenza, and later in potteries in Liguria, such as

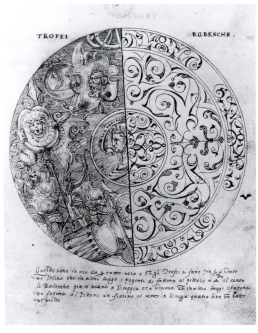

Albisola and Savona. This latter also made blue-painted wares of a very high quality.

The art of maiolica painting travelled across the Alps, and took root in France, firstly in Rouen, where the Frenchman Masseot Abaquesne provided tile-panels for Constable Anne de Montmorency's château at Ecouen in 1542–49.[71] Another great centre for painted tin-glazed ware was Lyons, where there was an established Italian community, and whose Cardinal Archbishop de Tournon was, as we have seen, the patron of Piccolpasso. Work generally attributed to Lyons includes plates decorated with scenes from the *Quadrins historiques de la Bible* by Bernard Salomon (Lyons, 1533), though an Italian edition, which would have led to their being copied in Italy, was produced in 1554 (fig. 35). Similarly an illustrated edition of Ovid's *Metamorphoses* by Salomon was produced in France in 1557 and Italy in 1559. Often the style of painting is sketchier (fig. 36), though possibly the only way of distinguishing between those painted in France and those painted in Italy is the use of language on the back.[72]

The figurative style of painting was continued by a group of Italian potters who moved to Nevers, between Lyons and Paris, under the patronage of Luigi Gonzaga, Duke of Nevers (1539–95). The impetus seems to have been the Italian potters Giulio Gambin from Lyon and the Conrade brothers from Albisola, who started making pottery in the *istoriato* style in about 1580. The most famous work is a large, oval dish in the Louvre signed on the back *Fesi a Nevrs 1589*.[73] In 1603 the Conrade brothers received a monopoly from Henry IV of France for making coloured and white ware in the manner of Faenza; the pottery continued to receive royal approval in the mid-seventeenth century, Antoine Conrade being appointed *faïencier ordinaire* to Louis XIV in 1644. He continued the Italian *istoriato* style, using prints and drawings, well into the seventeenth century.[74] Further south, tin-glazed ware was made at Nîmes, Montpellier and Narbonne from about 1570–80. The best-known painter is Antoine Sigalon of Nîmes.

The technique of maiolica spread throughout the world, dominating the middle market for ceramics through to the end of the eighteenth century. Inevitably, it gained its most-powerful foothold where the market for Italian maiolica was strongest. In Spain important centres of figurative maiolica were Castile, Seville and Talavera, the latter assuming dominance in the seventeenth century.[75] The production of tiles and tile-panels became especially important in the peninsula, and huge schemes, comprising many individual tiles, were produced to cover whole walls. As time went by, the *istoriato* tradition became increasingly crude and provincial, and single decorative motifs, set against a white background in the manner of Faenza, became dominant.

However, the tradition of treating the plate-surface as a vehicle for decoration survived and indeed flourished in the seventeenth century, though increasingly such plates were clearly primarily intended for display. Magnificent plates showing men in fighting dress were made in Montelupo in Tuscany; the style of painting is quite sketchy which suggests they were not made for the highest market. Maiolica painters of the seventeenth century had access to a much wider range of prints than their forebears. One of the most dynamic centres for the production of *istoriato* maiolica was the small town of Castelli in L'Aquila, where Francesco Grue founded a dynasty of pottery painters who used prints as sources for decoration.[76] In 1688 his son Carlo Antonio (1655–1723) approached the minor decorative painter Francesco Bedeschini for designs for the borders, versions of which survive in the Victoria and Albert Museum (fig. 37).[77] This led to the development of borders featuring putti among scrolling foliage which continued to be used until the mid-eighteenth century (fig. 38). Carlo Antonio's son Francesco Antonio Xaverio Grue (1686–1746) continued the tradition into the eighteenth century, with the help of his own sons.[78]

Similar lavishly decorated maiolica was made in Siena by the painters Ferdinando Maria Campani (1702–71) and his rival Bartolomeo Terchi (1691–after 1753), using prints

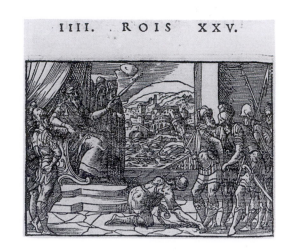

35 Woodcut of *Zedekiah before Nebuchadnezzar* from *Quadrins Historiques de la Bible*, Lyons, 1555.

36 Dish painted with a scene of *Zedekiah before Nebuchadnezzar*. Tin-glazed earthenware, painted in colours. Probably Lyons, *c.*1580–90. British Museum, London

37 Design for a maiolica plate. Pen and brown ink, 57 × 57 cm. Francesco Bedeschini. Victoria & Albert Museum, London.

38 Plate painted with a scene of *The Triumph of Bacchus* after Pietro Testa. Tin-glazed earthenware, painted in colours. Castelli, workshop of Carlo Antonio Grue, *c.*1690. Private Collection, Italy.

Overleaf, detail of fig. 49. Spouted vessel.

after the Bassano family; Terchi in fact worked for a time at the town of Bassano Romano in Lazio. Bartolomeo's son, Antonio, may have worked at the pottery in the Hungarian town of Holitsch, where a pottery was set up by Francis of Lorraine in 1743, in whose Italian possessions the town of Castelli also lay. This seems to have sparked off the last-surviving flowering of the *istoriato* style, using prints after such seventeenth-century artists as Stefano della Bella (1610–64). His last recorded work is a crudely painted plaque of *Christ Carrying the Cross*, signed and dated Viterbo (in Italy) in 1790.[79] This was the last gasp of a pictorial tradition whose origins lay at the very heart of the Italian Renaissance.

'Court Styles' of the Renaissance: Urbino Maiolica, Saint-Porchaire and Palissy Ware

So far we have discussed maiolica as an aspect of Italian Renaissance painting; that is, the use of the relatively flat surface of a plate as a vehicle for a pictorial composition. However, we should also remember that these pieces of pottery presumably had some kind of utilitarian function. It is not clear to what extent they were made for everyday use on the dinner table, and to what extent they were made for display. However, given the relatively good condition in which they have come down to us, we can assume that they were little used and may even have had a specific display function, perhaps on a *credenza* (the modern Italian name for a sideboard, formerly given to a dinner service). It may be significant that an *istoriato* service made for Pope Clement VII was described in a letter of 1528 as being used only when cardinals were present.[1]

We know very little about the organisation and arrangement of a Renaissance dinner (I use the term 'dinner' rather than 'banquet' as this latter had more precise connotations in the past). It would seem to have followed medieval precedent, with the lord sitting at High Table by himself or accompanied by selected guests, with a display of plate on a sideboard at the side, and certain ceremonial items of plate, such as the salt, directly in front of him. Such a dinner is shown in *Les Très Riches Heures du Duc de Berry* of about 1410[2] and the *Grimani Breviary* of about 1500.[3] We know even less of what they ate and the dishes on which the food was served. The *Harleian Household Regulations*, dating from the late fifteenth century, show that in England and presumably France a dinner consisted of two courses made up of numerous dishes, supplemented by 'potages' (soups). The tendency for the courses to move through meats to end in sweets appears to be a development of the fifteenth century.[4] The arrangement of the meal was supervised by various officers of the household, such as the Carver (for cutting the meat in the days before knives and forks), the Sewer (Server) and Cupbearer, who held the cup up to the lord. The diners ate off slabs of bread and shared a central dish of food for four, or 'mess'; this was shared between two in the case of more elevated people and of course one for the lord himself. The tradition of displaying silver and gold plate on another table, where the wines would be poured, was the origin of the French *buffet* (sideboard) of the late seventeenth and eighteenth centuries and continued well into the nineteenth century.[5]

There seems to have been some variation in Italy, where the diners occupied only one side of the table, leaving themselves free to be served from the other by the servants. Such scenes are shown in various Italian paintings of the fifteenth and sixteenth centuries (fig. 39).[6] Our best guide to the kinds of food eaten at a sixteenth-century dinner in Italy is probably Bartolomeo Scappi, who published *The Art of Cookery* in 1570. He was the *cuoco secreto* (personal cook) to Pius V, and responsible for the preparation and display of the food at the Papal Court. In it he gives sample menus

39 Sandro Botticelli (1445–1510), *Scene from the Story of Nastagio*. Oil on panel, 83 × 142 cm. Prado, Madrid (photograph courtesy of the Bridgeman Art Library).

for dinners according to season, dividing the courses into hot (served from the kitchen) or cold (already prepared and laid out on a sidetable). A meal that he prepared for Pius V in 1570 consisted of four courses, each comprising a wide variety of foods, but carefully divided into hot and cold courses. The first course consisted of cold foods from the sideboard – marzipan, wine, ham, cold song-birds and suchlike. The second was of hot foods sent up from the kitchen: roast pigeons, rabbits, pastries, veal, goat and almond-cream soup. The third course consisted of more cooked foods from the kitchen, including boiled meats and stews, goose, veal, and pies with custard cream. The fourth was a forerunner of what was to become the *dessert* course in the eighteenth century and consisted of fruit: quinces, pastries, pear tarts, parmesan cheese, and chestnuts.[7] The divisions between courses may have been influenced not by choice of foods but by method of cooking, ranging from boiled (*lesso*) to fried (*fritto*), stewed (*umido*) to roast (*arrosto*).[8] Throughout a meal such as this the emphasis was on display, and presenting the food in as elaborate a way as possible. Scappi had already worked for Cardinal Campeggio, who in 1536 gave a dinner to the Emperor Charles V, which consisted of ten courses laid out for twelve people. As it was Lent, only fish was served, with crayfish cooked in wine with their claws silvered and gilded, gold and silver forks used for the sweetmeats course, and live birds which were released from the complicatedly folded napkins – an art in themselves in the sixteenth century.[9]

We do not know the more mundane facts about everyday food and display; for instance how foods were laid out on the table, and whether dishes of a certain size or shape were associated with specific foods in particular courses in our present-day manner. The earliest depictions of table-layout suggest a high degree of informality in the setting, with a wide variety of trenchers, dishes and others utensils set out on the table with the largest in the centre.[10] Early Italian depictions of dinners and feasts show an array of different-sized round dishes supporting a variety of foods, without any suggestion that they were intended for specific items;[11] what would have been required would have been simply a variety of plates of various sizes which could be disposed as necessary (fig. 40).[12]

However, it would appear that the concept of a dinner service, consisting of different but matching items of tableware was current from Medieval times onwards. Charles VI of France ordered six dozen pewter dishes and twelve dozen porringers in 1393, although this was not necessarily a complete table service, and we do not know if the items matched.[13] A maiolica service made in Montelupo in 1518 by the potter Lorenzo di Piero di Lorenzo for Clarice Strozzi de' Medici comprised the following items: eleven large *piatti* (plates), twelve middle-sized plates, twenty five smaller; sixteen large *schodelle* (cups or basins), sixteen *schodellini*, and four large *mezzine* (the meaning of these latter terms is unclear, but must refer to some kind of medium-sized plate or dish).[14] Thus a basic dinner service consisted of three sizes of plates supplemented by various broth bowls. The Duke of Ferrara ordered a dinner service in 1530, including candlesticks, basins and ewers.[15] Some of these items are described in Piccolpasso's treatise on maiolica painting,[16] and the basins and ewers would have been used for washing one's fingers at a feast in the days before knives and forks.[17]

Throughout meals like these, the emphasis was on ingenuity and display; the meal was not intended to feed so much as delight the senses and impress the guest with the host's wealth and sense of hospitality (fig. 41).[18] It was customary to provide table decorations in the form of small-scale sculptures made out of marzipan or sugar-paste.

40 Bowl inscribed *Per meter uno pesco di vitello alleso 1577* (for placing a piece of boiled veal, 1577). Tinglazed earthenware, diameter 27cm. Probably Padua, 1577. The Bowes Museum, Barnard Castle, Co. Durham. The bowl must be a potter's sample, and perhaps refers to a change in European eating habits described by William Harrison in his *Description of England*, 1576/7: *Dishes and platters in my time begin to be made deep like basins, and are indeed more convenient both for sauce, broth, and keeping the meat warm.*

41 Crispin der Passe the Elder (*c.*1564–1637). *Dives and Lazarus*. Engraving.

These were called 'sobleties' in Medieval England, and were brought around at the end or beginning of each course. Their subject could be chivalric or classical, and they might furthermore provide a conversation piece for the diners themselves.[19] Such sculptures came to be especially associated with the last course, which in England in the sixteenth century was called a 'void' or later a 'banquet'. This was a light repast of sweet wines and preserved fruit (sugar was thought to have medicinal properties), often taken out-of-doors or in special pavilions outside, or even on the roof of a great house.[20] This 'banquet' became the origin of the eighteenth-century 'dessert', a separate meal taken after dinner that came to provide enormous stimulus for ceramic production (fig. 42).

In meals such as these the table utensils had to be of the most fashionable design, and by the early sixteenth century the design of gold and silver began to reflect the developments that were taking place in Italian painting. We know relatively little about the design of earlier secular gold and silver, since it was melted down for reasons of finance or simply changes of fashion. However, from the 1520s, the history of metalwork-design can be traced, not only from surviving objects, but also from drawings of metalwork and the publication of prints or motifs for decorative wares. The impetus probably came from the artists Raphael (1483–1520) and Michelangelo (1475–1564), both of whom are recorded as having designed metalwork.[21] The explanation for the use of major artists to design apparently lesser objects lay in their knowledge of *disegno*, or the art of design. This implied not simply drawing skills, but a knowledge and perception of the underlying structure of the world, as laid down by God in the Creation, which the artist should attempt to recreate in ideal form by studying the beauties of nature and trying to depict their underlying perfect form, rather than the specific detail.[22] The greatest exponent was of course Michelangelo, whose work is a continuous testimony to the search for ideal form in the nude, but once artists had this knowledge, they were considered capable of

42 Early seventeenth-century 'banquet' as laid out by Ivan Day at The Bowes Museum in 1994, showing large decorative 'marchpanes' and a central artificial garden of coloured fruit pastes after designs in William Lawson, *The Country Housewife's Garden*, London, 1627.

43 Below. Giulio Romano (*c.*1499–1546). Drawing of an ewer for Cardinal Ercole Gonzaga. Victoria & Albert Museum, London.

44 Right. Giulio Romano (*c.*1499–1546). Detail of the fresco of *The feast of Cupid and Psyche*, showing a sideboard laid with plate. Palazzo del Te, Mantua.

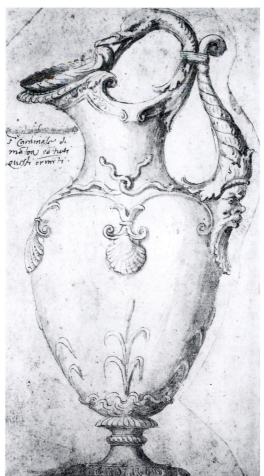

designing anything from a silver plate to a major work of architecture, such as St Peter's in Rome, the crowning achievement of Michelangelo's last years.

With this knowledge of *disegno* also came *licenzia*, that is, the ability to transgress the rules in the cause of variety and novelty. Hence the origins of caricature in sixteenth-century Italy, and the development of mannerist architecture, where the rules of the classical architecture of Greece and Rome are knowingly broken. These ideas affected metalwork-design in two ways. Firstly, it became general to use the human figure as a decorative motif, twisting it round and adapting it from its classical origin to produce handles on jugs and suchlike. Secondly, the variety and number of design sources now increased, to include grotesque faces, imitation leather 'strapwork' interlace, and other forms of ornament.

The most important designer of gold and silver of the sixteenth century, judging from the number of surviving designs, seems to have been Raphael's pupil Giulio Romano (1499–1546). He had assisted Raphael directly in his work in the Vatican and elsewhere in Rome. In 1524 Romano went to Mantua where he worked for Francesco Gonzaga, and part of his work there seems to have been designing objects of silver and other precious metals. He made numerous designs which combine naturalistic and grotesque features, as in a basin and ewer which feature fish in the sea.[23] A drawing in the Victoria and Albert Museum, inscribed for Cardinal Ercole Gonzaga, shows his use of natural forms (fig. 43), with decoration combining shells, snakes, bulrushes and a swan's head with a grotesque mask at the base of the handle. The great sixteenth-century art-historian and biographer, Vasari, refers to the 'bizarre vases, basins, jugs, cups . . . fashioned in various forms and fantastic styles' which appear on the credenza in his fresco of *The Feast of Cupid and Psyche* of about 1524 (fig. 44), which is of documentary interest for his design of metalwork. The silver is clearly intended to display the owner's taste and wealth, with only the wine-coolers below having practical use.

It would appear that many of these pieces were thought to be imitations or reproductions of pieces from classical antiquity; derivations of Giulio's designs were engraved by Agostino dei Musi, who published a series of prints of vase designs each entitled *Sic Roma antiqui sculptores ex aere et marmore faciebant* (Thus worked the ancient Roman sculptors in bronze and marble) in 1530–1, and Enea Vico (*c.*1520–63) who published a series of fantastic vase-designs of *Romae ab antiquo repertum* (Found in Rome from the Antique) in 1543.[24] The title suggests that they are taken straight from the Antique, though in fact they show a variety of naturalistic and fantastic ornamentation which places them well within the Italian Renaissance tradition. These prints would have propagated three-dimensional ideas to the makers of utensils in the same way that prints by Marcantonio Raimondi propagated the two-dimensional designs of Raphael and his school, and allowed ceramic manufacturers to develop ideas close to those of silver and precious metalworkers.

There thus arose in Italy a tradition of making vases and other decorative items in maiolica which rivalled the finest works of bronze and silver workers. The main centre for the making of elaborate maiolica seems to have been the workshops of the Fontana family and the Patanazzi in Urbino. Orazio Fontana, son of Guido Durantino (the family had assumed the name 'Fontana' by 1553) set up a separate workshop from his father in 1565.[25] The major products of Orazio's workshop appear to have been large tri-lobed wine-coolers, flagons in the shape known today as 'pilgrim flasks', salts, plates and other items for the table in the most up-to-date manner (fig. 45). The style of painting was usually that of the grotesque, but this time painted on a white background. Some remarkable pieces survive from various great services, for instance, from a service painted with scenes from the popular romance of *Amadis of Gaul*, apparently created for a Spanish patron,[26] or pieces made for the court of the Medici in Florence. A speciality seems to

45 Wine-cooler. Tin-glazed earthenware, painted in colours, inscribed on the base in blue F.F.F./URBI-NI/1574. Urbino, probably by Flaminio Fontana, the nephew of Orazio, 1574. Height 40 cm. The Wallace Collection, London.

46 Maiolica vase with serpent handles, mounted in eighteenth-century French gilt-bronze mounts. Workshop of Orazio Fontana, Urbino, *c.*1565–71. Bought by Horace Walpole in Paris in 1765–6. The British Museum, London.

47 Flask painted with the coat-of-arms of Philip II of Spain. Soft-paste porcelain, painted in underglaze blue. Height 27.6 cm. Florence, Medici workshop, *c.*1581. Musée National de Céramique, Sèvres.

have been large and elaborate vases with snake handles, of uncertain usage; one survives in the British Museum, in eighteenth-century gilt-bronze mounts, inscribed 'FATE.IN BOTEGA.DE ORATIO.FONTANA' (fig. 46). The style of the Fontana workshop was continued by that run by the Patanazzi family from 1580 to 1620; their products are often impossible to distinguish from those of the Fontana workshop, which also made great maiolica services for noblemen, such as the Count of Lemos in Spain.[27]

Though the workshop of the Fontana was run privately, many rare and precious items were made in court goldsmith's workshops. The most famous were those of the Medici in Florence, set up under Cosimo I (1537–74), and continued by his successors Francesco I (1574–87) and Ferdinand I (1587–1609). Their interest was not simply in the products but also the method of production, to such an extent that Francesco I was something of an accomplished goldsmith himself. Items were kept in his *studiolo* in the Palazzo Vecchio, which survive to this day with paintings by the most famous artists of the time depicting the process of the manufacture of precious goods. Such *studioli* were at first intended as studies in the modern sense, but with time came to be used for the storage of precious, rare and personal items;[28] as such they functioned as the forerunners of the French *cabinets* of the seventeenth century. When the ducal workshops were transferred to the ground floor of the palace of the Uffizi, in 1588, rare and precious items in the collection were moved to the famous *Tribuna* of the Uffizi, designed by Francesco's chief designer Bernardo Buontalenti (1531–1608).[29]

One of the most interesting aspects of the work of the Florentine workshops was the first successful attempt in Europe to make porcelain, which was highly sought after by Western princes and the Medici in particular.[30] The attempt was actually only partly successful since what was produced was not true 'hard-paste' porcelain of the Eastern kind, but a 'soft-paste' variety which was closely akin to glass, and which actually used ground-up glass in its composition.[31] Francesco utilised the services of Flaminio Fontana,[32] nephew of the pottery-maker Orazio, and in 1575 the Venetian ambassador was able to report that Francesco had met with success.[33]

Medici porcelain tends to divide stylistically into two types. A certain amount shows a clear debt to Chinese porcelain, virtually all items being painted in underglaze blue (cobalt oxide),[34] in the Chinese or Turkish manner, with large flowers stencilled on, as in a flask now in the Getty Museum.[35] There also exist a small number of plates painted in the centre with Evangelists from the series engraved by the German artists H. Aldegrever (1502–*c.*58) after G. Pencz (1500–*c.*50), or with a central medallion of the *Death of Saul* from the illustrated Bible by Hans Sebald Beham (1500–50).[36] A number of square flasks bear the coat-of-arms of Philip II of Spain, indicating a commission from, or gift to, him (fig. 47).[37]

Some items of Medici porcelain are straight copies from existing types, such as the tall-necked 'pilgrim' flasks (derived from leather water-bottles) (fig. 48), the double-spouted ewer in the manner of Montelupo maiolica,[38] or the tall vase with a mask head and handles above, which is a close copy of a model already found in Urbino maiolica.[39] However, the most ambitious seem to owe a debt to the work of metalworkers and in particular show the influence of two court goldsmiths, the aforementioned Bernardo Buontalenti and Giovanni Bilvert (1550–*c.*93). Bernardo Buontalenti had been a pupil of Vasari and supervised the firings of the porcelain; in Vasari's *Lives of the Artists* of 1568 he is described as being on the brink of success. He had worked in the ducal workshops on gold and precious stones, and Vasari praises his 'ingenious fantasies' (*ingegnose fantasie*) but unfortunately described them as too complex to describe (*che il tutto qui raccontare sarebbe lunghissima storia*). However, a certain number of carved objects in precious stones survive which are attributable to his hand and suggest he had a major role in designing the forms of Medici porcelain. The majority of

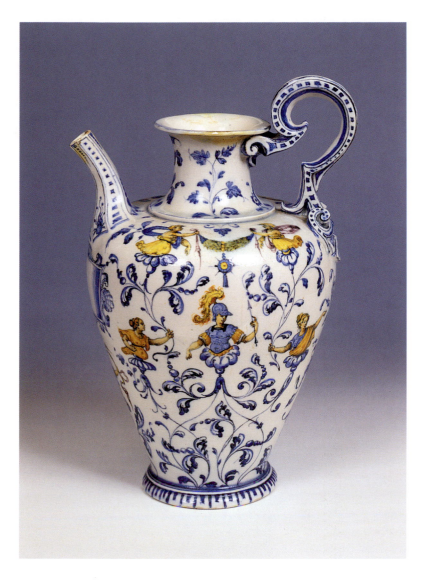

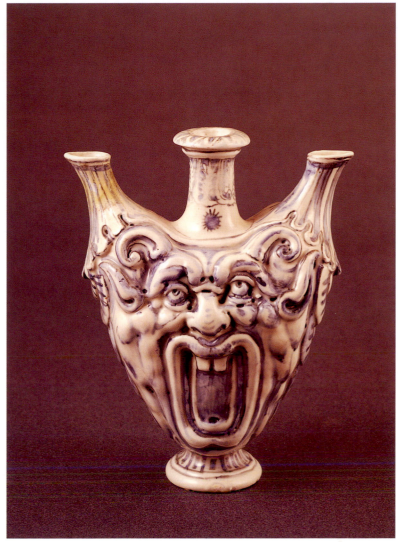

48 'Pilgrim' flask. Soft-paste porcelain, painted in underglaze blue. Height 26.4 cm. Florence, workshop of the Medici, c.1575–87. The J. Paul Getty Museum, Los Angeles.

49 Spouted vessel. Soft-paste porcelain, painted in colours. Height 27.5 cm. Florence, workshop of the Medici, c.1575. Private collection, courtesy of Marc Ferri, Paris.

50 Flask with three spouts with grimacing face. Soft-paste porcelain, painted in underglaze blue. Height 19.7 cm. Florence, workshop of the Medici, c.1575. Sévres, Musée National de Céramique.

these items are vases and ewers of concave shape, often with handles raised above the rims (fig. 49). Many have applied spouts or handles – sometimes in the form of dragons – a device which is associated with Buontalenti's metalwork.[40] A remarkable piece is the double-spouted flask in the form of a grimacing face,[41] a device often found in mannerist art and used to front an artificial cave in the gardens at Bomarzo, Lazio (fig. 50). The most ambitious piece is perhaps a ewer which bears the coat-of-arms of Medici-Austria and is marked on the base with the Medici *palle* (balls) and the initials 'FMMED II' for Francesco de' Medici.[42] One of the last pieces of Medici porcelain seems to be a biscuit (unglazed) plaque with a bas-relief of Francesco himself, dated '1586',[43] and production of Medici porcelain seems to have tailed off after Francesco's death in 1587.

These works were all part of an international culture which dominated the court art of Europe in the period 1530–1630. The emphasis was on fantastic design, invention, and variety, creating an art which would be fully understood only by those educated and initiated into these ideas; this rather self-conscious art has been christened 'mannerism' by modern art-historians. If some of these products seem a little over-ingenious to us, it is because we can no longer follow the Renaissance delight in ingenuity and craftsmanship. The objects were judged not by their restrained or harmonious appearance, but by their creator's ability to make something that could be seen as a rival to the natural world. This delight in artificial forms was not confined to Italy, but soon spread throughout Europe.

The first country to be directly and vividly affected by the influence of the Italian Renaissance was France. Here the king, François I, deliberately introduced Italian artists and craftsmen, mostly to decorate his new palace at Fontainebleau from 1532 onwards. Among the most famous were Rosso Fiorentino (1495–1540) and Primaticcio (1504–70), a former assistant of Giulio Romano. In 1540–59 they decorated the Gallery of Ulysses (demolished 1738–9), which gave rise to a whole school of print-makers, led by Antonio Fantuzzi (active 1537–50) and the master L.D.[44] The emphasis was on decoration using human forms, scrolled decoration called 'strapwork', and an overall refusal to obey the laws of classical composition. The style was reflected in architecture by Jacques Androuet du Cerceau (c.1515–c.84) and in design in general by Etienne Delaune (1518–83).

French patrons had already seen pottery of a high standard. Girolamo della Robbia, one of the great Della Robbia family of Florence, had decorated the Château de Madrid in the Bois de Boulogne with glazed-terracotta plaques, though unfortunately the château was destroyed and the terracottas ground up at the time of the French Revolution. The great military leader Constable Anne de Montmorency (1493–1567), supporter of the royal family during the Wars of Religion, owned a maiolica service made by Guido Durantino of Urbino. There also flourished in France pottery with strong local traditions: for instance, tablewares of high-fired pottery with fine relief decoration from Beauvais decorated with a blue, green or yellow glaze, or flagons of double-walled pottery from La-Chapelle-des-Pots, Saintonge, decorated with piercing and emblems such as monograms or coats-of-arms.[45] A pilgrim flask in the Louvre is decorated with the coat-of-arms of the aforementioned Anne de Montmorency, High Constable of France. The constable made several visits to Saintes in the Saintonge, and the inventory of his possessions in 1568 mentions ewers and flagons of Saintes earthenware.[46]

Anne de Montmorency was apparently also a patron of some of the finest French pottery of the sixteenth century that has come down to us, today called 'Saint-Porchaire' ware. This name is ascribed to a small but coherent body of about sixty finely decorated pieces of low-fired pottery for which no firm attribution is known, and whose origin has been the subject of much speculation over the last 150 years.[47] Today it is generally accepted that the pieces originate from the village of Saint-Porchaire, which was a feudal dependency of Bressuire between Poitou and Saintonge, a domain of the house of Laval-Montmorency whose arms occur on four of the recorded pieces.[48] Some items bear the arms of Anne de Montmorency, or Henri II, or the salamander of Francis I. However, no written records exist as to its date or place of manufacture, although fragments of moulds for wares similar to Saint-Porchaire have recently been excavated in Paris.[49]

There would seem to have been two main phases of production. The first comprises a range of types closely based on simple metalwork-shapes and forms – flagons, standing cups, or 'biberons' (a spouted drinking vessel now associated with children) (fig. 51). A covered cup in the Cluny Museum is clearly based on a pre-Renaissance metal prototype. However, its decoration, of bands of ornament in black, dark-brown or red encircling the item, bears no relation to medieval types and can only be paralleled with new developments in ornament that took place in sixteenth-century Europe, most notably the development of the 'arabesque' style based on the interlaced designs of Venetian-Saracenic metalwork.[50] These were copied and developed by a whole host of ornamental engravers in sixteenth-century Europe, one of the first being Francesco Pellegrino in his *La Fleur de la Science de Pourtraicture* (Paris, 1530). Pellegrino was an associate of Rosso at Fontainebleau and it is reasonable to believe

51 Spouted vessel. Earthenware, with stamped and inlaid clays. France, Saint-Porchaire, c.1540–50. The British Museum, London

that the style reflects types of decoration popular at court. His engravings are supposed to have been a major influence on the school of bookbinders which arose in the sixteenth century, and indeed the only specific link between the decoration on Saint-Porchaire ware and other goods is on a flagon of the first period in the Louvre where one motif has been found to recur on a Milanese or Venetian bookbinding.[51]

Models of the later period show a greater dependency on the shapes and forms of Renaissance metalwork, and include candlesticks, covered bowls, salts and jugs, all decorated with a maximum degree of elaboration. The surfaces are now covered with a variety of interlace arabesque decoration of different colours (black, red, brown) of the most complex pattern. These layers were apparently applied to a separate layer of clay which was then attached to the main body of the item.[52] These later productions often bear moulded ornaments of Renaissance form, separately cast and applied; putti, grotesque masks, shells and even small animals such as snakes and lizards in the manner of contemporary Palissy ware, glazed in different colours. The most important is perhaps the ewer in the Royal Museum of Scotland, which is clearly based on a metalwork prototype[53] (fig. 52).

In contrast to our lack of any documentation for Saint-Porchaire ware, we have an abundance of literature on the work of the French potter Bernard Palissy, whose reputation from the nineteenth century onwards has been that of one of the great figures of ceramic history. His work is especially characteristic of the Renaissance in that it combined an interest in science and the natural world with a belief in God and divine order. His theories were a curious mixture of economic and religious thinking, as evidenced by his two books, the *Recepte Véritable Par Laquelle Tous les Hommes De La France Pouront Apprendre À Multiplier Et Augmenter Leurs Trésors* of 1563 and the *Discours Admirables de la Nature, des Eaux, des fonteines, tant naturelles qu'artificielles, des métaux, des sels, des salines, des pierres, des terres, du feu et des émaux* of 1580. As these titles suggest, he was far more than a simple potter, and saw his work as an aspect of research into the natural world, which in turn was an aspect of his belief in God and his duty to study God's creation, and discover its laws and order.[54]

Palissy was born in about 1510 in Agen. He trained as a glass painter, which would have given him knowledge of enamel colours, and travelled throughout France, Flanders and the Rhine area, before settling in Saintes, about sixty miles from Bordeaux. In about 1539 he was shown:

> an earthen cup, turned and enamelled with so much beauty, that from that time I entered in controversy with my own thoughts . . . I began to think that if I should discover how to make enamels, I could make earthen vessels and other things very prettily, because God had gifted me with some knowledge of drawing [presumably meaning *disegno* or knowledge of the underlying structure of things]; and thereafter, regardless of the fact that I had no knowledge of clays, I began to seek for enamels, as a man gropes in the dark.[55]

In this passage we can sense him making his own myth, with a kind of religious conversion just as potent as St Paul's; we do not know for certain what this white earthenware cup was, but Saint-Porchaire, the probable place of manufacture of the inlaid white wares, was only nine miles from Saintes and has been suggested as its origin.

Palissy seems to have developed a variety of enamel colours, which he combined to produce the effect of jasper. Jasper was a popular semi-precious stone of the time, often carved into intricate shapes which would then appear in a princely treasury; several survive from the collections of Lorenzo de' Medici and today are in the Palazzo Pitti, Florence.[56] In his *Arts de Terre* Palissy gives the basis of many of his enamel colours; tin, lead, iron, steel, antimony, *saffre* (cobalt oxide), copper, sand, *salicort* (ashes made from the lees of wine), litharge and stone of Périgord. These could be used for tinting the lead-glaze into various colours,

52 Ewer. Earthenware, with stamped and inlaid decoration. Height 34.6 cm. France, Saint-Porchaire, *c*. 1545–55 (?). Royal Museum of Scotland, Edinburgh.

and Palissy soon developed them for counterfeiting a variety of natural products, although he admits to having great difficulty in controlling the colours in the kiln.[57]

Palissy's great fame in the sixteenth century seems to have rested on his ability to make artificial animals and rocks for 'grottoes', or those outdoor creations wherein all the features of the universe were on display. They derive from Roman versions which were at first situated in natural caves and were dedicated to some pagan deity; as time went on, artificial ones began to be built. They were discussed by the architectural theorist Alberti (1404–72) in his *De re aedificatoria* (1452) who observed that they were decorated with an artificially rough surface composed of small chips of pumice or spongy travertine, mixed occasionally with green ochre to simulate patches of green moss. He had also, he writes, seen a classical example decorated with oyster shells arranged in patterns. The taste was revived in the Renaissance by Giovanni da Udine at the Villa Madama at Rome and Giulio Romano at the Palazzo del Te in Mantua. The taste soon spread to France, where Primaticcio constructed a grotto in the Jardin des Pins at Fontainebleau and another for the Cardinal de Lorraine at Meudon.[58]

Palissy's work on grottoes seems to have resulted from a meeting in the 1550s with Anne de Montmorency, who was in Saintonge to crush the revolt against the *Gabelle* (salt tax), and seems to have commissioned him to create a grotto at his château at Ecouen in about 1555–6. It was also about this time that he appears to have received a visit to his workshop from the Cardinal of Lorraine and Henri II, to whom he offered one of his first *bassins rustiques*, a basin encrusted with fish, lizards, molluscs, and other creatures of the grotto, with which the name of Palissy is most commonly associated today.[59] It may be significant that it was Montmorency's patronage that got him out of many difficul-

53 Illustration of a grotto, from a drawing attributed to Bernard Palissy formerly in the Destailleur collection (illustration taken from Philippe Burty, *Chef d'Oeuvres of the Industrial Arts*, London, 1869). Kunstbibliothek, Berlin.

54 Dish with moulded animal decoration. Earthenware, painted in coloured glazes. French, workshop of Bernard Palissy (*c.*1510–90). Width 36 cm. The Wallace Collection, London.

55. Oval basin with moulded animal decoration, *c.* 1550. Lead-glazed earthenware French, workshop of Bernard Palissy (*c.* 1510–90). Width 48.2 cm. The J. Paul Getty Museum, Los Angeles.

ties, as when in 1562 he was imprisoned for founding a Protestant church at Saintes, but was released and invested with Montmorency's help with the title *inventor de rustiques figulines du Roi*. In about 1565 he came to Paris to work for the queen, Catherine de' Medici, on the now-destroyed grotto in her palace of the Tuileries, which may have been similar to the grotto recorded in a drawing now in the Kunstbibliothek in Berlin (fig. 53).[60]

There is thus comparatively little documented ware from Palissy; attributions to the potter's own workshop must be made on the basis of a close relationship with surviving fragments from excavations near the Tuileries grotto.[61] These fragments suggest that the grotto was decorated with applied reptiles, such as frogs, lizards, and fish, which were often modelled from nature, dead or newly killed specimens being used. Related to these are the large number of plates, decorated with such reptiles painted with coloured glazes (figs. 54 and 55). Similar decoration appears on plates by the German goldsmith Wenzel Jamnitzer dating from the 1550s.[62] A common theme in most of these plates is the snake wriggling down the centre, and it may be that the meaning is that of the serpent in the Garden of Eden, which makes all the other creatures flee. It may be that the animals, fish and birds that decorated these grottoes were considered appropriate to the level of nature that they occupied – the air, earth, or water, and that grottoes represented to Palissy a microcosm of the universe, and the artificial creatures he created were intended to deceive real ones.[63]

Palissy's later career is a sad one, with many problems resulting from his strongly held Protestantism. It is not clear to what extent he continued the manufacture of ceramics, but from 1575 to 1584 he organised conferences on natural history. He was imprisoned again in 1586, only to die, apparently of starvation, in the Bastille in 1590. However, he had started a whole movement of elaborately moulded plates and other objects decorated with coloured glazes, although the creative spirit in other hands was

less vigorous, and the elements became more decorative. After 1576 he had been associated with the Protestant goldsmith Jean Chipault I (working 1576–99), *émailleur du roi*, the first in a long line of family potters, who could have been responsible for a Palissy-style ewer and basin moulded directly after pewter models by the goldsmith François Briot (figs 56 and 57). He was working at a pottery at the royal palace of Fontainebleau before his death in 1599, and his work was continued by his son Jean II (d. 1611), in association with Claude Beaulat and Claude Bertélémy (*c.*1555–1626), Jean Chipault I's son-in-law, in a house just outside the main courtyard of the palace of Fontainebleau. The pottery must have been productive, as an inventory of 1620 of his house and workshop lists figures, dishes, basins, candlesticks, openwork-bowls, vases, urns, ewers, cups, salts, bottles and even picture frames, some described as *terres sigillées* or *jaspées* or *agatées*, showing that they were in the manner of Palissy ware.

Many of the products of this pottery reflect court styles and may have been modelled by the court sculptor Guillaume Dupré (1579–1640) or the medallist Giovanni Paolo (active *c.*1598–1612). Dupré may have modelled a figure of Henri IV as Neptune with an infant dolphin to celebrate the birth of the dauphin in 1601, and a pottery figure of a nurse and child which was presented by the dauphin to Madame de Montpensier in 1608, which could correspond with a well-known model in Palissy ware (fig. 58). Other

56 Ewer moulded from a pewter example by François Briot. Earthenware, decorated in coloured glazes. Height 26.5 cm. French, follower of Bernard Palissy (Jean Chipault I?), *c.*1600. The Wallace Collection, London.

57 Basin moulded from a pewter example by François Briot. Earthenware, painted in coloured glazes. Diameter 41 cm. French, follower of Bernard Palissy (Jean Chipault I?), *c.*1600. The Wallace Collection, London.

models represented a bagpiper, a hurdy-gurdy player, a boy with puppies and a shepherd. The dauphin himself owned a large collection of Fontainebleau figures and animals bought on his frequent visits to the pottery.

In 1620 Chipault II was joined by Jean Bertélémy, which may have led to wares with coloured glazes being made at La-Chapelle-des-Pots, also at Avon, under the Clérissy family. This later type seems to comprise designs with interlaced and radiating patterns, the so-called *style rayonnant*, but always of a quality and invention somewhat below that of the first Palissy-type pieces. Other centres for the production of similar ware in the seventeenth century may have been Manerbe, and Pré d'Auge, near Lisieux in Normandy. The gradual dispersal of the potters may have been due in part to the measures taken against the Protestants in France in the later seventeenth century, but it is also likely that changes in taste and manufacturing technique meant that Palissy-type wares were simply less sought after by the end of the seventeenth century.[64]

58 Figure of a nurse holding a baby. Earthenware, decorated in coloured glazes. Height 22.9 cm. Fontainebleau, *c.*1602–5. Musée National de Céramique, Sèvres.

Overleaf. Detail of fig. 68. Bottle/jug. Brown stoneware.

CHAPTER 4

The Stoneware Tradition

Although pottery in sixteenth-century Europe could be an article of high fashion, for most people it retained a more utilitarian function. Simple low-fired earthenware vessels continued to be made for eating and drinking and were used by lesser folk, along with wooden trenchers and other items in everyday use. This class of ceramic was probably the standard for most people, though it is known more through fragments from archaeological excavations than examples which have survived intact.[1] It is doubtful whether ceramics of this type would have been valuable enough to be exported. However, there arose in Germany a new class of ceramic which imbibed the ideas of the Renaissance without attempting to hide its utilitarian nature. This was the tough and durable stoneware of Germany, which combined utility with decorative influences from printed designs and other sources.

Although we can speak of a German culture, sharing a common visual style and (to a lesser extent) a common language, Germany itself in the sixteenth century was not a single political nation, neither sharing common laws nor a single prince. It was a mixture of over 1,000 principalities, bishoprics and independent Free Cities, such as the important trading towns of the *Hansa* in the North and the metalworking towns of Augsburg and Nuremburg in the South, all under the nominal tutelage of the Holy Roman Empire. However, this federation was beginning to break down, most obviously with the divisions caused by the Reformation from 1517 onwards, in which certain princes and towns openly defied the emperor on the issue of religion. These divisions were exacerbated by divisions within German society itself, exemplified by the Peasants War of 1522–5 and the growth of religious dissidents such as Anabaptists. However, the vigour with which activities such as painting, architecture, print-making and metalworking were pursued testifies to the internal dynamism of the economy.

Germany had led Italy in the production of books and prints from the fifteenth century onwards, although the new techniques of copper- and woodblock-printing had their first recognisable influence on ceramics in Italian maiolica. The process of printing using moveable type had been developed by Johan Gutenberg (c.1398–1468) by 1456; before that, printed books had been made by means of cutting a whole woodblock and then binding the pages together. Many of these were illustrated, as in the *Biblia Pauperum*. The great painter Albrecht Dürer (1471–1528) himself was one of the producers of separate woodcuts, publishing the great *Apocalypse* in 1498, and the *Large Passion*, the *Small Passion* and the *Life of the Virgin* in 1511. These were widely copied and disseminated, even across the Alps, where Marcantonio Raimondi was responsible for a pirated edition of the *Life of the Virgin* which may have been copied by maiolica painters.[2]

There was thus a strong native tradition of printmaking, closely linked to book illustration, whose main exponents have been christened the 'little masters' (*Kleinmeister*),

59 Stove with tiles moulded with scenes from *The Lives of the Patriachs* and *The Divinities of the Planets* after Sebald Beham, and *The Crucifixion* after Virgil Solis, signed and dated by Hans Kraut in the Black Forest. Earthenware, painted with coloured glazes or tin-glaze. Height 238.7 cm. Victoria & Albert Museum, London.

on account of the small scale of much of their work.[3] Their prints had great popular appeal and were frequently used in several editions of the same book in different languages. The most famous are perhaps Hans Holbein's illustrations to the Bible published in the *Historiarium Veteris Instrumenti Icones* of 1526, and in expanded form in Froschauer's Bible published in Zürich in 1531, and the Bible illustrations of Hans Sebald Beham (1500–50) published in German in Frankfurt in 1533, and in Latin in 1537, 1539 and 1557. Most popular and widely reproduced were perhaps the 147 illustrations by Virgil Solis (1514–62) published in the Bible of Sigmund Feyerabend in Frankfurt-am-Main in 1560.[4] These books were distributed internationally and can often be traced as sources for pictorial design in various of the decorative arts.

German patrons were aware of developments in ceramics in Italy, since there were strong trading links between the large towns in southern Germany and Italy. These links seem to have led to a number of commissions from such great banking centres as Nuremburg and Augsburg for maiolica services, for example one bearing the arms of Johann Neudörffer (1497–1563), a distinguished teacher in Nuremburg,[5] or a service made on the occasion of a marriage between the Christell and Mayr families of about 1593.[6] A small amount of painted German tin-glazed earthenware is known, probably the result of influences from Italy, as for example the case of the potters Hans Nickel and Sowald Reinhardt, who went from Nuremberg to Venice before 1531, and may have brought the secrets of maiolica painting back with them.[7] Tin-glazed earthenware made in sixteenth-century Germany included stove-tiles, and a small number of blue-painted jugs in the form of owls (*Eulenkrüge*), dated 1540 to 1561. A small group of tin-glazed wares was made in the stoneware-making town of Creussen, some of which are dated 1618. The tradition continued in the seventeenth century in the town of Winterthur in Switzerland, where guild regulations had been introduced in 1637. A group of at least ninety-six potters, most famously the Pfau family, made a wide range of tin-glazed earthenware, including tiles, jugs, plates and dishes painted with fruit, coats-of-arms and other motifs in a distinctive style that owed little to the *istoriato* tradition of maiolica painting.[8]

Much of our knowledge about the production of the decorative arts in sixteenth-century Germany comes from the surviving records of the different tradesmen's guilds. These were, in origin, medieval institutions which existed to protect the rights of their members and maintain standards of workmanship. By the sixteenth century, however, they had become institutions which tended to protect the rights of the more powerful members against the lesser. Often they had rights of representation on the city councils, in common with the old-established rich families and the 'honourable' (*ehrbar*) middle ranks.[9] In general, German guild organisation was much more strict and rigid than its Italian counterpart, operating a system of exclusion for outsiders, even those patronised by the Crown.[10] However, except in the most specialised fields of pottery production, there were no guilds of potters as such, their better members being members of the Builders' guild (for tiles and bricks), the painters and sculptors (for painted and moulded decoration), or, for the owners of large workshops, members of the Sellers of Glass and Earthen Pots.[11] It was only in the production of items of highly decorated ceramic, with large workshops headed by a Master, that guild organisation played a major role.

An important part of the ceramics industry in Germany and Austria was devoted to the production of large and elaborate lead-glazed stove-tiles, for the decoration of the great stoves that were to remain a feature of continental rooms into the nineteenth century. The main centres were Cologne,[12] Nuremburg, and the Tyrol in Austria (fig. 59). The decoration on early tiles, made before 1500, consisted mostly of moulded decoration formed by squeezing the flat clay of the tiles into a mould, which were then fired and glazed in green or brown lead-glazes. The first styles of moulded decoration were derived from traditional heraldic or plant forms in the Gothic manner, but soon classical motifs inspired by the Renaissance made their appearance, sometimes mixed with the older styles. The famous late-Gothic stove, dated 1501, in the castle of Hohensalzburg, is decorated with caryatids and pilasters in the classical manner, together with figures of Roman emperors and the apostles. The stove showing Renaissance ornamentation at Cracow of 1506–18 has tiles with polychrome decoration of different coloured glazes. The names of some of these early potters and tile makers are known, for instance Hans Bermain of Augsburg, some of whose pieces are dated 1562.[13] It is not known when the ideas of the Renaissance first came to have an influence on the German decorative arts, and artisans had to dispense with traditional patterns handed down over the years. It may be significant that in 1535 the Nuremberg Guild of Goldsmiths no longer forced the applicants to produce their own design when submitting their masterpiece to gain admission to the guild, suggesting that by then they needed professional help to produce designs.[14]

The making of coloured stove-tiles led to the development of brightly coloured so-called *Hafnerkeramik* (potter's ware), painted in various coloured glazes, in the second third of the sixteenth century, mostly in southern Germany and Austria. The glazes were white, yellow, brown, red-brown, purple, green and blue in the manner of Palissy ware. Again the main feature of the decoration is ornamentation made by producing the vessel in a mould, but with a greater range of shapes and types, such as large jugs which bear on the main body religious or other scenes, with applied or incised decoration on the other parts. The best-known maker of *Hafnerkeramik* whose name has come down to us is Paul Preuning of Nuremberg, who in 1541 was convicted, along with his workman Kunz Preuning, of having made a blasphemous jug decorated both with scenes of the Crucifixion and representations of fifers, drummers and dancing peasants. A number of pieces are attributed to him on this evidence (fig. 60).[15] Another centre of *Hafnerkeramik* was Salzburg, which probably made the Gotchi stove of 1501, and produced an elaborate *Zunftkachel* (guild-sign) of 1561 formerly in the Figdor collection.[16] Less elaborate Hafnerware was made in the Cologne region, mostly simple jugs and beakers with applied decoration with green or yellow glazes.

Though Italy dominated the field of luxury ceramic tablewares with its elegantly painted tin-glazed earthenware, there existed in the North a wholly different ceramic type. This was the German tradition of large stoneware jugs and flasks for beer called *Humpen*. In order to make them non-porous, the clay was fired to a high temperature of at least 1,200°C, which resulted in a vitrified body characterised by its toughness and durability (*stoneware*). The main centres for its production were the region around Cologne in Germany, Raeren on the border with modern-day Belgium, and the mountains and forest regions of the South and East. These wares were in great demand throughout Europe and beyond and formed a flourishing export trade from the fourteenth century until well into the eighteenth century.

Stoneware first appeared in Germany in the Rhineland. New types of jug in a hard-fired fabric, with a grey core and reddish or greyish surface fired to 1,000–1,050°C, began to appear during the first quarter of the thirteenth century in the area around the town of Siegburg near Cologne.[17] During the first half of the second quarter of the thirteenth century a slip was added to create a glassy reddish or brownish effect. As the strength of the body was increased, the walls of the vessel became thinner and the firing temperature rose to 1,050–1,200°C. It should be stressed that the production of stoneware proper required special clays which could withstand these high temperatures, which led to a certain amount of regional specialisation, with a range of places in the Rhineland and Lower Saxony being identified as centres of stoneware production in medieval times.[18]

60 Jug. Earthenware, painted in coloured glazes. Height 53.3 cm. Nuremberg, workshop of Paul Preuning, c.1550. The Victoria & Albert Museum, London.

61 Moulded jugs (*Bartmannskrüge*). Brown stoneware.
Heights 14.2, 11.2 cm. Cologne, *c.*1520–45. The British
Museum, London.

A major technical development of the early sixteenth century was 'salt-glaze', in
which a more refined clay was glazed by throwing salt into the kiln during firing.
During the process the soda in the salt combines with the silica and alumina in the
body, leaving a thin, colourless, glassy film on the body, akin to the texture of orange
peel, making the pot non-porous without the need for a further firing. This led to the
development of a whole group of export wares whose manufacture continued into the
eighteenth century.

The characteristic product of the early period was the brown mug or jug made at
Cologne and its neighbouring town of Frechen (from 1544 onwards[19]) which began
to appear around 1500. The clay has a grey body when fired in the kiln and so was
coated with a brown slip before firing.[20] The pot was thrown on the wheel, and handles or other parts added by hand. After drying, the jug was often given more decoration by cutting, or applying decorative motifs cast from moulds (*Stege*), which had
appeared by 1500. The best-known type was the *Bartmannskrug*, a large bulbous bottle
or jug decorated about the neck with the mask of a bearded man (fig. 61). This was
made by pressing a piece of clay into a negative mould bearing the imprint of a bearded face and applying it to the body when it was 'leather-hard', just before firing.
Sometimes the face was developed into a figure with arms reaching down the body of
the jug, or an applied or 'sprigged' decoration of trailed oak leaves was also added. Such
decoration was first seen on mugs and jugs, but soon appeared on bottles as well. They
often bear decoration associated with Cologne, such as small coin-like medallions, or
lion masks, with acanthus leaves issuing from a central band, sometimes inscribed with
a motto, such as *Trink und Esst, Gots Nicht Vergesst,* (Drink and Eat, but don't forget
God), or *Wann Gott Willt, So Ist Mein Zeilt,* (God's Will is My Aim).[21]

Four main workshops for stoneware in Cologne have been identified, located in the
Maximinenstrasse, which flourished from 1520–50, the pottery of Herman Wollters in
the Komödienstrasse (to about 1570), the Eigelsteinstrasse, and the Streitzeuggasse.[22]
The pottery in the Maximinenstrasse seems to have originated a range of so-called

Interim jugs (after the religious Interim of 1548–52) or *Antichristschnelle*, which featured applied moulded decoration of an anti-papal character. Cologne itself remained Catholic during the sixteenth century,[23] and some potters may have migrated or returned to Frechen on account of religious persecution, as well as severe restriction of their operations within the town.[24]

A different type of finely moulded and delicate-bodied wares were made in the outlying town of Siegburg. The local clays were of very fine texture and turned white in the kilns, giving Siegburg wares their characteristic pale appearance. Here we have the benefit of a vast body of guild records and regulations dating back to 1400 which enable us to identify individual potter's work and suggest a fairly precise stylistic evolution of shapes and styles of decoration.[25] The guild itself came under the Grand-Mastership of the abbot of the monastery which dominated the town, and the records of the guild of potters (*Zunft*) have been preserved in the church archives, giving a fairly full account of the trade.

Our basic knowledge of the industry comes from three *Zunstbriefe* (guild statutes, approved by the abbot) for the years 1516, 1531, 1552, which give detailed descriptions of the workings of the industry. The whole working of it was carefully regulated, in an effort to maintain the standards of pottery and keep the business within the town. The craftsmen involved in the production were divided into three types: apprentices, workmen and masters, but there were unskilled workers also. An apprenticeship lasted six years, most apprentices being bound to their fathers. Unskilled workers, such as carters and woodmen, who had access to the workshops and kilns, were sworn to secrecy so as not to divulge the secrets of the process to outsiders. Strict regulations kept rivals out of the system, breaking down only after the town was sacked in 1632 and the abbot sought to attract new workmen from elsewhere. An apprentice qualified as a workman by showing that he was skilled in throwing and turning all manner of pots, and capable of making moulds and applying them, as well as devising new shapes and decoration. A master had to know about the types of clays and sands needed for stoneware, as well as supervising the firings himself and checking the quality of the resulting items. The quantity and quality of production was carefully controlled. A master was allowed only sixteen firings a year, fewer if his number of workmen dropped below the requisite total. The working of the pottery was halted between Martinmas and Ash Wednesday, and it was not allowed to function by candlelight. The aim was to divide the industry up between the skilled members of the guild, and keep production within the local area.[26]

The size of pots, their prices and method of sale was also controlled. The potters were mostly based in the suburb of the *Aulgasse*, not actually within the town itself.[27] Large orders of pottery went through the guild, which divided the request up among the potters. The arms of the country of export were required to be on the pots, which accounts for the large number of wares bearing foreign coats-of-arms. The guild marketed its wares with all kinds of limitations; for instance, merchants from Cologne who bought the goods could only sell them outside of Cologne itself, the Cologne merchant Dietrich Dulman being granted the privilege of selling Siegburg stoneware in Hamburg till 1599.[28] Obviously, these restrictive regulations could only survive as long as Siegburg wares were in such great demand that they had few rivals; the 'golden period' of Siegburg was the second half of the sixteenth century, when the industry concentrated on the production of high-quality wares.[29]

It is possible to chart a particular line of development for Siegburg wares, since many are dated and bear the initials of the master potter who supplied the moulds, which, according to guild regulations, were meant to have been cut by the potters themselves,[30] although they may well have taken advantage of specialist mould-cutters.[31] The earliest products of the town, produced before the wares were marked, seem to have been the so-called *Jacoba* jugs, which were exported to the Low Countries, formerly thought to have been made in the potteries of the Dutch Countess Jacoba between 1401 and 1436.[32] However, by the mid-sixteenth century the characteristic product of the town was the very tall tankard (*Schnelle*), whose large surface area gave plenty of scope for moulded and applied decoration. This usually took the form of biblical and historical scenes, which were cast from moulds and applied to the main body of the vessel before firing. As with Italian maiolica, the designers of the matrices made much use of prints and ornamental engravings by the 'little-masters' (*Kleinmeister*), and particular scenes can be associated with particular workshops.

For many years pottery manufacture in Siegburg was in the hands of a few families, the most famous being the Knütgen, Simons, Flach and Omian. These dominated the trade and led to internal disputes between the potters; in 1564 the potter Peter Knütgen was prosecuted for selling goods directly to foreign dealers, and accused of selling more wares than all the other potters put together.[33] The best-known potter is his father Anno Knütgen, who with a monogrammist FT (usually thought to be Frans Trac) made many of the finest Siegburg moulds, dated from 1559 to 1568. His earliest work seems to have been a *Schnelle* of 1559 decorated with scenes of the *Raising of Lazarus* copied from a print of 1525 by Jörg Breu (*c.*1475–1537). Here we see the characteristic style of Siegburg already fully developed, with a long conical body densely covered in pictorial scenes. Many of Trac's sources have been identified as the Bible illustrations of Virgil Solis of 1560, as well as prints from the *Neuwen Biblischen Figuren* of Jost Amman of 1564.[34] Two other members of the Knütgen family were the aforementioned Peter Knütgen, whose signed work dates from 1569–71, and his brother Christian Knütgen, whose earliest signed work is a *Schnelle* dated 1568, and is especially associated with a group of spouted jugs embossed with animals. The Knütgen family also made *Schellen* decorated with scenes of *Esther* and the *Drunkenness of Noah*, the latter based on a print by Hans Sebald Beham (1500–50).[35] Other types of vessel are also attributed to the Knütgen family, including *Birnkrüge* ('pear-shaped jugs'), *Pullen* (footless globular bottles with a short neck) and *Leuchtervasen* (large jars or cisterns with the handles formed as sockets for candles) (fig. 62). As with many wares, they show a tendency towards increasing elaboration of applied and moulded decoration which gives these objects as ceremonial rather than utilitarian character.

The identification of these wares is usually based on the initials they bear, which can be linked with names in the guild lists. The letters 'HH' are believed to refer to the potter Hans Hilgers, whose signed pieces range from 1569–95 (fig. 63). He seems to have been less innovative than other potters and indeed borrowed or copied their matrices. This is also true of the monogamist LW (worked 1572–9), who may be identified either as Lorenz Wolter[36] or Lomjer Wilhelm.[37] Most of his works fall into the Siegburg tradition of tall *Schnellen* decorated with moulded scenes of coats-of-arms or biblical episodes. However, he apparently has the distinction of being the first to adapt as frieze decoration the *Dance of Peasants* by Hans Sebald Beham, which appears on the number of jugs.

Although Siegburg was clearly the most innovative and productive centre for high-quality stonewares in the sixteenth century, it was not long before other parts of Germany with suitable clays came to rival its ascendancy. Raeren, to the south of Aachen (in modern Belgium; hence the nineteenth-century term for German stoneware *grès de flandres*) was a major producer of stoneware from the middle of the fifteenth century until the eighteenth century. Its early products are indistinguishable from those made at Aachen and the production of ornamented wares seems to have commenced about 1560. Whereas the guild of potters at Siegburg is well-documented, little is known of Raeren potters, since no guild was formed till 1619[38] and much knowledge has depended on excavations.

62 Candelabarum. Salt-glazed stoneware. Height 55 cm. Siegburg, *c.*1570–80. Trier, Rheinisches Landesmuseum.

63 Tall mug (*Schnelle*). White stoneware with moulded decoration, by Hans Hilgers, 1591. Height 21 cm. The Bowes Museum, Barnard Castle, Co. Durham.

64 Jug. Brown stoneware, with an applied body-frieze moulded after scenes from Sebald Beham's *Das Bauernfest* (*Dance of the Peasants*) and dated 1576. Height 22.8 cm. Raeren, workshop of Jan Emens Mennicken. The British Museum, London.

The wares of Raeren are quite different from those of Siegburg – most obviously, they lack the white body of the latter – but they are not immune to the stylistic changes taking place in Siegburg. The most-famous master was Jans Emens Mennicken, whose signed works date from 1566 to 1594, but whose matrices remained in use into the seventeenth century, long after his death. His first works were tall brown *Schnellen* close to the work of Anno Knütgen of Siegburg, but he seems to have specialised in the creation of matrices. His great innovation seems to have been the introduction of the wide horizontal belt around the middle of the body of the jug, as a vehicle for frieze decoration. His best-known works in this field are jugs with the *Dance of the Peasants* by Hans Sebald Beham (fig. 64), jugs depicting *Susanna and the Elders* based on a print by Conrad Goltzius, the *Paris* jugs after Adrian Collaert, and jugs with a frieze of soldiers in niches. He seems to have had a pupil, Engel Kran, who is also known for jugs with scenes from Goltzius's *Susanna and the Elders*.

Emens's main rival seems to have been Baldem Mennicken, whose signed works date from 1575 to 1585. Much of his output is related to the that of others, with friezes taken from Anno Knütgen, the maker LW, Jan Emens and others. He adopted something of Emens' innovation of the central band/frieze, but retained in an ovoid form. His son, Jan Baldems Mennicken, whose works are dated 1589–1613, adopted a less architectural style of decoration, with stamped lines, arabesques, scales and palmettes forming the basis of the decoration.

The decorative tradition in stoneware became increasingly influenced by a technical innovation: from about 1585 the potters of Raeren began to produce grey stoneware partly decorated with blue glaze (*Blauwerk* or 'bluework'), firstly in the form of random splashes, later in the form of all-over decoration. This innovation heralded the beginning of a much more purely decorative phase of German stoneware, in which printed sources, and the use of the human figure in general, become much less important and were replaced by naturalistic or patterned decoration. The earliest marked piece of *Blauwerk* is thought to be a pilgrim bottle dated 1582, but the type did not really become general until around 1587. The shape of the jugs was modified to include a faceted body with nipped-in top with a handle, as well as the three-handled *Dreihelkelkrug*.

In the late sixteenth to early seventeenth centuries tight guild regulations and the wars that plagued Europe – most notably the Thirty Years War of 1618–48 – caused a vast amount of disruption to economic activity and led to the dispersal of stoneware production from its traditional centres. The town of Siegburg was sacked in 1632, never to regain its former supremacy, and its potters, and those from Raeren, fled to the villages of Grenzau, Grenzhausen and Höhr in the Westerwald, a district on the east side of the Rhine opposite Koblenz. Anno Knütgen had already arrived there with his sons Rutger and Bertram in 1590, and was soon followed by another son Herman, the Mennicken and Kran families, and Jakob Remy from Lothrungen. Some kind of guild regulations were introduced in 1591 and in 1614 Bertram was granted a privilege by Count Ernest of Isenberg and Grenzau with a gift of land and exemption from taxes, although he still had to pay 'six ridergulden, the amount to which are taxed the other potters of Raussbach'.[39] However, as the area came under the jurisdiction of three rulers it was not until 1643 that they achieved single guild status, ratified by the rulers of Trier, Wied, Isenburg-Grenzau, Sayn-Wittgenstein and Metternich.[40] These regulations were much less restrictive than before and enabled the industry to flourish. By 1700, there were about six hundred potters working in the region.[41]

The stonewares of the Westerwald are characterised by the fulfilment of the purely decorative tendency that began at Raeren and indicates production for a broad market. The Westerwald potters gradually developed their own distinctive style, based on the decorative innovations developed at Raeren, using sharply defined, applied moulded designs and washes of blue or blue and manganese oxide before salt-glazing. Many of their pieces are grey-bodied and covered in a blue glaze. Some of their designs continued to use the human figure, for instance friezes of soldiers or musketeers, but much decoration was either all-over leaf decoration, or in bands. In about 1620 they devised an eight-panelled jug showing the *Seven Works of Mercy*, copied from a print published in Augsburg in about 1620.[42] Vast quantities of these wares were exported to Holland, France and England, which were slow in developing stoneware of equal quality, and often bear these countries' coats-of-arms or portraits of their rulers (fig. 65).

The major technical development of enamelling on stoneware took place at Creussen near Bayreuth in the South, which had been a centre for lead-glazed stove tiles with relief-moulded decoration. Again, there was no guild to regulate the production and our knowledge of the workings are dependent on a few scattered church records and the wares themselves. The church registers record the following potters: Gaspard Vest (1574), Hans Vest (1576), Hans Schmidt (1643–56), Balthazar Seiler (1653), Johan Georg Seiler (1686–91) and Johann Schmidt (1766).[43] The stonewares made there were created from a grey ferruginous clay which fired to a reddish colour, so to improve their appearance, they were coated with a very dark brown slip before firing. The shapes of the tankards were short and squat (*Humpen*), with moulded decoration in the form of hunting scenes or rows of figures depicting saints, Apostles, the planets or local dignitaries. The first works seem to be the products of the Vest family, and matrices survive dated to 1602. After 1625 many pieces were painted in coloured enamels in the manner of Bohemian glass (fig. 66). A *Humpen* decorated with representations of the planets by Abraham Humbes survives in Hamburg Museum; the first known date of mugs with representa-

65 Brown and blue-decorated stoneware jug with an image of Mary II of England. Height 26.5 cm. Westerwald, *c*.1690. The Bowes Museum, Barnard Castle, Co. Durham.

tions of the Apostles, Five Senses and hunting scenes is 1627,[44] which proved to have a long life. Jugs with figures of Ceres and Pomona after Heinrich Goltzius, and pilgrim flasks are also known.

The story of German stoneware in the later seventeenth and eighteenth centuries is one of the increasing diffusion of the technique throughout Germany, with a corresponding increase in the number of local styles, mostly with particular decorative devices. In Saxony the jugs were glazed with a brown rather than a salt-glaze. The main long-term rival seems to have been at Waldenburg. This was at first derived from Rhenish influences, but by the mid-sixteenth century had developed its own style, with tall figures or medallions decorating the brown body. Elongated egg, beehive and barrel shapes are known. Similar decorations appeared at Annaberg, only with overlapping-scale patterns, applied rosettes and palmettes, pomegranates and portraits on jugs. The colours make great use of white, yellow, blue and gilding. Altenburg developed in the second quarter of the seventeenth century, directly inspired by Waldenburg. Altenburg wares are characterised by deeply incised profiles, stud decorations and, most famous of all, a pearl-like decoration developed in the eighteenth century. In the same tradition are the products of Freiburg in Saxony and Muskau in the Lausitz region on the Polish border. Freiburg stoneware is characterised by carved patterns derived from stylised foliage motifs, rosettes and lion-head friezes, which were frequently enamelled and gilded. Muskau wares, on the other hand, developed their own particular style, using segments of circles filled with various decorations as well as cobalt-blue and manganese, and included a large number of novelty wares, such as angular bottles with a metal top (*Schraubflaschen*) and bottles in the form of barrels. Another centre of stoneware production was Bunzlau; especially esteemed are the so-called melon jugs of the seventeenth and eighteenth centuries, glazed in brown, green or black. The well-known Bunzlau clay-washed wares with white applied decoration were first produced at the beginning of the eighteenth century. By this stage the clay being used in the production of stoneware was much finer than that of earlier periods, and the shapes more varied and elegant.

66 Tankard (*Humpen*). Brown stoneware, with moulded decoration and painted in enamel colours. Height 21.5 cm. Creussen, dated 1705. The Bowes Museum, Barnard Castle, Co. Durham.

The Influence Abroad

German stoneware was exported throughout the world from medieval times into the eighteenth century. Its toughness and durability made it ideal for objects in everyday usage and it was found in most countries in Europe, as well as further afield. It is often depicted in Dutch paintings of the time (fig. 67), perhaps most famously in Jan Vermeer's *The Procuress* of 1656 in Dresden, which depicts a jug of Westerwald type, and it is sometimes recovered from the wrecks of ships trading with India and the East.[45]

One major country of export was England. The English seem to have imported Rhenish stoneware from the fourteenth century onwards, aided by the settlement of German merchants at the Steelyard in Windgoose Lane, London; the earliest imports seem to have been pitchers and cups of white stoneware from Siegburg.[46] The London port book of 1567/8 records the import of 200 stone pots on the *Lion* of Lee, and all the cheaper ranges have been found in excavations in London, most especially the ubiquitous *Bartmannkrüge* from Cologne[47] (today called *Bellarmines* in Britain after the notorious Catholic Cardinal Bellarmino).[48] An English peculiarity seems to have been to mount these cheap wares in silver or silver-gilt mounts, even though the mounts were worth many times the value of the clay vessel.[49] Since these tough stonewares were in such common use, they attracted the attention of the Crown for taxation purposes and Queen Elizabeth granted a monopoly on the import of 'all manner of stone pottes earthen pottes stone bottles and earthen bottles' to one Henry Noell (or

67 Jan Steen (1626–79). *Twelfth Night Feast*, featuring a Westerwald stoneware tankard. Oil on canvas, 40 × 54 cm. The Royal Collection © 2001, Her Majesty Queen Elizabeth II.

Nowell) for fifteen years in 1593, which led to many disputes and infringements of the monopoly.[50] It is estimated that ten million stonewares may have been imported into London in the period 1600–40.[51]

Thus it is not surprising that the English themselves attempted to break the monopoly or make substitutes for stoneware. Locally made copies in lead-glazed earthenware have been excavated in London, apparently dating from the seventeenth century. A kiln that made crude copies of German stoneware, dating to the second quarter of the seventeenth century, has been excavated at Woolwich in south-east London, and in 1671 a Captain William Killigrew petitioned for a stoneware patent, probably using the services of the Wooltus family from Germany.[52] However, the first Englishman to make stoneware on a large scale seems to have been John Dwight of Fulham in London, who in 1672 obtained a patent to make 'the mistery of transparent earthenware commonly knowne by the names of porcelaine or China and Persian ware, as also the misterie of the stoneware vulgarly called Cologne ware'.[53]

68 Bottle/jug. Brown stoneware, with two bands of marbled decoration and applied moulded decoration including busts of William and Mary. Fulham. Height 19.4 cm. Workshop of John Dwight, c.1690. The Fitzwilliam Museum, Cambridge.

John Dwight is one of those interesting figures who played a part in both artistic and scientific thought in the seventeenth century in a way which would not be possible today. He had studied law, physics and chemistry under Robert Boyle while at Oxford in the 1650s, and in about 1660 became secretary to Bishop Hall of Chester and in 1665 registrar at Wigan. There in his house at Millgate, he set up a laboratory to study clays with such enthusiasm that when Hall died in 1668, Dwight was accused of using church funds for the purpose, and had to sell his church appointments and move down to London! He had more success there, and was encouraged in his researches by the scientists Robert Hooke and Robert Boyle, leading to his patent of 1672.[54]

It was at Fulham in London that Dwight commenced the manufacture of stoneware.[55] The site of his pottery at Fulham has been excavated and yielded a great number of finds, including failed test-piecess, which testify to his experiments and versatility. The bulk of the discoveries are fragments of the reddish *Bellarmine* jugs and mugs of the type imported from the Cologne region, many stamped with tavern signs such as the device of the Cock-Ale House at Temple Bar, but some exact copies of Westerwald stoneware tankards were also found, complete with the blue splashed glaze.[56] Later examples from the pottery seem to have become increasingly sophisticated, with moulded or applied decoration and splashed or irregular glazes (fig. 68).

The most ambitious pieces from the pottery are some figures, which are among the most remarkable products of the seventeenth-century pottery industry in England. They are made of fine white clay, carefully and deeply modelled, giving them the appearance of carved stone sculpture, and are the most obvious ceramic rivals to the art of sculpture since the works of the Della Robbia family. The most imposing are perhaps the busts of Charles II in the Victoria and Albert Museum and Prince Rupert in the British Museum, which are in the full Baroque tradition, modelled with great attention to the details of the hair and clothes. All these figures are finely sculpted with great characterisation of expression; the most famous is perhaps the moving bust of the young Lydia Dwight on her deathbed, who died on March 3rd, 1673 (fig. 69). No single sculptor has been suggested for their work, and it has been suggested that they are the work of at least four modellers, namely John Bushnell (d. 1701),[57] Caius Cibber (1630–1700), Grinling Gibbons (1648–1720) and Edward Pierce (d. 1698).[58]

A possible technical and artistic rival to Dwight was the York artist Francis Place, who ran a pottery from about 1678 to about 1694. A handful of his products are known, including some fine white tankards (fig. 70), although he does not seem to have managed to copy Dwight's technique of using mixed clays to create a marbled effect. Although his wares are distinguished by a high level of quality, he never seems to have succeeded commercially, and his work must have remained an experimental sideline.[59]

In 1684 Dwight obtained a fourteen-year patent which included 'white Gorges marbled Porcelane Vessels Statues and Figures and fine stone Gorges and Vessells never before made in England or elsewhere'. However, by the later seventeenth century he seems to have lost the exclusive secret of making stoneware in England, and other regional centres of the industry, such as Staffordshire, had appeared. Much of Dwight's time in the 1690s seems to have been occupied in prosecuting other potters in London and Staffordshire for alleged infringement of his patents, testifying to the vigour of their industry. A number of rather crude brown mugs with speckled dip are known, suggesting that these potters did not rival Dwight artistically.[60] Dwight himself died in 1703, leaving the pottery to his wife Lydia, which continued into the nineteenth century.

The tradition of fine quality stoneware continued to flourish in other parts of England, most notably in Nottingham, where the potter James Morley had been pros-

69　The infant Lydia Dwight on her deathbed. Height 28.5 cm. Stoneware. Fulham, workshop of John Dwight, *c*.1673. Victoria & Albert Museum, London.

70　White stoneware mug attributed to Francis Place, *c*.1690. Royal Museum of Scotland, Edinburgh.

71　Tradecard of James Morley of Nottingham, showing a variety of stoneware pieces, *c*.1700. Engraving.

72　Mug with sprigged decoration of hunting scenes. Stoneware. Height 17.2 cm. Probably London, Vauxhall, *c*.1730 The Bowes Museum, Barnard Castle, Co. Durham.

ecuted by Dwight in 1695. A range of pieces are associated today with Nottingham, including cylindrical mugs, two-handled mugs, and figures of chained bears. Morley's tradecard survives and shows a range of wares made for the fashionable market, including teapots, decanters and a *capuchine* (coffee-cup?) (fig. 71). Most interesting is his technique of *carved* ware, in which an outer wall of clay is pierced and cut-through with decoration, suggesting manufacture for a luxury market.

However, the great majority of English stonewares were essentially utilitarian in character and made for heavy and prolonged usage, presumably in taverns. They are more usually associated with beer and spirits than the more elegant beverages of tea and coffee and continued to be made well into the eighteenth century. Some of the finer items continued to have attractive 'sprigged' (applied) decoration on their surface, or were moulded with figures from popular entertainment. The main centres of later stoneware production were Derbyshire, Nottingham, London (Vauxhall) and Bristol, which all competed to make utilitarian wares. A list of prices of 'Brown Stoneware' published by the London manufacturers in 1795 lists bottles and jars, 'gorges', mugs, barrels, beer-barrels and shop-pots all in different sizes.[61] The best-known of the eighteenth-century types were the 'hunting mugs', large mugs for ale or beer, particularly associated with the London pottery at Vauxhall, so called because of the applied sprigged decoration in the form of hunting scenes with packs of hounds which decorated their surface. A characteristic of these was that they were often dipped in a white slip to improve their appearance, the base or top being left in their natural clay colour (fig. 72). They are often finished with a silver, or silver-plated rim, at the top, which can sometimes be used to give them a precise dating.

Overleaf, detail of fig. 85. 'Hampton Court' vase.

CHAPTER 5

The Influence of the East

The products of the East, most notably silks and spices, were the great luxury goods of Medieval Europe. They were brought overland via Persia and Turkey, a journey which lasted several months and added greatly to their value, resulting in large profits for the merchants involved. What little the West knew of the Far East was a vision of a fabulously wealthy distant land of 'Cathay', a fantastic vision of Oriental splendour that coloured the West's perception of the East well into the nineteenth century. The lure of goods and spices led European explorers to seek a sea-route to the East which cut out the laborious overland journey, an aim finally achieved in 1497 when the Portuguese explorer Vasco da Gama rounded the Cape of Good Hope and discovered the sea-route to China. From then on, the Portuguese, and later the Dutch and the English, dominated and tried to monopolise the trade with the Far East.

One of the products from the East that was highly prized was the hard and durable high-fired ceramic called 'porcelain'. True Chinese or 'hard-paste' porcelain was created by the fusion at high temperature of two naturally occurring minerals, china clay (Chinese:*gaolin* [formerly *kaolin*], named after the 'high-ridges', where it was found) and china stone (Chinese:*baidunzi* [formerly *petunse*], or 'little white bricks', the form in which it was taken to the potter).[1] These were blended, and fired in a kiln to a temperature of at least 1200°C, similar to that of European stoneware. It thus had the hardness and durability of stoneware, but was infinitely lighter, and translucent when held to the light. Its precise origin is unclear, but it seems to have been discovered and developed through a different amalgam of clays in China in the sixth to the tenth centuries, and subsequently developed into a national industry, with the kilns centred on Jingdezhen (formerly known to the West as Ching-tê Chên) in southern China, which had good river connections to the port of Nanjing (formerly Nanking). These kilns have remained in operation to the present day and produced the vast majority of Chinese porcelain imported into Europe.

The European name 'porcelain' appears to have derived from the travels of Marco Polo to the court of the Chinese Emperor Kubla Khan (1272–92), who records seeing what he described as *porcellana* ('little pig') or the name given to cowrie shells or mother-of-pearl. He may possibly have brought back the piece that still survives in the Treasury of St Mark's on his return to Venice in 1295. A very few pieces of porcelain filtered through to Europe before the sixteenth century, mostly through the overland route via Syria. They were highly prized and often mounted in gold or silver to protect and enhance them,[2] and feature in the inventories of the very rich and powerful.[3] The most famous example is perhaps the Chinese porcelain vase called 'the Gaignières-Fonthill Ewer', which was probably mounted as a coronation gift from Louis the Great of Hungary (1342–82) to Charles III of Durazzo, who was crowned King of Naples in 1381 (fig. 73). It survives today, sadly without its mounts, in the National Museum in Dublin.[4]

Much of the porcelain that was imported in this early period was of the blue-and-white variety, where the body is painted with grey-black cobalt-oxide before glazing and firing, which becomes a rich blue in the kiln ('underglaze blue'). This had been developed in China during the Yuan dynasty (1271–1368) specifically for export to the Arabic Near East, using cobalt imported from Arabic territories in Persia. Decoration of this early period consisted of scrolling foliage, possibly based on Greek acanthus motifs, as well as Chinese symbols such as dragons or Buddhist emblems. It was not until the sixteenth century that Chinese porcelain came to be imported into Europe on a regular basis. The first Portuguese ship arrived in Canton in 1517, and by 1522 the Portuguese government had ruled that a third of the cargoes of the ships coming from India had to consist of porcelain. The trade centred on the island of Malacca in present-day Malaysia, where the Portuguese bargained with Chinese merchants. Some of the styles of design and decoration began to reflect European taste, and there exist pieces of Chinese blue-and-white porcelain decorated with the arms of King Manuel of Portugal (1469–1521). By 1580 there were half-a-dozen shops in Lisbon where porcelain could be bought.[5] Portugal was annexed by Philip II of Spain in 1581, who encouraged the trade and is supposed to have amassed a collection of over 3,000 pieces of porcelain. There are in existence a number of porcelain flasks with tall necks bearing his coat-of-arms in underglaze blue (fig. 74), which can be compared with the European versions of square form bearing his coat-of-arms in Medici porcelain. However, porcelain remained the prerogative of the very rich into the early years of the seventeenth century, denoting special status and wealth, and was kept in a collector's cabinet rather than the living rooms, kitchen or pantry.

Porcelain came to be more generally available among other classes in Europe as a

73 Gaignières-Fonthill Ewer. Chinese celadon vase of the late thirteenth century mounted in silver-gilt mounts. Drawing by Roger de Gaignières, 1713. Bibliotèque Nationale, Paris.

74 Flask of Chinese porcelain bearing the coat-of-arms of Philip II of Spain (1556–90). Hard-paste porcelain, painted in underglaze blue. Height 30.5 cm. Jingdezhen, China, late sixteenth century. Courtesy of Christie's, London.

75 *Still life*. Jacob van Hulsdonck (1582–1647). Oil on panel, 65.4 × 106 cm. The Bowes Museum. Barnard Castle, Co. Durham.

result of the political upheavals of the early seventeenth century. The rebellion in the Low Countries in the late sixteenth century, with the consequent formation of Holland as the world's dominant trading nation, usurped the traditional monopolies of the kingdom of Spain. The Dutch at once attempted to break into the market with the East, forming their own East India Company, the VOC (*Vereenigde Oost Indische Compagnie*), in 1602, with a trading base in Batavia (present-day Djakarta). The papers relating to their Chinese trade survive and can be used to study its workings.[6]

In 1601 the Dutch were successful in capturing the Portuguese ship the *San Jago* off the coast of Saint Helena; similarly in 1604 Jacob van Heemskerck captured the *Catharina* near Patani (Malacca). These victories marked the entry of the Dutch into the trade of Chinese porcelain, as both ships carried extensive cargoes of porcelain, which were sold at auction for high prices. Soon, however, the Dutch entered the trade on their own account, the first truly Dutch cargo of porcelain arriving in 1604 from Bantam.[7] In 1613 the Portuguese successfully retaliated and sank the Dutch ship the *Witte Leeuw*, whose cargo has since been retrieved and gives us a good idea of the range of items imported at this early date. The finds from this wreck are mostly blue-and-white of the kind associated with the reign of the Chinese emperor Wanli (1573–1620). Typical examples included dishes of various sizes with segmental borders filled with Chinese characters and a central panel with a bird, grasshopper or other animal motif, as well as small bowls painted with foliage or other naturalistic ornament.[8]

This kind of export porcelain was called *Kraak* porcelain after the ships or so-called carracks in which it was carried, and was imported into Europe in vast quantities, where it came into everyday use (fig. 75).

The papers of the Dutch East India Company show that certain items and shapes were made specially for the European market.[9] In 1635 special wooden models of mustard pots, tankards, and jugs painted with all kinds of figures, which the Chinese porcelain dealers had declared that they could copy, were made in Batavia and sent to China. The resulting pieces arrived in Holland in 1637. Styles also changed according to fashions in eating; for instance, orders for vegetable dishes appear in 1643 and in 1644 further items were ordered according to samples sent from Holland.[10] As the century progressed, the styles of decoration began to reflect European influences as well. Decoration and patterning in the style of tulip petals is thought to have appeared on Chinese porcelain around 1634–7, at the time of the tulip boom then going on in Holland. By 1647 over three million pieces are thought to have been imported into Holland.

It was this kind of porcelain that began to be imitated by the tin-glazed earthenware makers of Holland. The technique of making tin-glazed pottery had come to Holland in the late sixteenth century, when imitations of Urbino maiolica were made at Antwerp and elsewhere, sometimes by potters who had emigrated from Italy. Their products were at first closely modelled on the colours and patterns of Italian maiolica, including polychromatic bowls and dishes with a pattern based on pomegranates. A special feature of their work was the production of tiles, often of the pomegranate pattern, and they are recorded in a inventory of 1603 which calls them 'orange apples'.[11]

However, by the mid-seventeenth century a style of decoration based on blue-and-white Chinese porcelain had become the dominant fashion. The Italian Piccolpasso had already described a kind of Chinese-style scrolling decoration as '*alla porcellana*' on Italian maiolica, but this was limited to the borders of plates (fig. 76). In Holland the Chinese-style decoration covered the whole object, so that it closely resembled a genuine piece of Chinese porcelain. The main centre of manufacture was the town of

76 Dish painted *alla porcellana*. Tin-glazed earthenware, painted in blue. Diameter 24.3 cm. Cafaggiolo, *c.*1500–25. The J. Paul Getty Museum, Los Angeles.

77 Plaque. Tin-glazed earthenware, painted in blue. 32 × 24 cm. Delft, by Frederik van Frytom (1632–1702). Courtesy of Aronson Antiquairs, Amsterdam.

Delft near Rotterdam, which came to dominate tin-glazed earthenware manufacture in Holland (hence the generic name 'Delftware' for this type of ceramic), with two factories, the *Porceleyne Lampetkan* and the *Porceleyne Schotel*, making especially fine wares.[12] Since the majority of Chinese porcelain of the early seventeenth century still consisted of sets of plates, the Delftware factories made a variety of other goods, such as jugs, vases and mustard-pots with Chinese decoration. Production diminished with the import of a wider range of pieces of Chinese porcelain from 1637 onwards, but resumed after 1647, when civil wars in China damaged the porcelain trade.

The Delftware industry developed rapidly after 1654, when the town had been virtually destroyed by a gunpowder explosion. This resulted in many vacant sites, some of which were taken by pottery factories. The most famous are *De Dissel* (The Pole) , *Het Jonge Moriaenshooft* (The Young Moor's Head) (1660–92), *De Grieksche A* (The Greek A) (1674–1722), *De Metalen Pot* (The Metal Pot) (1670–1721), *De Roos* (The Rose) (1662–1712) and *De Paeuw* (The Peacock) (1651–1705). We know about the workings of the industry from the records of the Guild of St Luke, the painters' guild which also included related trades such as printers, picture- and print-dealers, and tin-glazed pottery makers. The branch in Delft was founded on 29 May, 1611; with the potters being classed as *plateelbakker* (dish makers) to distinguish them from tile-makers. An apprenticeship for a potter ran for six years, under three master potters. According to the regulations of 1654 a thrower had to show that he could throw a ewer, a salad bowl and a salt-cellar with a hollow stem ('thrown from one piece of clay'), and a painter had to decorate six dishes of the largest size and a fruit bowl, as well as throw or paint a pile of thirty plates. The successful apprentices marked their sign in the guild registers.[13]

Although each pottery was meant to be in the hands of a master potter, in practice they were run by rich merchants, a potter being appointed 'shopkeeper' or manager to front the commercial interests behind it. For instance, in 1655 Wouter van Eenhoorn (d. 1679) bought *De Porcelyne Fles* (The Porcelain Bottle) through a potter, Quirinus van Cleynhoven, who was to act as shopkeeper and instruct van Eenhoorn in the art of pottery. In 1658 van Eenhoorn also bought *De Grieksche A* factory, acting as shopkeeper himself, and was its sole owner from 1663–78, although his son Samuel took over the management in 1674. Van Eenhoorn was also at various times co-owner of *De 3 Vergulde Astonnekens* (The Three Golden Ash-Barrels), *Het Hooge Huys* (The High House), and *De Paeuw*.[14]

The early wares of Delft bear decoration derived from both European figurative styles and Chinese influences, and include some fine wall-plaques by the professional landscape painter Frederik van Frytom (fig. 77).[15] However, most Delftware of the second part of the seventeenth century was painted in the Chinese style, and the better pieces came increasingly to imitate Chinese porcelain both in painting and thinness of potting. The finest copied the so-called *Kaapsche Schotels* or plates from the Cape, which were produced in the workshops of *De Metalen Pot* in the time of Lambert Cleffius (1661–91) or his successor Lambert van Eenhoorn (1691–1721). Here the contours of the design were carefully outlined in dark blue or black (*trek*), a style of decoration probably invented in the workshop of Samuel van Eenhoorn, and the quality enhanced by a covering of lead-glaze (*quaart*), giving a sheen something akin to that of porcelain. Such pottery was described as *Hollantsporceleyn* to describe its fine appearance (figs. 78 and 79).[16]

An important part of Delftware production was devoted to the production of decorative tiles, mostly in blue-and-white, but sometimes coloured, for grander furnishing schemes. These could be for damp cellars (to keep out moisture), for the skirting of floors (for cleaning, and to keep out mice), or the lower half of entrance-hall walls,

78 Illustrations of 'geeven' (glazing) from Gerrit Paape, *De Plateelbakker of Delftsch Aardewerk Maaker*, 1794.

79 Dish. Tin-glazed earthenware, painted in blue. Diameter 35 cm. Delft, De Dobbelde Schenckan. The Bowes Museum, Barnard Castle. Co. Durham.

to prevent whitewash from rubbing off onto the clothes of visitors. They could also be used for complete furnishing schemes in specialised buildings, such as dairies and pleasure pavilions, and were exported across Europe. Rooms decorated entirely with Dutch tiles, from floor to ceiling, still exist at the Château de Rambouillet in France (about 1715–34) and the Amalienburg at the Nymphenburg in Munich (1734–39), where the main decoration consists of panels of flowers in vases. The latter are attributed to one of the Rotterdam factories.[17]

The porcelain trade with China was only resumed later in the century, after the Emperor Kangxi (1661–1722) consolidated his hold on southern China after 1683. Precise evidence of the kind of Chinese porcelain imported at this time has been demonstrated by examining the cargo of an Asian trading vessel found off Vung Tau on the southern coast of Vietnam, which appears to be that of a ship bound for Batavia that sunk in about 1690. It includes a wide range of decorative pieces, sets of vases, covered beakers, and some cups and saucers.[18] By this time Chinese styles of decoration were much changed. The human figure now featured much more prominently as a decorative motif, particularly figures of tall, draped women and dancing children (called in Holland *zotjes* or 'sillies'), as well as flora and fauna, and a kind of patterning called *Franse-punt* (French point) in the borders. The rarer designs are likely to be private-trade items or commissions, carried on the ship by the officers as a way of supplementing their income.

Among the most popular items imported were vases in groups of five or more, based on the sets of vases made for Chinese altars. Such 'garnitures', as they came to be called, grew increasingly sought-after and were used for the decoration of rooms and (especially) chimney pieces well into the nineteenth century. The standard set seems to have consisted of three covered round 'baluster' vases, or ginger jars,, interspersed with two tall flaring beakers, or two round 'double gourd' vases, (figs 80 and 81). Groups of such vases were made by all the leading factories in Delft, in varying degrees of closeness to Chinese models. The most innovative factory in Delft seems to have been *De Griecksche A* factory, which is best-known for its fan-shaped tulip holders. With the factory of the Young Moor's Head it began to develop a 'mixed' technique, adding further colours and gilding to the blue-and-white wares in further firings in a glass painter's 'muffle' kiln. A further development (by 1700) was the use of a dark-brown or black ground covering the whole body of the object in the manner of Oriental lacquer, to which decoration in polychrome enamels was also applied.

Porcelain came to be an important feature of room decoration, and came increas-

80 Vase. Tin-glazed earthenware, painted in blue. Height 58 cm. Delft, *c*.1680. Courtesy of Aronson Antiquairs, Amsterdam.

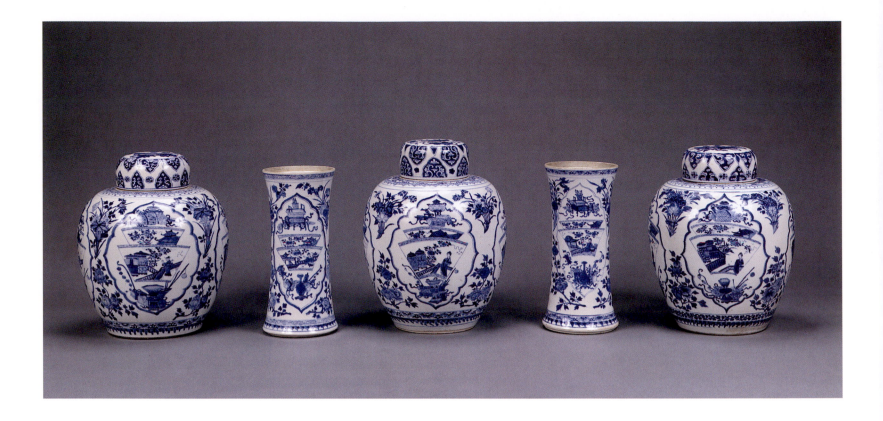

ingly to dominate the interiors of the rich. Early seventeenth-century depictions of Dutch rooms sometimes show a row of blue-and-white plates set along a plate-rack on wall, although whether of porcelain or Delftware we cannot be sure.[19] By the later seventeenth century Chinese porcelain was so readily available that whole rooms could be filled with it, and there may even have been a glut on the market, as by 1681 Chinese porcelain was being withdrawn from auctions as it was failing to meet its reserves.[20] The most famous 'china cabinets' (as they were called) were those of Mary II of England, wife of William of Orange, at her Dutch palace at Het Loo and in her London residences Kensington Palace and Hampton Court. Here masses of porcelain were piled-up high on shelves, or stood in pyramidal groupings, a motif very popular in the late seventeenth century.[21] A 1697 inventory of Kensington Palace records 7,800 pieces of china in the closet, drawing-rooms, supper-room, bedchambers, backstairs, old bedchambers and Queen's Gallery.[22] Although these schemes do not survive, an engraving by the court designer Daniel Marot (1663–1752) may illustrate one of Mary's china cabinets, perhaps that at Hampton Court (fig. 82).

Another fashion of Eastern origin was the taste for tea drinking, which led to an enormous demand for porcelain or pottery drinking-vessels. The key factor here was the durability of the hard-paste porcelain vessels, as the wares had to be strong enough to withstand boiling water and everyday usage. The craze for tea drinking (and the related Eastern drinks of coffee and chocolate) began to sweep across Europe in the later seventeenth century. Europeans had already heard of the fashion for tea drinking from such travellers as the Portuguese Caspar da Cruz, or the Dutchman Jan Huygen van Linschoten, but it took a while for the fashion to become generally established. By 1637, however, the VOC was ordering 25,000 teacups from China.[23] Tea could be drunk once or twice daily, but afternoon gatherings soon became the rule; this necessitated the apparatus of tea-kettle (for hot water), teapot (for keeping the concentrat-

81 Garniture of five vases. Hard-paste porcelain, painted in underglaze blue. Height of lidded vase 31.8 cm. China, Jingdezhen, *c*.1690. The J. Paul Getty Museum, Los Angeles.

82 Design for the decoration of a room with Chinese porcelain. Engraving. Daniel Marot (1663–1752).

ed liquid), tea-bowls and saucers, as well as slop bowls (fig. 83). Also considered necessary were small tables on which to serve it, and a certain type became standard in Holland, with an oval top and a column-shaped stand on a tripod base, made by a special section of the Dutch woodworkers guild. They seem to have been based on the idea that the Chinese drank their tea served from special tables shaped like a drum, as seen in engravings of 1682 by Romeyn de Hooghe and Petrus Schenk. There also came into existence hanging-shelves for porcelain (*tablet*) on which were stored the items for tea making.[24]

It was about this time that the low, horizontal teapot that we know today developed in Europe from the Chinese porcelain wine-ewer. Although a number were made in Delftware, the necessity of their having to hold boiling water led to a stronger material being copied. This was Chinese Yixing red stoneware, a kind of plain, red stoneware which held the heat well and did not crack when filled with boiling water. They were simply decorated, often with only a few sprays of trailing prunus blossom applied to the surface. A consignment of 320 'figured red teapots' was imported from Macao as early as 1680,[25] and they were soon imitated in Holland.[26] These Dutch imitations were very close to the Chinese in appearance and technique, being made out of a reddish clay with 'sprigged' decoration in the form of sprays of prunus blossom trailing over the side. Some deviation from Chinese models came later, as when in 1691 Cleffius's successor, Lambert van Eenhoorn, hired a trained wood-carver, Guillaume Neuillet of Le Havre, to model red teapots. His contract was renewed for another ten years in 1693, although the designs were to remain the property of De Metalen Pot factory. A rival firm of Ary de Milde's,

83 Attributed to Nicolas Verkolje (1673–1746). *A Dutch family at tea*. Oil on canvas, 63.5 × 76.2 cm. *c*.1715–20. Victoria & Albert Museum, London.

84 Teapot. Red stoneware. Height 11.5 cm. Delft, factory of Ary de Milde, *c*.1690. Musée National de Céramique, Sèvres.

at *De Gecroonde Theepot* (The Crowned Teapot), produced a finer and harder version of the same material, and in 1680 obtained a fifteen-year patent of Ary de Milde's products with a factory mark (fig. 84).[27]

Much of the finest and most-elegant Eastern porcelain of the late seventeenth and eighteenth centuries came not from China, but from Japan. With the collapse of the Chinese market due to civil war around 1645, the Dutch had turned to Japan as a source of porcelain, which had imported the techniques of porcelain production from Korea late in the sixteenth century. In 1659 the Dutch sent an order for 56,700 pieces. Samples were sent, and 1660 saw the first Japanese versions sent to Holland.[28] However, the Japanese porcelain trade was never commercially successful, as the Japanese authorities placed too many restrictions on it, and Japanese potters could not achieve the thinness of the Chinese examples. Much of the profit, in fact, went into the hands of the officers via private trade.[29]

Much Japanese porcelain imported into Europe consisted of vases, large plates and other forms of room decoration, and falls into three stylistic categories: blue-and-white, imitating the Chinese; pieces with delicate asymmetrical *Kakiemon* decoration, and richly coloured *Imari* porcelain.[30] The blue-and-white was very similar in design to the Chinese, although Japanese porcelain was greyer in paste, with a matt appearance to the glaze sometimes described as close to linen. This appears to have been the kind of blue-and-white porcelain that was most imitated at Delft in the years 1660–80.[31] The delicate asymmetrical, coloured style of decoration known as *Kakiemon* porcelain came later, and is traditionally based on a type of decoration developed by the Kakiemon family of potters. The motifs used were birds in flowering trees or

85 'Hampton Court' vase. Hard-paste porcelain, painted in enamel colours. Height 36.5 cm. Arita, Japan, *c*.1690. The Bowes Museum, Barnard Castle, Co. Durham.

86 Pair of vases painted in the *Imari* style. Tin-glazed earthenware painted in colours and gilt. Height 28 cm. Delft, The 'Greek A' factory, *c*.1700. The Bowes Museum, Barnard Castle. Co. Durham.

87 Plate painted with *'parasol ladies'*, after a design by Cornelis Pronk. Hard-paste porcelain, painted in enamel colours. Diameter 15.7 cm. China, Jingdezhen *c.*1740. The Victoria & Albert Museum, London.

prunus blossom, quails in tall grass, or lions and bamboo, portrayed delicately in a limited range of colours of blue, green, brown and red, which left much of the beautiful white body of this kind of ceramic undecorated.[32] *Kakiemon* shapes were often moulded rather than thrown, as in dishes moulded in the shape of chrysanthemum leaves, or hexagonal vases, which were listed in the inventory of Queen Mary of 1694.[33] They are to this day known as 'Hampton Court' vases, after the pairs at Hampton Court thought to be from her collection (fig. 85).

More widely distributed were the lavish *Imari*-style wares imported from Japan. These wares, so-called because they were imported through the Japanese port of Imari, were made specifically for export to Europe, and consisted of vases and large plates, decorated in a rich combination of under- or overglaze blue and red with much gilding. Popular designs included a basket or vase of flowers and fanciful Japanese motifs. The general quality of decoration was much poorer than that of the *Kakiemon* wares and such pieces were not intended for the home market. However, at a distance they look extremely impressive and the *Imari* style remained popular in Europe on and off into the nineteenth century. These wares were much imitated by *De Grieksche A* factory in Delft, which made fine quality tin-glazed earthenware decorated with colours and gilding (*Delft doré*) in a glass-decorator's 'muffle' kiln (fig. 86).

Regular trade with China had resumed by about 1730, but by then rather different styles of decoration had become current. The seventeenth and eighteenth centuries saw the development of painting in coloured overglaze enamels in China, the decoration being fired onto the glazed pots in a muffle kiln. Much of this decoration is supposed to have been applied at the port of export at Canton. The designs consisted most notably of figures at play, birds or other animal motifs, or trees and landscapes. At first green was the predominant colour; after 1720 a red or rose colour became popular, a colour based on gold which was discovered in Europe in the seventeenth century and used in enamels on copper; however, its use was recorded in China before 1720.[34] Designs became increasingly elaborate as the century progressed, and resulted in some over-lavish productions by the end of the eighteenth century. These styles were christened *famille verte* (green family) or *famille rose* (pink family) by the great historian Albert Jacquemart in the nineteenth century, though it should be emphasised that differentiation is simply a matter of degree.

Such coloured decoration was copied by the more ambitious factories in Delft, and a wide variety of pieces were made, including large interlocking groups of plates which form a single set. It is about this time that the birds and flowering-tree pattern known today as 'Indian tree' developed, and was soon copied and developed by European ceramic manufacturers. Such wares were developed by factories such as *De 3 Vergulde Astonnekens*, where the painter Ary van Rijsselberg worked in the years 1718–35, producing close approximations of Chinese designs.

It was logical in the context of this burgeoning demand to let the Europeans dictate their own taste, especially as the Chinese style as such was becoming somewhat hackneyed in the eighteenth century. Accordingly, the Dutch East India Company began to commission its own designs, which were sent out to the East to be painted onto wares.[35] This seems to have resulted in an agreement with the painter Cornelis Pronk (1691–1759) to provide drawings for a year for porcelain 'with their colours properly put in, blue as well as gilt and other colours, and in various fashions'.[36] About a dozen designs are attributed to him, some of them verified by copy drawings in The Rijksmuseum, Amsterdam. The most famous is the design of 'parasol ladies', that is, two women under parasols, which appears on both Chinese and Japanese porcelain (fig. 87).

Holland continued to be a major importer of Chinese porcelain well into the eighteenth century, although increasingly it had to compete with the British and

Scandinavian East India companies. The most remarkable relic of this trade is the consignment of the Dutch ship the *Geldermalsen* which sank off the coast of Batavia in 1752, and was recovered in the 1980s. On this cargo were dinner services, tea sets, and the full range of types made for export to Europe. The vast majority were painted with landscapes and Oriental motifs in underglaze blue, sometimes with the addition of overglaze red and gold to convert them into imitations of the ever-popular Japanese *Imari* style.[37] By this time Chinese porcelain was no longer an article of luxury, so much as of everyday ware, and was decidedly second-best to the new European porcelain factories that were beginning to spring up.

The Spread of Delftware in Europe

Versions of Delftware were made in other countries in Europe, such as Germany, aided by the migration of Dutch potters. The best-known factories are those at Hanau and Frankfurt; characteristic of their wares is a narrow-necked ewer called a *Enghalskrug*.[38] Versions of blue-and-white Delftware were made also in Frankfurt, where in 1666 the Frenchman Jean Simonet obtained permission to start a factory with six year's privilege.[39] A number of tin-glazed earthenware factories flourished on the shores of the Baltic, most notably at Copenhagen, which made good quality blue-and-white wares in a style derived from Delft. Their most distinctive product is the large punch-bowl in the shape of a bishop's mitre.

A similar situation existed in Great Britain, where close trading ties with Holland meant that there was a continual influx of Dutch potters (and pottery) into the eighteenth century. 'Galleyware' (the old English name for tin-glazed earthenware which later fell out of use) had been recorded in the inventories of Henry VIII,[40] but the first known potters in England producing tin-glazed earthenware are thought to be Jacob Jansen and Jasper Andries, two potters from Antwerp who settled in Norwich, and Aldgate in London, in about 1567. Few examples of 'delftware', as tin-glazed earthenware is called in Britain, are dated, but a large dish ('charger') painted with a scene of *Adam and Eve* bears a date 1635,[41] and is apparently based on a metalwork prototype.[42] Some jugs and mugs dated to the 1630s from Southwark in London are painted in a crude version of Chinese Wanli porcelain (fig. 88).[43] Plain utilitarian wares made in quantity at this time include a large range of plain white tall-necked wine bottles, based on the German *Engelhalskrug*, inscribed with the name of the drink ('sack', 'claret', 'whit') and a date in blue, apparently sold by Apothecaries.[44] Although most early identifiable wares seem to have been made in London, records indicate that the industry had spread to Brislington outside Bristol by about 1650.

The industry did not become widespread in England until the later seventeenth century, by when even the kind of lead-glazed ceramic made in Fontainebleau by the followers of Bernard Palissy had been copied.[45] Some of the finest wares were flat slabs made for the rolling of pills; these are frequently painted in blue with the coat-of-arms of the London company or trade guild for which they were made. Also made were numerous blue-and-white tiles, after the model of Delft; these were often incorporated into fireplaces where they could be used to teach biblical and other stories.[46] The grandest pieces of all, however, were large two-handled 'posset' pots, for a kind of mixture of milk and ale served at the time, often surmounted with a lid finely modelled in the form of a crown (fig. 89). A characteristic product of the later seventeenth and early eighteenth centuries was a range of cups, mugs and plates painted with depictions of the reigning monarch. The series seems to have commenced with the coronation of Charles II in 1660 and continued well into the reign of George II (d. 1760). Such decorative plates are

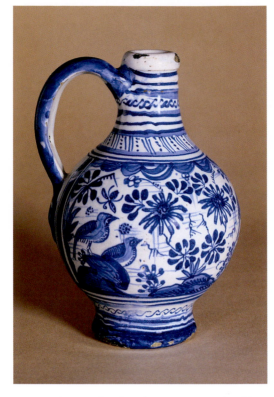

88 Bottle. Tin-glazed earthenware, painted in blue. Height 19.4 cm. London, Southwark, 1628. The Fitzwilliam Museum, Cambridge.

89 Posset pot and salver, the bases inscribed 'T/C.A./1685' and 'T/C.A./1686'. Tin-glazed earthenware, painted in blue. Height of pot 31.1 cm. Probably London or Bristol, 1685/6. The Fitzwilliam Museum, Cambridge.

90 Plate painted an image of George I (reigned 1714–27) and a 'blue dash' border. Tin-glazed earthenware ('delftware'.) Possibly Bristol, c.1720. The Royal Museum of Scotland, Edinburgh.

often painted around the borders with a staccato decoration of blue dashes applied at an angle with a paint brush – the so-called 'blue-dash chargers'(fig. 90).[47]

Many other wares of varying quality were made as well. The most important are the large group of apothecary's drug-jars, painted with the name of the drug in Latin, complemented by the distinctively shaped bleeding or barber's bowl, so-called for its use in shaving. A vast quantity of drinking-pots were produced, including novelty items such as 'fuddling' cups (linked cups) and 'puzzle jugs', where the unfortunate drinker had to stop up holes in the body in order to stop the liquid from spilling out. Porringers, plates and pedestal salts were also made. Particularly interesting is the series of six plates, called 'Merryman' plates, after the inscriptions that they bear: 'What is a Merryman/ Let him do what he can/ To entertain his guests/ With wine and merry jests/ But if his wife doth frown/ All merriment goes down.' These are known bearing dates from 1684 to 1742.[48]

By the mid-eighteenth century the industry had spread to Liverpool, Glasgow in Scotland, and Dublin and Limerick in Ireland. Unfortunately, although we have records of a pottery industry in these places, there are relatively few documentary pieces which show what was made there. Our best evidence comes from the excavation of kiln-sites. This shows that a wide range of rather crudely painted wares in the Dutch or Oriental manner was made throughout Britain. As the eighteenth century progressed, the variety of British delftware constantly increased, including styles after the Chinese, a type of the Italian *bianco sopra bianco*, where white slip is applied above a blue-coloured ground, and the so-called 'fazackerly' decoration of brilliant polychrome enamels, named after a village outside Liverpool (fig. 91). Such wares became common throughout Britain, and were presumably the standard kind of ceramic for many people. As in Holland, delftware came to incorporate new varieties of decoration that became current in the eighteenth century. However, production declined sharply in the second half of the eighteenth century, when the county of Staffordshire produced many more refined types of earthenware for everyday consumption.

91 Selection of British delftware from the period 1700–60, including a water-flask, flower brick, and a bowl painted with *bianco sopra bianco* decoration. Height of flask 25 cm. The Bowes Museum, Barnard Castle, Co. Durham.

The Influence of the Court of Louis XIV

Though styles emanating from the East were perhaps the most popular and widely disseminated types of decoration in seventeenth-century Europe, there was one style whose prestige remained overwhelming in higher circles. This was a style based on the classicism of ancient Greece and Rome. Even though classicism as a style might seem more applicable to architecture or sculpture than to the decorative arts, it retained a prestige that gave it a special attraction for those who were trying to assert the validity of their authority rather than demonstrate the novelty of their taste. A severe and moderate classicism remained an important influence in the art of seventeenth-century Italy, contrasting with the more lively and undisciplined *barocco* (Baroque) art of Gian Lorenzo Bernini (1598–1680) and his followers.

The re-introduction of classicism into the mainstream of Western decorative design was due largely to the personal policies of King Louis XIV of France (1638–1715), who took up direct rule in 1661. His aim was to establish his position in France and indeed Europe as a whole, and to this end the entire apparatus of the French state was channelled; it even extended to forms of production and manufacture.[49] His chief minister had been the Italian Cardinal Mazarin, who had invited prominent Italian artists and craftsmen such as Giovanni Romanelli (1610–62) and Domenico Cucci (c.1640–1705) to execute lavish paintings and decorations for the royal apartments in the Louvre or the Palais Royal. The elaborate decoration of the *Galerie d'Apollon* of 1661–4 survives in the Louvre today and gives a foretaste of the heavy classical style that was to become associated with the court of Louis XIV. The rather heavy-handed use of classical gods and goddesses to celebrate the virtues of the Crown, above all the use of the sun god, Apollo, to parallel the new Sun King, Louis XIV is prominent.[50]

Under the influence of Louis' chief finance minister, Jean Baptiste Colbert (1619–83), all the arts of France were regimented in order to secure cultural domination of the western world to the glory of the king. This was done not simply to boost the prestige of the Crown, but as a matter of sound economic policy. Colbert's economic thinking was dominated by 'mercantilism', a now discredited economic theory which maintained that the quantity of the world's trade was finite, and that it was up to each country to secure as large a share as possible. This had been traditional economic thinking for some time; in the sixteenth century the celebrated philosopher Montaigne had written an essay entitled 'one man's profit is another man's loss', ('le profit de l'un est dommage de l'autre'). Colbert's policies included the encouragement of national industries, the abolition of internal tariffs, the raising of external customs, and imports of precious metals with a consequent rapid circulation of money. The basic aim was self-sufficiency for France, with other countries being dependent on her, for the benefit of the Crown's prestige.[51]

The chief executor of artistic policy was the court artist Charles Le Brun (1619–83) who promoted a version of a classical style of unparalleled richness. The gods and goddesses of antiquity were introduced into decorative schemes executed in the most costly of materials. The major project was the rebuilding of the king's great palace at Versailles outside Paris, as well as other palaces, to provide an appropriate setting for the king himself. In 1663 Le Brun was made director of the *Manufacture Royale des Meubles de la Couronne*, established at the Gobelins factory, where all kind of luxury goods, from tapestries through to inlaid furniture, were made. A famous tapestry from the Gobelins factory shows the king visiting the factory and admiring many of its products, which, although missing today, are traceable in inventories; particularly prominent is the silver furniture commissioned for the Hall of Mirrors at Versailles itself.[52]

The chief examples of the classical court-style of Louis XIV as exemplified in ceramics were made, not in the Gobelins factory in Paris, but at Delft in Holland, by *Der*

Grieksche A factory. This was a commission for a large number of flower vases and other items for the palace of Hampton Court, outside London, which was being renovated for William III of England and his wife Mary Stuart. The designer in charge was the French Huguenot designer Daniel Marot, who had trained at the court of Versailles, but left Paris in about 1684–5, around the time of the Edict of Nantes, which expelled all French Protestants from France.[53] The apartments themselves have long been swept away; however, what remains of this commission is an intriguing series of tall vases and flower-holders in the French classical taste, clearly designed as decoration for the main rooms, and a group of elaborately decorated tile-panels and milking pans from Queen Mary's dairy, all bearing the royal monogram, and all painted in blue.[54] They show many of the characteristics of French classicism, including an insistence on proportion and symmetry. There are also some tall, pyramidal flower-holders, comprising different interlocking sections, which became a well-known (if scarce) product of delftware, which are probably also Marot's design (fig. 92).[55] Similar vases attributable to Marot are also found in England in houses owned by courtiers in William III's circle, such as Uppark, Chatsworth and Dyrham, showing that the taste spread among the British aristocracy.[56]

Delftware seems also to have been imported into France, where it was used as a sub-

92   Vase, from a design by Daniel Marot (1663–1752). Tin-glazed earthenware, painted in blue. Height 100 cm. Delft, the Greek 'A' factory, *c*.1690. The Royal Collection © 2001, Her Majesty Queen Elizabeth II.

93   One of a pair of pyramidal tulip-holders. Tin-glazed earthenware, painted in blue. Delft, The Greek A factory, *c*.1690. The Royal Collection © 2001, Her Majesty Queen Elizabeth II.

stitute for expensive Eastern porcelain.[57] Louis XIV naturally had a collection of true Eastern porcelain, some presented at the visit of the ambassadors from Siam in 1686, who brought Chinese and Japanese porcelain with them as gifts to the Crown.[58] Here Louis was following the taste of Mazarin and Fouquet, which was catered for by many dealers in Paris, such as Ducaurray, who imported statuettes and Chinese and Japanese porcelain, for which there was a vogue in 1692. However, not all of these items were purely decorative, as porcelain began to feature regularly in new modes of dining that Louis introduced.

For grand public occasions Louis XIV still retained the medieval style of dining, in which the separate status of the lord was emphasised, whether king or, as in other countries, one of his deputies in the form of duke, marquis or earl, seated in the centre of the dining chamber in the centre of his palace.[59] Such a meal required the maximum use of expensive items of plate if it were to have its desired impact. The buffet or sideboard was decorated, as in medieval times, with great quantities of silver and gold laid out solely for display. This was complemented by dining utensils of the greatest refinement and elaboration, many with a specialised function, and often made to match each other. It is in the mid-seventeenth century that we get our modern idea of a dinner service, with sets of differently shaped dishes meant for different foods to occupy a particular place on the dinner table, with specific types of plates appearing by the mid-century.[60]

However, in contrast to this Medieval grandeur, a more informal style of dining arose, that rapidly became known throughout Europe as 'service à la française', to emphasise its French origin. As before, the meal was divided into two (or more) courses followed by a dessert consisting of fruit and jams. The essential point was that all the separate dishes in each course were laid out at the same time, *around* the table symmetrically in groups of four, and kept warm by means of covers or underdishes of hot water (fig. 94). In the centre was a metal and glass container for condiments or spices called a 'surtout de table' which became a decorative feature in its own right. Diners could thus serve themselves, unless they desired a dish from the other side of the table, in which case a servant would be sent to get it. What would surprise modern taste would be the variety of foods available in a single course ('service'). The first course consisted of various soups and a kind of Spanish stew of mixed meats and vegetables called an 'olio' (from the Spanish *olla podrida* ('rotten pot'), a mixture of meats and vegetables boiled slowly together).[61] Stews were a great feature of French cooking and were sometimes served separately for meals outside the dining room in small covered bowls on stands called *écuelles*, which were occasionally included in toilet services for the morning.[62] Stews and soups at the dinner table were supplemented by side-dishes of prepared meats (*entrées*) and smaller dishes of great refinement and preparation (*hors d'oeuvres*). The second course consisted of the roast, accompanied by salad *en jatte* (in a bowl, often of Japanese porcelain, as metal would have been stained by the acidic dressing); this was supplemented by side-dishes called *entremets*, consisting of cooked vegetables followed by cooked puddings.[63] These first two courses would have been served on gold or silver, as befitting the grandest ceremony of the day.

Dinner was always followed by a separate meal of fruit called *le fruit* or later *dessert* (from *desservir*, to clear the table) (fig. 95).[64] This was an entirely separate meal of fruits, jams and ice-cream, with a light-hearted character, and was often accompanied by music, dancing or other entertainment. For this lighter course the delicate material of porcelain was considered especially appropriate, contrasting as it did with the heaviness and formality of the gold and silver used for the previous two courses. The moulded shapes of Japanese porcelain were especially favoured. Dessert was usually associated with the garden and the outside world, and was often laid out in the form

94   Drawing showing the layout of dinner at the Château de Marly in 1702. Nationalmuseum, Stockholm.

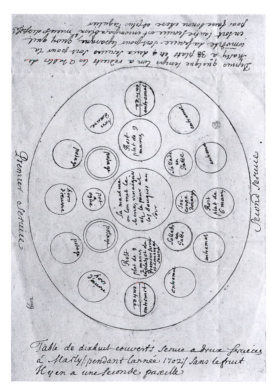

95 Reconstruction of a late seventeenth-century dessert in the manner of Massialot, *Le Cuisinier Royal*, 1698, using Chinese and Japanese porcelain with biscuits and preserved fruit, by Ivan Day at The Bowes Museum, 1994.

of a garden, with small statues in sugar-paste to mimic those that could be found in stone in the real garden outside. The fruit was often served in wicker baskets that guests could take away with them, or between elaborate schemes called *parterres* after the layout of gardens.[65] The special association with porcelain meant that the fruit – fresh or dried – was piled up high in several layers on dishes called *pourcelaines*, though they could be, in fact, of metal.[66]

The French pottery industry was slow to react to developments at court and remained strongly influenced by Italian maiolica until the end of the century. Tin-glazed earthenware or 'faïence' in the Italian style continued to be made at Nevers or Rouen, especially at Nevers where magnificent ewers and plates painted using prints after the French classical artist Michel Dorigny were made. Towards the middle of the century the taste for Chinese-style decoration began to creep in, including painting in colours

96 Jean Berain (1640–1711), Design for a silver ewer. Pen and black ink with grey wash, 40.2 × 26.7 cm. Nationalmuseum, Stockholm.

97 Drawing of a faïence ewer from Rouen (from Pottier, *Histoire de la Faïence de Rouen*).

on a blue-glazed background in imitation of Eastern wares, the so-called *bleu persan* ground, and a specific variety of vases with twisted rope-like handles was produced. Fragments of such vases have been found in excavations of the *Trianon de Porcelaine* at Versailles, a summer pavilion for the preparation and consumption of entremets, decorated with porcelain and tin-glazed tiles, which unfortunately did not outlast a series of severe winters.[67]

However, the numerous wars in which Louis XIV indulged had a profound effect on the status of tin-glazed earthenware in France. In 1689 the first of many financial crises led to a general calling in and melting down of silver and plate. Everyone was expected to bring his or her silver to the Crown to contribute to the national coffers; another great melt-down occurred in 1708, and again in 1759, which explains the paucity of French eighteenth-century silver surviving to the present day.[68] This encouraged the French faïence industry to produce substitutes for silver items for the dinner table for the very rich. The main centre of production was the factory at Rouen, run by Edme Poterat, which was even allowed to use the fleur-de-lis as a mark in 1713.[69] The range of shapes made included salt-cellars, casters, shaped dishes, and even centrepieces (the *surtout de table*), although on a smaller scale. The shapes often owed little or nothing to the potter's wheel and were based on fashionable silver shapes, characterised by heavy forms, vessels of segmental shape, often decorated with 'gadrooning' (convex fluting) on the base of the vessel. The best-known is the helmet-shaped ewer, which seems to have originated with the king's designer Jean Berain (1640–1711) as a design for silver (figs 96, 97).

More interesting are new kinds of objects that made their appearance with the development of *service à la française* and its attendant luxury items. The most famous today is perhaps the two-handled vase for cooling individual bottles of wine (*seau à bouteille*). The bottle rested in a bed of ice (preserved outside in deep pits of snow from the winter) on the dinner table until its contents were thoroughly chilled. The wine glasses themselves were cooled in a bowl with serrated edges (*verrière*). Here the glasses were laid head down in a bed of ice, with the stems supported on the serrations.

This fashion spread to England, where they were christened 'monteiths' after a nobleman of that name who favoured a serrated edge on his cloak. Such costly items epitomised the taste for excessive luxury of Louis' court.

The painted ornamentation on these items also followed silver decoration, characterised by strapwork and foliate ornament. The dominant decorative style for round items such as plates again followed that of silver and is known as the *style rayonnant*, in which the border patterns radiate outwards, or are inverted on hollow wares. Individual motifs included spiral or leaf designs in white on a blue ground or vice-versa, and *lambrequins*, a trefoil with spirals reserved on a blue ground copied from Chinese Kangxi porcelain. Swags of fruit also appear, and kinked scrollworks similar to ironwork (*ferronerie*). Most pieces were painted in blue, but for more ambitious pieces a range of *grand feu* colours were used as in Italian maiolica (so-called because of their ability to withstand high temperatures in the kiln), including blue (cobalt), green (copper oxide), purple (manganese), yellow (antimony) and orange (iron). Polychrome pieces were also especially popular in this later period, as well as 'armorial' wares, or dinner wares decorated with a coat-of-arms in the centre identifying the owner, a practice also favoured on imported Chinese porcelain.

As the eighteenth century progressed, the faïence of Rouen became increasingly a product for a less aristocratic market, and the style of its ceramics was increasingly left behind by developments in fashionable taste. Some large jugs decorated in the *rayonnant* style for cider or ale are dated from 1708 onwards and inscribed with the owners' names, in the manner of much popular pottery. By the mid-eighteenth century, polychrome high-fired decoration *à la corne* had become popular, where the dominant motif is a large cornucopia-like object surrounded by flattened Eastern-style floral decoration (fig. 98). This decoration is similar to 'bizarre' woven silks of Lyons, which were popular throughout Europe in the late seventeenth and early eighteenth century, and reflects

98 Dish with decoration *à la corne*. Tin-glazed earthenware, painted in colours. Rouen, *c*.1750–60. Width 43 cm. The Bowes Museum, Barnard Castle, Co. Durham.

99 Designs from plate borders, painted in blue. (from Pottier, *Histoire de la Faïence de Rouen*, pl.XVIII).

100 Jean Berain (1640–1711), *Grotesque*. Engraving.

the importance of textile design as a source of inspiration for luxury goods.[70]

Other centres of faïence existed in southern France, in the region around Marseilles. The village of Moustiers, about sixty miles north-east of Marseilles, contained several different factories which made it an important centre. It is best known for the products of the factory owned by Pierre Clérissy, which were painted in a revival of the 'grotesque' style introduced by the court designer Jean Berain (1637–1711) (figs 100,

101 Dish. Tin-glazed earthenware, painted in blue. Moustiers, factory of Clérissy, *c.*1710. Width 33.5 cm. The Bowes Museum, Barnard Castle, Co. Durham.

102 Tray. Tin-glazed earthenware, painted in colours. Moustiers, *c.*1740. Diameter 44.8 cm. The Bowes Museum, Barnard Castle, Co. Durham.

101). This style had developed by the end of the seventeenth century, when people had grown tired of the overwhelming heaviness of most classical decoration, and in 1698 the king himself told his architect Mansard on seeing new plans for room decoration that 'there should be something youthful in what is done' in new room decorations, though apparently this was in reference to the decoration of children's rooms.[71] Berain adapted the grotesque style, in which classical characters are retained, but within such a decorative framework that their symbolism and seriousness is diluted. Classical gods and goddesses now peer at each other among the scrolling foliage, which supports a weight of fanciful ornament that would have been impossible in a more architecturally organised design. This was a naturally flat style, intended for wall decoration, which was best suited to large platters or dishes.

Most colourful decoration was introduced by another factory, that of Joseph Laugier and his brother-in-law, Joseph Olerys, set up in 1739. They developed a style consisting of a central panel with religious or mythological scenes, surrounded by a border of hanging festoons, painted in the high-fired colours of blue, orange-yellow, violet and yellow-green. A related factory was set up at Saint Jean du Désert near Marseilles, when in 1677 Joseph Clérissy, the brother of Pierre, arrived from Moustiers and established one which ran till 1733. This made some magnificent large plates with a central scene in the manner of those from Nevers. It closed in 1748. By then the faïence of Moustiers itself was increasingly crude in quality, although inventive in style, characterised by a decoration of fantastic human or animal figures scattered over the surface with sprays of foliage (fig. 102).

Overleaf, detail of fig. 103. Ewer and basin.

CHAPTER 6

The Discovery of True Porcelain in Europe

We have already seen, in Chapter 3, the attempts made in sixteenth-century Florence to discover the secret of true porcelain. They were based on the assumption that porcelain was a kind of glass, made with similar ingredients. The limited success achieved at the Medici court seems to have gone largely unchallenged for a hundred years, with the exception of some interesting experiments made in Padua in the seventeenth century. Two bowls in the Victoria and Albert Museum inscribed 'I.G.P.F. 1627' and 'G.G.P.F. 1638' may be the results of these experiments, the last two initials meaning *Padorano fece*.[1] The style of these bowls, with their painting of birds and plants in underglaze blue, is a version of Chinese blue-and-white porcelain of the reign of Wanli (1573–1620).

The next attempts seem to have been made in France.[2] The first was undertaken by the dealer Claude Révérend, supplier of faïence to the *Trianon de Porcelaine*, who obtained a licence to make porcelain in 1664, but with no apparent result. In 1673, however, Louis Poterat of the Rouen pottery took out a patent for the making of porcelain, which was renewed in 1694 when his pottery patent of 1644 was coming to an end. He seems to have produced a little soft-paste porcelain in the Rouen-pottery style and died in 1696 'crippled in his limbs by the ingredients used in his porcelain'.[3] Greater success was obtained by the soft-paste porcelain factory at Saint-Cloud, on the outskirts of Paris, set up in about 1693 by the family of Pierre Chicaneau under the patronage of the king's brother, the duc d'Orléans.[4] The factory seems to have produced a range of blue-and-white cups, with saucers featuring a deep recess to hold the cup, as well as little objects, such as knife-handles and salt-cellars, painted in underglaze blue (fig. 103).[5] The factory continued to make soft-paste porcelain versions of articles normally made in silver, such as bottle-coolers, albeit in a rather heavy paste and in an increasingly old-fashioned style; it clearly could not compete with other factories in the later eighteenth century and was closed in 1766 after a number of changes of ownership.

The knowledge of making true hard-paste porcelain, like the Chinese, was not generally known in Europe until the later eighteenth century, although the Jesuit missionary Père d'Entrecolles, in his letters of 1712 and 1722, showed awareness of the process in China itself.[6] Its secret (or *arcanum*, the Latin name used) was also sought in Germanic countries, where demand for porcelain was stimulated by the new fashions for tea and coffee drinking, which necessitated a range of light but tough containers for the different liquids involved. Coffee houses had spread to Paris in 1643, London in 1652, Hamburg in 1671, and Vienna in 1683, but with the greatest concentration in Germany.[7] A print by the engraver Johann Elias Ridinger (1698–1767) shows a fashionable couple in undress (presumably they have just got up) drinking coffee and chocolate from handleless or two-handled cups with saucers, clearly of fine porcelain, with a coffee pot and presumably a chocolate pot on the table (fig. 104).

103 Left. Ewer and basin. Soft-paste porcelain, painted in underglaze blue. Height of ewer 17 cm. Saint-Cloud, mounted in silver mounts of 1717–22. The J. Paul Getty Museum, Los Angeles, California.

104 Above. J. D. Ridinger (1698–1767), *Kaffee und Chocolata*, copper-engraving, *c*.1730.

Porcelain was also preferred in Germany for the dessert, called the *Konfekt* ('confection') on account of the numerous sweet and sugary pastries that were supplied by *Konditerei* (confectionery), the equivalent of the French *Office* (pantry), the department of the kitchen responsible for preparing cold foods. The use of porcelain specifically for the dessert course was recommended in Maria Sophia Schellhammer's book *Die wol unterwiesene Köchinn*, (Brunswick, 1697), and the great traveller Lady Montague observed the practice of using porcelain for the dessert in Vienna in 1716. This could well have been Japanese porcelain,[8] as this was the most fashionable style at the time, and came in a variety of shapes that were thought suitable for the layout of a dessert course.[9]

The prospect of Germans buying Eastern porcelain ran contrary to the prevailing economic doctrine of mercantilism, which as we have seen meant countries producing their own goods and exporting to others in the belief that international trade was a finitquantity to be divided up between countries. In Germany a version of the doctrine called 'cameralism' (from *Kameral-wissenschaft*, a type of political and administrative investigation) obtained, which emphasised the importance of strengthening the State within its own territory, rather than expanding its borders, and at the same time restricting imports from abroad.[10] In these circumstances it made sense for the state to subsidise research into the secret of making porcelain and other luxury goods, in order to retain specie in the country.

The greatest prince in Germany was perhaps Augustus II of Saxony (1670–1733), called 'the Strong' for his capacity to father illegitimate children. He was dedicated to building up his country geographically and financially in the manner of Louis XIV of

France, a policy which led him into several wars, including one with Sweden (1700–6), and the incorporation of Poland within his kingdom. His capital, Dresden, thus became the capital of one of the most prosperous kingdoms in Europe. The wealth of Saxony was based on its rich mineral deposits in the *Erzgebirge* (the Ore mountains), which also yielded deposits of semi-precious stones. Augustus set up a court workshop for the making of precious objects, reminiscent of the workshops at the sixteenth-century Medici court, whose products were stored in the *Grüne Gewölbe* (Green Vaults). These were recreated in 1723 directly under the king's private apartments in the Royal Palace, and remain on view in Dresden today.[11]

A great king such as Augustus was naturally also an avid collector of porcelain, and he went to extraordinary lengths to obtain rare specimens. Much of his collection still survives, filling several galleries and storerooms with shelf upon shelf of rare and beautiful Oriental porcelain. His most celebrated exploit as a collector came in 1717, with the exchange with Friedrich Wilhelm I of Prussia, of 600 soldiers from his army in return for 151 large Chinese blue-and-white vases from the palaces of Oranienburg and Charlottenburg in Berlin. They still exist in Dresden today and are called 'Dragoon' vases after the unfortunate soldiers.[12]

Augustus naturally encouraged attempts to discover the secret of making porcelain, employing the scientist Ehrenfried Walther von Tschirnhaus (1651–1708), who knew the Delftware factories in Holland and had visited the porcelain factory at Saint Cloud in 1701.[13] Greater prominence is generally given to his assistant, Johann Friedrich Böttger (1682–1719), an alchemist who had escaped from the custody of the King of Prussia,[14] only to be similarly confined by Augustus the Strong in the castle of the Albrechtsburg in the town of Meissen on the outskirts of Dresden, as an assistant to Tschirnhaus.[15] Although the scope of their operations is still unclear, in 1707 Tschirnhaus and Böttger succeeded in producing a very hard red stoneware of great beauty, similar to Chinese red stoneware, which could be cut and polished on the wheel, like glass (fig. 105). Its commercial possibilities were immediately perceived and in 1708 a factory was opened in Meissen with the help of 'Dutch masters and potters' from Amsterdam.[16] It produced a wide number of very fine pieces, most notably items for tea and coffee drinking, as well as decorative vases and figures copied from Chinese originals in Augustus's collection. Some models based on metalwork prototypes were designed by the court goldsmith Johann Jacob Irminger (died *c.*1726), who made models in copper in his studio in Dresden which he sent to Meissen.[17] Some pieces were gilded and painted by the court painter Martin Schnell, who appears in the list of staff and wages of 1712, in the style of oriental lacquer (fig. 106).

Böttger's stoneware was an immediate success and the secret of its manufacture jealously guarded. However, despite strict precautions and regulations on the movement of staff, some workmen managed to escape, attracted by bribes and offers of high pay from other countries. The compounder and kiln-master at the factory, Samuel Kempe, offered the secret of the red stoneware to the Prussian minister Friedrich von Görne, who was able to establish a rival factory in Berlin (Plaue-am-Havel) in 1713, and whose products were on sale at the Leipzig Trade Fair by 1715. Böttger's stoneware was also imitated at the faïence factory at Bayreuth, which made incised and dark-glazed wares of a great delicacy and quality.

However, a much greater venture was by now in hand. Von Tschirnhaus and Böttger had continued their ceramic research and on 15 January 1708, they appear to have succeeded in making true hard-paste porcelain like the Chinese, although by October 1708 von Tschirnhaus was dead and the credit is now usually given to Böttger alone. The discovery was proclaimed to the world on 28 March 1709, and the creation of a royal porcelain factory was announced on 23 January 1710, in a proclamation written in four languages: German, Latin, French and Dutch. The manufacture was based on clays found at

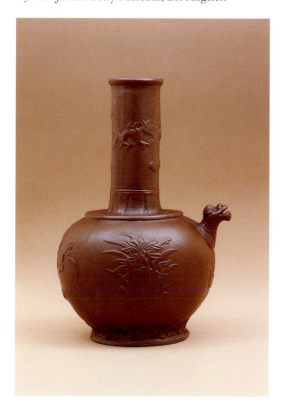

105 Wine bottle of Böttger stoneware, based on a Chinese prototype. Height 16.5 cm. Meissen, *c.*1710–15. The J. Paul Getty Museum, Los Angeles.

Aue in Saxony. Production was sufficiently advanced for pieces to be displayed at the Leipzig trade fair in August,[18] and a showroom was opened in the Albrechtsburg in 1711; another one was set up in Dresden itself in 1715.[19] Specimens were exhibited at the trade fairs at Leipzig, or the Peter and Paul Fair in Naumburg, and a travelling salesman, Johann Wilhelm Stürtzel, was appointed.[20] Böttger succeeded in establishing his position as chief administrator of the nascent concern in 1711, but was by this time broken in health. He was granted his freedom in 1714, but sadly died on 13 March 1719.[21]

In general, Böttger's porcelain seems to have used the same forms that were available in the red stoneware and it is reasonable to assume that they were made concurrently; in the repertoire we find, for instance, almost exact copies of Chinese *blanc-de-chine* (pure white) figures of the goddess Kouang-Jin, or the four-sided *saké* bottles. The great body of production was devoted to tea and coffee wares in the European taste, including a teapot copied from a shape in the French designer Jacques Stella's *Livre des Vases* of 1667, and delicate tea-bowls and saucers, some with applied mouldings or trailing vine leaves. More ambitious were the pieces decorated with pierced or cut-away decoration, and some large vases with mask handles that seem to follow designs by the Frenchman Reymond Leplat, which still exist in the archives there. Other remarkable pieces include a drinking vessel in the form of a great key, which appears to have been used by Augustus the Strong during his stopover at Meissen on his way to the Leipzig trade fair in 1714.[22]

Although much of Böttger's porcelain was left in the white, some was also decorated with gilding and colours, in the manner of glass. 'Painters of good porcelain' were taken on as early as 1711, though it took some years to develop a range of colours.[23] In the absence of in-house decoration, much Meissen porcelain was painted outside the factory by independent decorators called *Hausmaler* ('home-painters'), who had their own workshops with muffle kilns for the firing of enamel decoration and gilding onto undecorated pieces. They were active in the seventeenth century when they decorated glass and pottery, with their own trade guild.[24] *Hausmaler* who

106 Coffee pot. Brown stoneware, painted in enamel colours. Meissen, *c*.1715. The British Museum, London.

107 Leaf-shaped dish, with enamelled decoration attributed to Ignaz Preissler. Hard-paste porcelain. Meissen. Height 4 cm, *c*.1715–25. The J. Paul Getty Museum, Los Angeles.

108 Tureen and cover. Hard-paste porcelain, painted in black. Vienna, factory of Du Paquier, *c*.1725. Courtesy of Christies, New York.

decorated Meissen porcelain include the Dresden painter Johann Georg Funcke (active 1713– 26), who seems to have specialised in gilding,[25] and Ignaz Preissler (active 1720– 39)[26] of Breslau (fig. 107), who specialised in working in *schwarzlot* (literally, 'blacklead', but in fact a transparent black enamel painted onto the surface and scratched through with a needle before firing). It was in this period that the first engravings intended specifically for *Hausmaler* were made.

The most famous *Hausmaler* were based in the old metalworking town of Augsburg. They include members of the Auffenwerth family, headed by Johann (1659–1728) and continued by his daughter Sabrina (1706–82), the decorator Ignaz Bottengruber[27] and the engraver Bartholomäus Seuter. Their speciality seems to have been Chinese figures in gold applied to the white body of the porcelain, in the fanciful European version of the Chinese style termed 'chinoiserie'. The Chinese are portrayed in a charming but perhaps rather patronising manner at their pursuits; drinking tea, making offerings to gods, and smoking. Such scenes were copied or derived from prints of travel books to Asia, and adapted by decorative engravers such as Wolff (fig. 109).[28]

It was at this period that an employee of the Meissen factory, Christoph Hunger, a gilder and decorator, betrayed his employer's trust and took the secret of porcelain production to Vienna. This led to the beginnings of porcelain production in Vienna, under the administration of the courtier Claude Innocent du Paquier, inspired perhaps by a patent encouraging new commercial undertakings issued by the Emperor Charles VI in 1717 (fig. 108). The factory's own patent dates from 1718, and survived until 1744, when it was sold to the Empress Maria Theresa and the factory became a state concern.[29]

Under Du Paquier it had made some of the most distinctive porcelain of eighteenth-century Europe, in a version of the Baroque style that even then was going out of fashion. The potting is generally heavy and was in 1735 compared to Delft pottery.[30] The range seems to have consisted primarily of tea and coffee wares, with an especial line in heavily potted plates, tureens, pilgrim flasks, and even wine-coolers for the dinner table,[31]

109 'Chinoiserie' scene, engraving by Jeremais Wolff (1673–1724).

110 Engraving of *Laub-und Bandelwerk* for a (silver?) broth bowl and cover by Johann Jacob Baumgartner, *c.*1730.

111 Bowl painted with 'Cephalus and Procris' after Antonio Tempesta. Hard-paste porcelain, painted in enamel colours. Diameter 17.2 cm. Venice, factory of Francesco and Giuseppe Vezzi, *c.*1725. The Bowes Museum, Barnard Castle, Co. Durham.

and the earliest-known porcelain clockcase.[32] Decoration on Vienna porcelain is comparatively restrained, consisting of motifs in black or coloured enamels silhouetted against the white porcelain.[33] It tended to follow styles already in use by metalworkers or *Hausmaler*, such as *Laub-und Bandelwerk* (leaf and strapwork) so characteristic of the early eighteenth century (fig. 110) Figurative engravings were also used, as in the famous *Jagd* (hunting) service, decorated with hunting scenes after Johann Elias Ridinger, published in 1722–38. In about 1735–44 the factory supplied a dinner service to the Empress Elizabeth of Russia, decorated with her coat-of-arms. Other painted decoration imitated Chinese or Japanese styles, presumably copied directly from Japanese or Chinese laquer-panels or porcelain.[34] The Du Paquier factory also has the distinction of producing the first specially manufactured room entirely decorated with porcelain, the Dubsky room now in the Museum of Decorative Arts in Vienna, which comprises 1,400 plaques of Vienna porcelain on the walls, and where the furniture, and the sconces, chandeliers and even the fireplace is made of the same. The fireplace in particular is painted with '*deutsche Blumen*' – naturalistic sprays of cut flowers in the European taste – which had appeared on a tankard with hallmarks of 1729 (such flowers had of course already appeared on German faïence). These were rapidly copied by other European porcelain factories, and became a dominant style of decoration in European ceramics for the rest of the eighteenth century.[35]

In 1720 Hunger moved on to Venice, where he met the brothers Francesco and Giuseppe Vezzi, both goldsmiths, who had amassed such wealth that they were able to spend 100,000 ducats on titles of nobility. Together with two other gentlemen, they set up a factory which was in production by 1723, by which time they had invested 30,000 ducats. The source of china clay was Aue in Saxony. They seem to have made a variety of useful wares, including a large service for an unknown bishop comprising tureens, coolers, dishes and plates. Painting included both Chinese-style and figurative

112 Teapot. Hard-paste porcelain, painted in enamel colours and gilt. Height 12.3 cm. The teapot bears the 'MPM' mark for 'Meissner Porzellan Manufaktur', dating it to 1723–24. The Bowes Museum, Barnard Castle. Co. Durham.

113 Engraving of *Chinese scene* by J. G. Höroldt, 1726.

decoration (fig. 111). Their best-known productions are the hexagonal tea and coffee pots with handles, the panel decorated with a variety of designs. However, the factory soon fell on hard times; it seems to have closed at the end of 1727, since the treacherous Hunger was by then back in Dresden and had revealed its source of china clay to the king, who then forbade its export.[36]

The impetus had by now passed back to the factory at Meissen, which had entered its great phase known as the 'painter's period', when styles and decoration were dominated by a number of distinguished porcelain decorators (fig. 112). The painter Johann David Köhler perfected decoration in underglaze blue, and by 1731 the pattern known today as the *Zwiebelmuster* ('onion pattern') was in use, copied from a Chinese pattern of melons.[37] But the great glory of Meissen decoration lay not in its blue-and-white wares, but in its coloured wares, which were developed by Viennese decorator Johann Gregor Höroldt (1696–1775).[38] He joined the factory in 1720,[39] after having vandalised and damaged works at Vienna, a measure of the strength of competition between the two factories. The use of colour seems to have been established by 1723,[40] and the painters' workshop was reorganised to cope with the increased demand.[41] In 1725 the rate paid to the painters was no longer decided by the autocratic Höroldt, but paid according to piecework by the factory commission.[42] By 1731 there were forty painters working in the factory.[43]

In the 1720s two styles of decoration became general, both attributable to Höroldt. The first style is a version of chinoiserie, with scenes of Chinese men and women at work and play, which were introduced in about 1722; figures were at first shown half-length, and framed in gold cartouches, or very rarely in underglaze blue.[44] Their origin is difficult to determine, but they may be based on Dutch engravings by Petrus Schenk (1660–1718/19) and Martin Engelbrecht (1684–1756) of about 1680, later

114 Melchior Küssel after Johann Wilhelm Baur (d. 1640). *Harbour Scene*.

115 Plate, Christie-Miller type. Hard-paste porcelain, painted in enamel colours and gilt. Diameter 29.5 cm. The Victoria & Albert Museum, London.

copied at Augsburg.[45] A number of Höroldt's own designs are preserved in the Schulz codex in Leipzig, depicting a wide variety of slight, comical tall figures, dressed in heavy robes with exaggerated hats.[46] A particular development was to show the scene as if taking place on an island surrounded by the white beauty of the porcelain. A vase in Dresden is a rare signed work, dated 1726 on the base. It was also in this year that Höroldt produced a series of engravings of similar Chinese scenes (fig. 113).[47]

The second of these styles was the depiction of shipping or harbour scenes (fig. 113), usually showing classical buildings surrounding an expanse of sea, copied from engravings by Johann-Wilhelm Baur (d.1640) (fig. 114). Here the depiction could be exceedingly atmospheric, with the sails of the ships billowing in a windy sky. They seem to have been introduced at Meissen about 1723–5;[48] however, similar scenes appear on the great gold coffee service, made for Augustus the Strong by the court goldsmith J. M. Dinglinger (with enamel decoration by his brother Georg) of 1697–1701.[49] Such scenes are often attributed to Höroldt's pupils J. G. Heintze (born 1706) and C. F. Herold (1700–79). Their best-known depiction occurs on the lavishly decorated Christie-Miller service of the 1740s (fig. 115). The interior panels in the borders are painted *en camaïeu* or in rose, the colour developed in China from European models. Such scenes, both Chinese and European, were set off by gilding of the highest quality, often featuring drawn-out 'C' scrolls and a four-petalled flower of a type often attributed to the factory gilder Johann Georg Funcke (active 1713–26).

As the factory developed its own range of styles, it became more reluctant to allow outside decorators to use its pieces and thus dilute the market. In 1722 the famous crossed-swords mark, based on the coat-of-arms of Saxony, began to be painted in underglaze blue on the base of objects before glazing, to distinguish between *Haumalerei* and proper factory-decorated ware. This mark has remained in use to this day.[50] The mark 'AR' entwined in underglaze blue is thought to have been used on items for the Crown's own use, and features on some magnificent display vases which are highly sought-after today. It was consequently much copied in the nineteenth century.

Also in the 1720s Meissen developed an important and long-standing feature of Western ceramic design. This is the use of a central panel or 'reserve' framed by 'ground' colours which cover the rest of the body. Colours developed included yellow, pea-green, celadon-green, cobalt-blue, red, purple and even black. These early colours are generally restrained and slightly pale in tone, and form a beautiful complement to the often colourful decoration that accompanies them.[51]

However, the most fashionable style of the early eighteenth century in porcelain was neither Chinese or European, but Japanese. Japanese porcelain had become the height of fashion in Holland in the late seventeenth century, when the *Kakiemon* and *Imari* styles dominated the market, and rapidly spread across Europe. The mood had been anticipated in the introduction to J. Stalker's *Treatise of Japanning* of 1688, which proclaimed the superiority of Japanese designs over Chinese or European.[52] Meissen responded to the Japanese taste in two ways. Firstly, it developed a wide range of *Kakiemon* and *Imari* decoration of its own, often copied from specimens in Augustus's collection.[53] Two services made for the king in about 1728–31 were decorated with a 'yellow lion' (in fact, a tiger with bamboos and a plum tree) and a pattern of birds and dragons coiled into rings, the so-called 'red dragon' service.[54] A particularly amusing type is the 'Flying Fox' pattern, based on a *Kakiemon* design, whereby a tree-squirrel is transmuted into a red fox that leaps through trees. Sprays of flowers and foliage, flattened in the manner of Eastern designs, developed into a style of decoration called *Indianische Blumen* (Eastern flowers) (fig. 116). Some pieces in this style may have been ordered by the Parisian dealer Rodolphe Lemaire, who ordered versions without the factory mark in order to deceive, and whose close involvement with the factory led to suspicions of industrial espionage and his eventual deportation from Saxony in 1733.[55]

Secondly, Meissen developed a figurative version of the *Kakiemon* style, in which Eastern figures make their way around exotic landscapes and forests. One of the earliest painters who seemed to have specialised in such scenes was Johann Ehrenfried Stadler, who had worked at Eggebrecht's factory in Dresden-Neustadt.[56] The style was further developed by the great painter Adam Friedrich von Löwenfinck, who was apprenticed to Höroldt in 1727 at the age of thirteen. Though relatively few items can be definitively ascribed to him, he is credited with the fine pseudo-Eastern decoration on items such as the Jersey service, and a number of fine tankards. Löwenfinck's time at Meissen was short and he left on 6 October 1736, to begin a series of journeys round Europe that touched on ceramic factories wherever he went.

The most important manifestation of the Japanese taste was Augustus's purchase of the Dutch Palace in 1717, which was enlarged in 1729 and renamed the Japanese Palace in 1730. The idea was to create a kind of large pavilion filled with porcelain, some Chinese, some Japanese, some from Meissen itself, all of which were listed separately in the inventories of 1721–7.[57] The palace comprised thirty rooms, each with

116 Vase. Meissen, *c.*1735. Courtesy of Christies Images, New York.

its own colour scheme in which the appropriate porcelain was displayed, such as 'dark-blue and gold' or 'peach bloom with gold.' The whole must have appeared to be a vast china cabinet. Much of this porcelain survives today in the museums in Dresden and elsewhere, identified by its inventory number scratched on the back.

The decoration of the Japanese Palace led to one of the most important commissions of the Meissen factory: a gallery 270 feet long decorated with 'all sorts of native and foreign birds and animals of pure porcelain furnished in their natural sizes and colours'.[58] These were a vast number of large, realistically modelled animals, up to two or three feet in length, today mostly encountered in plain white, since various firing cracks in these big pieces meant that they were unsuitable for enamelled decoration.[59] The first animals were modelled by the sculptor Johann Gottlieb Kirchner (b.1706), who was employed from 1727, replaced by the ivory-carver Johann Christoph Ludwig Lücke in 1728, but reinstated in 1730, only to be dismissed again in 1733. He is thought to be the modeller of the first series of animals, which shows a high degree of fantasy and personality. Although their representations are seldom accurate, they show great stylisation and inventiveness (fig. 117).

Kirchner was succeeded in the commission by the greatest modeller in the history of Western ceramics, the sculptor Johann Joachim Kaendler (1706–75). He had trained in the workshop of the court sculptor Benjamin Thomä, and his great achievement was to blend the accuracy and sophistication of the monumental sculptor with a high degree of liveliness and characterisation in his models, suitable to the lighter medium of porcelain. It is generally thought that his figures for the Japanese Palace have more naturalism than Kirchner's, and are based on close observation of the king's menagerie at Moritzburg. The details of anatomy and fur and feathers are exceptionally fine. Not only was he responsible for a large number of the animal figures, but he went on to model porcelain figures of Apostles for the chapel of the palace in a vigorous Baroque style, fully

117   Lion, modelled by Kirchner. Hard-paste porcelain. Meissen, c.1730. Royal Museum of Scotland, Edinburgh.

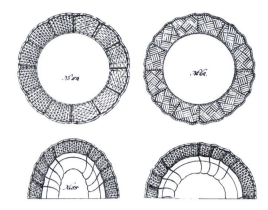

118 Borders of eighteenth-century Meissen dessert wares, from a catalogue of the early nineteenth century.

the equal to that of the finest sculptors in Rome.

A change of direction for the factory came in 1733 with the death of Augustus the Strong. His successor, Friedrich Augustus II succeeded as Augustus III, and took less interest in the factory than his predecessor, preferring to devote himself to building up the great collection of pictures which today forms the basis of the Gemäldegalerie at Dresden. The factory, however, was retained and developed under the minister Count Heinrich von Brühl, who retained this position until his death thirty years later in 1763. Brühl was in the enviable position of being able to requisition whatever porcelain he liked as a perquisite. Under him the factory tended to downplay the great individual commissions, such as the animals for the Japanese Palace, and concentrate instead on goods with commercial possibilities, such as dinner services, although standards remained high. A shop had been opened in Warsaw in 1731 and by 1733 the factory had agents in thirty-two German cities.[60] In 1734 links with Paris were renewed when Lemaire's partner, Jean-Charles Huet, was appointed agent, with the occasional use of a dealer called Bonnet in 1740 and 1746–7.[61]

Meissen was the first European factory to produce a complete porcelain dinner service; it appeared in the Meissen price lists in 1731, comprising tureens (but no soup plates), meat and dinner plates and salad plates in the Japanese manner.[62] A complete dinner service was made in 1733 for the court (the *Jagd* or hunting service), which had a yellow ground enclosing hunting scenes. In general, the enamelled decoration at this time was sparse, consisting mostly of coats-of-arms and tiny sprigs of *Indianische Blumen* or other eastern patterns.[63] The service made for Count Sulkowsky of 1735–7 has an evident debt to silver in its modelling, shown in double-curving profiles, gadrooning and strong volute-scrolled 'S' shaped feet, as well as handles with female heads and half-figures.[64] By the mid-1740s European or 'German' flowers (*Deutsche Blumen*) stiffly painted in the manner of woodcuts had come into vogue, and appear on the service presented to the British envoy Sir Charles Hanbury-Williams in 1746.[65]

Dessert services in porcelain continued to be considered as separate from dinner services and were decorated with new styles of moulded border decoration, based on relief patterns.[66] These included imitation basketwork (*Ordinar Ozier*) in 1732, the more elaborate *Neuozier* in 1742 and, in 1744, a pattern of raised flowers created for the Berlin merchant Gotzkowsky (fig. 118).[67] Some dessert wares were simple copies of natural shapes, such as vine-leaves and flowers, and in 1746 the now-familiar dessert dish based on a peony was modelled by J. G. Ehder, and remained in the sales catalogue of 1765.[68]

The greatest service of all was made for Count Brühl himself in 1737–41. This was the great 'Swan' service, a triumph of modelling and firing, which was clearly designed to show off the capability of the factory at its highest level (fig. 119). The whole service was conceived as a tribute to water, possibly inspired by the meaning of Brühl's surname (meaning 'marshy-ground'). The published records of orders show that the first pieces to be ordered by Count Brühl were for the *Konfekt* course.[69] It finally comprised a central *plat de ménage* (centrepiece), round and oval tureens, covered entrée dishes, *wärmeglocken* (dish covers), meat and soup plates, tea- and coffee pots, cups and saucers, and a host of other modelled wares for the dinner and dessert table, with splendid figures modelled by Kaendler. Count Brühl's pastrycook is rumoured to have contributed to the modelling of this service, which is not improbable, as he would have had knowledge of modelling swans for table decoration.[70] The vessels in the form of nereids holding shells are known to be the work of J. F. Eberlein, who had come to the factory as Kaendler's assistant in 1735; however, the general conception of the service must be due to Kaendler, which amply demonstrates his astonishing fertility of imagination.[71]

Kaendler's greatest forte seems to have been the modelling of small porcelain figures for use as table decorations, which has led to this period being called the 'mod-

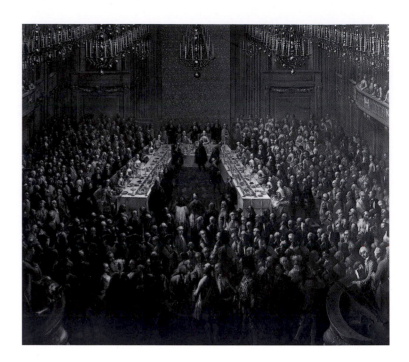

ellers' period. These figures had a distinguished history going back to medieval times when they were modelled, often by pastrycooks, out of sugar-paste.[72] They seem to have reached an apogee in the seventeenth century, when celebrated sculptors were involved in their modelling and design, especially in Italy. Naturally no sugar-paste examples survive, but we do have depictions and engravings of them, such as those for a feast for the Earl of Castlemaine in 1687 or Queen Christina of Sweden in 1688.[73] In Germany figures seem to have been used mostly for the final *Konfekt* course prepared by the pastrycook, and figures and architectural decoration of Meissen porcelain are listed under the *Konditorei* (confectioner) in the inventory of Count Brühl's possessions of 1763.[74] It is not always clear how such elaborate confections could be brought into the dining-room, but smaller decorations would have been brought in on mirrored trays.[75] This arrangement would appear to be confirmed by one of the few surviving depictions which show an eighteenth-century table layout with figures, the feast at the wedding of Joseph II and Isabella of Parma at Vienna in 1740 (fig. 120).[76]

Porcelain figures had already been made at Meissen, most notably the figures of Chinamen by Georg Fritzsche (*c.*1725), but Kaendler developed the genre into the vast array of animated figures that we are familiar with today. The earliest date from about 1735 and the precise date of the modelling of many of them is known from the *Taxa*, the record of work that Kaendler kept for the years 1740–5.[77] The first, *Harlequin Playing the Bagpipes*, heralded a huge range of figures representing the *commedia dell'arte* character figures, which would have been considered a suitable after-dinner entertainment.[78] This was developed into a great series representing virtually the whole of the Italian comedy, including figures of Harlequin (the clown), Mezzetino or Scapino (an intriguer), Pulcinello (another clown, but of less tractable disposition than Harlequin, and the origin of the English 'Punch'), Pantalone (a comic old man of amorous tendencies), the Doctor (a pedant), the Captain (a braggard), Columbine (the maid) (fig. 121), as well as the central loving couple, so essential to the plot.[79] Often two figures were modelled as a group, responding to each other with animated expressions, as in the group of *Harlequin and Columbine* of 1741. Kaendler's intention is avowedly satirical, and the figures misbehave with a licence and frivolity that could only have been countenanced during the light-hearted dessert course.[80] The ill-

119 Plate from the 'Swan' service. Hard-paste porcelain, painted in enamel colours and gilt. Meissen, *c.*1738. Victoria & Albert Museum, London.

120 Detail from Martin van Meytens, *The Wedding of Joseph II and Isabella of Parma*, 1740. Schönnbrunn, Vienna.

tempered *Scowling Harlequin*, and the *Harlequin Twisting a Dog's Tail as a Rummel Pot* of about 1738, are the best-known of this type (fig. 121). Kaendler similarly modelled figures of court jesters Joseph Fröhlich (1737) and the postmaster 'Baron' Schmiedel who would have been allowed to behave in this way.[81] A further series of *commedia dell'arte* figures was modelled for the Duke of Saxe-Weissenfels in about 1744, copied from Riccoboni's *Histoire du théâtre italien*, Paris, of 1728.[82]

Kaendler also developed a wide range of characters beyond the *commedia dell'arte* figures. He introduced a range of folk types, including Tyrolese dancers and figures of miners, so important to Augustus's economy. The figure of the tailor riding a goat of 1737–40 apparently refers to an old tradition that the weakest member of a farmer's family did not work on the land but became a tailor; the goat is clearly representative of his bodily weakness and aristocratic aspirations. Kaendler also modelled figures of exotic subjects such as Chinamen and Turks. But his other great contribution to figure modelling involved the figures relating directly to court life, and especially the rituals of love and seduction, the so-called 'crinoline' groups, whereby a fashionably dressed lady partakes of tea, or entertains a gentleman visitor, attired in a huge crinolined dress (fig. 122). This series was begun in about 1737, the best-known of which is *The Handkiss*. He was also capable of fine direct sculpting, best seen in the two heads of about 1753 of Prince Louis-Charles and Princess Marie-Zéphérine de Bourbon, children of the Dauphin of France

121   Figures of Harlequins, including the *The Scowling Harlequin* and *Harlequin Twisting a Dog's Tail as a Rummel Pot*. Hard-paste porcelain, painted in enamel colours. Average height 16 cm. Meissen, *c*.1740. The Victoria & Albert Museum, London.

and his wife Maria Josepha of Saxony, daughter of Augustus III.

As the century progressed, desserts came to be artistically and intellectually ambitious, and copied the formal gardens of the period. Figures became increasingly sculptural in style and began to consciously copy garden sculpture rather than the gaudy, coloured work of the pastrycook. Kaendler is recorded as modelling a series of figures of Apollo and the Graces for Frederick the Great of Prussia in 1743–4. In 1745 Kaendler, assisted by Eberlein, copied in porcelain a fountain with statues which had been erected in Brühl's garden by the architect Zacharias Longuelune and the sculptor Lorenzo Mattielli.[83] A version of the ensemble survives in the Victoria and Albert Museum, and reproduces the Dresden fountain with considerable fidelity in white undecorated porcelain (fig. 123).[84]

In the 1750s more allegorical subjects became popular, such as groups of gods and goddesses, the Four Seasons, and the Five Senses. These latter figures were often modelled by Kaendler's assistant, J. F. Eberlein. The introduction of scrolled bases is thought to be the

122 'Crinoline Group'. Hard-paste porcelain painted in enamel colours and gilt. Meissen, c. 1740. Victoria & Albert Museum, London.

123 Table-centrepiece in the form of a fountain. Hard-paste porcelain. Meissen, 1745. Victoria & Albert Museum, London.

responsibility of the court sculptor Friedrich Elias Meyer (1723–85), brought in from Weimar in the 1750s. Such figures became standard items of tableware throughout Europe. The Englishman Horace Walpole, wrote in *The World* on 8 February 1753, on the changes that had taken place in garden design, which were reflected in the dessert course:

> Jellies, biscuits, sugar plumbs [sic] and creams have long given way to harlequins, gondoliers, Turks, Chinese and shepherdesses of Saxon china. But these, unconnected, and only seeming to wander among groves of curled paper and silk flowers, were soon discovered to be too insipid and unmeaning. By degrees whole meadows of cattle, of the same brittle materials, spread themselves over the whole table; cottages rose in sugar, and temples in barley-sugar; pigmy Neptunes in cars of cockle-shells triumphed over oceans of looking glass or seas of silver tissue, and at length the whole system of Ovid's metamorphosis succeeded to all the transformations which Chloe [a cook] and other great professors had introduced into the science of hieroglyphic eating. Confectioners found their trade moulder away, while toymen and china-shops were the only fashionable purveyors of the last stage of polite entertainments. Women of the first quality came home from Chenevix's [a fashionable china-dealer] laden with dolls and babies, not for their children, but for their housekeeper. At last even these puerile puppet shows are sinking into disuse, and more manly ways of concluding our repasts are established. Gigantic figures succeed to pigmies, and if the present taste continues, Rysbrack, and other neglected statuaries, who might have adorned Grecian salons, though not Grecian desserts, may come into vogue.[85]

This period also saw the development of new types of painted decoration, most famously that of scenes copied from the French painter Jean-Antoine Watteau (1684–

1721) and his followers. They are first recorded on porcelain made in 1745 and sent to Augustus's daughter, Maria Amalia Christina, in Naples in 1747 (not 1738, as is often stated).[86] The figures are presented in green on islands in panels against a gold background, and, as is usual in aristocratic commissions, the owner's coat-of-arms feature prominently. 'Watteau scenes' were to remain a prominent type of decoration in the mid-eighteenth century, being mentioned in the 1765 price-list when they would have been quite out of fashion in France itself.

124 French eighteenth-century clock with figures from a 'Monkey band'. Hard-paste porcelain, painted in enamel colours and gilt. Height 14.3 cm. Meissen, c.1755. The National Trust, Waddesdon Manor, Aylesbury.

125 Chamber pot (*bourdalou*). Hard-paste porcelain, painted with European flowers in enamel colours and gilt. Meissen, *c*.1740. Courtesy of Brian Haughton Antiques, London.

A more striking use of French influence lay in the production of the famous 'monkey band' of 1747, a complete orchestra of monkeys dressed as musicians (fig. 124). The motif stemmed from an ancient tradition of the depiction of monkeys as imitating human activity, a parallel for the way in which art imitates life. There was a vogue for such decoration (*singeries*) in France in the 1740s, most famously in the room painted by Christophe Huet (1700–59) in the Château of Chantilly. The Meissen band seems to have been based on drawings by Huet supplied to the Meissen factory by his namesake the Parisian dealer Jean-Charles Huet for sale in France; to this extent, they are a measure of how much French taste was coming to dominate Germany. In about 1757 the Meissen factory produced a further series of figures based on drawings on Huet, the 'Cries of Paris', featuring thirty-six Parisian street-traders, mostly food sellers, crying their wares in miniature over the dessert table.[87]

Parallel with this taste was a taste for novelty items or *Galanterien*, that is, small objects of porcelain that were partly functional and partly decorative. They comprised a wide range of snuff-boxes, scent bottles and bobbin cases, all executed with the most exquisite refinement in the most elegant taste. Such items were largely intended for the gift market and were called 'toys' in Britain. Many were decorated in purple alone (*camaïeu*). Most curious to modern audiences is the small slipper-shaped lady's chamberpot called a *bourdalou* (fig. 125), after a French preacher of exorbitantly long sermons which left no time for relief. This was intended for daytime use, avoiding the necessity of the lady having to take off her heavy garments, when underclothes were often non-existent or minimal!

Indeed, the tendency at the Meissen factory in the 1740s and 1750s was to produce items to impress the French market, a tendency increased by the marriage of Augustus's daughter, Maria Josepha, to the French Dauphin in 1749. Needless to say, these wares were always the largest and most elaborate that the factory could produce but ironically, the more they strove to show off the factory's inventiveness, the more they merely reflected the dominance of French taste. A peculiarity is the way in which they are encrusted with figures and three-dimensional flowers of the most elaborate kind. A set of five vases symbolising the elements was made for Louis XV in 1741–2; it was of flam-

126 Vases from a set of *The Elements*. Hard-paste porcelain. Meissen, *c.*1750. Courtesy of the Antique Porcelain Company, London.

boyant form with much applied decoration, recalling elaborate vases of the kind made by the Italian bronze-caster Massimiliano Soldani-Benzi (1656–1740). The central vase was smothered in porcelain flowers or *Guelderrosen*, which were to become a feature of the more elaborate products of Meissen in the 1750s. A set of seven vases was sent to the Empress Elizabeth of Russia in 1744; that of Phoebus Apollo is perhaps the most attractive, with applied branches of bay which are very reminiscent of the applied floral decoration that we find on Böttger porcelain. In 1747–8 Brühl himself ordered a set of vases symbolising the Four Elements, which are conceived in three-dimensional terms with decorations of flames, clouds, plants, rocks and even a lobster-pot (fig. 126). Most flamboyant of all would have been the mirror-frame and console table made in 1748–50 as a belated wedding present for the marriage of Augustus' daughter, Maria Josepha, to the Dauphin of France in 1749. They were taken to Paris by Kaendler himself, accompanied by the factor Helbig, in 1750. These were heavily encrusted with applied flowers and their fragility meant that they did not survive the French Revolution, although the moulds survived in Dresden, which have enabled reproductions to be made. It is ironic that this tribute to German skill and industry was also a demonstration of the extent to which French taste was now pervasive throughout Europe.

Detail of fig. 121. Figures of Harlequins.

Overleaf, detail of fig. 136. Vase *pot-pourri fontaine*.

CHAPTER 7

French Rococo: The Ascendancy of Sèvres

Though Germany had dominated the world in the development and decoration of porcelain, France remained the acknowledged ruler of taste, supplier of luxury goods, and arbiter of fashion to the whole of Europe. The tradition which started under Louis XIV continued under his successor the *Régent*, Philippe, duc d'Orléans, who ruled during the minority of Louis' great-grandson, Louis XV. Under the regent the centre of fashion again shifted back to Paris, where he kept court at the Palais Royal, his residence opposite the Louvre. His aim in government was domestic retrenchment and the avoidance of wars, and, in his personal life, luxury and debauchment.

The style of his rule, the *Régence*, had none of the bombastic leanings of that of Louis XIV, and was in general a much lighter and more fanciful style. It was a development of the grotesque style favoured by Louis XIV's chief designer, Jean Berain, in which the gods and goddesses of the ancient world are treated as decorative figures. The most famous painter and designer of this period is Jean-Antoine Watteau (1684–1721), whose elegant pastorals and *fêtes galantes*, engraved in the *recueil Julienne* of 1727–35, had already been used on Meissen porcelain.[1] The emphasis was on small-scale luxury rather than grandeur, with smaller rooms dominating the domestic interior, but decorated with greater refinement of taste. The decorative interior style was developed by the regent's chief architect Gilles-Marie Oppenord (1672–1742) in his interiors for the Palais Royal. The straight and ponderous lines of the classical style begin to break down and become curved; light-hearted motifs, such as children or fanciful figures appear, and gods or goddesses are no longer depicted as solemn statues but feature as vase supports or as decorative motifs.[2] In general, a lighter, more 'feminine' style became popular,[3] to provide a setting for the smaller parties and less grandiose entertainments, often held by women rather than men. In this respect, tea and coffee drinking and smaller dinner-parties could play a part; the print by L. Jacob after Watteau's follower Nicolas Lancret, showing a woman at breakfast with friends, gives a flavour of the age (fig. 127).

This new taste led to a demand for knick-knacks and small-scale objects that was catered for by the *marchands-merciers* of eighteenth-century Paris. They comprised a separate trade-guild which specialised in luxury goods and expensive objects: porcelain, furniture, fans, snuff-boxes, and small decorative objects of all sorts. Their function was to tempt and titillate jaded appetites and create a market for unnecessary and pointless items; the critic Diderot in the great *Encyclopédie* called them 'makers of nothing and dealers in everything'.[4] We have already encountered a number of them selling goods to Louis XIV, or as dealers in Meissen porcelain in Paris. The most famous is the dealer Lazare Duvaux, whose account books for the years 1748–58 survive, listing many noble and aristocratic customers, including Louis XV's mistress, Madame de

Lancret pinxit   LE MATIN   Llacob Sculp

127   L. Jacob after Nicolas Lancret (1690– 1743): *Le Matin*. Engraving.

Pompadour.[5] She was a client over many years and is recorded as buying everything from a 'trictrac' board of ebony and ivory, with green and white pieces, to 'two Japanese monkeys with nodding heads' along with various pieces of lacquer.[6]

Some of the demand for porcelain was supplied by French factories. There were a number of porcelain factories in early eighteenth-century France, which made soft-paste porcelain, similar in body to Medici porcelain, rather than the true hard-paste porcelain of China, Japan and Meissen. In addition to the existing factory at Saint Cloud, which was under the patronage of the duc d'Orléans, a factory was founded at Chantilly in about 1730, under the patronage of Louis-Henri de Bourbon, prince de Condé, who continued to subsidise it until his death in 1740.[7] This made wares in the Japanese *Kakiemon* style, which was highly fashionable in France during this period, appearing in sales catalogues with the description 'first rate enamelled Japanese porcelain' ('premier qualitié coloré de Japon') to contrast with the coarser *Imari* type decoration. It is thought that the factory was inspired by *Kakiemon* porcelain in the duke's own collection, which was directly copied at the factory.[8] As the quality of the paste was not good, the early wares were covered in an opaque tin-glaze to hide deficiencies. It tended to make smaller wares, for tea or coffee, and *galanterie*, such as snuff-boxes and walking-stick handles, though there also exist a small number of tureens and wine-coolers. A small range of figures was also produced; most remarkable are the *magots* or grotesque figures of Chinese gods, based on Chinese models, sometimes supporting a flowerpot, or mounted in ormolu. Another soft-paste factory was set up at Mennecy in about 1750 (formerly in the Rue de Charonne, Paris) under the patronage of the duc de Villeroy.[9] This made a similar range of objects, but the decoration tended to consist of bunches of flowers in the tradition of European flowers at Meissen, and the range tended to be confined to tea-wares.

Some of the porcelain sold by the *marchands-merciers* was not sold plain, but mounted in extravagant gilt-bronze (*ormolu*) mounts; this reached a height in Paris in the 1740s and 50s when the flamboyant mounts came to smother the actual object. Some of the mounts can be dated to 1745–9 by the mark of the crowned '*C*' that appears on them, a hallmark indicating copper content.[10] The preferred objects for mounting were Chinese vases with a *celadon* (pale-greenish) glaze (fig. 128); however, porcelain (including that of Meissen) and other objects could also be used, often incorporated into more fanciful items, such as clocks. Duvaux's favourite craftsman for the mounting of porcelain seems to have been the metalworker Jean-Claude Duplessis (d. 1774) from Turin, who had come to Paris in 1740, and brought with him Italian skills in modelling three-dimensional objects.[11] Many of these wares were sold to Madame de Pompadour, who had an especial liking for flamboyant objects of the highest quality.

Most of these gilt-bronze mounts are in the new 'rococo' style, which became dominant in France and Europe in the mid-century. The term 'rococo' is a late eighteenth-century term, conflated from the Italian *barocco*, or Baroque style and the term 'rocaille', which was the contemporary word for the types of rocky ornament found in the grottoes that were so popular at this time. Its three major characteristics were the use of 'C'- and 'S'-shaped curves in the design; the use of asymmetry (in that the left-hand side of the design did not correspond to the right), and the use of naturalistic decoration involving animals, fruit and fish, often mixed together without any sense of their relevant proportions. In the eighteenth century, the term for rococo in painting was '*genre pittoresque*', a picturesque style, which shows the rough texture and movement of the surface that is characteristic of much eighteenth-century art. It was propagated by means of ornamental engravings by such designers as Nicolas Pineau (1684–1754), Jacques de La Joue (1686–1761) and, above all, the great Turinese gold-

128 Pair of Chinese celadon vases mounted in French gilt bronze mounts. Height 60 cm. The mounts bear the crowned 'C' mark, dating them to 1745–9. The J. Paul Getty Museum, Los Angeles.

smith Juste-Aurèle Meissonnier (1695–1750), in whose work we first encounter the rococo style in its fully developed form (fig. 129).[12]

The print of 'rocaille' decoration is by one of the leading contributors to the rococo style, the French court-painter François Boucher (1703–70). No other painter has had so considerable and pervasive an influence on the decorative arts, blending as he does both the fine and the decorative arts into one glorious whole (fig. 130). He had spent his youth making engravings after the work of Jean-Antoine Watteau, and was familiar with the light-hearted decorative style that Watteau had introduced into French painting. Boucher's work owes its genesis to Watteau's dreamy world of the *fête galante*, a world in which people disport themselves outside in fancy dress, masquerades, and other manifestations of the elegant art of pleasure. However, Boucher's world is much more dynamic and physical, the world of the 'pastoral', in which shepherds and shepherdesses disport themselves in the process of flirtation and the preliminaries of love-making. To add a certain innocence to these proceedings, the participants are frequently depicted as young children, directly related to the chubby 'putti' of Italian Baroque sculpture. Boucher was a particular favourite of Louis XV's mistress, Madame de Pompadour, and became court painter in 1760. It was the works of Boucher, translated through the medium of prints by skilful engravers such as Gilles Demarteau and Jean-Baptiste Le Prince, that made these themes so popular in the decorative arts (fig.131).[13]

Though Boucher's influence is pervasive throughout the rococo period, his work is associated most closely with the products of one porcelain factory, that of Vincennes, which later moved to Sèvres, just outside Paris. This factory was to make some of the most beautiful porcelain produced in eighteenth-century Europe; the body of the wares is of a beautiful milky-white soft-paste, and the forms and decoration are due to the finest designers and decorators that France could produce. It was the envy of other nations and provided a lead in the provision of new forms and styles of decoration throughout the rest of the eighteenth century. Though its products have lost something of the kudos that they possessed in the eighteenth century, mainly due to a growing appreciation of the work of the individual craftsman-potter in the twentieth century, many of the products of the factory must still be considered among the high-points of European ceramic art.

129 Juste-Aurèle Meissonnier (1695–1750), *Design for a Table Centrepiece ('Surtout de table') for the Duke of Kingston*. 1735. Engraving.

130 François Boucher (1703–70), *Rocaille*. Engraving.

The original factory was set up in the old royal castle of Vincennes, east of Paris, in about 1740, with the help of two brothers who had previously worked at the Chantilly factory, Robert and Gilles Dubois. The guiding lights, however, seem to have been two government officials, the brothers Philibert Orry de Vignory and Jean-Henri-Louis Orry de Fulvy, who saw the factory through its early years and set up a joint-stock company in 1745, to make porcelain 'in the manner of Saxony painted and gilded with figure subjects'.[14] This suggests that the factory was intending to make wares in imitation of Meissen. The secrets of the establishment were jealously guarded in the manner of all early porcelain factories, and employees were not allowed to leave without written permission. Sales rose from virtually nothing in 1745 to 31,738 livres in 1748; however, this was not enough to make a profit and the king started to take a personal interest in the factory in 1751. The factory was reconstituted in 1752 with the king as the principal shareholder, others being friends of the king's mistress, Madame de Pompadour, who maintained close links with the factory throughout her life. Probably at her suggestion, the factory moved to Sèvres in 1756, to be closer to the court at Versailles (the factory will be called generally 'Sèvres'), and in 1759, after further losses, became the personal property of the king himself, in the manner of the great porcelain factories being set up in Germany.[15]

One of the remarkable features of the factory is its relatively intact factory records, which often enable us to identify individual items and trace their original purchaser. Furthermore, since Sèvres was a royal factory, it adopted as its factory mark the two interlaced 'L's of Louis XV painted in blue, together with a series of date letters which run from 1753 to 1792. There were also separate marks for painters and gilders (the factory had been given a monopoly of the use of gilding on porcelain to enable it to maintain its supremacy in France). These marks and records enable us to trace many single examples from the eighteenth century, and reconstruct their early manufacture and ownership.

In its early days the factory seems to have made a specialty of producing porcelain flowers, which would have been scented in imitation of real flowers. These were often mounted on ormolu stalks and sold in porcelain vases of European or Eastern manufacture. The dealer Lazare Duvaux was selling such items in 1747 and 1748.[16] One of the earliest pieces from the factory, now in Dresden, is the large bouquet of porcelain flowers set on an ormolu base, with two undecorated porcelain figures, which was sent by the German Princess Maria Josepha, wife of the dauphin, as a present to her father Augustus III of Saxony in the spring of 1749. A similar piece with 480 flowers had been presented to Queen Marie Leczinska, in 1748. Though it is a great *tour de force*, the quality of the white figures is not such as to worry the owner of the Meissen factory. They represent 'Music' and 'Astrology', and were part of a number of figures made in the beautiful unpainted soft-porcelain of the early years of the factory. Similar figures were made at Mennecy. Other figures made at Vincennes include river gods and goddesses, sleeping women and a remarkable clock-case intended to symbolise Zephyrus and Flora.[17] Some of these may have been modelled by the sculptor Louis Fournier, who worked at Vincennes from 1747–9, and Chantilly from 1752–6; he subsequently founded a porcelain factory at Copenhagen (1759–66), which made ware reminiscent of early Sèvres.[18]

Despite the aims of the 1745 petition to set up the factory, which were to produce coloured figures in the manner of Meissen, Vincennes/Sèvres showed less interest in the kind of coloured figures that were made at other factories to act as table-decoration during the dessert. Instead, they developed a line in unglazed 'biscuit' porcelain figures which were first made in 1751.[19] The earliest models were done after designs by François Boucher himself, who provided thirteen drawings of children, one of which, *Le Petit Jardinier*, survives in the factory's archives today. The designs were

131   Jean Baptiste Le Prince (1734–81) after François Boucher (1703–70), *La Chasse*. Engraving.

translated into three-dimensions by the sculptural team at the factory in 1753–5: Blondeau, La Rue, Fernex and Suzanne. Some were even modelled by the great sculptor Etienne-Maurice Falconet (1716–91), who worked at the factory from 1757 to 1766. They well capture the chubby-faced innocence of Boucher's designs, as well as advertising the sculptural possibilities of biscuit porcelain.[20] Their fragility was judged such that prints after some were engraved and advertised in *L'Avant-Coureur* in 1761 and 1763, in order to record their appearance (figs 132 and 133).[21]

132. Unglazed (biscuit) figure of 'The Little Confectioner' modelled by Etienne-Maurice Falconet after François Boucher, 1757, together with engraving. Musée National de Céramique, Sèvres.

The emergence of a distinctive style in more everyday items came with the employment of the bronze-caster Jean-Claude Duplessis, who was in charge of modelling from 1752 until his death in 1774. He is credited with a large number of forms for the factory in its early days. At first they are rather heavy and cumbersome; for instance, a rather heavy bottle-cooler with leaf moulding at the side,[22] but later he devised a lighter and more successful range of shapes, which were to remain standard for a great many years.[23] These included tea and coffee wares, which were often sold in the form of small services for one or two people with a tray, called a *déjeuner*, or sometimes a *cabaret* (from the tray on which it was served).[24] Such sets were in production at Sèvres from 1753 onwards. The items ranged from cups and saucers and sugar bowls in the form christened *Hébert* (possibly after a famous marchand-mercier of that name), with a milk jug and sometimes a small teapot[25] (fig. 134).

133 Group of *The Flute Lesson*. after François Boucher. Soft-paste porcelain, unglazed. Height 22.3 cm. Sèvres, *c.*1757–66. The J. Paul Getty Museum, Los Angeles.

134 'Déjeuner' set. Soft-paste porcelain, painted in enamel colours and gilt. Length of tray 32.2 cm. Sèvres, 1764. The Bowes Museum, Barnard Castle, Co. Durham.

The factory was especially distinguished for the quality of its painted decoration and gilding. The work was overseen by the artist Jean-Jacques Bachelier (1724–1805) who was appointed *directeur artistique* in 1751 and in 1753 opened a school for trainee painters. He was responsible for the purchase of prints for the nascent factory.[26] Early painting was comparatively restrained, and often featured landscapes, flowers or birds painted in a European style in central panels (*réserves*), or putti or pastoral scenes after François Boucher. The latter were a speciality of the painter André-Vincent Vielliard (fig. 135).[27]

Possibly Sèvres' greatest contribution to European ceramic design was the development of rich ground-colours under the direction of the chemist Hellot, often enriched by lavish gilding. The most famous are underglaze dark-blue (*bleu lapis*), developed in 1751, followed by overglaze turquoise-blue (*bleu céleste*) (1753), green (1756) and pink (*rose*) (1757). Sometimes these colours were used in combination, such as pink and green or blue and green.[28] Gilding was lavishly applied from the 1750s in the *caillouté* pattern, resembling small stones, or *vermiculé*, resembling worm-casts. Patterns were also devised in which the ground colour was patterned to produce a marbled (*marbré*) ground; it should be emphasised that these ground colours were expensive and greatly added to the cost of porcelain.

The greatest achievement of Duplessis is probably the series of flower vases and vases with pierced lids for pot-pourri of the 1750s, which show a consistent development into richer and more extravagant forms. They are perhaps not entirely to the taste of the twentieth century, but until well into the nineteenth century they were the most prized objects a porcelain collector could aspire to. Early models include the urn-shaped *pot-*

pourri pompadour of 1752, pierced with openings for the scent to pass through at the top of the body; the *vase à oreilles* (1754), with curved handles at the top resembling ears; the fan-shaped flower vase, the *vase à l'hollandoise* (1754), with a pierced base for watering the plants in the container above; *pot-pourri gondole* (1756), with an extravagant pierced lid on a curved base resembling a gondola; the remarkable *vase 'à tête d'éléphant'*, with two elephants' heads at the top with the trunks curving round to support candle-arms (*bobèches*), based on Japanese birdcage vases copied from Meissen; the *cuvette Mahon* (1756), *vase Boileau* (1758), *pot-pourri girandole* (1759), and the *pot-pourri fontaine* (1756), in the form of a fountain with water tumbling down and splashing back up the sides (fig. 136). The greatest of all was perhaps the *pot-pourri à vaisseau* or *en navire*, today often called a *vase vaisseau à mat,* of 1757. This was an extravagant creation in which the pot-pourri was modelled in the form of a ship with sails, the scent of the pot-pourri coming up through the holes in the rigging (fig. 137). Fewer than fifteen were made and were apparently sold mostly to the royal family or members of the king's immediate circle.

An interesting and unexpected development of the late 1750s and 1760s was the filling of the *réserves* with tightly painted scenes of harbours or soldiers, in the manner of Meissen, or even peasant scenes after such Netherlandish artists as David Teniers.[29] This decoration contrasts strangely with the rococo form of some of the products, but seems to have been considered very fashionable, as there was a great rage for the work of Teniers and other Dutch paintings of the seventeenth century, in mid-eighteenth-century Paris.[30]

Often these vases were decorated and combined in the form of 'garnitures' of three or five in the manner of sets of vases from Delft, Meissen or elsewhere. The most famous are the two garnitures made for Madame de Pompadour, now divided between several institutions, and recently identified through their peculiarities of decoration. The first comprises a *pot-pourri à vaisseau*, which formed a garniture with two *pots-pourris girandole* and two *pots-pourris fontaine* (Getty Museum), all decorated with rare chinoiserie decoration and a unique combination of pink, blue and green ground-colours. They were sold from the factory, with two wall-lights, on 30 May 1760, and later listed as

135 Pair of bulb-holders (*vases à oignon*). Soft-paste porcelain, painted in enamels with figures after François Boucher by André-Vincent Vielliard and gilt. Sèvres, 1756. Probably the pair sold by the dealer Lazare Duvaux to Mademoiselle de Sens in December 1757 for 312 livres. The Bowes Museum, Barnard Castle, Co. Durham.

136 Vase *pot-pourri fontaine* painted with Chinese scene against a pink, green and blue ground. Soft-paste porcelain, painted in enamel colours and gilt. Height 29.8 cm, Sèvres, 1760. The J. Paul Getty Museum, Los Angeles.

137 Overleaf. Pot-pourri vase in the form of a ship (*vaisseau à mat*), with a central panel of figures after David Teniers. Soft-paste porcelain, painted in colours framed by ground colours in pink, green. Height 37.5 cm. Sèvres, about 1760. The J. Paul Getty Museum, Los Angeles.

138 Vase *Duplessis à enfants*. Soft-paste porcelain, painted in enamel colours with a green ground and gilt. Height 24 cm. Sèvres, 1756. Adrian Sassoon, London.

139 Pair of pot-pourri vases (*pots-pourris Pompadour*). Soft-paste porcelain, painted in enamel colours by Morin and gilt. Height 25 cm. Vincennes, 1755. The J. Paul Getty Museum, Los Angeles.

140 Reconstruction by Pierre Ennès of a garniture made for Madame de Pompadour, featuring a *pot pourri vaisseau* and accompanying vases

141 Reconstruction by Pierre Ennès of a garniture made for Madame de Pompadour, featuring a clock and accompanying vases.

being on the chimney piece of Madame de Pompadour's bedroom in Paris on her death in 1763. Another garniture, comprising a clock, two *pots-pourris girandole* and two *pots-pourris à feuillage*, was sold to Madame de Pompadour on 25 June 1762, and has recently also been identified (figs. 140 and 141).[31]

The early dinner wares of Vincennes tended to follow Meissen shapes and styles. However, a range of its own beautiful shapes were soon created by the factory. The credit for these is also given to Duplessis, who presumably supplied them for a service ordered by Louis XV in 1751, which was delivered between 1753 and 1755.[32] They were to remain standard in Sèvres dinner services right into the 1790s,[33] and imitated throughout Europe.

Chief among the new forms was a set of two pairs of tureens and stands to be arranged symmetrically around the centrepiece. Those made by Sèvres exhibited close parallels with contemporary silver design, copying its curved legs and naturalistic decoration. They would have been equipped with a metal liner to contain the soup or stew while it was hot, in order to prevent the cracking or crazing the soft-paste porce-

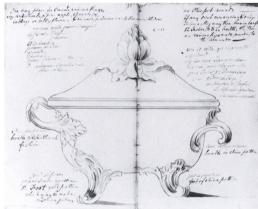

142 Tureen and stand painted by Rosset. Soft-paste porcelain, painted in enamel colours and gilt. Sèvres, 1755. Adrian Sassoon, London.

143 Drawing from the Leeds pottery pattern books showing an *olio* pot in both silver and china shapes. Victoria & Albert Museum, London.

lain.[34] They came in two kinds, one tall and round for the *olio*, the other low and oval for the *terrine* (fig. 142), following the fashion of metalwork, as Meissonnier's engravings make clear.[35] Both tended to be decorated with finials in the form of animals or vegetables, reflecting their contents, as is shown in a late eighteenth-century drawing in the Leeds pottery pattern-books in the Victoria and Albert Museum (fig. 143). They would have been arranged around the centre of the table (fig. 144).[36] Other new shapes include separate plates for the side-dishes of the first two courses, *plat d'entrée* and *plat d'entremets*,[37] and a wide variety of bottle-coolers in different sizes, and wineglass-coolers. These came in different sizes for bottle, half-bottles, liqueur bottles, and individual wineglasses (fig. 145).[38] Wineglasses could also be cooled rather more economically all together in a serrated edge wineglass-cooler, in which the bowls of the glasses were laid together face-down in a bed of ice (fig 146). For meals outside the dining-room, portions of soup could be served in an *écuelle* or covered broth-bowl and stand, which were often individually decorated (fig. 147).

Sèvres became the standard supplier of dinner services to the rich throughout Europe; though other factories of course made their own designs, the models began to be copied from Sèvres shapes. Here Sèvres seems to have started the trend in the use of porcelain instead of silver at fashionable dinner tables, for as late as 1751, Gilliers, *Chef d'Office* (Master Confectioner) to the King of Poland, in his influential *Le Cannameliste Français* had mentioned that porcelain was used at table only for covered dishes, salad dishes, fruit dishes and plates.[39] The general aim at Sèvres was to encourage the rich to consider porcelain as a fashionable alternative to using gold and silver. This tendency was reinforced by the king's habit of presenting a dinner service of Sèvres porcelain as a diplomatic gift, to advertise the products of the factory and the supremacy of French design. Recipients included the Empress Maria Theresa (1758), the Duchess of Bedford,

144 Setting for a dinner of fifteen or sixteen dishes, engraving from Vincent La Chapelle, *Le Cuisinier moderne* (The Hague, 1742).

145 Pair of bottle coolers ('seau à liqueur rond'). Soft-paste porcelain, painted in enamel colours by F. Binet and gilt. Sèvres, 1754–55. Adrian Sassoon, London.

146 J. B. Moreau (Moreau le Jeune), *Le Souper Fin*, engraving from *Le Monument de Costume* (Paris, 1783), showing a wine-glass cooler (*verrière*) on the side-table.

147 Écuelle with the monogram of Madame Louise, daughter of Louis XV. Sèvres, 1764. Soft-paste porcelain, painted in enamel colours and gilt. The J. Paul Getty Museum, Los Angeles.

wife of the British Ambassador (1763), whose service still survives at the family's ancestral home of Woburn Abbey, Bedforshire, and the Scandinavian Kings Christian VII of Denmark (1768) and Gustav III of Sweden (1771).[40]

Another influential development at Sèvres was the creation of specialised shapes for the dessert service, which kept its garden-like character, as is shown by an illustration in Gilliers' *Le Cannameliste Français* (1768).[41] These included a shell-shaped dish, designated 'compotiers coquille forme nouvelle', of 1752,[42] and an ice-pail, a deep-lidded container for ice-creams and sorbets,[43] which preserved the coldness by storing the

sorbet or ice-cream between two layers of ice kept in the lid and the base (fig. 148). Ice-creams (*glaces*) were made in tin boxes filled with fruit juices, chocolate or cream, and left to freeze in urns containing ice and salt. They were drunk semi-liquid in small *tasses à glace*, which were often served on a tray.[44]

The result of all these innovations was that Sèvres porcelain became *the* dominant luxury porcelain used at the dinner table in Europe in the eighteenth century. As such, it was internationally recognised as a mark of wealth, good breeding, and luxury, and considered the height of refinement for anyone who wanted to impress a guest.[45] However, it was expensive and most Frenchmen continued to eat off pottery, be it tin-glazed ('faïence') or lead-glazed. Contemporary advertisements in papers stress that faïence was as good as Meissen porcelain and cost a good deal less, although it might share the dinner table with objects in more prestigious materials.[46] When the Swiss miniaturist Rouquet commented on the relatively small amount of silver in use in England, he noted that it was never 'mixed with this ignoble material, known under the name of *faïence*', implying that this was the practice on the Continent.[47]

Since pottery had to take the place of, or mix with, silver on the dinner table, as with porcelain the shapes tended to follow silver forms. A splendid earthenware centrepiece from the Pont-aux-Choux factory in Paris, founded in 1743 by Claude-Humbert Gérin, with its flamboyant curves and rococo base, is essentially a pottery version of the metalwork-styles propagated by Meissonnier and his followers (fig. 149). The factory also made a wide variety of good-quality unpainted moulded dishes, covered tureens and other articles with carefully modelled naturalistic decoration. The body was a fine white pottery similar to that of imports from Staffordshire in England, hence its title '*Manufacture royale des terres de France à l'imitation de celles d'Angleterre.*' Such pottery was very popular in France where it was called *faïence fine*, and tariffs had to be imposed on English imports in 1741 and 1749.[48]

However, the vast majority of good-quality pottery made in eighteenth-century France was tin-glazed ('faïence'). Its popularity was aided by the development of *petit feu* enamel

148 Drawing of an ice-pail, annotated to show its use. Victoria and Albert Museum, London.

149 Tureen with cover and stand in the rococo style. Lead-glazed earthenware. Paris, Pont-aux-Choux factory, c.1750. Height of tureen 30.5 cm. The Art Institute, Chicago.

colours, that is, a new range of colours mixed with powdered glass, which could be fired at a lower temperature in a muffle kiln, in the same way as on porcelain. The new colours consisted of vermillion-red, crimson, pink and leaf-gilding, which allowed these factories to rival – in appearance at least – the porcelain creations of China, Japan or Meissen, but in pottery.

The main factory for the development of faïence painted in *petit feu* colours was that of Paul-Antoine Hannong at Strasbourg in eastern France in the period 1747–9. The factory had been founded by his father, Charles-François, in about 1709, with a sister branch at Haguenau, and Paul-Antoine was director from 1739 to 1760. Owing to a peculiar system of customs duties, wares made in Alsace, Lorraine and the 'Three Bishoprics' of Metz, Toul and Verdun, paid lower customs duties if they were sent to Germany rather than to central France. Consequently a great export trade developed with Germany, Switzerland and the Baltic countries, where they were imitated. Many of the workers at the Strasbourg factory came from Germany, most importantly the various members of the Löwenfinck family from Meissen who arrived in 1748, followed by John Jacob Ringler from Vienna in 1753.

The main form of decoration was sprays of naturalistic cut-flowers, similar to those at Meissen or Mennecy. In addition Hannong also developed a range of ground colours, comprising blue, yellow, greens, and a very rich brick-red, as well as developing painting *en camaïeu* (monochrome colours). Gilding was prohibited by the ban on its use in factories other than Vincennes, although it is recorded in 1744 on pieces offered to Louis XV. Tureens were made in the shape of animals and animals' heads, as well as a range of figures in the manner of Meissen, and a spectacular clock-case with elaborate rococo mouldings (fig. 150).[49] The factory was later run by Paul's son Joseph, who also set up a porcelain factory, the huge running costs of which led to the closure of the parent pottery factory in 1779.

There were three further factories on the eastern border in Lorraine, which had the benefit of princely patronage. The factory at Lunéville, the home of the exiled Polish king, Stanislaw Leczinska (1677–1766), father of the queen, Marie Leczinska, was founded in 1749 by Jacques Chambrette. The factory is best remembered for the work of the modeller Paul-Louis Cyfflé, who founded his own factory in 1766. His principal production was a large number of figures of gods and goddesses, shepherds and shepherdesses and other ordinary folk at work or play, depicted with the slightly sentimental characterisation that is reminiscent of the work of the painter Greuze. They were made both in a fine glazed white pipe-clay and an unglazed biscuit hard-paste porcelain reminiscent of the work of Sèvres, called *terre de Lorraine* in order to avoid infringing the monopoly of the royal factory. The moulds eventually passed to the factory at Niderviller, set up in about 1754 by Baron de Beyerlé and his wife, which was eventually to produce them also in porcelain. Cyfflé in the meanwhile finished his career in Flanders, where his factory at Hastière was destroyed during the Revolutionary wars.

A more distinctly French style of faïence was made in the South, at Marseilles, where the Veuve Perrin took over her husband's pottery factory on his death in 1748 and ran it until her own in 1793. This factory made some of the most magnificent pieces of rococo faïence of eighteenth-century France, comprising great tureens and pot-pourri vases decorated in the most extravagant taste, with much moulded and painted decoration. The factory is perhaps best known for its large *bouillabaisse* (fish stew) tureens, often delicately painted with fish in *petit feu* colours. Other forms of decoration included flowers, figures in landscapes and chinoiserie in the manner of the decorative engraver Jean Pillement (1728–1808). Such decoration was imitated at the Marseilles factory of Joseph Robert (fig. 151), who was responsible for plates with finely painted decorative landscapes in the centre. The factory also made good quality porcelain in the twenty years following 1773.

150   Clock case. Tin-glazed earthenware, painted in enamel colours. Height 114 cm. Strasbourg, factory of Paul Hannong, *c.*1750. Victoria & Albert Museum, London.

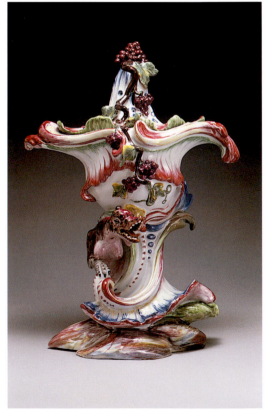

151 Tureen. Tin-glazed earthenware, painted in enamel colours. Marseilles, Robert factory, c.1770. Musée National de Céramique, Sèvres.

152 Vase. Earthenware, painted in enamel colours. Sceaux, c. 1755. The J. Paul Getty Museum, Los Angeles.

In 1761 the Veuve Perrin acquired a partner, Honoré Savy, who in 1764 set up his own factory which pioneered certain forms of decoration such as green enamel washed over black underdrawing. Savy was so successful that he maintained his own ship for exporting faïence to the Levant or the French Atlantic Islands. The factories of Savy and Robert allowed their painters to attend classes at the local academy, and the painter Leroy has left us some chalk drawings of flowers fron nature. Savy's apprentice, Antoine Bonnefoy, set up a rival porcelain and faïence factory in 1770, again known for the high standard of landscape painting. Ambitious pieces were also made at La Rochelle, where the factory of Piaud and Crespin created some extreme rococo models, including some wonderfully elaborate pot-pourri vases with applied ornament and flowers.[50] These are dated to 1777 and 1779, long after such items would have gone out of fashion in porcelain.

The faïence factory at Sceaux, being only five miles from Paris, was closest to trends of taste in the capital (fig. 152). This factory, dating from 1735, was under the patronage of the Duchesse du Maine; it was refused permission to make porcelain in 1749, on account of the monopoly held by Vincennes, but created some of the most delicate faïence made in eighteenth-century France.[51] Since it was only four miles from Sèvres it imitated Sèvres shapes, including the ewer and basin, the large tureens modelled by Duplessis, as well as the fan-shaped *vase hollandais*, all with a considerable degree of sophistication which belies the nature of its body. It was also able to poach skilled

153 Dish. Tin-glazed earthenware, painted in enamel colours. Diameter 26.7 cm. Meillonnas, c.1765. The Bowes Museum, Barnard Castle, Co. Durham.

painters from that factory, and copy Sèvres decoration with great exactitude. A 'feathered' border, copied from factories in Eastern France, is coloured blue as in Sèvres porcelain. After a series of changes of ownership, it was bought out by the duc de Penthièvre in 1775, and went on to produce porcelain.[52] Similarly elegant wares were made at Meillonnas, near Bourg-en-Bresse, where the Swiss painter Protais Pidoux was active from 1764, and produced flower painting of exceptional quality (fig. 153).

Overleaf. Detail of fig. 168, Vase with Personification of Venice.

Primo Esperimento in Grande
fatto li 15 Maggio 1769 Nella Prima
Fabbrica
di Geminiano Cozzi in Canalreggio

CHAPTER 8

The Spread of Porcelain Factories
throughout Europe

Europe in the eighteenth century was not the collection of nation-states that we are familiar with today. Much of central Europe and Italy remained a loose federation of states nominally under the authority of the Holy Roman Empire, as it was in the sixteenth century. However, the Thirty Years War (1618–48) had done much to undermine that authority and give the princes of Germany absolute power within their dominions, leaving the emperor with few sources of revenue in Germany other than the 15,000 florins he received annually for acting as Protector of the Jews.[1] Moreover, the devastation of Germany by war had undermined the development of a Germanic culture, and German princes looked to the court of Louis XIV of France, rather than that of the Holy Roman Emperor, for a model, strengthened by the fact that Louis paid them enormous subsidies for their political support, a sum apparently equal to almost the entire currency in circulation in Germany during the seventeenth and eighteenth centuries.[2] This led to much local resentment and hostility, often allied to moral objections against dissolute French life; the seventeenth-century German philosopher Christian Thomas commented on the prevalence of 'French clothes, dishes, languages, French customs and French vices',[3] which he thought were undermining Germany.

Each prince maintained an army, used more often for gorgeous parades than war, an opera and ballet troupe based on the French model, and a variety of summer and winter palaces, decorated with maximum richness of effect by craftsmen imported from France and Italy. The courts were staffed with a vast variety of placemen and petty officials, who occupied such unnecessary posts as Master of the Horse, Officer of the Hunt, or the purely nominal title of Councillor. Apart from these nominal posts, the courts were also overrun with a wide variety of entertainers, singers and dancers, jesters and court fools. The latter are especially interesting, as they sometimes doubled up as executioners and could punish courtiers with a beating, just as in turn they could be beaten by the prince himself. The courts also acted as magnets for any travelling mountebanks, alchemists and other tricksters, including those who professed to know the secret ('arcanum') of the making of true porcelain.[4]

A 'typical' example of a German eighteenth-century prince may be that of Carl Eugene of Württemberg. He had no doubt as to the divine origin of his status, declaring himself to be 'the Fatherland and the image of the Godhead on earth', and he acted accordingly. He maintained a household of over 1,800 officials, including a Court Chamberlain, a Cup-Bearer, pages, halberdiers, and 800 horses for his own use. He had travelled to Paris before he ascended the throne in 1747, and had met Louis XV and Madame de Pompadour, and had returned with a passion for all things French. He rebuilt the royal palace at Ludwigsburg with the help of French and Italian craftsmen in 1746, and in 1753 visited Italy, where he viewed the excavations at Pompeii and the newly founded royal porcelain factory at Capodimonte. His principal occupations seem to have been drilling his army and making enormous hunting expeditions into the countryside,[5] as well as attending the opera and ballet. Dr Charles Burney, the celebrated English musician, visited Württemberg at this time and commented that 'half the population of Württemberg consisted of violinists and theatre folk, the other half of beggars and paupers'.[6]

One of Carl Eugene's ambitions, in common with that of other sovereigns in Germany, was that of setting up and maintaining a porcelain factory, which was realised by the establishment of one in the grounds of his palace at Ludwigsburg in 1758. In its founding decree he stated that a porcelain factory was 'a necessary attribute of the glory and dignity of a prince [*notwendiges Attribut des Glanzes und der Würde eines Herrschers*]'. For a king a porcelain factory was both a symbol of prestige, a token of his country's capacity for industrial innovation, a means of keeping specie (gold and silver bullion) in the country, and a means of encouraging local industries and manufactures.

The spread of porcelain factories throughout Germany can be briefly chronicled as follows: Nymphenburg, near Munich, belonging to the Wittelsbach rulers of Bavaria, founded in 1747; Fürstenberg, belonging to the Duke of Brunswick, founded also in 1747; Höchst, near Mainz, belonging to the Elector of Mainz, in production from 1750 to 1796; Berlin, belonging to the King of Prussia, founded in 1751; Frankenthal, in the Electorate of Mannheim, which was in production from 1755 to 1794; Ludwigsburg, near Stuttgart, founded by the aforementioned Carl Eugene, in production from 1758 to 1824; and many lesser factories such as Kelsterbach, near Darmstadt, set up by the Landgrave of Hesse (1761–8, 1789–92, 1799–1802); Fulda, north-east of Frankfurt, supported by its Prince-Bishop of Mainz (1764–90); and Kassel, supported by Landgrave Frederick II of Hesse (1766–88). Of the twenty-eight factories on German-speaking soil, at least ten were begun by princes, and at least eight more encouraged or supported by them. The period 1746–80 was christened 'the great period of invasion by porcelain factories' as Franz Joseph Weber, former director of the Höchst factory, states in his book *Die Kunst das ächte Porzellain zu verfertigen* of 1798.

The ground for these porcelain factories had been prepared by the large number of German factories which made good quality tin-glazed earthenware, which were able to supply experienced personnel. They were supported by privileges from the local ruler, who was generally anxious to support industry in his own domains. Most made tin-glazed earthenware of high quality in imitation of porcelain, which was often misleadingly called 'faïence-porcelain'. Consequently they followed porcelain styles in decoration, making great use of low-temperature colours fired on in the muffle kiln. We have already noted the important factories at Hanau and Frankfurt; another was set up in Ansbach by Matthias Bauer and Johann Ripp between 1708–10 with the permission of the Margrave Friedrich Wilhelm of Brandenburg-Ansbach,[7] and is best known for its excellent copies of Chinese *famille verte* porcelain in green, yellowish green, iron-red, light, sulphur-yellow and black, as well as fine *Imari* patterns and plates painted with coats-of-arms surrounded by *Laub- und Bandelwerk*.[8] However, staff did not remain attached to one institution and Ripp went on to help run rival tin-glaze factories at both Nuremberg and Bayreuth.

The status of faïence was much raised by the contribution of painters from the Meissen factory, especially Adam Friedrich von Löwenfinck. He worked at Bayreuth in 1736 and at Ansbach from 1737 to 1740, and from 1741 to 1744–5 he was the chief enameller at the factory at Fulda north-east of Frankfurt, where the title 'court enameller' was conferred on him by the prince-bishop in recognition of his achievement in attracting trade and industry to the state. Löwenfinck also went on to found and direct a faïence factory at Höchst, west of Frankfurt, in partnership with the merchants Johann Christof Göltz and his son-in-law Johann Felician Clarus, who had obtained a

154 Plate with a scene after Jacopo Amiconi (1675–1752). Hard-paste porcelain, painted in enamel colours. Fürstenberg, 1758. Victoria & Albert Museum, London.

155 Johann Esaias Nilson (1721–88). *Neues Caffeehaus (New Coffee House)*. Engraving.

privilege for making porcelain in 1746. Although Löwenfinck never succeeded in making true porcelain, they made faïence of a notably flamboyant rococo character, including tureens in the shape of flowers or animals. Löwenfinck left after a dispute with Göltz in 1749, and went on to try (unsuccessfully) to establish a factory at Coblenz, before moving to Strasbourg, where he died in 1754.

Although a large number of ceramic factories were operating in Germany, the range of their products was very narrow and mostly in the rococo style of the period. However, the rococo in Germany has quite different characteristics from that in France; it is a more lightweight, less substantial style, in which the motifs are crowded together without any real regard for their overall effect.[9] The style was often propagated by French or Italian craftsmen called over for their particular skills, most notably in the work of the Frenchman Jean François Cuvilliés (1695–1768) who decorated the palaces in Munich in a notably flamboyant rococo style. What is especially noticeable about the German rococo is the way in the *Muschelwerk*, the rocky shell-like rocaille, developed into a rather sinister lifeform which spread sinister tentacles in the background, a style much imitated by the modellers at the porcelain factories. There were also a number of accomplished designers and engravers of ornament, most notably the engraver Johann Esaias Nilson of Augsburg (1721–88), whose work was often inspired or copied from the work of Jean-Antoine Watteau and François Boucher. Another important source for rococo design and decoration was the Italian painter Jacopo Amiconi (1675–1752), who worked in and around Munich (fig. 154). Their works were part of an international visual language, and the same print can be found as the source for the decoration on the products from a number of different factories.[10]

Porcelain was especially associated with the fashion for coffee and tea drinking, which reached a peak of fashion in the mid-eighteenth century. The lighter rococo style, with its borrowings from the East, was thought especially suitable for lightweight entertainment, as the engraving by Nilson of the *New Coffee House* shows (fig. 155). However, there were those who saw coffee drinking as a symptom of the degeneracy of the times and considered it foreign, unmanly and degenerate. Frederick the Great of Prussia banned its grinding and consumption at home in 1777,[11] even appointing former soldiers called *Kaffeeriecher* (coffee-sniffers) to literally sniff out any illegal private roasting and drinking.[12]

Frederick the Great dominated the political stage of mid-eighteenth-century Germany through his attempts to ward off the Austrian-Saxon alliance formed against him during the Seven Years War (1756–63). He thus played a major part in undermining the status of the great Meissen factory, when his troops invaded Saxony and damaged the kilns. He toyed with the idea of transporting the factory lock, stock and barrel to Berlin, but instead contented himself with appointing a factor, Georg Michel Helbig, to run the factory on his behalf. Much of the factory's output was now destined for Frederick, including six large dinner services, some of which were apparently designed by the king himself,[13] including two services painted with a chequered border called *Mosaique* in green and black or red and gold, which was to be copied throughout Europe and even appears on Chinese export porcelain.[14] In 1765 financial difficulties stimulated Meissen to issue a price-list '*Preiss-Courante von ordinairen Porcellainen*',[15] which lists items according to their model, pattern and type of decoration, as well as *Galanterien* and figures. A 'complete coffee service' at Meissen consisted of twelve coffee-cups with handles, six chocolate cups with handles, slop-basin, coffee pot, milk jug, teapot, sugar basin, tea caddy and a bread-and-butter plate. Prices ranged from eighteen Taler twenty Groschen for a coffee service in a plain shape decorated in underglaze blue to two hundred and forty-eight Taler eighteen Groschen to one painted with '*Watteauischen Figuren in zwei Parthien und mit Mosaique*'[16] (Watteau figures on both sides with mosaic decoration).

The factory at Vienna had lost artistic ground in the mid-eighteenth century, as the wares of the factory lost their Baroque individuality with the takeover by the State in 1744. The old director, Du Paquier, was forced to retire and artistic influence was dominated by Johann Joseph Niedermayer, a former teacher at the State Academy, who became chief modeller (*Modellmeister*) in 1747. With his colleague Leopold Dannhauser, a former *Bossierer* (repairer or assembler of figures), they produced a wide range of figures of high quality within the accepted range of German porcelain, including figures from the *commedia dell'arte*, and figures of peasants, perhaps reminiscent of the *Wirtschaft* or festival whereby the court imitated rural life.[17] The tablewares were also of high quality but unexceptional design, well-painted with pastoral figures and rococo decoration. The factory had the advantage of being able to sell its wares throughout the Holy Roman Empire and beyond, setting up showrooms in Karslbad, Trieste, Prague, Lemberg, Ofen and Brünn, and developing a market in small coffee cups with the neighbouring country of Turkey.

Meissen and Vienna remained the main factories making hard-paste porcelain in Europe until the mid-eighteenth century. The actual spread of porcelain factories in Europe was dependent on the services of that magical figure, the 'arcanist', the man with the secret of making porcelain. The eighteenth century saw the rise of several professional arcanists, adventurers who went from one court to another, selling the secret of porcelain manufacture that was thought to be so prestigious. Many of these arcanists were, in fact, spurious, such as the glass- and faïence-painter Johann Christoph Glaser, who offered the arcanum to Ernst Augustus I of Saxe-Weimar in 1740, and Elias Vater, who tricked the Elector of Bavaria in 1729. However, two figures were genuine, and gave rise to many of the porcelain factories in Germany; these were Johann Benckgraff (1708–53) and Joseph Jakob Ringler (1730–1802) from the Vienna factory.

Ringler and Benckgraff travelled round Europe, spreading the secret of porcelain wherever they went; in this respect they may almost be compared to bees, pollinating the flowers as they went around – albeit with a high degree of deceit and bribery involved. In 1750 they were summoned one after the other to Höchst by the merchant Göltz, one of the original partners of the faïence factory, which promptly commenced the production of true porcelain.[18] The first workers included eleven painters, five modellers, one turner, and one kiln master. Early products included copies of Meissen figures and tablewares, including the patterned borders associated with dessert wares. Painting of flowers was carried out by the faïence-painter Johannes Zeschinger, as well as landscape- and cattle-painting by P. J. Angele and J. H. Usinger. The standard is good but unexceptional; the most interesting products are perhaps a group of *commedia dell'arte* figures attributed to the modeller Simon Feilner, based on prints by the engraver Johann Jacob Wolrab which were published in Nuremberg in about 1720.[19]

Göltz now dealt with Benckgraff in the way that he had dealt with Löwenfinck, accusing him (correctly) of selling the secret to Berlin, and pressing charges against him, resulting in his dismissal. Göltz himself went bankrupt in 1756, whereupon the Elector of Mainz took over the factory; Göltz died a broken man the next year. The factory ran at reduced capacity until the administration was taken over in 1759 by Johann Heinrich Maas, but it had taken advantage of refugees from the factory at Meissen, including the modellers Johann Friedrich Lück, his brother Karl Gottlieb, and the painter Gottlieb Friedrich Riedel (1724–84).

Under Maas, Höchst developed a figure-style of its own led by the sculptor Laurentius Russinger, who is first listed in the records in 1753, and was *Modellmeister* from 1759 to 1767. He is thought to have executed a wide range of figures of farmers, monks, musicians, as well as two groups after the French artist Pater, *Le Baiser Donné* and *Le Baiser Rendu*.[20] The attribution of some fine models has frequently been disputed between him and the great J. P. Melchior, who succeeded Russinger as *Modellmeister* in 1767 at the age of twenty, and became court sculptor in 1770.[21] His models were

156 Group of *Le Songe Pastoral* modelled by Johann Peter Melchior. Hard-paste porcelain, painted in colours. Höchst, *c.*1770. The British Museum, London.

157 Plate from the service made for Frederick the Great for the Palace of Sanssouci. Hard-paste porcelain, painted in enamel colours and gilt. Diameter 25.2 cm. Berlin, 1769–70. National Museum of Wales, Cardiff.

clearly very heavily influenced by the biscuit models of Sèvres, and he produced many fine porcelain figures of children in the manner of the *enfants Boucher*, which show the same pinched facial expressions, as well as small figures of Turks.[22] His most ambitious works are probably the two groups of *Amynthas and Sylvia* and *The Slumber of the Shepherdess* after *Le Songe Pastoral* (fig. 156) and other prints after François Boucher. He also produced some fine sculptural portrait medallions, and a large group of *The Crucifixion*, with expressive figures of St John and the two Marys at the base.[23]

Meanwhile Benckgraff had indeed sold the arcanum to Berlin in 1752, where a factory had been set up by Wilhelm Caspar Wegely in 1751. However, the factory's operations were cut short by the Seven Years War, and Frederick the Great refused financial assistance,[24] perhaps because he had plans for a greater factory. In 1760, during the occupation of Meissen by Prussian troops, Frederick instructed the merchant Johann Ernst Gotzkowsky to set up a porcelain factory to rival it (Gotzkowsky had already travelled to Berlin to set up a silk industry to rival that of France.[25]) In 1761 the Meissen painters Carl Wilhelm Boehme, Johann Baptist Borrmann and the sculptor Friedrich Elias Meyer (a pupil of Kaendler) moved to Berlin. In 1762 Gotzkowsky was able to show Frederick first-class specimens of porcelain, but owing to financial problems Frederick took on the factory as a State enterprise in 1763.[26]

The factory produced some of the finest and most elaborate porcelain to come out of Germany in the eighteenth century. It developed a speciality in large dinner services, complete with *Wärmeglocken* (dish covers) as a separate article. An especially magnificent service, painted with a yellow border and Japanese figures, was made in 1769– 70 (fig. 157).[27] One of the most ambitious services was that made for the Empress Catherine II of Russia in 1770–2 which survives in the Hermitage, St Petersburg. The great centre-piece in undecorated porcelain was modelled by Friedrich Elias Meyer, and depicted the empress seated under a canopy surrounded by people from her empire paying homage.[28] He also produced a range of superbly modelled classical figures for the dessert table.[29]

In the meantime Benckgraff had left Höchst in 1753 with his colleagues, the modeller Simon Feilner and Johannes Zeschinger, and the flower-painters Geisler and Zisler, to go to Fürstenberg in Brunswick. Here Duke Carl I of Brunswick had attempted to set up a porcelain factory with the help of the incompetent and spurious chemist Johann Christoph Glaser.[30] With the arrival of Benckgraff the factory began to make real porcelain, and the modeller Feilner produced a large number of shapes for useful wares, as well as a series of *commedia dell'arte* figures in 1753–4 based on prints by the engraver Johann Jacob Wolrab that had been used at Höchst.[31] He also made figures of miners (1757–8) and lovers in fashionable dress, but was discharged for laziness and insubordination in 1768, leading to a decline in the number of figures produced. Early tablewares were of high quality and often moulded, with the details picked out in gilding. Painting reached a very high standard under Johann Christofkind and Carlo Gottlieb Albert, as seen in the service made for Duke Carl I with landscapes by Pascha Johann Friedrich Weitsch. It was presented to his daughter Caroline, Princess of Wales, and recently rediscovered in the British Royal Collection.

Meanwhile, the arcanist J. J. Ringler had been active west of the border at the faïence centre of Strasbourg in France. In 1752 he had assisted Paul-Antoine Hannong in setting up a porcelain factory there, but it was forced to move in 1754, when Louis XV proclaimed restrictions on porcelain production in France in favour of the royal factory at Vincennes. Hannong then moved the factory to Frankenthal across the border in Alsace under the patronage of the Elector of Mannheim, employing his eldest son Charles-François-Paul as director (to be succeeded on his death in 1757 by his younger brother, Joseph-Adam). The chief modeller of figures was Johann Wilhelm Lanz, who produced some wonderful works, complete with foliage backgrounds. There seems to have been some attempt to market these in France in competition with Sèvres porcelain, which made no coloured figures, since the French border was so close, with fewer customs duties. The group of lovers representing autumn, for instance, is advertised in the 1760 *Journal de Commerce* as 'Love inspired by wine', cost ninety-six florins with the arbor and sixty-six florins without. The factory was sold to the Elector himself in 1762, two years after Paul Hannong's death. Especially fine models were produced by the court sculptor Konrad Linck (1732–93), such as the figures of Neptune and other sea-gods in 1765 (fig. 158), and K.G. Lück (fig. 159) . Tablewares were sufficiently advanced for a price list to be issued in 1777.

In 1753 Ringler moved on to Neudeck near Munich in Bavaria, where the Elector Maximiliam III of Bavaria had set up a factory as a wedding present to his wife Marie Anna Sophie, one of the daughters of Augustus the Strong of Saxony. The potter Franz Ignaz Niedermayer had been recruited for the factory in 1747, as he was believed to have obtained the arcanum from a worker at the Meissen factory 'while they were enjoying some wine together and exchanging confidences'.[32] Although Jacob Helchis and Schreiber had been recruited from Vienna as well, success was not achieved until Ringler's arrival. Little is known of its early productions, except for fragments of a *Garten-dessert* modelled in 1755 by the sculptor Joseph Ponhauser of Vienna for the marriage of a Bavarian princess. The factory moved to the royal palace of Nymphenburg outside Munich in 1761.

This factory produced some of the greatest rococo porcelain in the world, both in

158   Figure of Oceanus. Hard-paste porcelain painted in enamel colours. Height 27.8 cm. Frankenthal, *c.* 1770. The Fitzwilliam Museum, Cambridge.

figures and modelled tablewares. The guiding spirit seems to have been the modeller Franz Anton Bustelli (1723–63), who worked at the factory from 1754. His origins are uncertain; his name suggests an Italian or even Swiss origin, possibly from the Ticino region, but he cannot be positively connected with anyone listed in local records. The sequence of his works can be reconstructed by factory lists from 1755 onwards and the price-list of 1767. They comprise an enormous variety of religious figures, Chinese figures, figures in fashionable dress, including large centrepieces of a girl awakening a slumbering gentleman (*The Sleeper Disturbed* and *The Impetuous Lover*). All these figures are modelled with a maximum of panache and expression, which hovers on the borders of Baroque satire and rococo exuberance. His greatest work was the series of *commedia dell'arte* figures of about 1760 which rank among the major achievements of eighteenth-century porcelain modelling (fig. 160). There are sixteen in all, which seem to form eight pairs where the figures turn round and respond to each other. The women are all dressed in the height of fashion, with tightly corsetted waists, and the figures are unmasked in the manner of the later *commedia dell'arte*. What is remarkable is the degree of characterisation put into each, which may reflect a central idea. Pantaloon's daughter Isabella rejects the advances of the Spanish Captain in favour of the elegant Octavio of noble birth. The enraged Captain draws his dagger while Leda tries to avert his anger with screams. Columbine dances with Scaramouche, while Pierrot is deceived by Mezzetin.[33] However, Bustelli seems to have got little credit for the exuberance of his figures, and died neglected in 1763.

Bustelli had also modelled tablewares, snuffboxes and other *Galanterien*, which appear in the price-list of 1767 (fig. 161). In that year the factory at Nymphenburg underwent a financial crisis, when its staff was reduced from two hundred to eighty, and production was put on hold in the famine years 1771–2. Although its range increased with the appointment of the modeller Dominikus Auliczek as director in

159   Top. Pagoda Group. Hard-paste porcelain painted in enamel colours and gilt. Frankenthal, modelled by K.G. Lück, *c.*1770. The British Museum, London.

160   Above. Figure of Columbine from the *commedia dell'arte*. Hard-paste porcelain, painted in enamel colours and gilt. Nymphenburg, modelled by Franz Anton Bustelli, *c.*1760. The Victoria & Albert Museum, London.

161   Tureen. Hard-paste porcelain, painted in enamel colours and gilt. Nymphenburg, *c.*1755. Bayerisches Nationalmuseum, Munich.

1773, the factory was relegated to second-best behind Frankenthal after 1777, when Bavaria was ruled by Elector Karl Theodor of Mannheim. Full-scale production was not resumed until the later eighteenth century.

Ringler travelled on from Nymphenburg to assist at short-lived factories at Schrezheim in 1757, and at Ellwangen in 1757–8, but his last port of call was Ludwigsburg, at the behest of Duke Carl Eugene in February, 1759, to help set up the factory that had been decreed by the duke on 5 April 1758. Here he settled and was to direct the factory for over forty years. The factory made relatively few useful wares, concentrating instead on figures, although domestic wares were also made, based on silver forms, often very elaborate, the most famous being the table and toilet service made for the Marchesa Giovanelli-Martinengo of Venice in 1763[34] (a faïence factory was run concurrently with the porcelain factory by the widow of Adam von Löwenfinck from 1762 to 1795). The factory developed a line in the painting and modelling of birds, as produced by Gottlieb Friedrich Riedel, the chief painter from 1759 to 1779. In 1770 he published a pattern book *Sammlung von Feder-Vieh besonders Haus-Geflügel, nützlich Fabriquen*, and four large vases survive in Stuttgart with such decoration (fig. 162).

The great glory of Ludwigsburg was its series of figures. The first modeller was Johann Carl Vogelmann, who arrived at the factory in 1759 and left to become chief modeller at Kelsterbach in 1764. A series of putti representing seasons is attributable to him. Another modeller was Joseph Nees (active from 1759 to 1767/80) who appears to have modelled a group of dancers with arms outstretched, and a charming series of small fairground booths showing print and drapery sellers. But the chief modeller was Johann Christian Wilhelm Beyer, who modelled a series of antique figures, as well as some superlative huntsmen and musicians (fig. 163). His sculptural abilities were such that in about 1767 he went on to Vienna, where he created some of the statues in the gardens of the Schönbrunn.

Although Höchst, Berlin, Fürstenberg, Frankenthal, Nymphenburg and Ludwigsburg were the major creative forces in eighteenth-century German porcelain, a number of shorter-lived factories also played their part. Since they were founded in smaller principalities, they had fewer resources to draw on and were less able to develop individual styles and forms. Their wares were more heavily dependent on stylistic influences from the larger factories, and their access to fine modellers and painters rather more limited. The factory at Ansbach, for instance, was set up in 1757 under royal patronage with the help of craftsmen from the Meissen factory, which at that point had been devastated by the Seven Years War, but Ansbach tended to follow the more fashionable forms of Berlin (fig.164). Similarly the porcelain factory at Kelsterbach on the River Main near Mainz was founded in 1761 with the help of the Meissen arcanist Christian Daniel Busch, and later supported by the Landgrave to the end of the century. Other State factories set up in this period include Fulda in Hesse-Nassau (1764), Kassel (1766), Pfalz-Zweibrücken (1768), Ottweiler in Nassau-Saarbrücken (1763).

Other countries, without a royal prince, were more tardy in the setting up of a porcelain factory, and more dependent on local support. In Zürich in Switzerland the use of porcelain for the dinner table was actually forbidden, until an influx of French and Italian refugees led to an economic expansion, including the establishment of silk and porcelain factories. A porcelain factory was set up by private enterprise in 1763 by members of the *Physikalische Gesellschaft*, a society founded for the discovery and exploitation of local mineral ores. Staff were recruited from the greater Germanic factories, including the painter Johann Daffinger from Vienna, and the modellers Josef Nees and Valentin Sonnenschein from Ludwigsburg. However, much of the artistic direction seems to have been under the painter and poet Salomon Gessner, who appears to have encouraged a taste for romantic-landscape painting on its wares (fig. 165).[35] The factory did not flourish, needing a lottery in 1774 to clear out unwanted stock, and was

162 Vase. Hard-paste porcelain, painted in enamel colours and gilt. Ludwigsburg, painted by Gottfried Friedrich Riedel, *c.*1765. Württembergisches Landesmuseum, Stuttgart.

163 Figure of a trumpeter. Hard-paste porcelain, painted in enamel colours and gilt. Ludwigsburg, modelled by Johann Christian Wilhelm Beyer, *c*.1760–65. Württembergisches Landesmuseum, Stuttgart.

164 Right. Coffee-pot. Hard-paste porcelain, painted in enamels colours and gilt. Height 17 cm. Ansbach, *c*.1770. The Bowes Museum, Barnard Castle, Co. Durham.

165 Plate. Hard-paste porcelain, painted in enamel colours and gilt. Diameter 23.8 cm. Zürich, *c*.1770. The Bowes Barnard Castle, Co. Durham.

dissolved in 1790.[36] Parallel with this venture was a faïence factory (also in Zürich) of good quality, imitating that of Strasbourg, and figures similar to those from Lorraine.[37]

Even lower down the scale flourished a wide range of faïence factories across northern and central Europe, especially on the north coast of Germany, and in Scandinavia, where there was less competition from porcelain factories. Their wares copied the rococo forms and decoration of France and Germany and included Crailsheim (1715–1827), Durlach (1723–1890), Künersberg (1745–67) Schrezheim (1752–1862) near Ellwangen in Württemberg,[38] and those in the Baltic Basin – Lesum (1755–1800), Eckernförde (1765–88), Kiel (1763–88), Schleswig-Holstein (1755–72),[39] Stockelsdorf (1771–*c*.1811) in Lübeck,[40] and Königsberg in East Prussia (1772–1811). Those on the Scandinavian coast have rather more individuality and include Copenhagen (1722–1814)

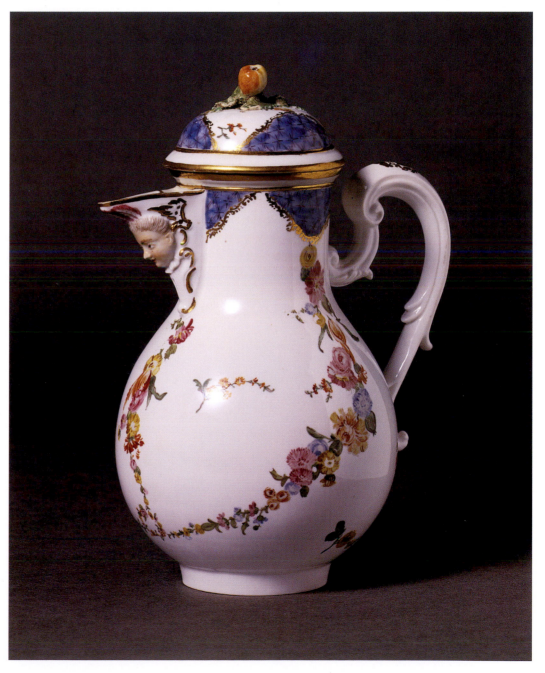

in Denmark and Rörstrand (founded 1725), Stralsund (1755–92) and Marieberg (1758–88) in Sweden. The latter factory was run from 1766 by Pierre Berthevin of Mennecy, who introduced the production of porcelain. A line particular to the faïence factory is the large rococo 'terrace-vase', a vase set on a platform, sometimes with the innovative addition of printed decoration (fig. 166).[41]

Faïence of good quality was also made at the great historic centres in Italy, which had, however, lost their artistic pre-eminence and produced items of a middle range in a mixture of eastern and rococo styles. The Savona faïence-maker Giacomo Boselli seems to have been the first to import the *petit feu* painting style of Strasbourg, possibly via a factory at Marseilles.[42] The main Italian factories were those of Felice Clerici (1745–*c.*1772) and Pasquale Rubati (*c.*1756) at Milan, Conte Camillo Ferniani at Faenza, Filippo Antonio Callegari and Antonio Casali at Pesaro (*c.*1763), and Rosetti and Ferretti at Lodi outside Milan. At their most inventive they produced finely modelled wares of imaginative and extravagant shapes, superbly painted in enamel colours, of great character and charm.

The many states of Italy also produced a number of fine porcelain factories, although their spread was nowhere near as pervasive as it was in Germany. They were a mixture of public and private initiatives, following the example of the Vezzi factory in Venice. Since Italy was traditionally a centre of taste and fashion, their wares often showed strongly individual features which are not paralleled in the work of other European factories. At Doccia outside Florence a factory had been set up in 1737 by Marquis Carlo Ginori, who had travelled to Vienna in that year and come back with a privilege for making porcelain and the *Hausmaler* Anreiter von Zirnfeld. As might be expected, the early products of the factory are severely Baroque in feel, with extensive debts to Viennese shapes. However, it should be noted that much of this porcelain was tin-glazed, rather than lead-glazed. Tableware was decorated *a stampino*, that is, ornaments were cut out of vellum, placed on the porcelain and then stencilled around, as well as with a pseudo-Chinese pattern 'a tuli-

166 'Terrace' vase, with printed decoration. Faïence. Height 25.5 cm. Marieberg, Sweden, *c.*1770. The Bowes Museum, Barnard Castle, Co. Durham.

167 *The Deposition* after Soldani-Benzi. Hard-paste porcelain. Height 28 cm. Florence, Doccia, *c.*1760. The British Museum, London.

pano'. Imitations of Meissen ('Miniatures in the Saxon manner with arabesques in red and gold') and cups decorated with fighting cockerels *a galletto* were also made. However, its great glory was perhaps the moulded undecorated figures, after classical statues or models by the Baroque sculptor Massimiliano Soldani-Benzi (1656–1740), which still survive in the factory[43] (fig. 167). The Anreiters returned to Vienna in 1746 and Carl died there in 1747, his son entering the Imperial factory.

Other Italian factories in private hands include the Venetian factories founded by the German, Nathaniel Friedrich Hewelcke (1758–63), who had left Dresden for the duration of the Seven Years War and gained a patent for making porcelain in the Meissen manner, and Geminiano Cozzi (1764–1812), who made a hybrid soft-paste porcelain in imitation of Meissen with painting '*ad uso del Giappon*' (in the Japanese manner) of high quality (fig. 168). Porcelain imitating that of Meissen and Sèvres was also made at Le Nove in Venetian territory from 1762 to 1825, often in the most extreme rococo shapes. The guiding spirit here was the faïence-maker Antonibon, who continued in the meantime to make a large range of good-quality faïence at his factory at Bassano.

Links with Germany and Austria were again apparent in the foundation of the

168 Neptune Vase and Vase with Personification of Venice. Hybrid soft-paste porcelain, painted in blue. Height 30 cm. Venice, Geminiano Cozzi, 1769. The J. Paul Getty Museum, Los Angeles.

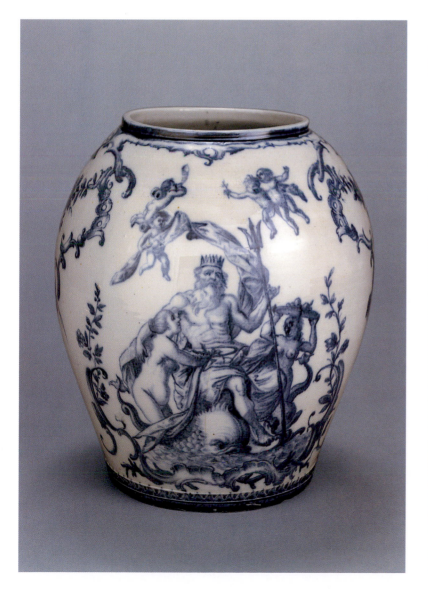

Capodimonte factory at Naples. Charles of Bourbon had married Maria Amalia of Saxony, daughter of Augustus III, one of the three 'porcelain princesses' who were to influence the development of porcelain in Europe so much. He immediately set about founding a porcelain factory, and in 1740 shipments of clay were brought from Cantanzaro to the workshops in the gardens of the Royal Palace. Unsuccessful attempts were made to attract workmen from Meissen, as well as Anton Wagner and Jacobus Helchis from Vienna. The paste eventually produced was soft, rather than hard, but was of great beauty, which attracted the praise of visitors from abroad such as the Abbé de Saint-Non.[44] The factory developed a reputation for fine painting; for instance, battle scenes by Giuseppe della Torre, or flower painting by Maria Caselli. The chief modeller was Giuseppe Gricci, who modelled a charming series of small groups depicting religious scenes, street criers or local types. Some extraordinary rococo snuff-boxes were made in the form of shells, as well as a bizarre ewer and basin of *rocaille* encrusted with *frutti di mare* (marine life) motifs. Most remarkable is the great porcelain room from the Palace of Portici, today in the museum at Capodimonte in Naples. It was produced in 1757–9, modelled by Giuseppe and Stefano Gricci, and painted by J. S. Fischer and Luigi Restile (fig. 169). The factory was moved in its entirety to Buen Retiro near Madrid when Charles succeeded his half-brother Ferdinand VI as King of Spain in 1759. This naturally produced stylistically similar wares, including another porcelain room for the Palace of Aranjuez, south of Madrid, in 1763–5.[45] The factory lasted until destroyed during the Napoleonic Wars in 1812.

Little porcelain was made in Spain outside Buen Retiro other than some at the factory at Alcora, where a tin-glaze factory had been set up in 1727 by Don Buenaventura, Count of Aranda, largely to benefit the local town and to employ apprentices from the nearby schools. Some of its wares, particularly busts, were made out of fine pipe-clay (*tierra di pipa*).[46] Good quality *faïence* was also produced in Portugal at Oporto (1766–1819) and Rato (1767–c.1814), mostly in the northern-Italian style.[47] Portugal was also an important centre of tile production, much of it decorated with paintings after figurative prints.[48]

The last outpost of the once-great Holy Roman Empire was the Austrian Netherlands, which retained many local privileges. From 1741 it was governed by Charles of Lorraine, the brother-in-law of the Empress Maria Theresa, for nearly forty years. He kept the country out of the Seven Years War and encouraged a policy of economic expansion and a distant attitude to Vienna. A faïence factory had been founded at Brussels by Philippe Mombaers in 1724, which made a variety of tureens in the shape of animals, birds and vegetables. A rival factory was set up by his son-in-law with the protection of the Empress Maria Theresa.[49] The first porcelain factory was set up at Tournai in 1751 by François-Joseph Peterinck with the assistance of the city council and a licence from the empress. Robert Dubois of the Chantilly and Vincennes factories was appointed director in 1753. The factory produced works in a modified rococo style, heavily dependent on French influences, but less ambitious in character, and in the medium of soft-paste (fig. 170). It produced many works using Sèvres blue ground colours, and was especially notable for its successful imitation of the Sèvres biscuit figures. The chief painter was Henri-Joseph Duvivier (d.1771), who is said to have studied in England. It had access to fine Flemish sculptors in the persons of Nicolas Lecreux, Antoine Gillis (1702–82) and Joseph Willems (d.1766), and the Frenchman Nicolas-François Gauron, who had probably worked at Mennecy and Vincennes,[50] and was later to work in Holland and England.[51]

In 1787 it produced a fine service painted with birds after the naturalist Buffon in the ornate Sèvres manner for the French prince of the blood the duc d'Orléans, though it is not clear why the duke did not go directly to Sèvres itself (fig. 171).

The most independent country in Europe, Holland, was late in developing a porce-

169 Section of the porcelain room from the Palace at Portici. Museo di Capodimonte, Naples.

170 Ewer and basin. Soft-paste porcelain painted in underglaze blue. Height of ewer 21.8 cm. Tournai, *c.*1770. The Bowes Museum, Barnard Castle, Co. Durham.

171 Pieces from a service for the duc d'Orléans. Soft-paste porcelain, painted in enamel colours and gilt. Tournai, *c.*1787. The Royal Collection, Windsor Castle, England.

172 Tea and coffee service. Hard-paste porcelain, painted in red enamel. Height of coffee-pot 25.5 cm. The Hague, *c.*1780. The Bowes Museum, Barnard Castle, Co. Durham.

lain factory, as it lacked a centralising prince to control its economic activity, and the old faïence industry (Delftware) remained healthy, increasingly adapting itself to the rococo style of the mid-eighteenth century. The first porcelain factory in Holland was founded in about 1757 at Weesp, near Amsterdam with the help of German workmen thrown out of work by the Seven Years War. It made porcelain of a very high standard, mostly in Meissen style, although it failed to make a profit and existed only with the support of Count Gronsfeldt-Diepenbroek. It was sold in 1771 to Pastor Johannes de Mol, who transferred it to his impoverished parish of Oude Loosdrecht in an effort to create work for the unemployed. Wares were made in the newly fashionable French taste. On the death of Mol in 1782 it was sold and moved to Amstel in 1784. By contrast, a rival factory at The Hague was founded by the German porcelain-dealer Anton Lyncker (1718–81) in 1770s, but made few new models; at one stage it seems to have painted Ansbach and Tournai porcelain (fig. 172). It fell into debt and closed in 1790.

Overleaf. Detail of fig. 180. *The Music Lesson.*

CHAPTER 9

Porcelain in Eighteenth-Century Britain

Britain in the eighteenth century was fast on her way to becoming the powerful and dominating world power that she was in the nineteenth century. The population of Britain was, at about five to six million in the mid-century, only about a third of that of France, yet Britain defeated its great rival on two occasions in the eighteenth century: in the War of the Spanish Succession (1701–13) and the Seven Years War (1756–63), gaining on both occasions substantial overseas territorial possessions. English exports doubled in value, and agricultural and industrial production rose by 60 per cent. Much of this wealth went straight into the hands of the old aristocracy, who had dominated the political scene in England since the accession of George I in 1714, yet much also found its way down the social scale, buttressing the position of the professional and merchant classes.[1] Visitors from abroad commented on the 'luxury' of the times; especial mention was made of the wealth of what we would now call the middle-class, whose luxury and extravagance had 'risen to such a pitch as never before seen in the world'.[2] Furthermore, their lifestyle was imitated in turn by the labouring and servant classes, which led to an increased demand for goods. This tendency for wealth to descend the social scale was noticed by foreign visitors and the general ownership of goods among all classes has caused this century to be christened 'the birth of a consumer society' by some modern historians.[3] These conditions led to a boom in the ownership of household objects throughout Britain,[4] with a consequent growth and stimulus to the decorative arts.

Economic writers in eighteenth-century England shared many of the concerns of their contemporaries abroad, stressing the need to stimulate industry, both to create wealth and to mop up the unruly hordes of the unemployed that posed such a threat to public order. However, they did not necessarily share the obsession of mercantilism with tariffs on imports and indeed the writings of Adam Smith (1723–90) tended to favour a free market with a lack of state intervention. Britain did not have the strong unified authority of the centralised monarchies of the rest of Europe, for although the king possessed great powers by way of influence and preferment, he was ultimately not able to dictate the country's growth and direction in the manner of a continental monarch. Both Church and State colluded in a kind of *laissez-faire* economic policy which left British manufacturers to cope as best they could with competition from their subsidised European competitors without any kind of State support.

There did exist certain organisations, however, which attempted to raise the standards of British industry in the mid-eighteenth century. The most famous was The Society of Arts, which was a forum for the discussion of new technology in the industrial arts, and offered encouragement in the way of prizes and scholarships for gifted designers.[5] A principal concern was the textile industry, which was the major form of luxury spend-

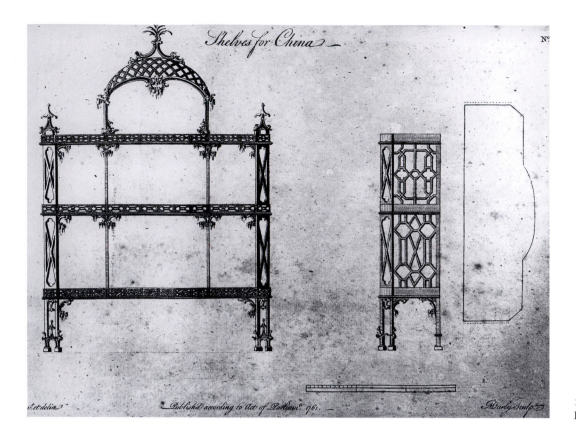

173 Matthias Darly, *Shelves for China*, c.1754. Engraving.

ing of the rich, and the cause of many imports from France. Another interest was the porcelain industry; although Britain had been a major ceramics producer for some years, this had been in the form of pottery rather than porcelain, and until the mid-century Britain was dependent on imports of porcelain from China, or France and Germany.[6]

The most fashionable types of porcelain in Britain – the sort preferred by the aristocracy – were those from Meissen and Sèvres. For these there existed a steady market, although the import of European porcelain for sale was illegal. However, some came through purchases made abroad or diplomatic gifts, such as the magnificent Meissen service presented to Sir Charles Hanbury-Williams, the British envoy at Dresden in the years 1747–50 and 1751–5 by Augustus III of Saxony,[7] or the great Sèvres service given to the Duke of Bedford by Louis XV after the Treaty of Paris of 1763.[8] The richly coloured and gilded porcelain from Sèvres was the preferred type for the very rich by the 1760s, and virtually every wealthy British visitor to Paris seems to have come back with some decorative pieces.[9] The only deterrent to this rage for Continental porcelain seems to have been high customs duties on imports, which reached 150 per cent in 1775,[10] and led to a number of aristocrats cancelling orders.[11]

Another factor in the appreciation of Continental ceramics was the collecting of ceramics for themselves, a development of the 'chinamania' of the late seventeenth century. 'China-closets' continued to be in fashion, and, following the taste of Mary II, china cabinets were often associated with women.[12] Famous china cabinets were established by Lady Betty Germaine at Drayton, 'crammed with old china' as Horace Walpole described it in 1763,[13] by the Countess of Suffolk in the gardens of her villa at Marble Hill in Twickenham on the banks of the river Thames, and the Duchess of Portland at Bulstrode.[14] There also began a certain interest in the collecting of historic ceramics, best demonstrated by the collections of Andrew Fountaine at Narford Hall and Horace

Walpole at Strawberry Hill,[15] where the centrepiece of the china room was the Saint Porchaire ewer now in Edinburgh, which was then attributed to Giulio Romano.

It was during this period that porcelain 'escaped' from the china room or china-closet and became a general means of furnishing a room, especially the drawing-room, which was seen as a feminine preserve. One fashion was to incorporate it into pieces of furniture, such as girandoles and chimney pieces[16] or to show it in china cases or hanging shelves (fig. 173). By the mid-century, the porcelain figures intended for the dessert became to be valued for themselves and began to appear as decoration on the chimney piece.[17] The most valued items of china for furnishing were large porcelain jars which stood in the corner of rooms or long galleries; these were of Chinese manufacture, as only Chinese hard-paste was suitable for making such large objects.

Those that could not afford Meissen or Sèvres made do with Chinese export porcelain, which was used by the lesser aristocracy and the gentry. The British imported Chinese porcelain directly via the English East India Company which had been set up in the seventeenth century to wrest the trade from the Dutch.[18] Many of these first imports consisted of utensils for tea drinking, and it was in the eighteenth century that this became a national habit. Tea consumption rose from 1,493,626 lb in 1728 to 3,762,800 lb in 1767,[19] despite the high customs duties of about 100 per cent which were reduced to 12 1/2 per cent only in 1784.[20] The fashion was closely linked to porcelain, and 'chinamen' (dealers in china) often sold tea as well.[21] Demand was enormous and in 1776 the East India Company sold 168,000 blue-and-white cups and saucers and 35,000 dinner plates, while a whole tea set cost only about 12 shillings.[22] An anonymous English portrait of about 1720 shows a family proudly at tea, not only with silver utensils, but also tea bowls and saucers of Eastern porcelain (fig. 174).

174 Anonymous English, *c*.1720. *A Family at Tea*. Oil on canvas, 64 × 76 cm. Victoria & Albert Museum, London.

Chinese porcelain was used not only for tea drinking but also for large dinner services, a fashion which grew in the eighteenth century.[23] Visitors from abroad noted that the British preferred to use porcelain (presumably Chinese) rather than metal on the dinner table,[24] though for the grandest of the aristocracy a display of plate at dinner was still desirable.[25] As time went on, English buyers began to insist on conditions relating to the colour and the fineness of the Chinese porcelain.[26] Dinner services were frequently decorated with the owner's coat-of-arms, the so-called 'armorial porcelain', which grew very popular after about 1730. A print or drawing with the owner's coat-of-arms would be sent to China, where it would be copied in enamel with absolute fidelity in the centre of the dishes; the borders remained decorated in the Chinese taste, and can generally be dated to within two or three years by their design. The most famous service is that made for the Okeover family, whose original design of 1738 survives; a total of at least 120 plates and 34 dishes were delivered in 1740–3, at the high cost of £1 a plate (figs 175, 176).[27] Occasionally mistakes occurred; the unfortunate customer who wrote 'Our Coat of Arms' on his bookplate must have been dismayed to find the inscription carefully copied on the entire service of porcelain![28]

However, despite the underlying competition from the Continent and the East, there arose in England a large number of privately owned and financed factories that

175 Plate with the coat-of-arms of Leake and Mary Okeover, sent to England in 1740 or 1743. Chinese (Jingdezhen), hard-paste porcelain, painted in enamel colours and gilt. Diameter 22.8 cm. Victoria and Albert Museum, London.

176 Design for a plate sent by Leake Okeover to China in 1738. 22.8 cm. Private collection, England.

made porcelain to the taste of the upper and middle classes. They were not the great State-subsidised ventures that often obtained on the Continent, which were supported by the Crown and had access to court designers and artists. In Britain they took the form of commercial ventures masterminded by groups of private citizens with the risk – which frequently occurred – of going bankrupt. Of the seven or eight major porcelain factories set up in eighteenth-century England, only one, that of Worcester, was to survive with an unbroken history into the present day. Consequently we possess no complete set of records for them, as is often the case with the state-owned factories on the Continent, and the history of many British factories is a matter of conjecture and reconstruction. They virtually all produced soft-paste porcelain of varying quality and their chief interest lies in their technical and artistic development through the century.[29]

Successful experiments in the manufacture of porcelain seem to have taken place as early as 1743, when a Mr Bryand showed the Society of Arts 'fine white ware' which 'when broken appears like broken sugar'. The honour of producing the first porcelain in England is usually given to the factory in Chelsea in west London, set up in about 1744 by the Flemish Huguenot Nicholas Sprimont.[30] Sprimont was an accomplished goldsmith who made silver articles for the aristocracy and the Prince of Wales, and certain early models owe a clear debt to silver prototypes, such as the 'goat-and-bee' jug of about 1745 (fig. 177). This has goat supporters similar to Sprimont's later silver Ashburnham centrepiece of 1747 in the Victoria and Albert Museum. The famous crayfish salt of about the same date (fig. 178) is based on the silver-gilt salts of 1742–3 made for Frederick, Prince of Wales, which still survive in the Royal Collection (fig. 179). There exist also a certain number of plates and platters with borders which are clearly dependent on a silver prototype by Sprimont, as evinced by the sauce boat and saucer of 1746–7.[31] These early wares are sometimes marked with an incised anchor. Figures are rare, but a rival factory, operated by Sprimont's former partner Charles

177 'Goat-and-bee' jug. Soft-paste porcelain. Height 11.5 cm. Chelsea, incised *1744*. The British Museum, London

178 Crayfish salt. Soft-paste porcelain. Width 12.5 cm. Chelsea, *c.*1745–9. The British Museum, London.

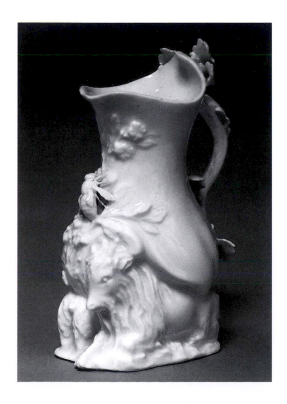

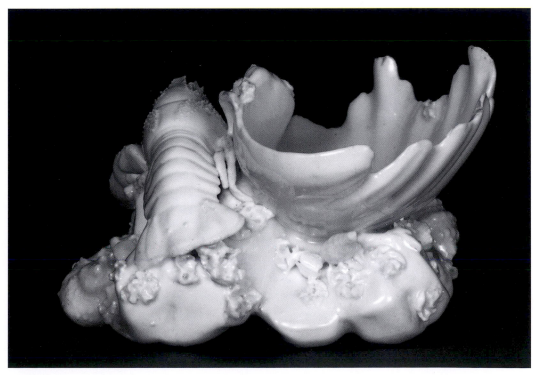

179 Pair of crayfish salts. Silver gilt, width 12.7 cm. London, Nicholas Sprimont, hallmarked for 1742–3. The Royal Collection © 2001, Her Majesty Queen Elizabeth II.

Gouyn,[32] made a range of scent bottles and figures, the most famous representing a girl on a swing, from which the factory formerly took its name.

During the 'raised anchor' period (1750–2) and the 'red anchor' period (1752–5), so-called after the factory marks on the base of products, Chelsea produced a range of beautiful soft-paste wares, delicately painted with patterns in the Japanese *Kakiemon* style, or sprays of flowers in the manner of Meissen.[33] One style of decoration which was a home invention are wares painted with 'fable' decorations after Aesop, which seem to have been painted by Jefferyes Hamett O'Neale, who later worked at Worcester.[34] A peculiarity of these early pieces is that many of them have a certain amount of tin in the glaze, to give them a milky whiteness, as at Chantilly in France.

Although Sprimont never gained a public subsidy, he did succeed in gaining the goodwill and patronage of the king's son, the Duke of Cumberland, who used his influence to further the factory's interests. The Duke of Cumberland's secretary, Sir Everard Fawkener, contacted the British ambassador in Dresden, Sir Charles Hanbury-Williams, in 1751, with a request to borrow some of his Meissen porcelain for the Chelsea factory to copy.[35] It has recently been shown that Chelsea copied details from the plates of the Meissen service, most notably the plate with the rhinoceros, and also a number of animal finials as separate figures.[36] This was in addition to a large number of figure-models copied directly from Meissen, most notably the famous *Monkey Band*.

Chelsea however found its own figure style in the work of the sculptor Joseph Willems (1715/16–66) from the Low Countries.[37] He seems to have been the modeller of a whole range of figures, from individual figures of the 'Seasons' through to ambitious groups such as the *Maypole Dancers* and the group of *Roman Charity*, based on a print after the artist Peter Paul Rubens. He presumably also modelled the group of the *Deposition* based on a sculpture by Nicholas Coustou;[38] Willems returned to Tournai for six months before his death in 1766, and significantly this group appears in Tournai biscuit porcelain just after that date.

Figure groups and vases of the 1760s are often exceptionally elaborate, with rich colouring and gilding in the Sèvres manner, and sometimes marked with an anchor in gold (the so-called "gold-anchor" period). The most famous groups are *The Music Lesson* and *The Dancing Lesson* based on engravings after François Boucher; they bear an elaborate background of leaves (*bocage*), indicating that they are clearly intended for mantelpiece rather than dessert decoration (fig. 180). The most notable vases are the

180 Group of *The Music Lesson*. Soft-paste porcelain, painted in enamel colours and gilt. Height 46 cm. Chelsea, *c.*1760. Victoria & Albert Museum, London.

181 Tureen from the Mecklenburg service. Soft-paste porcelain, painted in enamel colours and gilt. Height of tureen 23.7 cm. Chelsea, *c*.1763. The Royal Collection © 2001, Her Majesty Queen Elizabeth II.

rich flamboyant vases presented to the British Museum and the Foundling Hospital in 1763, and a group of seven elaborately moulded vases known as the 'Dudley vases' after a former owner. An especially ambitious attempt to rival Sèvres was the great dinner service prepared for the queen's brother, the Duke of Mecklenburg-Strelitz (now in the Royal Collection), which has the full complement of tureens, candlesticks, plates and a centrepiece in the flamboyant rococo style of the mid-century (fig. 181).[39]

Dinner services of English porcelain were still comparatively rare, at least until the end of the century. This may be due to certain technical problems, as large pieces of soft-paste are unstable in the kiln, and this may have created difficulty in the making of the large tureens so popular on the Continent.[40] Also the English did not share the same enthusiasm for stews and *bouillon*, preferring a roast joint of meat.[41] It is thus rare to find the great tureens and covered broth-bowls which are so characteristic of Continental porcelain, except in factories like Chelsea which imitated continental forms. As in France, dinner was followed by dessert for which Mrs Glasse, in *The Compleat Confectioner* (1760) included recipes for blancmange, syllabubs, ice-cream, dried cherries, trifle and compotes.[42] As we have seen, dessert services were often made of porcelain, and Chelsea made a full range in the shapes of leaves or fruit in the Meissen manner (fig. 182).

For many years Chelsea had few competitors in England. Its nearest rivals, in time at least, were two factories in the East End of London, a short-lived venture at Limehouse and a more important factory at what was then called Bow (now Stratford High Street).[43] This latter is best known for its porcelain in the Chinese manner, as its name, *New Canton*, suggests, although it also later made wares in the Sèvres style. Its products are often thickly potted, and distinguished by the addition of bone ash as a strengthening material, a substance which was to become the ingredient of the later bone china made in Staffordshire. Although the bulk of its production consisted of tea wares,[44] it did produce a number of figures, most famously the actor Henry Woodward and the actress Kitty Clive as the 'Fine Gentleman' and 'Fine Lady' in David Garrick's farce *Lethe* of about 1750 (fig. 183), which are based on prints after James McArdell and Charles Mosley respectively. It closed in about 1776 and the equipment was taken over by William Duesbury of the Derby factory.

Porcelain factories seem to have sold their wares through a variety of outlets, including their own showroom or warehouse in central London, through a specialist dealer or 'chinaman', or through an annual sale where the best of the factory's products was put up for auction, much being acquired by the aforesaid 'chinamen'. Some of these

182 Reconstruction of an English dessert on the French model by Ivan Day, at The Bowes Museum in 1994, using Chelsea 'Hans Sloane' plates, Derby figures and Worcester baskets, with a layout of a sugar temple, parterre and preserves based on Menon's *La Science du Maître d'Hôtel Confiseur*, 1768.

china-dealers seem to have had a tenuous foothold on the fringes of fashionable society, such as Mrs Chenevix and her sister Mrs Betrand, from whom Horace Walpole bought his suburban villa 'Strawberry Hill' and to whom he was later to show his cabinet of enamels in 1749.[45] They also doubled up as 'toy' dealers, selling a wide range of small objects and knick-knacks, many imported from abroad,[46] and they could be found in large towns across the country.[47]

The experiments at Chelsea in the naturalistic rococo style was seldom followed with such enthusiasm by other factories. An exception is the factory at Longton Hall in Staffordshire, set up in about 1750, and joined by William Littler in 1751, who had transferred his share to West Pans in Scotland by 1784. It is most celebrated for a wide variety of tureens and teapots based on naturalistic forms, such as lettuce leaves or cabbages, in the manner first seen at Meissen and Chelsea, as well as figures with a tree- or flower-ornament (fig. 184).

A more significant rival to Chelsea was the factory set up at Derby in about 1750 by the goldsmith of French descent, André Planché, who was joined by the London dealer and decorator, William Duesbury, in about 1756.[48] The factory is famous for its figures, including a group of fashionably dressed ladies and gentlemen representing the 'Senses', and important models of Chinese figures in a lively rococo style (figs. 185 and 186).[49] Its figures are usually unmarked, but distinguished by a 'dry edge', where the glaze was scraped away before firing, or three patch marks on the base, where the figure was supported during the firing. Some of the animal figures are especially lively in modelling. The factory was also distinguished for the quality of its fruit- and flower-painting on tea, coffee, and dessert wares, as well as lesser items painted in underglaze blue in the Chinese style.

In some ways the most innovative factory was that at Worcester, set up by Dr Wall and others in 1751. It produced some important decorative wares in the manner of the great Continental factories, but it is better known for its smaller items, such as tea

183. Figure of Kitty Clive in Garrick's farce *Lethe*. Soft-paste porcelain. Height 27 cm. Bow, *c.* 1750. The Fitzwilliam Museum, Cambridge.

184 Teapot in naturalistic form. Soft–paste porcelain painted in enamel colours. Height 15.5 cm. Longton Hall, *c.*1756. Victoria & Albert Museum, London.

185. 'Flying Chinaman'. Derby, c. 1752–5. Soft-paste porcelain painted in enamel colours. Derby Museums and Art Gallery, Derby.

186 Chinese group representing 'Hearing', from a set of the Five Senses. Soft-paste porcelain painted in enamel colours, height 20.3 cm. Derby, c.1752–5. Victoria & Albert Museum, London.

wares, made for the middle class. These had the advantage of not 'flying' or cracking when filled with hot-water, as the body was toughened with the addition of soapstone.[50] Many were decorated not with hand-painting, but with small line engravings, similar to the technique used for producing copper engravings for book illustration. The technique, arguably Britain's most important contribution to the history of ceramic decoration, seems to have been invented by John Brooks and developed at the Battersea enamel works in 1753–6,[51] and was soon used at Bow and Worcester factories.[52] It consisted of a 'pull' being taken from the inked plate onto tissue paper, which was then transferred onto the body of the object. The decoration was then fired on. A more sophicated variation involved transferring the design in oil onto a 'bat' or pad of rubber-like glue which, after being applied to the body, was then dusted with powdered colour before firing. This technique allowed the image to curve round vessels such as teapots and jugs, but had the disadvantage of not being suitable for underglaze printing.[53]

Many of the prints used in transfer-printing on porcelain seem to have been first engraved by Robert Hancock (1729/30–1817), who moved to the Worcester factory in about 1756. Stylistically, Hancock's influences are almost wholly French, as popularised by the artists who gathered around the immigrant engraver Hubert Gravelot (1699–1773)[54] at his drawing academy in St Martin's Lane, London. This 'school' or circle of engravers and painters is believed to have done much to popularise the rococo style in Britain.[55] Volumes of prints or patterns were freely available on the London market

187 Plate painted with a central scene of cut fruit. Soft-paste porcelain, painted in enamel colours and gilt. Diameter 22.5 cm. Worcester, painted in the workshop of James Giles, *c*.1765. Victoria & Albert Museum, London.

through the medium of such print-sellers as Robert Sayer of Fleet Street, who is perhaps best known for his collection of ornamental engravings published together as *The Ladies Amusement, or, whole Art of Japanning made Easy*.[56] The publication includes engravings of flowers, birds, insects, ships, figures after Watteau, 'chinoiseries' after the French designer Jean Pillement (1728–1808), landscapes and garden buildings in the Chinese taste. Details from the book have been traced on the porcelain of Chelsea, Bow and Worcester.

Such volumes were the inspiration for many independent decorators – the equivalent of the German *Hausmaler* – who were to be found throughout Britain.[57] The best-known, James Giles of London, was active from 1756 to 1776, when his business appears to have failed.[58] He seems to have used many Worcester blanks for decoration, to the extent that it is often very difficult to know what was decorated at Worcester and what was decorated in London. Some plates given by his descendants to the Victoria and Albert Museum in 1935 give the best clues to his workshop's style, and show painted landscapes in the centre, or depictions of game, while another shows cut-fruit in the centre surrounded by a Meissen-type mosaic pattern (fig. 187).[59]

However, the vast majority of everyday porcelain made in Britain in the mid-eighteenth century continued to be in an Eastern style, reflecting the continuing imports

188 Pull from the copper-plate with the 'Fisherman' pattern. Victoria & Albert Museum, London.

189 Pull from the copper-plate with an early version of the 'Willow' pattern. Victoria & Albert Museum, London.

of china from the East, with especial emphasis on the use of underglaze blue, the cheapest form of coloured decoration. Apart from Worcester, the main centres of production were Liverpool, and Lowestoft on the Norfolk coast, which all made Oriental-style wares of medium quality. In addition there were short-lived porcelain factories at Isleworth and Vauxhall in London, and Newcastle-under-Lyme and Baddeley at Staffordshire, which are only recently being discovered through excavation.[60]

Most larger wares, such as tureens, meat-plates and dinner plates, continued to be of imported porcelain, especially Chinese, which was considerably cheaper than that of Meissen or Sèvres. This was made according to English specifications and by mid-century the composition of a standard Chinese dinner service could be described thus: two tureens, covers and stands, thirteen dishes of various sizes, sixty dinner plates, twenty-four soup plates, eight salad dishes, one salad bowl, two sauce boats, and four salts.[61] Increasingly many of these dinner services were painted in simple underglaze blue, which the London market christened 'Nankin' or 'Nankeen' after the Chinese port through which they were exported. Motifs on these wares included quaint Chinese motifs so beloved by Europeans, including fishermen, trees, temples on islands and stylised flowers.[62] The vast majority of these goods were sold by the East India Company at auctions held twice yearly at their warehouses, the main purchasers being the professional china-dealers.[63]

Naturally factories in Britain were keen to fill the demand for dinner wares on a large scale, but with little success until the activities of Thomas Turner of the Caughley factory in Shropshire, which was set up in about 1772. He made a wide range of middling wares in transfer-printed blue-and-white, very similar to those at Worcester, using similar or identical prints, and in particular two Chinese-style patterns, the 'Fisherman' pattern (fig. 188), showing a Chinese fisherman at work, and the 'Broseley' pattern, featuring a willow tree, island and bridge (fig. 189). This is often seen as the basis of the modern 'Willow' pattern, a term in use by 1799.[64] The original copper plates survive, showing the characteristic pagodas and willows, although at first without the bridge.[65] In the period 1795–7 the factory shifted from the production of soft-paste soapstone porcelain, of the kind manufactured at Worcester, to a hybrid hard-paste type, which was suitable for larger items. However, Caughley porcelain still seems to have been more expensive than Chinese, and the factory suffered from such competition until the end of the century.[66]

By the end of the eighteenth century, the East India Company's trade in porcelain began to lose its profitability. This was probably due to rivalry with Staffordshire pottery, and also machinations among the London china-dealers, who combined to form a 'ring' (an agreement not to bid against each other) at auctions, leading to loss of profit for the company itself. Problems were recognised from about 1779 onwards,[67] and in December 1791 the Court of Directors gave orders that no china should be imported except as 'flooring' (ballast), and took legal action against the London chinamen for forming the 'ring'. This naturally upset the china-dealers, and the chinaman Miles Mason wrote to the court of Directors in April 1795 on behalf of the London dealers to learn on what terms of freight the company would allow their officers 'to import china ware',[68] that is, as private trade. Mason presumably received a negative response, and he re-appears in ceramic history as the manufacturer of British blue-and-white porcelain advertised in 1804 as 'British Nankin', not in London, but in the county of Staffordshire, a part of Britain which had become the prime ceramics manufacturer in the whole world.

Overleaf, detail of fig. 199. Teabowl, saucer and coffee pot.

CHAPTER 10

The Rise of Staffordshire

As we have seen, pottery centres existed throughout Europe in any place where supplies of clay and a ready market conjoined to create favourable manufacturing conditions. However, pottery remained the poor relation of porcelain, deriving its forms and styles from its more prestigious sister. This is perhaps not true for peasant pottery made for local markets – the *Bauerntöpferei* of central Europe – which used traditional techniques of decoration and patterns to good effect. However, the products made, though worthy, are not within the strict definitions of fashionable taste and so lie outside our story. Yet the eighteenth century saw the rise of one particular pottery district and its products which came to dominate fashionable tables throughout Europe.

The county of Staffordshire lies right in the centre of England. It had been a major centre of ceramic activity from medieval times onwards, based particularly on the area now comprising the six 'pottery towns' – Stoke, Hanley, Burslem, Fenton, Tunstall and Longton, today all swallowed up in the modern town of Stoke-on-Trent. Its importance for the development of ceramic design lies not so much in its use of particular designers or painters, but in the technical developments made by the craftsmen, often anonymous, who worked in the district. Their achievements have been the subject of much analysis and speculation from the early nineteenth century onwards, a process hampered by the fact that so few early pieces are securely documented or marked.

Since there are relatively few written records for the many individual makers and workshops that abounded in the district, we have to use two main published sources that purport to set out the story. The first is Dr Robert Plot's *The Natural History of Staffordshire* (1686), a survey of its structure and industries, characteristic of the scientific interest of the later seventeenth century. Plot took great care to describe the various processes and workshops that he visited, identifying Staffordshire as an area of major industrial activity. The second source is Simeon Shaw's *History of the Staffordshire Potteries* of 1829, written when this area was the most productive ceramic-making centre in the world. Like all such histories, it tends to interpret the story in terms of significant personages who made individual discoveries and improvements, at the expense of many other potters who probably also made contributions that are now unrecorded; as such, it has a bias which has become accepted tradition and is impossible to correct. These books can also be supplemented by contemporary records relating to sales, taxes and rates, and petitions to Parliament. Most recently, archaeological excavations of tips and waster sites have given concrete evidence of the kind of pottery that certain manufacturers made, and will probably lead to considerable rewriting of ceramic history in the future.

Staffordshire first came to prominence as a centre of ceramic manufacture in the seventeenth century, when references to local potters abound. Deposits of clay and coal co-existed with a good water-supply, and, within a short distance, deposits of lead, used for the making of glazes, and iron and copper, whose oxides were used for colouring them. In these circumstances, production could be organised on quite a small scale and operate as part of a 'cottage' industry, co-existing with other industries in the same household, since the materials lay more or less on the doorstep. Potters had only to dig clay from the road outside.[1] At this stage, pottery making was still very much a craft industry, comprising 'potworks' rather than factories, which sold their products to travelling 'cratemen' 'who carry them on their backs all over the country',[2] and sold them at country fairs. Pictures of such pot-sellers, sitting amid a pile of brown and brown-glazed pots, can be seen in depictions of such fairs right into the nineteenth century.

Contemporaries seem to have first become aware of Staffordshire as a significant centre for the production of pottery in the later seventeenth century, when the afore-mentioned Dr Robert Plot, in his *The Natural History of Staffordshire*, gave a detailed breakdown of the industry in scientific terms, mentioning the crude kinds of pottery that were made there. It is invaluable as he gives a full description of the types of wares made, describing:

> the greatest Pottery they have in this County is carried on at Burslem near Newcastle under Lyme, where for making their severall sorts of Pots, they have as many different sorts of Clays, which they dig round about the Towne, all within half a miles distance, the best being found nearest the coale, and are distinguish't by their colours and uses as followeth:
>
> 1. Bottle clay, of a bright whitish streaked yellow colour.
> 2. Hard-fire clay of a duller whitish colour, and fuller intersperst with a dark yellow, which they use for their black ware, being mixt with the
> 3. Red blending Clay, which is of a dirty red colour.
> 4. White-clay, so called it seems though of a blewish colour, and used for making yellow-colour'd ware, because yellow is the lightest colour they make any Ware of all which they call throwing clays because they are of a closer texture, & will work on the wheel.[3]

Plot here describes four types of clay, giving a range of colours from red through to yellow and black. It should be noted that nothing very refined is described, and he specifically states that yellow-coloured ware is the palest that they can achieve.

Forms and decoration were comparatively simple, closely related to the peasant wares made on the Continent and elsewhere in Britain. A favourite form of decoration on pots was in the form of 'slip', that is, a liquid coloured-clay that was trailed over the object to form patterns or designs. The decoration might take the form of a brown slip trailed onto the yellowish body, or else the whole object could be dipped into a dark slip, and white slip be trailed over. A variety of objects were made in slipware, the best-known being large chargers or display dishes decorated with crude but vigorous designs based on heraldic or religious motifs, such as coats-of-arms, mermaids, and the pelican in her piety. Other chargers depict royal portraits, Adam and Eve, and other subjects reminiscent of the types of decoration found on English delftware of the same period. A peculiarity of these dishes is that they are often inscribed at the base with a name, presumed to be that of the potter. Names on the signed pieces include John Wright and William Wright, Ralph Simpson, William Talor and George Talor. The best-known name appearing on the large dishes is Thomas Toft, which appears on dishes dated from 1671 to 1683 (fig. 190), or Ralph Toft, dating from 1676 to 1683. However, in spite of the fame that they have now achieved, neither person is traceable in the records as a potter.[4]

Another class of item featured drinking pots, 'tygs' (a jug with several handles for passing round a table), bleeding-bowls and jugs. Production of these was not confined

190 Dish with Adam and Eve. Red earthenware, covered in white slip with trailed red slip decoration. Signed *Thomas Toft 1674*. Diameter 55.9 cm. Staffordshire, Thomas Toft, 1674. Temple Newsam House, Leeds.

to Staffordshire, but was found in many places in Britain, such as Derbyshire, Yorkshire, and Wrotham in Kent.[5] Some pieces bear inscriptions such as 'The best is not too good for you', suggesting that they may have been intended as gifts. Developments in slipware in the early eighteenth century included the production of moulded items, whereby the dish is made by pressing moist clay into a mould, to produce a raised decoration which could then be emphasised with a different-coloured slip. The most famous exponent seems to have been Samuel Malkin (1688–1741), who made a dish moulded with a clock-face dateable to 1712, now in the British Museum,[6] and a press-moulded slipware dish in the Victoria and Albert Museum bearing the date 1715 (fig. 191).[7]

A more sophisticated use of slipware lay in combining different-coloured slips together to give the effect of marbling (fig. 192). A popular version comprised white and red slips trailed together and 'broken' with a wire brush, 'much after the manner they do when they marble paper, and then cloud them with a pencil when they are dry', as Dr Plot writes.[8] Such decoration is often seen on shallow serving dishes found all over Britain. The cruder wares have a 'combed' effect and were made in many parts of England well into the nineteenth century. These can be exceptionally difficult to date as the styles changed very little.

The major development in Staffordshire at the end of the seventeenth century was

191 Dish inscribed 'Wee three Logerheads' and initialled 'SM'. Earthenware, moulded and decorated with slip under lead glaze. Diameter 35.5 cm. Burslem, Samuel Malkin, *c.*1720–30. The Fitzwilliam Museum, Cambridge.

192 Jug. Buff earthenware, decorated outside with marbled and feathered slips under lead glaze. Height 26.5 cm. Staffordshire, *c.*1680–1710. The Fitzwilliam Museum, Cambridge.

the introduction of the manufacture of stoneware. As we have seen, this was first made in Britain by John Dwight of Fulham. A form of stoneware must have been made in Staffordshire from as early as 1693, when John Dwight successfully prosecuted John and David Elers of Fulham, James Morley of Nottingham, and three Wedgwoods of Burslem for infringing his patent on stoneware by gaining the secrets from his labourer John Chandler.[9] This marked the beginning of a burgeoning stoneware industry that dominated Staffordshire production into the mid-eighteenth century.

Some of the finest types of stoneware were made by the aforementioned Germans John and David Elers at Bradwell Wood, near Burslem. They are supposed to have worked as silversmiths before turning to pottery, producing red stonewares of the kind made in Holland by Ary de Milde and others in the tradition of Chinese Yixing stoneware.[10] Their wares include tea and coffee pots, cups, saucers and dishes; they are exceptionally finely made and trimly potted, and have a lightness of body not heretofore associated with Staffordshire wares. They were made by the technique of 'slip-casting', a process in which the ceramic body is built up with layers of liquid clay or 'slip' poured into a plaster mould, which absorbs the water to leave a thin-walled fine-bodied ware. It could subsequently be 'turned' or trimmed on a potter's wheel to achieve a more regular profile. Their wares, and those of their imitators (for it is often impos-

193 Mug and beaker. Red stoneware with sprigged decoration. Height of mug 11.8 cm. Staffordshire or London, possibly Elers workshop, c.1700. Temple Newsam House, Leeds.

sible to distinguish between them) are decorated with applied 'sprigged' decoration, often of Chinese motifs such as prunus blossom (fig. 193). These was made by impressing sharply cut metal-dies or stamps into pads of wet clay applied to the pot, and scraping away superfluous decoration from around the edges of the die. Such wares could be further decorated by way of gilding, indicating their use by the richer classes, and a mark a great refinement in the quality of ceramic made in Staffordshire.

Other early Staffordshire productions of stoneware seem to have been of rather coarse salt-glazed tankards for beer drinking, mugs or cups in the brown salt-glaze, similar to that of Nottingham, sometimes stamped with the excise mark 'WR' (for William III) or 'AR' (for Queen Anne) to guarantee a full measure of beer. The simpler 'crouch' ware was also produced, made from common clay and sand. These wares were all comparatively crude, and would have been used in drinking-houses or poor homes, rather than by people with a degree of wealth.

The need for a rise in quality was caused partly by changing tastes, such as the introduction of new hot drinks – tea, coffee and chocolate – to the country, with a corresponding increase in the need for fine-quality ceramics in which to serve them. Naturally the very rich used porcelain, but there existed in Britain a vast body of people of the middling sort who could not afford porcelain, but wanted ceramics that had something fashionable about their design. There came into being in Staffordshire a great number of potters who made stoneware of fine quality, which also had the required toughness to withstand boiling water. This led to the production of a vast range of novel teapots, tea-canisters, milk jugs, cups and saucers in various forms and with different decorations, which were made in considerable quantities by the mid-eighteenth century.[11] They were exported across the whole country, partly via the River Weaver, which was opened to river traffic in 1733, and led to a dramatic increase in trade. The quantity of goods carried on it rose from 100 tons per annum, to 1,800 per annum in 1760.[12]

One of the earlier kinds of mass-produced stoneware seems to have been a fine, thin-walled brown stoneware today called 'drabware', with the sprigged decoration being made of the fine white pipe-clay imported from Devon (fig. 194). The range of wares encompassed all the fashionable silver items of teapots, cream jugs, cups and saucers, and sometimes even larger vases similar to the Chinese. These wares were sometimes glazed in a second firing called a 'glost' firing, which gave the potters much greater control of the body and minimised losses in the kiln. Excavated wasters of such wares have been found in the pottery of Samuel Bell, dating from 1724 onwards.[13]

However, fashion dictated a search for ever-whiter varieties of pottery. One technique was to dip lighter-bodied unfired products of Staffordshire clay into a dip of white pipe-clay slip; calcined flint was later introduced into the slip to give an even whiter effect. Contemporary accounts differentiate between the two.[14] The latter innovation is often credited to John Astbury (1688–1743), and a number of small figures, decorated in coloured glazes, are also often attributed to his hand. However, by the 1720s a thin, white salt-glazed stoneware was made with a body that was a mixture of white pipe-clay from Devon and Dorset (so-called 'ball clay') and calcined flint; a patent of 1722 for making transparent earthenware obtained by Thomas Biling presumably refers to a refined version of this ware. These salt-glazed white-bodied wares were to dominate Staffordshire production for the next thirty years.

A sideline to these tea and dinner wares in the early eighteenth century were crude but attractive figures in white salt-glazed stoneware, often in the form of 'pew' groups, so called because they showed a person or people sitting stiffly in a pew in church (fig. 195). They generally show people in fashionable dress, the gentlemen in long coats and the women in wide, hooped petticoats, but are so crude in modelling that they can

194 Teapot. Salt-glazed stoneware (*drabware*), with applied decoration. Staffordshire, *c.*1740. Temple Newsam House, Leeds.

195 'Pew Group'. Salt-glazed stoneware, with details in brown clay and slip. Height 16.5 cm. Staffordshire, *c.*1740–50. The Fitzwilliam Museum, Cambridge.

196 Selection of salt-glazed stoneware, including two sauceboats and a mould. Staffordshire, c.1740–60. Courtesy of Phillips Auctioneers.

197 Salt-glazed stoneware sauce boat block attributable to Aaron Wood. Height 9 cm. Staffordshire, c.1760. The Victoria & Albert Museum, London.

hardly have been rivals to the porcelain figures of the great factories. They are presumably early examples of cottage chimney-piece decoration.

By mid-century the Staffordshire potters were making an enormous number of patterns, nearly all in the fashionable rococo or chinoiserie styles, which continued to be popular into the 1760s. Pieces vary from hexagonal or angled wares with panels of moulded ornament, including teapots in the shapes of houses, through to more obviously rococo pieces, such as items moulded with shell motifs (fig. 196). As with English porcelain, there was a tendency to make the smaller domestic wares, such as sauce boats and cream jugs, which might otherwise have been made in silver. A particular speciality seems to have been moulded and pierced wares, including plates and baskets, clearly imitating rococo silver of the mid-eighteenth century. By the second half of the eighteenth century elegant decorative items were made, such as wall vases in the shape of a cornucopia or with mask heads. The urge to imitate items of silver or porcelain was such that a version of the Chelsea 'goat-and-bee' jug was even made.[15]

These pieces could be mass-produced by means of the slip-casting technique, mentioned earlier, whereby a potter could make a 'block' or solid pattern which was used to create negative moulds of plaster-of-Paris, into which 'slip' or layers of liquid clay were poured to create the final ceramic. The blocks were frequently made of salt-glazed stoneware as this had the necessary toughness for many negative moulds be made. The earliest-known dated block in the British Museum is for a sauce boat and is signed and dated 'RW 1748'.[16] This is thought to stand for the potter Ralph Wood (1715–72) who, with his brother Aaron (1717–85), is credited with some of the finest and most inventive moulds.[17] A block for a sauce boat that may be his work was used, not only by the makers of salt-glazed stoneware, but also by Bow and the Longton Hall porcelain factory in Staffordshire, indicating the versatility of a fashionable shape between the different mediums (fig. 197).

By the mid-eighteenth century Staffordshire had risen to national economic importance, as improvements in manufacture and export facilities led to a vast increase in production. Output is thought to have increased in value from about £10,000 in 1710 to about £40,000 by 1760. By then it was no longer a local industry, using local materials, but an industry using resources from all over the country and exporting all over the world; white 'ball' clay had been imported from Devon and Dorset to improve the colour and texture of the body from about 1710. A windmill for grinding flints, also used in the body of paler wares, was established at Burslem by 1750.[18]

The result of this demand was increased specialisation of production, with the pottery workshops leaving behind their craft origin and changing into something akin to a modern industrial process, with much specialisation of labour on different sites. By the early eighteenth century production was on a par with minor industries; in 1710–15 a year's rent on a slipware pottery in Shelton was five pounds, twice that of a blacksmith's.[19] But in 1749 the lease on a pottery in Shelton listed as many as five separate houses. Specialised outbuildings, such as the 'Smoke-house', 'Throwing-house', 'Turning-House', 'Slip-House' and 'Saggar-House' were in existence by 1750, though smaller potteries were still run by men who also worked as farmers.[20] The typical number of employees for a production centre seems to have been about forty, as at Thomas Whieldon's in the 1760s,[21] and the total number of people employed in the potteries is thought to have risen from about 500 in 1710–15 to 15,000 in 1785.[22] However, it was not until 1867 that potteries became 'factories' by statute law.[23]

As the century progressed, we begin to get more familiar with the names of those potters who operated in Staffordshire, such as Enoch Booth, William Greatbatch, William Littler, Humphrey Palmer, Thomas Whieldon, and John and Thomas Wedgwood of the Big House, Newcastle-upon-Lyme, which has led to many individual attributions of unmarked wares. There seem to have been about 150 manufacturers in total. They all seem to have made a great variety of objects in different styles and techniques, sometimes sharing the same moulds; to add to the confusion, they frequently bought unglazed or undecorated wares from each other, or sent them out to the same firm of independent decorators to be decorated. In these circumstances, it is preferable to try and avoid precise attribution of pieces to a single maker, unless backed up by a firm provenance or inscription, or similarities with archaeological wasters.[24]

Painted and enamelled decoration was also applied, often reminiscent of the decoration of porcelain. A cheap form of decorating pottery was incising the decoration before firing and filling in the grooves with colour, usually blue made from zaffre (hence today's term 'scratch blue') (fig. 198). Most examples seem to date from between 1740 and 1780.[25] Completely blue overglazed wares, similar to the Sèvres *bleu-de-roi* ground colour, were made by dipping the ware into a slip containing zaffre, so that the resulting object, once fired, was covered in a glossy blue colour. The invention was credited by Shaw to the potters William Littler and Aaron Wedgwood, who shared a pot-bank at Brownhills.

Painted decoration of the kind seen on porcelain was often done by outside decorators, in the specialist workshops containing muffle kilns that we have already encountered with porcelain. The potting families of Daniel of Cobridge and Warburton of Hot Lane became specialists in the art of enamelling, taking in the work of other potters. For instance, on 24 September 1762, Thomas and John Wedgwood sent the Warburtons '2 Doz[en] White let in one dish (teapots)' to be enamelled.[26] The range of decoration was enormous, but painted chinoiseries and landscapes figured largely, closely followed by sprigs of flowers in the Meissen manner. Some exceptionally fine pieces are known featuring a portrait of the Young Pretender, Charles James Stewart, and must date to around the time of the Great Rebellion of 1745. By mid-century, some of this decoration appeared in coloured 'reserves' in the manner of Sèvres or the more ambitious English factories, indicating a high level of fashionable influence.[27]

The mid-century saw an increased development of earthenware techniques, with experimental use of clays and glazes, aided by the use of the second 'glost' firing for a clear and liquid lead-glaze, to produce ordinary earthenwares of greater quality. One of the great developments was the invention of a solid body called 'marbled' or 'agate' ware. Here several different coloured clays, tinted with metal oxides, were wedged together in layers (but *not* blended) so that they adhered to one another but still showed as separate sections of clay in the fired product. From the resulting block thin layers could be sliced off with a wire, showing the veining all the way through, which could then be pressed into a mould. The result was a body which had the appearance of marble or 'agate', and was much used for tea wares and decorative pieces (fig. 199). Great care had to be taken in potting so as not to blur the coloured clays; when such pieces were thrown on a wheel, they inevitably achieved a 'swirling' effect.

A similar effect was achieved by mixing coloured slips together, in the manner of the marbled or 'combed' wares made in the seventeenth century, and applying them to the

198 Mug, salt-glazed stoneware, with incised blue decoration, dated 1749. Temple Newsam House, Leeds.

199 Teabowl, saucer and coffee pot. Mixed 'wedged' lead-glazed earthenware (*agate ware*). Height of coffee-pot 25 cm. Staffordshire, *c*.1750–65. The Fitzwilliam Museum, Cambridge.

body to create different effects of marbling, making surface agate or marbled ware. Such effects were aided by a whiter, more refined body, which was becoming popular, using the white clays from Devon or Dorset,[28] which was to lead to the development of 'creamware' later in the eighteenth century. A particularly popular combination of metallic oxides producing brown and white colours, applied to the biscuit before a second firing with a clear lead-glaze, gave an effect of tortoiseshell, which was used on all kinds of goods, such as teapots, coffee pots (fig. 200), jugs and even large tureens and plates.

By the second half of the eighteenth century the potters of Staffordshire were the most advanced in the world. They made a wide range of light-bodied wares which had captured all but the richest market. The opening of new canals, such as the Newcastle canal from Stoke to Newcastle 1759, and the Cauldon canal from Shelton to Leek and Froghall in 1773[29] greatly increased their market and led to their wares being exported across the world. The economic importance of the industry can be gauged from the petition of the potters to Parliament in 1762 asking for a turnpike road from Burslem to Lawton in Cheshire, which emphasised their international trade.[30]

It was this fertile ground that gave birth to the most famous of all British potters, Josiah Wedgwood (1730–95). He was born, the last of twelve children, to Thomas Wedgwood, a potter at Burslem, a relative of the more successful Thomas Wedgwood, maker of salt-glazed ware who lived at the 'Big House' at Burslem. He was formally apprenticed to his brother Thomas in 1744 for five years, during which time he contracted smallpox, which was to lead to the amputation of his leg. In 1752 he joined the pottery of John Harrison and Thomas Alders at Cliff Bank, Stoke, who presumably made standard salt-glazed and lead-glazed wares, although nothing precise is known of their activity. However, his great breakthrough came in 1754, when he went into partnership with the highly successful potter Thomas Whieldon at Fenton Vivian. Whieldon's products are listed in an Account and Memorandum Book for 1749–53, which mentions a wide range of white salt-glazed stoneware, tortoiseshell-ware and pale lead-glazed earthenware ('creamware'), as well as some figures. Such wares were excavated from the site of Whieldon's pottery in the 1960s, although similar wares have also been found on other sites, such as that of Humphrey Palmer. It would appear that at this time Whieldon was already producing items such as teapots and milk jugs covered in a green glaze and moulded in the form of cauliflowers, pineapples, and other fruit and vegetables, similar to the rococo wares made in porcelain at Chelsea and Longton Hall (fig. 201). These became very popular in the 1760s and were supplied by a number of manufacturers, the best-known of which was the potter William Greatbatch (1735–1813), who had been apprenticed to Whieldon in 1749, but left him in 1759, going on to set up business independently in 1762. To him are also attributable the 'Landskip' teapots decorated with a house and garden in panels at the sides.[31]

We do not know the precise reasons behind the Whieldon–Wedgwood partnership, but it is clear that it gave Wedgwood the chance to experiment with a wide range of processes and techniques.[32] In 1759 he seems to have set up on his own account, leasing the Ivy House Works from his cousin John Wedgwood of the Big House, Burslem. One of his first employees was another of his cousins, Thomas. In 1763 he moved to larger premises at the Brick House Works, Burslem. His wares are not recorded, but presumably they consisted of tortoiseshell and cauliflower wares, using moulds obtained from Greatbatch or Whieldon. He seems to have had extensive business contacts, most notably with William Greatbatch and John Baddeley of Shelton, a distinguished potter who produced the full range of Staffordshire ware.[33] Wedgwood took not only blocks, but fired-wares from Greatbatch.[34] He also sent Greatbatch drawings which he could subsequently work up into blocks, illustrative of the close working procedures of the Staffordshire potters.

However, Wedgwood was soon developing trading links outside the Staffordshire

200 Two teapots and a punchpot painted in coloured glazes. Staffordshire, c.1750–60. Courtesy of Phillips Auctioneers.

201. Teapot in the shape of a cauliflower. Creamware decorated in coloured glazes. Height 12.7 cm. Staffordshire c.1760. The Wedgwood Museum, Barlaston, Staffordshire.

area, and in particular with Sadler and Green of Liverpool, who had developed a speciality in transfer-printing, using other potters' wares, beginning first with tiles, and from 1761 using blanks of tea and tablewares from Wedgwood, although nothing seems to be precisely dateable to this early period. This trading link led to his friendship (and later partnership) with the Liverpool merchant Thomas Bentley, who could put him more directly in contact with fashionable taste. This was now moving away from the colourful wares of the rococo period towards something more austere and learned, and heralds a new chapter in ceramic history. In 1766 we have records of Wedgwood exchanging cauliflower blocks for manufactured cauliflower cups and saucers from the potter John Baddeley; this may be seen as the termination of his manufacture of green cauliflower ware and other pottery imitating naturalistic motifs.[35] Although other potters in Staffordshire such as Greatbatch continued to produce coloured wares into the 1770s, the market henceforth lay in styles of ever-increasing severity, which can only be understood in relationship to an enormous change in the intellectual and philosophical basis of European society itself.

Overleaf, detail of fig. 231. *Pegasus* vase.

CHAPTER 11

The Classical Revival

Classical art – the art of ancient Greece and Rome – was a major influence on the art of Western Europe from the fifteenth century to the late nineteenth century. We have seen how in the fifteenth and sixteenth centuries the Renaissance ('rebirth') in Italy tried to emulate and rival some aspects of the antique. But their Renaissance was very much a re-creation of the past in which the styles of classical art were adapted to a new form. Many specific instances are known of direct borrowing from classical art, but in general the intention was to surpass rather than simply copy the art of the past. The resulting products could seldom be mistaken for real specimens of classical art, even if at the time contemporaries thought that artists and sculptors had produced items of equivalent value. The eighteenth-century movement we are now dealing with laid claims to be a much more exact imitation of classical art, especially with regard to items for the domestic interior, reproducing details of the antique with apparent understanding and taste. But we shall also see how the movement was in fact very eclectic, deriving inspiration from a wide range of sources, and using them to create a version of the antique that suited the norms and forms of eighteenth-century society, and could fit into a more modern way of life.

This revival was closely linked to trends in eighteenth-century thought, known as the 'Enlightenment'. This was an intellectual and social movement which sought to understand the world in rational rather than emotional or religious terms, supplanting the Bible and religion as the ultimate authority in favour of the study of human society and nature through scientific observation. It had its roots in the scientific advances of the seventeenth-century, but differed from them in that it did not necessarily accept the existing organisation of the world as divinely ordained, an idea which was eventually to undermine the whole principle of a hierarchical society, headed by a God-given king. The individual's allegiance to a divinely ordained king was replaced by the concept of the virtues of public responsibility and citizenship. These ideas tended to undermine a hierarchical society based on birth in favour of the belief that the individual could achieve personal status through the execution of selfless and altruistic deeds, in the manner of the heroes of classical antiquity. Thus the classical age was seen as both more 'natural' and morally better than eighteenth-century society, and its disciplined artistic style superior to that of the unrestrained rococo.

The date of the first signs of the appearance of this emerging classical style in the decorative arts has occasioned the most furious debate among art historians. While it is generally agreed that it had its epicentre in Rome, much ink has been spilt on whether it was France or England that held the lead in reintroducing classical forms – straight lines, the Greek key pattern, muted colours and severe outlines – into the repertoire of the decorative arts. The origins and introduction of such features as the straight neo-classical chair leg have occasioned much virulent and learned argument.[1] However, these rigid nationalistic borders would not have been recognised in the eighteenth century; 'neo-classicism' (as the movement was termed in the late nineteenth century) was an international movement whose main proponents were in contact with each other, producing different manifestations in each country.

We should first be aware of discontentments with the rococo style among architects and people with pretensions to taste. The rococo style had its detractors even at the apparent height of its success. Much of the criticism came from architects and sculptors, who, as we might expect, would find faults in an 'irrational' style which owed its origins to the work of goldsmiths and ornamental print-makers, and was so unsuited to the straight lines and levels of building work.[2] These complaints were closely linked with dissatisfaction with the court of Louis XV, with its emphasis on small-scale luxuries and minor pieces of architecture – the taste of the king's mistresses – quite apart from its tendency to lose wars; it was contrasted unfavourably with the glorious days of Louis XIV, when France was the dominant nation in Europe. Similar objections to the rococo style were raised by architects in Britain,[3] though they were overlaid with patriotic connotations, as France was England's traditional enemy.[4]

As a constant background to these stylistic and nationalistic attacks on the rococo was the feeling that the art of Greece and Rome, with its emphasis on order, balance, symmetry, straight lines and restraint, represented the ideal which all should follow. This feeling was encouraged by the popularity of the Grand Tour, the process by which a gentleman, brought up on a classical education, traversed the Continent with Rome as his ultimate goal. It was especially popular with the nobility of Great Britain, where power lay in the hands of the aristocracy rather than the Crown. They had successfully created their own architectural style, Palladianism, based on the work of the classicising Italian architect Andrea Palladio (1508–80), whose work was imitated by the British architect Inigo Jones (1573–1652). The classical style in architecture held constant sway in Britain during the eighteenth century, aided by the publication of such books as James Stuart's and Nicholas Revett's *The Antiquities of Athens* in 1762 and Robert Adam's *Ruins of the Palace of the Emperor Diocletian at Spalatro in Dalmatia* in 1764. These books served to stimulate a taste for the classical ideal, which was continued in interiors and even filtered down to the furniture and decorative details.

The classical style was also held in high regard in mid-eighteenth-century France, but its ideals were upheld by the French Academy in Rome rather than in France itself. This had been set up in the seventeenth century in the Villa Medici as a training academy for young painters, sculptors and architects, subsidised by bursaries from the Crown. Prominent students in the 1740s and 1750s include the painter Jean-Baptiste Marie Pierre (1713–89), the architect Jean-Laurent Le Guay (1710–after 1786),[5] the sculptor Jacques-François-Joseph Saly (1717–76) and the painter Joseph-Marie Vien (1716–1809). They all rejected the flamboyance of the rococo style in favour of an approach that had something of the purity and simplicity of the ancients. Though as students they had little chance of giving permanent expression to their views in the form of a major public building, they could demonstrate their ideas in temporary decorations for the Roman Festival called the *Chinea*, which acted as a vehicle for new styles of decoration. Furthermore, they publicised their ideas and their abilities through the means of decorative prints, showcasing their ideas in two-dimensional form.

One important visitor to the Academy in the 1750s was the brother of Madame de Pompadour, the Marquis de Marigny. He had been travelling in Italy in the years 1749–51 with the intention of improving his taste so that he could take over the influential post of *Directeur-Général des Bâtiments, Jardins, Arts, Académies et Manufactures Royales* on the death of the then incumbent. He was accompanied on his journeys by the Abbé Le Blanc, the architect Soufflot,[6] and the draughtsman Charles-Nicolas Cochin (1715–90),[7] who encouraged him to view classical buildings favourably and avoid the rococo.

A further stimulus to the development of neo-classicism was the discovery and illustration of new archaeological sites. In particular, the excavations at Pompeii and Herculaneum meant that far more was known about the daily life of Ancient Rome, especially through the recovery of small items relating to the domestic interior. Their serious excavation commenced in the eighteenth century,[8] and in 1753 the excavations at Pompeii had even been visited by the flamboyant Carl Eugene of Württemberg, though it is probable that he was probably more captivated with the porcelain factory at Capodimonte.[9] The results of the excavations were published in book form in the *Antichità d'Ercolano* from 1757–92, although these do not seem to have been generally available at first, and the discoveries at Pompeii did not have their fullest impact on the decorative arts until the *style étrusque* in France at the end of the century.

These volumes were simply one of a great number of such works which appeared in the middle of the century, disseminating classical ideas to the educated public. Books about classical antiquities had of course been published much earlier, for instance Bellori's *Admiranda Romanorum Antiquatum* of 1693 and Montfaucon's *L'Antiquité Expliquée* of 1719–20; however, it was the publications of the mid-century that stimulated the greatest interest. They generally appeared with a text that explained the meaning of their contents to the public, as in the comte de Caylus's *Recueil d'Antiquités* published in 1752–3, and Giovanni Battista Passeri's *Picturae Etruscorum in vasculis* published in Rome in 1767–75.[10] The greatest and most influential volume was perhaps d'Hancarville's *Collections of Etruscan, Greek, and Roman Antiquities from the Cabinet of the Hon. W. Hamilton* (1767–76), which portrayed the collection of Greek vases (then thought to be Etruscan as they were excavated in Italy) which the British envoy, Sir William Hamilton, had assembled during his stay in Naples (fig. 202). Its introduction expresses the hope that it will be used by designers. These volumes led to a renewed appreciation of true classical vases as decorative motifs, though they seem to have been considered most appropriate for libraries, where, with classical busts, they decorated the tops of bookcases.[11]

However, it was Greece that provided the main focus for intellectual discussion. This was despite the fact that few of its proponents had visited it, and knowledge had to come from publications such as Stuart and Revett's *Antiquities of Athens* or prints published by Robert Sayer. The main prophet of this movement, Johann Joachim Winckelmann, was neither French nor English, but German. He had studied science and theology at the Universities of Halle and Jena, before going to Dresden in 1754 to act as librarian for Cardinal Passionei. This introduced him to classical works of art, and in 1755 he published *Reflections on the Imitation of a Greek Art in Painting and Sculpture*, in which he criticised the 'caricatura-carvings, and favourite shells' of the rococo as being as false as the grotesques criticised by Vitruvius.[12] In 1758 he became librarian to Cardinal Albani in Rome and published his *History of Ancient Art* in 1764, in which he praised early Greek art for simplicity, even though he knew it only through Roman copies. It was this kind of propaganda which led to the revived classical style of the second half of the eighteenth century being christened, with very little justification, the *goût grec* (the Greek taste) in its earliest stages.

There is much dispute as to which country showed the first signs of a classical revival in the decorative arts. In France the designer Louis-Joseph Le Lorrain (1715–59) supplied neo-classical designs for the francophile Count Tessin in Sweden as early as 1754, and went on to design a suite of furniture for comte de La Live de Jully which was reminiscent of the severe and sombre work of the great cabinet-maker André-Charles Boulle (1642–1732).[13] By contrast the first signs of a classical revival in Britain are generally held

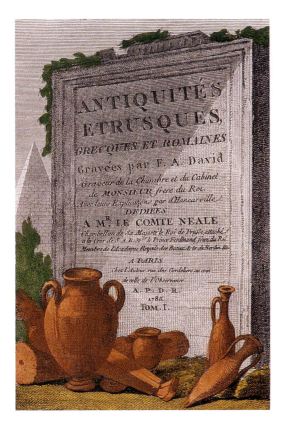

202 Frontispiece to d'Hancarville's *Antiquités Etrusques, Grecques et Romaines*, French edition, Paris, 1785.

to be James 'Athenian' Stuart's designs for the painted room at Spencer House, London of about 1759, which are altogether lighter in feel, with painted decoration in the form of pilasters and grotesques, and suggestions for classical straight-legged furniture against the walls.[14] For many British patrons this was simply a perpetuation of their long-standing Palladian classicism, and visitors to France, such as Horace Walpole, were unable to understand why the French considered the *goût grec* to be new.[15]

Though the origins of neo-classical art in Europe are still not entirely clear, it is certain that, in Paris at any rate, by the mid 1760s neo-classicism had become the dominant mode of taste for any persons with aspirations to be in fashion, and was

203 Vase 'antique ferré'. Soft-paste porcelain, painted in enamel colours by Jean-Louis Morin and gilt. Height 35.8 cm. Sèvres, 1769. The Wallace Collection, London.

204 Group of five Sèvres vases in the neo-classical taste, the smaller pair datemarked for 1764. Height 53.8 to 38 cm. Photograph courtesy of Antique Porcelain Company, London.

noted as such by visitors from abroad.[16] It soon descended to such items as millinery and braids, and was clearly a 'selling point' for modern goods.[17]

The *goût grec* made its first appearance in ceramics at the royal porcelain factory of Sèvres, where designers of the most fashionable taste were employed. It manifested itself first in display pieces such as vases, which could be prominently displayed as proud testimony of their owner's advanced taste. They might stand, in garnitures of three or five, on the chimney piece, or singly, on a pier table in front of a looking glass.[18] This was a great deal cheaper than rebuilding one's town house or remodelling the main apartment in the new taste! Sèvres developed a range of vases based on the motif of the fluted classical column, of ponderous outline and sombre dark-blue colour, which contrast with the brightly coloured and gaily decorated pot-pourris which Sèvres manufactured in the 1750s and early 1760s.[19] The function of these new vases was not to hold flowers, fresh or dried, but to act as minor works of architecture or sculpture in themselves, embodying in miniature all the taste and ingenuity that one might find in a palace or pavilion.

A vase christened *urne antique* in a restrained rococo manner had been produced at Sèvres from as early as 1755.[20] However, this was presumably just a temporary fashion, and it was not until 1761 that we encounter the first true manifestations of the *goût grec* at Sèvres, in a version of the famous *pot pourri à vaisseau* with a severe neo-classical base and gilt-bronze stand.[21] From 1762 onwards the factory began to produce an enormous range of vases of classical form, which made a considerable impact on European ceramic history. The well-known *vase ferré* is thought to date from about 1762, possibly one of the models exhibited by the sculptor Falconet at Versailles in December, 1762.[22] This was a design in which four large oval panels are moulded as if tied to the body of the vase by clamps or rings. These provided vehicles for the painters to produce painted *réserves* of military or harbour scenes (fig. 203). A low oval vase *à feuilles d'acante*, known from 1763 is, as its title suggests, moulded with acanthus leaves on the base.[23] *Vases grecs à rosettes* were produced from 1764. They well illustrate the ponderous nature of French neo-classicism in its early phases, with the Greek key pattern around the neck, incised straight fluting, heavy festoons, and the ungainly handles with a right-angle turn *à la grecque*. They possibly represent an unsuccessful attempt by Jean-Claude Duplessis to accommodate himself to the exigencies of the neo-classical style;[24] an ungainly garniture of five dates from 1764 (fig. 204). Other, more attractive, sets of vases are the vases *à jets d'eau*, and vases *avec des cygnes* possibly designed by Duplessis around 1765.[25] They are essentially a neo-classical reworking of the vases *pots pourris fontaines* that he had designed in the 1750s, with broken columns replacing the curved body of the earlier vases.[26]

205 Vase in the neo-classical taste, probably designed by E. M. Falconet. Soft-paste porcelain, painted in enamel colours with a scene of Pygmalion after a group by Falconet and gilt. Height 46.5 cm. Sèvres, *c*.1765–70. The National Trust, Waddesdon Manor.

Though Duplessis was still head of the modelling studio, some of the new designs may be due to the sculptor Etienne-Maurice Falconet (1716–91), who was in charge of the artistic direction at Sèvres until 1766.[27] In 1763 he was praised specifically for the new shapes that he had invented (fig. 205).[28] The artistic adviser Bachelier took over Falconet's responsibility for sculpture in 1766 and in the annual lists of new models for vases during the period 1765 to 1768 six were specifically attributed to him. In turn he relinquished responsibility to the sculptor L. S. Boizot in 1773, who held the post until 1800. Since it is difficult to link models listed in the factory records to existing examples, there is often an element of doubt as to their designer.

Many of these early vases are quite rare and one must assume that their ponderous nature made them commercial failures. Rather more attractive are the *vases Danemark à godrons* of 1764 in which neo-classicism appears in a lighter vein. They were copied from a book of designs written by the sculptor J. J. Saly which he published in Rome in 1746.[29] Other popular vases included the *vase à panneaux* of about 1766, possibly designed by Falconet, and the *vase à glands* of about 1768.[30] These latter especially seem to have been made with the intention of exhibiting some finely painted panels in *réserve*, an increasingly important preoccupation as neo-classicism developed.

Falconet seems also to have been behind a major stylistic change in figure-modelling at Sèvres, leading to the production of biscuit figures that no longer imitated sugar sculpture but full-scale classical or classical-style sculpture. This presumably reflects his own interest in producing small-scale decorative marble sculptures for the drawing-room rather than the garden or the sculpture gallery.[31] Naturally some copied his own full-scale models (fig. 206); these figures now seem to have had a dual function, acting either as small-scale decorative features for room decoration, often under glass, or as major centrepieces for dessert or table decoration that grew increasingly didactic as time went on, with attempts to educate the diner in classical history or mythology while he enjoyed his meal!.[32]

Neo-classicism took correspondingly longer to affect the design of whole dinner services, where modifications in modelling would have had to be made to every item in the service. The first signs of neo-classicism in table wares were in the individually decorated *écuelles* of the 1760s, and in the enamelled decoration of certain table services, such as the *Service avec Petits Vazes et Guirlandes* delivered to the king's mistress, Madame du Barry, in 1771. Here the border design of garlands and vases may be due to the painter Augustin de Saint-Aubin.[33] However, the old rococo forms of Duplessis continued to dominate the manufacture of table services to the end of the century, although he modified his designs for tureens incorporating classical features such as husks of corn in about 1775.[34]

The greatest example of neo-classicism in dinner services was the 'Cameo' service ordered by Catherine the Great of Russia in 1776. Her agent, Prince Grigori Potemkin, wrote that the service should be 'in the best and newest style, with Her Majesty's monogram on every piece' and 'without any deviation from antique models, with reproductions of cameos'.[35] It comprises a range of plates and bottle-coolers, wineglass-coolers, ice-cream pails, and other items for the dessert, all modelled in the new taste with straight sides and cameo decoration. It was intended for sixty people, with a centrepiece of ninety-one biscuit figures centred on a bust of Minerva (representing the empress) surrounded by the muses sculpted by the sculptor Boizot, who had already worked for Catherine in 1769. The great innovation (and expense) was in the cameo decoration, which in the bottle-coolers and ice-pails consisted of inlaid medallions carved from layers of porcelain, made in a grinding shop specially set up for the purpose. The resulting service is one of the great triumphs of neo-classicism, although few today would want to reproduce its style exactly (fig. 207).

206 Figure of Cupid by Falconet. Soft-paste porcelain, unglazed, on a stand painted in enamel colours and gilt. Inscribed around the base 'Omnia Vincit Amor'. Height 30.4 cm. Sèvres, 1761–63. The Wallace Collection, London.

207 Ice-pail from the service for Catherine the Great of Russia. Soft-paste porcelain painted in enamel colours and gilt. Height 23.7 cm. Sèvres, 1778, The Wallace Collection, London.

Developments in England

The English porcelain factories, though similarly obsessed with the need to provide a wide range of neo-classical vases, were perhaps less innovative stylistically. They lacked the fashionable in-house designers that existed at Sèvres, and were much more dependent on published designs for ideas and inspiration, as well as copies and variations of Continental models. Here the market for what was essentially chimney-piece decoration was catered for by the great porcelain factory of Chelsea (soon to be run in tandem with that at Derby), and in pottery by the up-and-coming Wedgwood factory. Both were in competition with makers of chimney-piece deco-

208 Engraved trade card of William Duesbury's premises in Covent Garden, *c*.1773–4.

ration in other materials, such as the metalworker Matthew Boulton of Birmingham, who specialised in sets of vases in polished stone, such as Derby Bluejohn, mounted in elegant gilt-bronze mounts.[36] Both the products of the factory at Chelsea, run by William Duesbury of Derby, and Wedgwood's work in Staffordshire are documented by two remarkable survivals of business correspondence; that of William Duesbury and his son of the same name with his London agent, Joseph Lygo, preserved in Derby Public Library, dating to the later eighteenth centur; and that of Wedgwood with his London agent Thomas Bentley, which survives in the Wedgwood archives at the University of Keele. Both sets of correspondence are invaluable in tracing the day-to-day development and running of a fashionable ceramics factory in response to changes in taste in late eighteenth-century England.

The factory at Chelsea had been taken over in 1770 by William Duesbury, the independent decorator who had been proprietor of the Derby factory since 1756. He ran it concurrently with the factory at Derby until 1784, when the Chelsea factory was closed down and the remaining stock and wares were sold. He seems to have been instrumental in introducing new shapes and styles of decoration to the factories, including painted decoration copied from the Paris edition of Ovid's *Metamorphoses* of 1768–1771, whose elegant neo-classical designs were used by a number of ceramic factories throughout Europe.[37] These are listed in the 1771 auction catalogue, which also includes some vases which are clearly straight copies of recent Sèvres shapes. In 1773 he opened new shop premises in Bedford Street, Covent Garden, London, which presumably showed his new range of ornaments in the neo-classical taste, as evinced by his trade card (fig. 208).[38]

Duesbury seems to have commissioned a new range of vases based on printed designs. These have been shown to derive from engravings from the school of Raphael of the sixteenth century, through to vase-types designed by French classical designers of the seventeenth and eighteenth centuries. A pair of vases in the Victoria and Albert

209 Jacques-François-Joseph Saly (1717–76). *Design for a vase*. Engraving.

210 Vase on stand. Soft-paste porcelain, painted in enamel colours and gilt. Derby, *c*.1773. Victoria & Albert Museum, London.

Museum are derived from engravings after Raphael's pupil Polidoro da Caravaggio,[39] and other designs were taken from the group of French designers working in Rome in the 1740s and 50s. This includes those of Edme Bouchardon (1698–1762), featuring a design for a vase with a river-god handle and spirally-fluted neck,[40] and Jacques-François-Joseph Saly (1717–76) (figs 209, 210), whose design of an egg-shaped vase with two facing sphinxes acting as handles on the top appears in a pair of Derby vases on the Long Gallery chimney piece at Syon House, Middlesex, neatly contrasting with the Greek vases ranged above the bookcases above them.[41]

An important development at Derby consisted of figures in unglazed 'biscuit' porcelain, in imitation of those made at Sèvres and Tournai. They first appear in the Derby sale catalogues for 1771. The best-known are derived from prints after the famous woman artist Angelica Kauffmann (1741–1807), including a famous group of 'Three Graces' copied from a print published in 1776 (figs 211, 212). A well-known group of George III and his family after Zoffany is probably modelled by the sculptor John Bacon, as it is stylistically similar to his marble bust of the king. It is noticeable that such groups were more expensive in biscuit than enamelled, since the body had to be perfect. However, we should beware of thinking of all later eighteenth-century Derby production as purely neo-classical, as the auction catalogues testify to the endless groups of shepherds and shepherdesses, and putti in the rococo style. Some of these may have been by the Tournai modeller Nicolas Gauron, who was recommended to Duesbury by the china-dealer Thomas Morgan in 1770.[42]

Derby continued to make biscuit figures, with a resurgence of energy coming in the later eighteenth century (1784–90) under William Duesbury II, partly due to commissions and encouragement from the London-based royal clock-maker Benjamin Vulliamy.[43] Some may have been modelled by John Deare, an assistant of the sculptor

John Bacon, including a large clock, decorated with biscuit figures from Derby, inscribed 'designed by Benjamin Vulliamy, clockmaker to the King' (fig. 213).[44] These works are all in a somewhat frigid neo-classical style, with few concessions to more popular taste. Works of greater charm were supplied by the Swiss modeller J. J. Spaengler (active at Derby 1790–5), who created a range of figures of sentimental character, often of shepherds and shepherdesses, from about 1790 until his dismissal in 1795.[45]

Developments in neo-classical design were picked up by a number of other porcelain factories and decorators in London, and rapidly spread through all the factories, although never completely dominating total output. The London decorator James Giles appears to be responsible for a large number of items of Worcester porcelain, mostly tea-wares, decorated with festoons of husks and paterae, a design which also appears on items of glassware attributed to him.[46] His work shows how the neo-classical style was applied not just to large vases for display (to which it could claim some historical links), but also to modern fashions such as tea and coffee drinking, which could reflect the advanced taste of the hostess.[47]

One of the most innovative factories for neo-classical design was the hard-paste porcelain factory at Bristol, which used china-clay found in Cornwall under patent. It had moved from Plymouth in about 1770. Under the proprietorship of Richard Champion many of its products were decorated in an austere classical style, with festoons linking cameos in the manner of the Sèvres dinner service for Madame du Barry of 1771. Champion also made some very fine figures, including two groups of figures of the *Elements* and the *Seasons*, which he commissioned from an unknown modeller to whom he wrote some still-surviving letters, explaining that he wanted the figures to be in classical garb (fig. 214).[48] He also made a number of small oval biscuit-plaques with coats-of-arms in high-fired porcelain as gifts to prominent patrons and influential politicians. However, Champion was in the event unsuccessful, as the patent was restricted to porcelain only, and he moved up to Staffordshire

211 William Wyland, after Angelica Kauffmann. *The Three Graces Adorning Pan*. Stipple Engraving, 1776.

212 Group of 'The Graces Adorning Pan'. Unglazed (*biscuit*) porcelain. Height 27.9 cm. Derby, *c*.1776. Royal Museum of Scotland, Edinburgh.

213 Clock by Benjamin Vulliamy (1747–1811), the case with Derby biscuit porcelain figure set on a marble base inset with a Wedgwood cameo. Height 35 cm. Derby Museums and Art Gallery, Derby.

by November 1781, where a consortium of potters used it to found the successful and productive factory of New Hall.[49] In the meantime, Cornish clays were to be used by one of the great potters of the age – Josiah Wedgwood.

We have already encountered Wedgwood as an important pottery maker in Staffordshire in the early 1760s, where he was a proponent in the development of coloured glazes and finer earthenware for everyday use, with which he had achieved great success. These would have been for a largely middle-class market, and Wedgwood seems at this stage to have been content to follow taste and fashion rather than to initiate it. However, over the course of the next ten or twenty years he developed a new range of techniques and designs which made him the leading ceramics manufacturer throughout the whole of Europe.

The basis of Wedgwood's success lay in two things: firstly his ability to refine pottery in such a way that the body became acceptable to the upper classes, and secondly, his attention to design and marketing, so that his wares were sought by fashionable society throughout Europe. He was greatly aided by the regularity of neo-classical ornament, which meant that he could take advantage of new techniques such as engine-turning, whereby grooved and incised ornament is applied to a round body by means of a lathe. Although he is perhaps the first manufacturer to fully exploit the processes of mass-production, it is a fallacy to suppose that he achieved his success by offering his goods more cheaply than other manufacturers; his products were offered to the rich first – at higher prices – before he sought a more middling market.[50] His success lay in gauging fashionable taste at any one time and then creating products which mirrored the perceived social need.

This success was achieved with the help of his London partner, the Liverpool merchant Thomas Bentley.[51] Bentley was, like Wedgwood, a Dissenter, but better educated and in touch with metropolitan fashion. Wedgwood maintained a showroom in Liverpool, which sold lesser items,[52] and also opened a London showroom in Charles Street in 1765, for grander wares, which moved to larger and more extensive premises in Great Newport Street in 1767, and finally on to Greek Street in 1774.[53] In 1767 Wedgwood and Bentley drew up an agreement to divide decorative or 'ornamental' wares between them, the domestic or 'useful' wares being sold on Wedgwood's behalf, which became official in 1769.[54] Bentley wrote more-or-less weekly to Wedgwood, keeping an eye on Wedgwood's decorating works at Chelsea, which ran from 1771–4, and commenting on taste in the capital. In turn he received Wedgwood's news of developments at Burslem. In 1773 they published the first *Ornamental Catalogue*, the first illustrated catalogue of shapes published by a ceramic manufacturer. This partnership lasted until Bentley's death in 1780 (when their joint stock was auctioned) and led to the development of Wedgwood as a manufacturer of international importance.

Their most important products were vases in the neo-classical taste that was a direct response to what Wedgwood called the 'vase madness' that affected Britain in the later 1760s. Bentley wrote to him in May, 1769, that 'Vases was all the cry' in London.[55] The first Wedgwood vases, dating from the mid-1760s, seem to have been some rather cumbersome examples in the Palladian style, made in the pale earthenware body subsequently to be called 'creamware', which Wedgwood was developing at that time.[56] But Wedgwood soon developed a more successful range of vases imitating marbles and coloured stones using the traditional Staffordshire techniques of coloured clays, or coloured slips, in imitation of stone or marble. Granite was imitated by applying powdered oxides onto the surface, a product which Wedgwood called 'pebble ware'.[57] In partnership with Bentley he made a wide range of regularly-shaped oval vases, the bodies in imitation of polished stones, sometimes with the addition of a medallion in the classical taste, and always monumental in effect (fig. 215). The handles of these vases

214 Figure of *Fire* from a group of *The Elements*. Hard-paste porcelain, painted in enamel colours. Bristol, *c*.1775. Royal Museum of Scotland, Edinburgh.

are almost invariably gilded, imitating the gilt-bronze handles applied to mounted stone-vases of the kind made by Matthew Boulton of Birmingham, with whom, in 1768, Wedgwood had talks on possible collaboration, but without result.[58] Such gilding was to prove unpopular, and Wedgwood reduced the amount of 'offensive Gilding' in response to suggestions from Sir William Hamilton in 1772.[59]

The most important of Wedgwood's early achievements in vase production was the perfection of the black stoneware body, which he called 'basalt'. This body could imitate the colour and shapes of 'Etruscan' or Greek vases which were being excavated in Italy and had become so fashionable, principally through the publication of d'Harcanville's *Collections of Etruscan, Greek, and Roman Antiquities from the Cabinet of the Hon. W. Hamilton* (1767–76).[60] The first such items were put on the market in 1768, unpainted vases which Wedgwood himself christened 'Etruscan'.[61] When, in June of 1769, Wedgwood opened a new factory on a site north of Stoke that he christened 'Etruria', he threw six classically formed black basalt vases, while Bentley turned the wheel. Their form and decoration was copied from a plate in Hamilton's vases, in a technique which he christened 'encaustic' after the description of the comte de Caylus.[62] They were inscribed on the reverse: 'JUNE XIII .M.D.CC.LXIX./One of the first Days Productions/at/Etruria in Staffordshire,/by/Wedgwood and Bentley' (fig. 216).

Wedgwood dedicated much research to the different types of vases to be made, clarifying, with the help of the architect Sir William Chambers, the distinction between 'vases' and 'urns', the latter being more monumental and lacking handles.[63] His letters to Bentley of the later 1760s testify to his relentless search for new vase types, as well as a showroom in which to display them.[64] A great number of these vase shapes were derived from prints by French designers of the seventeenth and eighteenth

215   Group of vases, with decoration in imitation of agate and granite. Cream-coloured earthenware, decorated in coloured glazes and gilt. Height of tallest 17 cm. Staffordshire, factory of Josiah Wedgwood, 1769–80. The British Museum, London.

centuries in the classical tradition, which, as we have seen, were also used at Derby. The vase with a handle in the form of a fishtail (fig. 217), dating to about 1770, appears to be derived from a print after Jacques Stella (1596–1657), whose volume of vase designs, published in 1667, was much plagiarised by Wedgwood (fig. 218). Like Duesbury at Derby, he also copied designs by Jacques-François-Joseph Saly (1717–76) and Edme Bouchardon (1698–1762), whose work had been pirated by the English engraver Vivares in 1771. Both Derby and Wedgwood were to copy a Bouchardon design of a vase with a clam-shaped base with mermaid handles in black basalt, transforming the mermaids into mermen.

Wedgwood also turned to ready-made models and casts supplied by professional sculptors and modellers. The sculptor John Bacon was supplying neo-classical models to Wedgwood by 1769, and continued to do so until at least 1777. Wedgwood had also attempted to buy models from model-supplier Mrs Landré as early as 1769. However, the most famous of all model-suppliers was the sculptor John Cheere, whose premises on the corner of Hyde Park were one of the first sights to greet a traveller to London. Here he sold statuary in lead or plaster, the latter sometimes bronzed to look like metal. The works were by a variety of artists, old and new, including Cheere himself. In 1774 he sold Wedgwood four plaster busts of Shakespeare, Plato, Aristotle and Homer at 10/6 each, intended, with true Greek vases, to act as decoration above library bookcases, where they added to the serious nature of the room. Wedgwood went on to make purchases from his former employees James Hoskins and Benjamin Grant in 1774, 1775, and 1779 of busts of Addison, Chaucer, Congreve, Horace, Johnson and Swift (fig. 219).[65]

Wedgwood was always conscious of the rivalry with other manufacturers, most

216 'First day' vase. Black stoneware (*basalt*), painted with 'encaustic' painting after a vase from the collection of Sir William Hamilton. Height 25.5 cm. Staffordshire, factory of Josiah Wedgwood, 1769. The Wedgwood Museum, Barlaston, Staffordshire.

217 Title page from the *Livre de Vases* by Jacques Stella, Paris, *c.*1667.

218 Vase. Black basalt. Height 31.3 cm. Staffordshire, factory of Josiah Wedgwood, 1773–80. The Royal Museum of Scotland, Edinburgh.

219 Bust of Jonathan Swift. Black basalt. Staffordshire, factory of Josiah Wedgwood. Royal Museum of Scotland, Edinburgh.

obviously Matthew Boulton of the Soho works in Birmingham, as well as the products of the Derby factory. Boulton's polished stone vases in ormolu mounts had become so fashionable that Queen Charlotte asked him to replace the china vases on her bedroom chimney piece with his own in 1770. However, they were not a commercial success, and he began to wind down production after 1773, when the rage for chimney-piece ornaments among the aristocracy had run its course.[66] Wedgwood was also aware of developments at Sèvres,[67] and developments in the mounting of vases in ormolu in Paris.[68] In general he seem to have wanted to create a fashionable style appropriate to the bodies that he had devised, and anticipated the thrill of beating the French at their own game, as in 1769, when he had discovered to his amazement that the French had renounced the rococo style – what he called 'frippery' – and were favouring the neo-classical style.[69] However, he was still interested in Sèvres shapes and styles, and by November he was having drawings made of Sèvres vases in the possession of the china-dealer Thomas Morgan and also Lord March,[70] though Bentley was dismissive of them when he visited the factory itself in 1776.[71]

Wedgwood was also developing other bodies and by 1775 he had developed a version of the hard red Staffordshire stoneware, which he christened 'rosso antico', whose 'extreme vulgarity' reminded him of earlier Staffordshire teapots.[72] He preferred the light 'fawn-coloured' wares, which were later issued as 'caneware', used for a variety of small, decorative pieces, including a teapot in the form of bamboo leaves based on a Chinese design. However, this body was not perfected by Wedgwood until about 1787, after Bentley's death in 1780, using local yellow clays, rather than trying to tint the body.[73] It was used for imitations of pie-crust in tureens, a fashion started during a flour shortage.[74] He also seems to have developed a fine white ceramic akin to porcelain.[75]

Wedgwood's great contribution to everyday ceramics was the development and production of 'creamware', which was especially useful for table or 'useful' wares, which he produced in partnership with his cousin Thomas Wedgwood, independently of Bentley. This was a light-coloured earthenware covered in a clear lead-glaze made in Staffordshire from the 1740s onwards; in France it was known as *faïence fine* and the subject of import regulations from the 1740s. Wedgwood improved the body through the use of Cornish clays for which Richard Champion of the Bristol factory held the patent in porcelain production, the subject of much parliamentary dispute with Wedgwood. Wedgwood's creamware was in production from as early as 1763, when he described it as 'a species of earthenware for the table, quite new in its appearance, covered with a rich and brilliant glaze bearing sudden alterations of heat and cold, manufactured with ease and expedition, and consequently cheap having every requisite for the purpose intended'.[76]

Wedgwood's domination of the creamware market began in about 1765 when he was the only potter prepared to execute a 'complete sett of tea things, with a gold ground and raised flowers upon it in green' for Queen Charlotte, wife of George III.[77] Soon after that he christened his creamware 'Queen's ware',[78] and launched a ceramic body whose supremacy in the world markets would remain unchallenged for nearly fifty years. The earliest pieces seem to have been sent for decoration to the Liverpool transfer-printers John Sadler (1720–89) and Guy Green (retired 1799), and were printed in red, black and even purple.[79] In 1765 he made creamware copies of the Duke of Bedford's Sèvres dinner service for tableware shapes.[80] However, Wedgwood developed the style of the shapes more and more in the neo-classical mode.[81] He was soon able to offer a range of standard shapes to his customers, with sample border patterns to chose from pattern books kept on the premises of his London showroom at Greek Street, of which copies were kept at Etruria, for the reference of the painters there (fig. 220).[82]

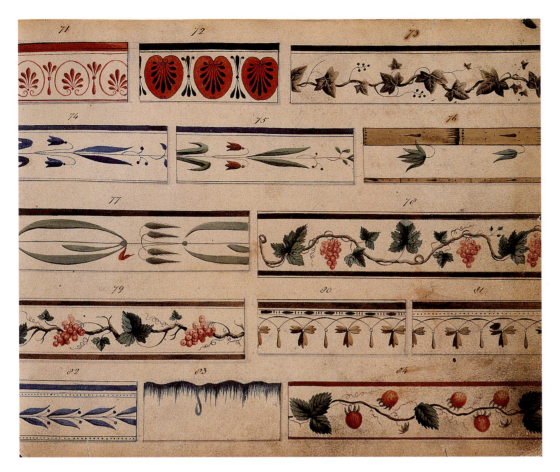

It was at this time that British dinners took on their traditional character of meat and vegetables that we know today, although they followed the basic overall symmetrical layout of *service à la francaise*, often using a creamware service. Parson Woodforde of Norfolk, a man of gargantuan appetite, had acquired 'a compleat Table service of the cream-coloured ware, with some other useful things' by 1777.[83] Elizabeth Raffald's *The Experienced English Housekeeper* of 1769 shows how these were laid out in the first and second courses of dinner (figs 221, 222). In the first course there are a pair of 'transparent' and 'Hare' soups, which were 'removed' to make way for other dishes, and a wide variety of hams, turkey, beef, lamb and pork, surrounded by dishes of vegetables, in the second course. This tallies with one of Parson Woodforde's descriptions of dinner in 1794 which consisted of:

> First Course at the Upper End, stewed Tench, Veal Soup, best part of a Rump of Beef boiled, 2 rost [sic] Chicken and a Ham, Harrico [sic] Mutton, Custard Puddings, backed [sic] Mutton Pies, mashed Potatoes in 3. Scollop Shells browned over, Roots. 2 Dishes. Second Course. At the upper End, Rabbitts fricasseed, at the lower End Couple of Ducks rosted, Trifle in the Middle, blamange, Cheesecakes, Maccaroni, and small Rasberry-tartlets. Desert of Fruit mostly that sent by me to them, Peaches, Nectarines, and three kinds of Plumbs.[84]

Wedgwood was especially keen to develop the export market,[85] and his greatest opportunity for international renown came in 1773, when he was commissioned, via Lord Cathcart, the British Ambassador to Russia, to make a service for Catherine II.

220 Page from a Wedgwood pattern book showing borders for creamware. The Wedgwood Museum, Barlaston, Staffordshire.

221 Layout of the first course of dinner, from Elizabeth Raffald's *The Experienced English Housekeeper*, 1769.

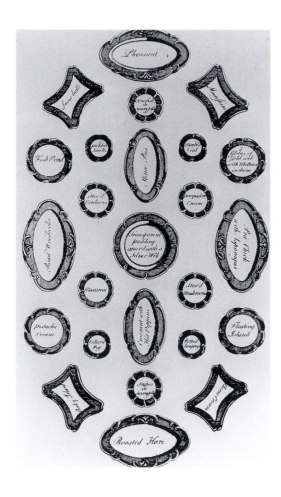

222 Layout of the second course of dinner, from Elizabeth Raffald's *The Experienced English Housekeeper*, 1769.

Wedgwood had already supplied a simple dinner service of standard shapes decorated with husks and flowers in mulberry pink, but this newer service was to be more ambitious, with specially modelled items. It was to comprise 952 pieces, each painted with a different view of a scene in the British Isles, 'the noblest plan ever yet laid down or undertaken by any Manufacturer in Great Britain,' as he wrote to Bentley in July, 1773. Each scene was painted in what Bentley called 'a delicate black' (in fact, grey to dark-purple brown) and the borders consisted of leaf decoration containing a medallion painted with a frog in green, as the service was destined for the palace at *La Grenouillière* ('the froggery', so-called after its marshy site) (fig. 223). Wedgwood had originally intended that each scene should be individually studied, and hired a professional artist, Stringer, to make drawings; however, it was clear that this was too ambitious, and he had recourse to prints and paintings lent by owners, or books such as George Bickham's *Beauties of Stowe* (1750–6) and Sir William Chambers' *Descriptions of the Garden and Buildings at Kew* (1771). Most of the painting was carried out in Wedgwood's decorating studio at Chelsea.[86] Although many of the shapes were derived from his standard repertoire, some unusual items, such as the ice-pail surmounted by a figure of 'Winter', were made specially for the service. It was shown at the new premises at 12/13 Greek Street in 1774, and cost Wedgwood £2,290, of which

223 Plate from the 'Frog' service. Creamware, painted in enamel colours. Length 35.5 cm. Staffordshire factory of Josiah Wedgwood, *c*.1773. The British Museum, London.

224 Cruet set. Creamware with enamelled inscriptions. Height 21.5 cm. Probably Leeds, *c.*1770. Temple Newsam House, Leeds.

only £51 was for the pottery itself, the rest being paid for the elaborate decoration; Catherine paid £2,700 by October 1774. As Wedgwood had said, his aim was not to make a vast profit, but to demonstrate the capabilities of his factory to all the world.[87]

Queen's ware came to dominate dinner tables not just in Britain, but the whole of the Western world. It was soon copied in England by a great number of other manufacturers, who produced similar pattern books, inscribed in several languages, with which their products could be sold internationally. The main centres of production seem to have been Staffordshire and south Yorkshire, in the area around Leeds (fig. 224). The best-known manufacturer after Wedgwood seems to have been the Leeds firm of Hartley, Green's and Co., which issued a pattern book with texts in German in 1783, and French in 1785. It offered an enormous range of objects 'Enamel'd, Printed or Orna-mental with Gold to any Pattern, also with Coats of Arms, Cyphers, Landscapes, &c, &c.'.[88] One of the specialities of Leeds creamware seems to have been the delicate

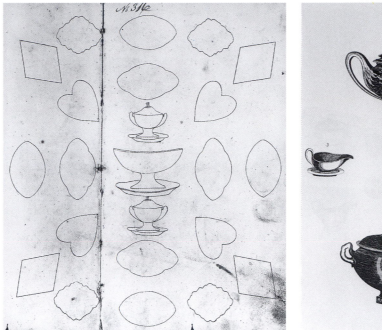

225 Drawing of the layout of a dessert service, showing the arrangement of the differently shaped plates, with tureens in the centre for cream and jam. *Leeds Pottery Pattern Books*, Courtesy of Leeds Public Library.

226 Page from a pattern book issued by Whitehead's of Hanley, 1798, showing the design of tureens and sauceboats.

227 Jug, decorated with colours ('Prattware'). Staffordshire, *c*.1800. Royal Museum of Scotland, Edinburgh.

hand-piercing of the surface of the body, much imitated in the later nineteenth century. This was especially suitable for the making of dessert wares, and an illustration from the factory record books gives us our best surviving illustration of the symmetrical layout of these services, with heart- and trapezoidal-shaped dishes, all surrounding central comports and tureens for fruit and jams (fig. 225).[89]

Pattern books were also issued by a number of other potteries, including Dunderdale (1796) and Whitehead's of Hanley (1798) (fig. 226). The objects depicted in these catalogues are often virtually identical, and thus cannot always be used as guides to identifying the manufacturer. Often such items were transfer-printed with popular subjects in black by outside workshops, such as that of John Robinson (formerly employed by Sadler and Green of Liverpool), Thomas Fletcher or Thomas Baddeley, both of whom signed prints.[90] Much was exported to Holland, where it was decorated, often with religious imagery, at Delft and other centres.[91] Most obviously, it put many continental tinglaze manufacturers out of business; as early as 1765 MacPherson, in the *Annals of Commerce*, observed that 'Formerly, we ate all our meat off plates made in Delf [sic] in Holland; now the Dutch generally use our Staffordshire plates.'[92]

The utilitarian body of creamware was also developed for a much more popular market by the Staffordshire pottery makers. The shapes and styles of decoration are much cruder than those made by the greater potters and are indicative of a lower market. Moulded items with splashes of red or yellow decoration were made, today often attributed to the Pratt family of Staffordshire (fig. 227).[93] The search for a body that could act as a substitute for porcelain continued and by the 1780s a variant of creamware, with a whiter body covered in a slightly blue-tinted cobalt glaze had been developed, called pearl-ware; Wedgwood refers to a 'Pearl White' ware as early as 1779.[94] The blue in the body produces a brilliant white effect which, combined with the lighter body, can be extremely effective in imitating porcelain. Staffordshire potters referred to it as 'china-glazed', and it was often transfer-printed in blue, so that it looks (and feels) very like English blue-and-white porcelain; in this respect it is the

228 'Toby' jug. Cream-coloured earthenware, painted in enamel colours. Height 25 cm. Staffordshire, *c*.1800. The Bowes Museum, Barnard Castle, Co. Durham.

229 'Fair Hebe' jug. Earthenware, painted in coloured glazes. Height 22 cm. Staffordshire, *c*.1788. Royal Museum of Scotland, Edinburgh.

immediate precursor of the vast quantities of blue-and-white pottery made in Staffordshire in the early nineteenth century.

The potters of Staffordshire also continued the making of wares in naturalistic shapes decorated in coloured glazes, but their main market now was outside the centres of fashionable taste, and they concentrated on the making of decorative figures for chimney pieces, distant relatives of the figures made by the great porcelain factories. The major makers of figures seem to have been the brothers John and Ralph Wood II, sons of the block-cutter Ralph Wood I (1715–72), who made a wide range of works of popular appeal. The most famous is perhaps the 'Toby' jug, a drinking-jug in the form of a stout eighteenth-century gentleman seated holding a jug. It was apparently based on a legendary drinker called Toby Fillpot (real name Henry Elwes) who is reputed to have drunk 2,000 gallons of 'stingo' (a very strong ale). The earlier ones are decorated with high-temperature underglaze colours of blue, yellow, brown, green and black. The design seems to be based on a print of 1761 and was made with variations by innumerable firms in Staffordshire (fig. 228).[95] Another satirical piece is the group of *The Vicar and Moses*, showing the vicar in church asleep above the preacher. All these works were made by a wide range of potteries in the region.[96] They were presumably modelled by independent sculptors, who sold their models to a number of different potters. The best-recorded of these was Jean Voyez, who in 1769 was working with a rival of Wedgwood's, Humphrey Palmer, producing black basalt vases in the neo-classical taste. In 1773 he issued a *Catalogue of intaglios and cameos . . . made by J. Voyez, sculptor*. However, his work did not long remain at this elevated level, and in 1788 he signed a well-known jug in the popular taste representing a rural courting couple inscribed 'Fair Hebe', often found decorated in coloured glazes (fig. 229).

Meanwhile, Wedgwood had been busy developing what remains to this day his best-known invention, the coloured stoneware called 'jasperware'. This is a kind of stoneware either coloured all the way through, or just on the surface ('dip'), with applied sprigged decoration in the classical style, to reproduce the effects of carved classical cameos. It was first marketed in the form of small medallions which had the appearance of carved cameos from classical antiquity. Some of the inspiration may have come from the work of the Scotsman James Tassie (1735–99), who won a prize from the Society for the Encouragement of Arts, Manufacturers and Commerce in 1766 for his paste portrait-medallions and reproductions of antique cameos;[97] about half the designs in Wedgwood and Bentley's first catalogue were taken from his models.[98]

Wedgwood began his experiments in the making of jasperware in about 1771,[99] but it was not until 1779 that he could advertise the product under its new name – 'Jasper' – in the sales catalogue of that year. The range of colours, which include pale blue and lilac, are reminiscent of the colour-schemes of fashionable architects such as Robert Adam (1728–92) and James Wyatt (1746–1813) in the later eighteenth century, and small plaques of jasperware did in fact feature in chimney pieces and furniture decoration.[100] The technique was soon imitated by other potters in Staffordshire, although frequently for the more mundane objects such as jugs for ale or water.

Wedgwood employed a variety of fashionable artists to provide him with designs for this new material that would prove attractive to a public demanding novelty. He used the artists Lady Diana Beauclerk (1724–1808) and Lady Templetown (1747–1823) to provide designs of children at play and maternal scenes called *Domestic Employments*, which were to have a long life and prove popular on domestic wares such as tea sets (fig. 230). The best-known association is that of the artist George Stubbs (1724–1806), who modelled two jasperware plaques of a *Frightened Horse* and *The Fall of Phaeton* in 1780, as well as using unglazed creamware plaques as a basis for enamel painting in the period 1775 to 1795.[101] The most important artistic link was with the sculptor John

230 Teaset decorated with scenes from *Domestic Employment* by Lady Templetown. Tinted stoneware (*Jasperware*). Width of tray 35 cm. Staffordshire, factory of Josiah Wedgwood, *c.*1790. Royal Museum of Scotland, Edinburgh.

231 *Pegasus* vase. Blue-tinted stoneware (*Jasperware*) with applied moulded decoration. Height 46.5 cm. Staffordshire, factory of Josiah Wedgwood, 1786. The British Museum, London.

Flaxman (1755–1826), nurtured by Wedgwood's business partner Thomas Bentley. By about 1775 Flaxman was producing wax models in London on commission from Wedgwood, which were sent up to Etruria to be translated into ceramic by such distinguished modellers as William Hackwood, Wedgwood's most accomplished 'repairer', one of a number of skilled modellers and assemblers of objects that Wedgwood encouraged.[102] By 1778 they had produced the large jasper reliefs of *The Dancing Hours* and *The Apotheosis of Homer*, the latter after a design in Hamilton's vases.[103] This was utilised on the *Pegasus* vase that Wedgwood presented to the British Museum in 1786, named after the figure of the flying horse Pegasus on its cover (fig. 231). Wedgwood records in his correspondence with Sir William Hamilton that he had thought at first of sending the vase to the King of Naples, priced at 20 guineas!

Wedgwood's most famous, though not perhaps the most artistically remarkable, product was the copy of the Roman Portland vase (fig. 232). This was a Roman cameo-glass vase, today in the British Museum, formerly in the collection of Sir William Hamiliton and sold to the Duchess of Portland in 1783. Wedgwood immediately asked the duke if he could copy it. Four years of painstaking work ensued, at first under the direction of Henry Webber; the first copy was presented to Erasmus Darwin in 1789. Copies were put on public view in the summer of 1790. It was an immediate success, and recognised as a real *tour de force*, but it does leave one wondering whether Wedgwood should have been concentrating his efforts on reproducing facsimiles of other works of art, rather than commissioning original designs.

Josiah Wedgwood died in 1795, leaving a son of the same name who was less successful in maintaining the firm's position as the most important ceramic-manufacturer in Europe. However, Wedgwood's activities inspired numerous imitators in

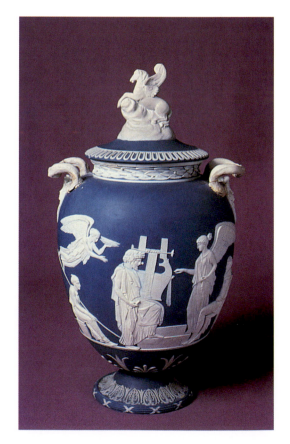

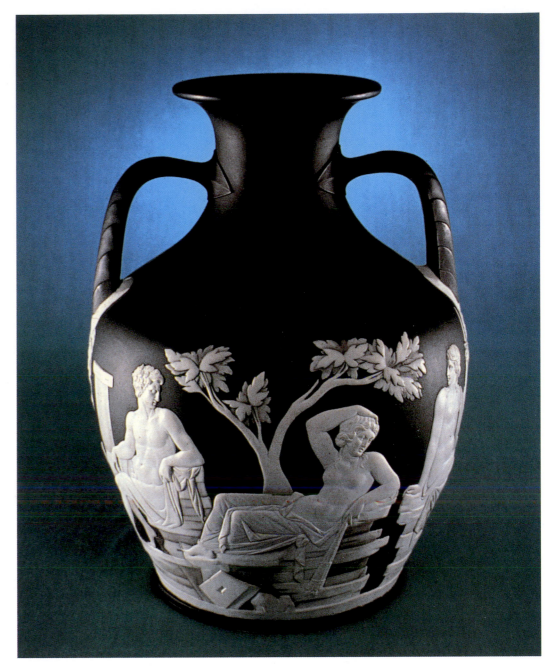

232 Reproduction of the Portland vase. Dark stoneware with applied decoration. Height 25.4 cm. Staffordshire, factory of Josiah Wedgwood, 1786–90. The British Museum, London.

233 Jug. Stoneware, with moulded decoration and a silver plated rim. Height 23.5 cm. Staffordshire, Adams, *c.*1800–10. The Bowes Museum, Barnard Castle, Co. Durham.

Overleaf, detail of fig. 255. Cup and saucer from the dairy service made for Rambouillet.

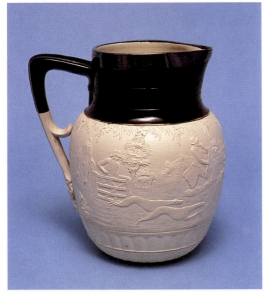

Staffordshire and elsewhere in England. The most famous are John Turner and his sons at Lane End (today Longton),[104] and William Adams of Tunstall (d. 1805), who made a variety of creamware and jasperware, but is best known for the production of a large number of moulded utilitarian items, such as beer-jugs moulded with hunting scenes, somewhat in the tradition of Nottingham stoneware hunting mugs.[105] The range of subjects also included archery lessons, cock-fights, and putti disporting themselves in the more classical Wedgwood style, according to the market they were intended for. Many of these jugs are mounted with a hall-marked silver rim, enabling a precise date – usually between 1790–1820 – to be given for their manufacture (fig. 233).

CHAPTER 12

The Spread of Neo-Classicism in Europe

The classical style spread throughout Europe in the late eighteenth century, although it did not penetrate all countries to the same extent. In general, it took longer to become established in Germany than in any other European country. The strength of the roco-co in Berlin and Munich meant that a style of straight lines and right angles was more difficult for fashionable taste to swallow than elsewhere. However, once established, it was with a dominance that contrasts with the variety of taste that can be found in other countries. In general, we can say that signs of the neo-classical style were very rare in Germany before 1760, were spreading by 1770, were in vogue by 1780 and well-nigh universal by 1790. By this time German courts and manufactories had adopted the style with a consistency and whole-heartedness that makes the products of other countries look rather tame. The engraving by Johann Esaias Nilson (1721–88), the engraver of the charming print of the *New Coffee House* of the 1760s (Chapter 8), of *Tearing up the Rococo* (fig. 234), makes the point about the severity of these changes.

There were of course isolated examples of the *Zopfstil* (severe style) as it was called in Germany before 1770, presumably in imitation of fashions in Paris. The picture of *The actors Clairon and Le Kain as Medea and Jason in the play 'Medée' by Longepierre* by Carl Van Loo (1705–65) of 1759 hangs in a heavy neo-classical frame in the picture gallery at Sanssouci quite at variance with the rococo frames around it.[1] A picture of the family of the goldsmith Müller of 1763 in the Historical Museum in former East Berlin shows a silver neo-classical vase prominently displayed. A painting of *The Love Letter* of 1760 by Johann E. Schenau (1737–1806) shows strict neo-classical detail in the furniture, but he was living in Paris from 1756–68.[2] The style appealed particularly to writers and thinkers: the title pages of Salomon Gessner's *Schriften* of 1762 make exten-sive use of heavy neo-classical detail.[3] More importantly, in 1764–5 Adam Friedrich von Seinsheim (1708–79), Prince Bishop of Würzburg, commissioned neo-classical decoration in his palace from the Bossi brothers of Stuttgart. However, the style was restricted solely to architectural features, for as late as 1768 statuary in the gardens was modelled after Meissen porcelain figures rather than true classical statues.[4]

The origins of this taste for classical art seem in part to have been a reaction against the pervasiveness of the French rococo style. The latter part of the eighteenth century saw the beginnings of a consistent national consciousness in Germany, and increased prosperity brought about the growth of a middle, intellectual class, which had no possi-ble allegiance, spiritual or political, to the court of Versailles.[5] Indeed, their reaction was one of mutual hostility. As early as 1740 the Frenchman Éléazar Mauvillon published his *Lettres françaises et germaniques sur les Français et les Allemands*, in which he asserted that Germans were incapable of artistic creativity.[6] A German response came in 1746 when Reiffstein published a polemic against rococo, making the usual criticisms of irrationality, asymmetry and departure from nature, coupled with a nationalistic and moral aspect to this degeneration, which his editor blamed on French influence.[7]

The greatest prophet of neo-classicism in Germany was of course the writer Johann Joachim Winckelmann (1717–68), who in his *History of Greek Art* singled out porcelain for criticism, describing it as a 'beautiful material' ('*schöne Materie*'), but claiming that it had never produced a real work of art, and that most porcelain was 'in childish taste' and was used mostly to make 'idiotic puppets', the charming little figures made for the dessert table that are so esteemed today.[8] The great German poet Goethe was aware of these changes and wrote a mock-serious lament for a rococo garden pavilion, stressing the severe nature of the innovations, in his poem *Hermann und Dorothea*, published in 1797.[9]

A major blow to the rococo style in ceramics was the diminution in the prestige of porcelain as a precious commodity in itself. No longer was it the 'white gold' of the early eighteenth century, whose secret had been sought by all the courts of Europe; in 1771 the comte de Milly published *L'Art de la Porcelaine* in which he described the manufacturing process of hard-paste porcelain, and publicised what had once been a closely guarded secret (fig. 235). The death-knell of the respect for porcelain as a material may be said to have come in 1781, when the new superintendant of the Art Collections in Dresden (and also director of the Meissen porcelain factory) Count Marcolini (1739–1814) cleared out the porcelain collection in the Japanese Palace in Dresden and stored it in the cellars, replacing it with a collection of books, coins and casts, some recently acquired from Rome from the collection of the neo-classical painter Anton Raphael Mengs (1728–79).[10] A visitor who saw it in store commented that 'Nothing about it is true at all!', which seems to be the beginning of a long history of porcelain as a 'false' and artificial material.[11]

Classicism was equated with nature, and the sense that a 'natural' world would be fairer and better if society were run by sense rather than tradition. The originator of the German literary revival of the later eighteenth century, the poet J. C. Gottsched (1700–66), had insisted that Nature was the sole arbiter of all taste and actions, and, being wholly reasonable, should be sought and imitated by all educated and literary men. The stress on finding a moral in things and the accompanying cult of 'Sensibility' – of cultivating and expressing emotions and responses to the natural world – was also thought to lead to man developing in his 'natural', unhampered state, freed from the fripperies and ceremonies imported from the court of Versailles.[12] The engraving by illustrator Daniel Chodowiecki (1726–1801) makes clear how classicism was seen as a return to nature, contrasting a couple in French court dress as *Af[f]ectation* with a seminude couple, reminiscent of classical models, as *Natur[e]* (fig. 236).

In the context of society, this approach tended to emphasise the central importance of civic duties, rather than allegiance to the person of the king and nobility, and led to a rise in the prestige of the administrative and professional classes. Personal worth now depended not on noble birth but on *Bildung*, a mixture of education and character formation, which led to the creation of a new, bourgeois, elite.[13] The cultural emphasis shifted from the court, in the sense of the palaces, ceremonies and other immediate appurtenances of the person of the sovereign, to the State, seen most clearly in the layout and development of towns and State institutions. This was the age of the rise of public museums and various academies designed to mould public taste. These were frequently under the artistic direction of one person who could thus impose a unified style on all buildings and royal manufactories (including the porcelain factory) within the State. Even the extravagant Carl Eugene of Württemberg, founder of the Ludwigsburg porcelain factory, began to reform his luxurious lifestyle. He dismissed the French Comedy, reduced his troupe of ballet dancers, and instead developed the

234 Johann Esaias Nilson (1721–88), *Tearing up The Rococo*. Engraving.

235 Painters at work. Illustration from the Comte de Milly, *L'Art de la Porcelaine*, 1771.

Afectation   *Natur*

236 Daniel Chodowiecki (1726–1801). *Af[f]ectation* contrasted with *Natur[e]*. Engravings from the *Göttinger Taschenkalender*, 1778.

public character of his domains, founding hospitals, a public library and museum, and botanic gardens in his native Stuttgart. He is best-known today as the overbearing patron of the poet Schiller.[14]

Apart from the loss of prestige of porcelain, the main problem for the German factories in this changing world was probably still the dominance of fashionable taste by France, represented by Sèvres, and rivalry with imports of pottery, especially creamware, made by Josiah Wedgwood and other manufacturers in England. These problems were exacerbated by increasing pressure from the various governments to make their State porcelain factories produce a profit, in line with new economic theories of the value of market forces which were becoming current. The two tastes tended to stimulate a certain polarity of taste; on the one hand, a taste for lavish all-over decoration, rich ground-colours and much use of gilding in the manner of Sèvres, for display or ornamental items; on the other hand, a tendency to produce objects of severe or austere character, with simple decoration and much of the body of the vessel left in the white, in the manner of English creamware. The design and decoration of much late eighteenth-century German porcelain tends to veer between these two extremes.

Most German factories were severely affected by the Seven Years War of 1756–63. The Meissen factory recovered only slowly from its ravages, since Frederick the Great of Prussia had invaded Saxony and expropriated much of the porcelain in the making at the Meissen factory.[15] With the coming of peace in 1763 the factory was put under a special commission, which complained that the painters at the factory clung to 'modern fantasy' and neglected the 'true beauty and antique'. An academy was set up in Meissen itself to teach drawing, which in 1764 was put under the charge of the court painter Christian Wilhelm Ernst Dietrich (1712–74), a friend of Winckelmann, heralding the beginnings of the so-called 'academic' period at Meissen. The factory now made a determined effort to study developments in other lands. In June of 1764 a special deputation of workers from the factory set off to study porcelain factories in other parts of Germany and France.[16] They brought back with them the minor French sculptor Michel-Victor Acier (1736–99), to supersede Kaendler, who worked in tandem with him until his death in 1775. He seems to have been responsible for modelling a number of important figure-groups in the style of the French engraver Moreau le Jeune (1741–1814), showing families in fashionable dress at work or at play (fig. 237). He seems also to have made putti and other groups, including clocks, on neo-classical pedestals often bearing a Greek key pattern, which were much copied in the nineteenth century. Ground colours were developed to rival those at Sèvres, and a dark-blue ground imitating *bleu nouveau* was achieved soon after 1768 by the arcanist Christian Daniel Busch, who had studied at Sèvres itself before returning to Meissen in 1765.

The factory also saw changes in management. After the 'academic' period, the courtier Count Camillo Marcolini was appointed to the directorship in 1774. He was responsible for the financial reorganisation of the factory, reducing the workmen's wages in 1776. As at Sèvres itself, the neo-classical style first made its appearance on vases and smaller items, before appearing on whole dinner services.[17] However, the most accessible vehicle for the new styles of decoration were the small tea or coffee services for one or two. Those for one or two people were called *déjeuners* at the time, although today the term *cabaret* is often used, referring to the tray on which the service is supported. Both are based on the *déjeuners* made at Sèvres in the 1750s and were taken up by virtually all the Continental factories thereafter, and were often vehicles for fashionable taste. The vast majority of these tea sets seem to have followed a simple pattern; teapots and coffee pots, often with right-angled handles *à la grecque*, as it was called, supplemented by cups and saucers and a tray, all with decoration in the new neo-classical mode[18] (fig. 238).

Dinner services at Meissen also eventually came under the classical spell, though being used less for display, they tended to retain old forms longer. Patterns described as 'à la grecque' were in use as early as 1766.[19] However, the first Meissen dinner service that seems to have shown any real concession to the new style was the service made for the Duke of Kurland in 1774, modelled by J. E. Schoenau and M. V. Acier. It was decorated with rams-head handles and garlands, and painted sparingly with a green ribbon mixed with flowers. A more severe service with right-angled handles was made in 1777 and modelled by the same two for the Elector Friedrich August III of Saxony. Here the decoration was of fruit and birds surrounded by a rich blue ground.[20]

The more serious nature of neo-classicism even had its impact on the dessert service, which up to now had been a fairly light-hearted display, to contrast with the heaviness and formality of the first two courses. Porcelain figures of the kind which Winckelmann decried were not abolished, but were regimented into complete allegorical displays based on certain metaphysical meanings, designed to instruct and educate rather than delight.[21] A *Frauenzimmer-Lexicon* (housewife's manual) of 1773 gives precise instructions for the decorations of dessert, insisting that the housewife has a good knowledge of history and classical mythology.[22] These displays seem to have been quite literally talking points: the confectionery of the Freiherr of Dalbert borrowed cork models of antique buildings for the dessert, so that 'guests were vouchsafed more knowledge and encouraged to use this in the discussion of the most ancient monuments and other works of art'.[23]

In keeping with the sculptural and classical tradition of these displays, many of these allegorical figures were not glazed and enamelled in the rococo manner, but made in unglazed biscuit porcelain in the manner of Sèvres, to resemble classical marble figures. Meissen made a wide variety of these figures, usually of classical gods and heroes, some modelled by Christian Gottfried Jüchtzer (1752–1812), who was appointed chief

237 Group modelled by M. V. Acier. Hard-paste porcelain, painted in enamel colours and gilt. Meissen, *c*.1774. The British Museum, London.

238 Saucer from a *déjeuner*. Hard-paste porcelain, painted in enamel colours with a scene from Goethe's *Werther* and gilt. Width 37 cm. Meissen, *c.*1785. Victoria & Albert Museum, London.

modeller in 1794, and made much use of the collection of casts from the Mengs collection. A group of *The Three Graces* after a classical prototype was first exhibited in 1785.

These developments were mirrored to some extent in all the other porcelain factories in Germany. The march of taste was all-pervasive, each factory wishing to emulate the others. Carl Eugene's factory at Ludwigsburg is thought to have been the first to make figures in the neo-classical taste, when in 1762 it recruited the aforementioned modeller Johann Christian Wilhelm Beyer, whom Carl Eugene had sent to study in Rome to introduce modern ideas to the factory. He made a wide range of elegantly modelled statues of naked athletes, gods and goddesses, in a particularly accomplished mode. After his death, the tradition was continued by the modeller J. J. Louis who was brought in from Tournai as *Oberbossierer* (chief modeller) in 1762–72. The severe course of neo-classicism in Germany can be judged by the monument to the director of the factory, von Kauffmann, his wife and their seven children, dating to 1789. It comprises a white biscuit tabernacle, pyramidal in form, guarded by two angels, with silhouettes of the deceased painted in black. It is essentially a piece of sculpture executed by a ceramic factory (fig. 239).[24]

The fashion for French modellers and craftsmen extended to the other factories. The factory at Fürstenburg obtained the services of the French sculptor, Desoches, to act as modeller as early as 1769. He made a range of figures in biscuit, the most notable being busts of Greek philosophers mounted on pedestals, as well as medallions of the royal family. The tradition was continued by the German modellers Carl Gottlieb Schubert and Johann Christoph Rombrich. An important range of vases was made from 1768 onwards, each new model being marked with a letter of the alphabet. The pricelist for 1779–85 features 'Sets of Urns after the Antique for chimney-pieces or table-settings'; their development was so rapid that by 1785 the letter 'Z' had been reached. These were not all classical-style vases, many of the first being pierced pots-pourris of the rococo kind; however, by 1779 straight copies of Wedgwood models were being made in gilded porcelain.[25] They also made a wide variety of tea and coffee services with trays;[26] these generally have severe right-angled handles *à la grecque* and are painted with cameos, silhouettes, and medallions of classical heroes or contemporary philosophers, in the manner of Meissen.

The factories of Höchst, Frankenthal and Nymphenburg all succumbed to the neo-classical spell, but in varying degrees at different times. A prime mover was the great modeller J. P. Melchior, who finished his days at Höchst by producing some fine portrait reliefs, including one of Goethe in 1775. In 1779 he became chief modeller at Frankenthal, supplanting Adam Bauer, who had already produced for the factory a number of portrait reliefs, busts and allegories. Neo-classical vases had already been made at Frankenthal by 1771,[27] and a set of three vases and a 'dejune [sic] finely painted in brown, Ovid's figures' is recorded in a London sale as early as 1774.[28] Researches into better pastes and colours continued under Simon Feilner, formerly of Fürstenburg; the British Museum and the Fitzwilliam Museum both have specimen plates painted with over sixty different colours, including seven different shades of green. As at Höchst a range of rather severe *déjeuners* were in production by 1775; some of these show great quality in the modelling, presumably due to Melchior.[29]

Melchior went on in 1797 to work at the factory at Nymphenburg, which had lain dormant since 1777, when Elector Karl Theodor had concentrated resources on the Frankenthal factory instead. The modeller Dominikus Auliczek had been appointed as successor to Bustelli and in 1792 produced the 'bead' service, a severe neo-classical service with a border of pearls ('beads') (fig. 240). Melchior himself was to produce small allegorical medallions and groups such as the one celebrating the birth of Prince Maximilian in 1800, before his retirement in 1822, and death in 1825.

Other factories, which were blessed with a strong monarchy, fared better in these difficult times. The factory at Berlin continued under the personal protection and interest of Frederick the Great until his death in 1786, and continued to make porcelain of a very high standard, albeit rather old-fashioned in taste. The first neo-classical vases, of restrained pear-shaped form but with fluted bases and tops, date to 1767, to be followed in the 1770s and 1780s by a garniture of five severely classical vases, modelled for the Duchess of Weimar in about 1785. The first truly neo-classical tea wares, described as 'vase-shaped with trellis work,' appeared in 1776.[30] The sculptor Wilhelm Christian Meyer had created figures of Hercules and Venus on round classical pedestals as early as 1769.[31] The neo-classical influence in dinner wares did not appear until the late 1770s, when patterns such as the *Englischglatt* (based on Wedgwood creamware) and the *Antiqueglatt* were produced. Most of these works retained a rococo element (for instance, in the use of sprays of enamelled flowers), and the severe classical style did not gain complete hold until after the death of Frederick, when the courtier Friedrich Anton von Heinitz (1725–1802) was put in charge of the Porcelain Commission and updated its wares in an effort to make a profit.[32]

The kind of very severe works made by the Germanic factories at the end of the eighteenth century are well demonstrated by the centrepiece from an ambitious dinner service ordered from Berlin by Frederick William II of Prussia in 1791 to the

239 Von Kauffmann memorial. Hard-paste porcelain, painted in enamel colours. Ludwigsburg, 1789. Kunstgewerbemuseum, Frankfurt-am-Main.

240 Tureen from the 'Bead' service. Hard-paste porcelain, painted in enamel colours and gilt. Nymphenburg, c.1792. Bayersiches Nationalmuseum, Munich.

241 Centrepiece in the form of a temple. Hard-paste porcelain, painted in enamel colours and gilt. Height 60.5 cm. Berlin, 1791–95. Victoria & Albert Museum, London.

designs of the architect Hans Christian Genelli, and carried out by the chief modeller Carl Friedrich Riese. The service is allegorical of 'the kingdom of Nature' and a contemporary critique by Feder Rosenthiels wrote that 'Nature is great in its underlying principles, incomprehensible in her workings; her products are a source of continual enjoyment to men and appreciated by sensitive souls'.[33] It is thought that the figure of Bacchus on the centrepiece (fig. 241) could have been modelled by the great neo-classical sculptor Johann Gottfried Schadow. This centrepiece is representative of a trend towards large presentation pieces, often included in a presentation dinner service.

A rival to the established State factories came with the foundation of many smaller factories in eastern Germany, in Thüringia, where deposits of kaolin had been discovered in about 1760. They included Gotha (1757 to date), Volkstedt (1760 to date), Kloster-Veilsdorf (1760 to date), Wallendorf (1764 to date) (fig. 242), Limbach (1772 to date), Ilmenau (1777 to date), Gera (1779 to date) and Rauenstein (1783 to date). Many were run or founded, not as luxuries by princes, but as commercial businesses by different members of the Greiner family of potters and painters, who continued them well into the nineteenth century. They all made vigorously modelled wares for a 'middle-class' market, the paste being of a thick greyish texture which gives them something of the heaviness of stoneware.[34] Their rate of production was astounding, and they produced vast quantities of rather inelegant tea and dinner wares in a plain neo-classical style, simply painted in enamel colours. Some of their interpretations of the classical ideal were bizarre in the extreme (fig. 243).[35]

Other countries succumbed to neo-classicism in varying degrees, and to varying purposes. Russia began to manufacture its own porcelain from 1766 when a factory was set up in Moscow by the Englishman Francis Gardner. Its employees included sixty-seven serfs bought for a total of 300 roubles, and, as it was established under a manufacturing edict of Peter the Great, the *Manufaktur Kollegiia*, and came under the

242 Figures in contemporary dress representing *The Seasons*. Hard-paste porcelain, painted in enamel colours. Height 30 cm. Wallendorf, Thüringia, *c.*1780. The Bowes Museum, Barnard Castle, Co. Durham.

Department of Manufactures, its employees were not subject to outside law for crimes other than murder, theft and treason. Its great achievement was the production of services with insignia for the annual ceremonial dinners for the Orders of St George (1777–8), St Andrew (1780), St Alexander Nevskii (1780) (fig. 244), and St Vladimir (1783–5), which took inspiration from the Berlin service sent to Catherine the Great in 1772.[36] A similar style can be seen in the wares of the porcelain factory set up under royal protection in about 1762 in St Petersburg. It was linked to the newly established

243 *Déjeuner* in the neo-classical taste, *c.*1800. Hard-paste porcelain, painted in enamel colours and gilt. Length of tray 37.5 cm. Ilmenau (Thüringia, Germany). Kunstsammlungen, Weimar.

244 Dessert basket and plates from the St Andrew, St Vladimir and St Alexander Nevskii services. Hard-paste porcelain, painted in enamel colours and gilt. Moscow, 1777–1800. Hillwood Museum and Gardens, Washington D.C.

245 Copy of plate from the *Flora Danica* service. Hard-paste porcelain, painted in enamel colours and gilt. Copenhagen, *c*.1871. The Bowes Museum, Barnard Castle, Co. Durham.

Academy of the Arts, under the direction of the Frenchman Jean-Dominique Rachette, who designed many services in the latest style, including the 'Arabesque' service of 1784, with a classical centrepiece of figures glorifying Catherine II's foreign policy, and the similar 'Cabinet' service of 1795.[37]

Large prestigious dinner services were made by all the major factories in Europe as a way of showing off a nation's skill and taste. The most famous service of all was made by the factory founded at Copenhagen in 1775, under the sponsorship of Queen Juliane Marie, a daughter of the Duke of Brunswick who had set up the Fürstenberg factory in Germany.[38] It is the great *Flora Danica* service, begun in 1790, apparently made for Catherine the Great of Russia. The shapes were based on the neo-classical 'pearl' service of 1783, where the rim of each piece was edged with a row of pearls, and each piece was painted with a plant from the great *Flora Danica*, a recently published illustrated compendium of Danish plants (fig. 245). Catherine died in 1796 and the production of the service was stopped in 1802, at 100 place-settings. It was kept in the court pantry and the pastry cook's account book reveals that one piece from it was broken nearly every time it was used.[39]

However, the true spirit of classicism was, not unnaturally, found most closely in its homeland of Italy. However even here the classicism of Wedgwood held sway over the Italian, and when the Englishman Arthur Young visited Vicenza in Italy in the late eighteenth century, he saw 'a magazine of earthenware in imitation of Mr. Wedgwood. It is surely a triumph of the arts in England to see in Italy Etruscan forms copied from English models. It is a better imitation than many I have seen in France.'[40] Imports of Wedgwood creamware put paid to the once-flourishing Italian tin-glaze market, although towards the end of the century the Giustianini factory in Naples made some fine creamware decorated in the Etruscan manner.

The porcelain factory that followed the classical style most consistently was that of Naples, close to the ruins of Pompeii and Herculaneum. King Ferdinand founded a new factory in the grounds of the royal palace at Portici, to the east of Naples, in 1771. In 1779 he appointed as director Domenico Venuti (1745–1817), a man of great learning and ability, the son of Marcello Venuti, one of the first excavators at Herculaneum.[41] He was himself involved in the restoration and publication of the Greek temples at Paestum, and, not surprisingly under his directorship a number of neo-classical services were made. These include the 'Herculaneum' service of 1781, made as a present for the Spanish court, and the 'Etruscan' service of 1785 presented to George III of Great Britain. They were full of neo-classical imagery, the useful vessels being copied directly from Greek vases (fig. 246).[42] The modeller Filippo Tagliolini (1745–1809) joined them from the Vienna factory in 1780, and modelled a wide variety of figures in the classical style, or copied from antique originals; his most ambitious work is a large biscuit centrepiece of many figures in contorted poses of *The Fall of the Giants* of 1787–92/99. Towards the end of the century, he seems to have been responsibe for some charming groups depicting fashionable figures at rest or play.[43]

Many of the products described above are in a rather ponderous style, not perhaps best-suited to the fragile beauty of porcelain. The remedy for this lay in the very same country that had sparked off the classical revival, namely France. Though the dominant style of the later eighteenth century continued to be classical, the range of types and decoration was expanded to include dainty flower motifs, a wider range of colours, delicate patterns, and even references to the Orient in a style harking back to the early eighteenth century. Style was dictated by such elegant anglophile architects as François-Joseph Belanger (1744–1818), who revived the grotesque/arabesque in his decorative panels for the bathhouse at the Hôtel de Brancas in Paris in the early 1770s, and was soon copied throughout France.

By now the court at Versailles was no longer the leading patron of the French decorative arts; instead, there had risen up in Paris a whole generation of rich millionaires, such as the tax-gatherers ('fermiers-généraux'), who patronised a variety of styles, the only common characteristic of which was the extreme refinement of design and detail which meant that even furniture was made with something of the minute attention that might have been given to a piece of jewellery. They were patrons of the *marchands-merciers*, the successors to dealers such as Lazare Duvaux of twenty years before, who innovated styles and techniques to tempt the jaded appetites of Parisians and rich visitors from abroad. They had the power to influence taste, and commissioned work for sale.[44] One of the most famous was Simon-Philippe Poirier, who kept shop at 85 Rue Saint-Honoré, and specialised in the mounting of Sèvres porcelain plaques, painted with flowers, into gilt-bronze on furniture, which was purchased by such fashionable clients as the king's mistress, Madame du Barry. From 1758 to 1770 he bought 1,400 plaques from Sèvres.[45] His preferred craftsman was the cabinet-maker Martin Carlin, whose stamp was often erased from the products, presumably to ensure their anonymity (fig. 247).[46] By the end of the century the luxury trade was dominated by Dominique Daguerre, a successful *marchand-mercier* who had many dealings with British aristocrats and even set up shop in London. Daguerre became Wedgwood's Paris agent and may have been responsible for applying Wedgwood's jasperware plaques to furniture.[47]

One kind of ceramics that the *marchands-merciers* promoted was the 'cabinet' cup and saucer. This was an individual cup and saucer of regular form decorated in the most lavish and fashionable taste; its main purpose seems to have been not to drink from, but to demonstrate taste and fashionable ornament, and designs were sometimes specially made (fig. 248). The Reverend William Cole records that his friend Horace Walpole bought one at Poirier's shop on their visit to Paris in 1765:

I was with Mr. Walpole one Day at a great shop in Paris, Mr. Poirier's, where [Sèvres porcelain] was sold, & saw him give 10 Louis or guineas for a single Coffee cup, Saucer, & a little square Sort of *Soucoupe*, or under-saucer, to set them on; they were

246 Plate from a service sent to George III in 1787. Diameter of plate 23.5 cm. Soft-paste porcelain, painted in enamel colours, Naples, Royal Factory. Royal Collection, Windsor Castle.

247 Table with inset Sèvres plaques by Martin Carlin. Height 80.5 cm. The porcelain, c.1765. The Bowes Museum, Barnard Castle, Co. Durham.

indeed the highest finished things of the kind that can be conceived: perfect Jewels that deserve to be set in gold Frames to be admired & looked at, but never to be used for Fear of breaking them.[48]

By the later eighteenth century the cylindrical form of the *gobelet litron* was preferred (which became the English 'coffee-can') to allow space for decoration (fig. 249); sometimes, the cup and saucers in a set were deliberately mismatched to create a 'harlequin' set.[49]

Many of these new products were in the new hard-paste porcelain, based on deposits of china clay found at Limoges in 1769 and made at Sèvres soon thereafter. Many hard-paste factories were set up in Paris to cater for this trade in middle-range luxury goods. Most were located in the artisans' quarter in the north-east of the city, a traditional centre for the manufacture of consumer goods such as furniture. A number of factories arose in the wake of the government's decision to allow some sort of expansion of trade in 1760, though at first the factories were allowed to make only undecorated porcelain, or wares painted with underglaze blue in the Chinese style.[50] An influx of makers from German states, such as Hannong from Strasbourg and Russinger from Höchst, took place, and some of the new factories gained the patronage of the royal family; Queen Marie-Antoinette supported a factory in Rue Thiroux, run by Lebeuf; the king's brother, the comte de Provence (later to reign as Louis XVIII) supported that at Rue de Clignancourt; the king's youngest brother, the comte d'Artois (later to become Charles X), that at Faubourg St Denis (Limoges, which supplied the clay, was in his domain); his son, the duc d'Angoulême, supported the factory run by

249 Cup and saucer with raised ('jewelled') decoration. Soft-paste porcelain, painted in enamel colours and gilt. Height of cup 6.9 cm. Sèvres, 1781. The J. Paul Getty Museum, Los Angeles.

250 Broth bowl and cover (écuelle). Hard-paste porcelain, painted in enamel colours and gilt. Stand 22.5 cm wide. Paris, Manufacture du Petit Carousel, 1774–1800. The Bowes Museum, Barnard Castle. Co. Durham.

251 Vase *bouc du Barry B*. Hard-paste porcelain, painted in enamel colours and gilt. Height 29.5 cm. Sèvres, 1778. The J. Paul Getty Museum, Los Angeles.

Guérhard and Dihl in the Rue de Bondy; and the duc d'Orléans supported a factory in the Rue Amelot. All these factories made a wide variety of elegant, simply decorated wares in the late eighteenth-century taste, often decorated with flowers; those painted with rather angular sprigs of cornflower in blue and white are known as Angoulême sprig, a pattern imitated across Europe. Some factories, such as that of the Manufacture du Petit Carousel, were only decorating establishments, using blanks supplied by other factories (fig. 250). They all had to suffer numerous disputes with Sèvres, which accused them of enticing away craftsmen and modellers with inflated wages, and even pirating designs, to the extent that a design for the king appeared in general circulation before the king had seen it! However, the general principle was conceded in 1784, when they were permitted to make everything except vases, pictures, bas-reliefs and groups, and even these were allowed to the factories with royal patronage in 1787.[51]

However, great artistic impetus remained with the Sèvres factory, which was in a position to develop new styles in a way denied to other, more commercial, factories, including some very refined pieces in the Chinese style[52] (figs. 251 and 252). The artistic director at Sèvres was still Jean-Jacques Bachelier, but in 1785 the neo-classical artist Jean-Jacques Lagrenée [*le jeune*] (1740–1821) was appointed artistic co-director. In 1787 he bought a '*suite d'arabesques de Raphael*' drawings for the factory, which seems to have been the beginning of much elegant arabesque decoration. The head of the painters' studio from 1753 to 1789, J. B. E. Genest, also supplied arabesque designs and selected models for painting.[53] A 'service arabesque', with individually designed pieces, had been begun for Marie-Antoinette in 1782. It was designed by the architect and engineer Louis Masson, and to speed up production, one of Masson's drawings was cut into three, so that three times the number of craftsmen could work on the project at the same time (fig. 253).

The delicate styles and forms of late eighteenth-century French classicism were to prove popular throughout the rest of Europe well into the nineteenth century. The arabesque became the basis of the lighter style that prevailed in all the more artistical-

252 Vases with Chinese heads. Hard-paste porcelain, painted in enamel colours by the decorator Schradre and gilt. Height 47 cm. Sèvres, 1780. The Royal Collection, London.

253 Plate from the Arabesque service made for Queen Marie-Antoinette. porcelain, painted in enamel colours and gilt. Sèvres, 1784. Courtesy of Christie's Images, New York.

ly advanced factories that operated in Europe at the end of the eighteenth century, such as that at the factory at Nyon in Switzerland, set up by the German Jacques Dortu in 1780.[54] Very fine wares in the late neo-classical taste were also made at the newly founded factory at Buen Retiro in Spain, under the guidance of the director José Gricci (1760–70) and Carlos and Felipe Gricci (1783–1803) including some very elegant vases supporting candelabra in the French taste, popularised at the court by the French designer J. A. D. Dugourc (1749–1825).[55] A particularly elegant and ambitious brand of late neo-classicism was developed at the factory at Vienna, with the appointment of the courtier Konrad von Sorgenthal as director in 1784. He tightened up the design and painting of the factory's wares, employing only painters who had successfully completed the drawing course of the Academy. Landscape and flower painting became especially prominent. With the new colours of blue and violet devised by the chemist Joseph Leitner and elaborate raised gilding devised by Georg Perl, the factory began to specialise in elaborate all-over decoration in the classical style of a type that rivalled Sèvres. A fine *déjeuner* in the British Museum is datemarked '[17]85' (fig. 254).[56]

The designer Dugourc claimed the credit for the last major style of the eighteenth century, the *style étrusque*, a more archaeologically accurate version of the neo-classical style, which exactly copied details from Grecian and Pompeian antiquity. It was distinguished by great refinement of detail, and the use of sombre or striking colours, some of the most popular being chocolate brown or acidic yellow as background colours, often without any gilding. The most famous example of the *style étrusque* in ceramics is

254 *Déjeuner*. Hard-paste porcelain, painted in enamel colours and gilt. Vienna, 1785. The British Museum, London.

the service of Sèvres porcelain of 1788 made for the dairy that was built for Queen Marie-Antoinette at the royal hunting lodge at Rambouillet. It was designed by Lagrenée and comprised a number of exotic items, the design of which was thought to mirror the fashions of classical Pompeii: milk pails shaped and painted as if made out of wood; bowls in the shape of breasts, and an elegant cup with high handles rising above the rim in the Greek manner, called a *gobelet à anses étrusque* (with etruscan handles). This was derived from two Greek vases acquired by Sèvres from the collection of the aristocratic art-collector and arbiter of taste, Baron Vivant-Denon, in 1786[57] (fig. 255).[58]

It should be realised that these refinements of taste were mostly for private consumption; for State occasions a heavier, more traditional style prevailed. The great sur-

255 Cup and saucer from the dairy service made for Rambouillet. Hard-paste porcelain, painted in enamel colours. Height of cup 11 cm. Sèvres, 1788. Musée National de Céramique, Sèvres.

256 Bottle-cooler from the service made for Louis XVI. Soft-paste porcelain, painted in enamel colours and gilt. Height 20.8 cm. Sèvres, 1790. The J. Paul Getty Museum, Los Angeles.

viving monument to official taste is the service begun for Louis XVI at Sèvres in 1783 and only half completed by the time of the king's execution in 1793. The style of the service is much richer than pieces in the Etruscan style, with central panels in a gilded frame against a rich *gros bleu* ground colour. The subject of the central panels are all classical, and come from a variety of sources, the most frequently used being the *Metamorphoses* of 1768–9[59] (fig. 256). Although the painting and modelling is of the highest quality, it does suggest a certain lack of artistic adventurousness on the part of official taste in the years immediately preceding the French Revolution.

Overleaf, detail of fig. 259. Teaset with cups in the 'Bute' shape.

CHAPTER 13

Ceramics in the Period 1790–1830

The beginning of the French Revolution in 1789 led to enormous changes among the governing classes of Europe which were to affect their patterns of spending and the objects they bought. Most of the French aristocracy lost that great surplus of wealth which is so conducive to changes in taste and fashion, and led to the commissioning of so many individually designed or decorated items. Furthermore they lost the respect which until then had been automatically granted to the Crown and the aristocracy, and with it the concept of developments in fashionable taste being a prerogative of the governing classes. This was affected most obviously by the destruction of the hopelessly profligate court at Versailles. The French monarchy was officially abolished in 1792 and Louis XVI was guillotined in 1793, and with that a system of French dominance of European taste that dated back to the court of Louis XIV in the seventeenth century, came to an end, at least temporarily. More practically for ceramic design and production, the system of massive State subsidies to the royal factory of Sèvres, either directly or through extravagant royal commissions, ended, only to be revived under the reign of Napoleon. However, by then all Europe was at war and the other European countries were beginning to display more individual national characteristics in design.

The factories in Britain that gained the most obvious benefit from the problems at Sèvres were those at Derby and Worcester. After the death of William Duesbury in 1786 the Derby factory was run by his son of the same name, who later took as a partner the miniature-painter Michael Kean. Many of its products were decorated in a rich style in imitation of Sèvres for which it is best known today, with a range of rich ground-colours, usually with elaborate gilding, which framed reserves containing painting of the finest quality. The factory developed especial skills in flower and landscape painting, with certain artists specialising in particular types of decoration, such as William Billingsley (1758–1828), who is noted for flowers, or landscapes by artists such as Thomas 'Jockey' Hill (1753–1827). An important part of the factory's production seems to have been the provision of lavishly decorated dessert services, often painted with botanical subjects, as was appropriate for something with garden connections. Such services had, of course, often been painted with flowers before, but the fashion now was to copy prints from botanical journals, so that the flowers are depicted in profile or section with considerable scientific accuracy, sometimes even showing the roots. The Prince of Wales bought a dessert service so decorated in 1792.[1] The names of the flowers are invariably inscribed on the back of the plates, possibly so that they could be a topic of discussion over dessert. Such depictions were painted on the white porcelain and framed with a simple border, often assigned a number to facilitate multiple production in the manner of creamware. The well-known simple yellow border (pattern 216) had appeared by 1796 (fig. 257).

Similarly the factory at Worcester began to produce richly decorated wares. Like so many factories it was in the hands of a retailer, having been bought by its London agent, Thomas Flight, for £3,000 in 1783. By 1789 he was also acting as the London agent for the French Angoulême factory, possibly because the Worcester factory was having technical problems with the manufacture of porcelain. A large dinner service was ordered by the Duke of Clarence in 1789; he was offered a choice of three specimen patterns, *Arabesque*, *Hope and Patience* and *Peace and Abundance*, of which he chose the second. The service was delivered in 1792, with a central panel in grisaille of a female allegorical figure and a border of gilded blue (fig. 258). In 1792, the merchant Martin Barr was made a partner, and the firm continued with variations of their two names until 1840.[2]

A rival factory had been set up in 1788 by a former Worcester employee, Robert Chamberlain, who had also first acted as a decorator. This firm had close links with the factory at Caughley, with much interchange and decoration of Caughley pieces at Worcester during times of shortage.[3] The firm also made lavish items of porcelain for the rich, including a dessert service for the Prince of Orange in 1796, comprising the full range of shaped dishes, comports, cream pots and ice-pails in the French manner.[4] Much ingenuity was employed in the designs of tea and coffee sets, which became a major aspect of production in this period. They seldom followed strictly classical mod-

257 Dessert plate painted with a design of *Hepatica*. Soft-paste porcelain, painted in enamel colours and gilt. Derby, *c.*1795. Royal Museum of Scotland, Edinburgh.

258 Plate from the 'Hope' service. Soft-paste porcelain painted in enamel colours and gilt. Worcester, Flight, *c.*1792. Courtesy of Phillips Auctioneers.

259 Teaset with cups in the 'Bute' shape. Soft-paste porcelain, painted in enamel colours and gilt in the *Imari* style. Worcester, (Flight and Barr), 1802–5. Courtesy of Phillips Auctioneers.

260 J. B. Papworth (1775–1847), a breakfast laid out, from Peter Coxe, *The Social Day*, 1823.

els, as in France, but showed varieties of attractive moulding, including curved fluting, and rich Eastern-style decoration.[5]

It was about this time that tea sets began to change their character altogether from their eighteenth century models, as they became larger and more adapted to entertaining large groups of people. The teapots themselves become larger and more elegant, and tea-bowls vanish in favour of large cups with handles. A standard tea set from Chamberlain of Worcester cost about three guineas and comprised a teapot and cover, a teapot-stand, a sugar basin and cover, a jug, a 'slop' (waste) bowl, two bread-and-butter plates, of slightly different sizes, twelve teacups (cheaper sets still had handleless tea-bowls), twelve (or fewer) coffee cups, and twelve saucers.[6] There was thus one saucer to both a teacup and coffee cup, as the hostess after dinner would normally offer her guests a choice of tea or coffee. Cups also began to take on regular forms which became standard for most manufacturers throughout Britain, with relatively simple shapes such as the *Bute* (with straight coffee cans and rounded teacups) (fig. 259) followed by the *London* (with concave-based coffee and teacups) profiles emerging in the early nineteenth century. It is clear that tea was beginning to be drunk in larger quantities, presumably with the regular addition of milk in the way that is familiar to us today, but the social ritual of daily afternoon tea did not come into being until the mid-nineteenth century, a result of the change in the dinner hour from four o'clock to about eight o'clock in the evening. Larger cups were made for breakfast services (fig. 260).[7]

The most beautiful porcelain made in Britain was perhaps that made at Pinxton in Derbyshire, a factory founded by the Derby flower-painter William Billingsley in 1795. Its wares were soft-paste, similar to that of Derby, but distinguished by painting and enamelling of the highest quality, with a softness about them reminiscent of the finest

261 Teaset with tray (*déjeuner*). Soft-paste porcelain, painted in enamel colours and gilt. Pinxton, *c.*1799. The Bowes Museum, Barnard Castle, Co. Durham.

work of Sèvres, and of the most elegant and delicate design.[8] The flower painting was naturally exceptionally good (fig. 261). Billingsley left Pinxton in 1799, going to Mansfield, and then subsequently pursuing his career at Torksey, Flight and Barr's factory at Worcester, and, most famously, at Nantgarw and then Swansea (1814–17) in Wales, at which locations he produced some of the most translucent and beautifully decorated porcelain ever produced. However, the cost of such items was prohibitive and both factories failed, forcing Billingsley to sign a seven-year contract with John Rose in 1820, who had taken over the old porcelain factory of Caughley in 1799 and produced the rich wares that we know today as Coalbrookdale or Coalport.

The quality of Swansea and Nantgarw porcelain was such that it was bought undecorated by various London retailers, such as Mortlock of Oxford Street, Pellat & Green of St Paul's Churchyard, and John Bradley and Co. of Pall Mall, who in turn employed local decorating firms such as Robins and Randall, Powell of Wimpole Street, and John Simms, to decorate it in an up-to-date manner. It is not always clear which pieces are factory decorated and which are London decorated, but it does reinforce the trend that successful porcelain factories needed to operate with a base or contact in London in order to keep their designs fashionable. The most famous independent workshop of all was that of Thomas Baxter at No.1 Goldsmith Street, Gough Square, Clerkenwell, from as early as 1797. Baxter brought to porcelain painting something of the quality of picture painting, possibly based on his studies at the Royal Academy School, where he exhibited paintings from 1802 to 1812. He seems to have had especially close links with the Worcester and Coalport factories, buying their products in the white, and firing on enamelled decoration in his own muffle-kilns. There exists a watercolour drawing of 1809 in the Victoria and Albert Museum (fig. 262), which shows the members of his factory at work, with a Coalport plate on the left depicting the commemoration of the death of Nelson, now also in the Victoria and Albert Museum (fig. 263). Baxter's workshop was not commercially successful and he worked for Flight, Barr and Barr at Worcester in about 1814, and later at the newly founded soft-paste factory at Swansea, before ending up with Chamberlain at Worcester.[9]

Many of the wares decorated at the factories themselves were painted in styles different from those used on the Continent. This was presumably because of the lack of a strict State-led (or imposed) taste in England. Rich Eastern-style patterns, based on Chinese *famille-rose* porcelains or Japanese *Imari* porcelains, continued to be very popular in Britain at the turn of the century, rivalling in richness the ground colours of Sèvres and its imitations. Worcester produced a version of a Chinese 'Dragons in Compartments' pattern as early as 1797–9, and Admiral Nelson was able to order a service in the 'Japan' (*Imari*) pattern from the factory in August 1802. These wares gradually supplanted the more restrained styles of the late eighteenth century, whose elegant painted borders, often of arabesques, left much of the body of the porcelain white, and seem to have been very popular in the early years of the nineteenth century.[10]

This was also the age of the economic expansion and worldwide dominance of the Staffordshire ceramic industry. The early nineteenth century saw the development of new bodies, and new techniques of decoration, which meant that manufacturers in Staffordshire could supply ceramics that were of as high quality, and in many respects more durable, than those of the great European factories. This became a source of considerable national pride, especially after the ending of the Napoleonic Wars in 1814/15, when employment was needed for considerable numbers of demobilised soldiers, as Jane Austen observed in *Northanger Abbey*.[11] By 1818, 144 master potters specialising in the manufacture of earthenware alone are listed in a directory of the district.[12]

The major technical developments in Staffordshire at the time were the creation of a new porcelain body called 'bone china' and a kind of strengthened pottery called 'stone-china'. The leading exponents were Josiah Spode II (1755–1827) and the family of the former London china-dealer Miles Mason (1752–1813) of Lane End. Bone china is thought to have been developed by Spode and others at Stoke-on-Trent from about 1800 onwards;[13] it was a kind of hard-paste porcelain strengthened by the addition of

262 Watercolour of the decorating workshop of Thomas Baxter, 1809. Victoria & Albert Museum, London. The plate in the lower left is painted with a scene of Britannia mourning the death of Nelson. See fig. 263.

263 Plate painted with a scene of Britannia mourning the death of Nelson. Porcelain, painted in enamel colours and gilt. Coalport, painted in the workshop of Thomas Baxter, signed and dated 1806. Victoria & Albert Museum, London.

264 Selection of Staffordshire ceramics of the period 1800–30, showing a Spode bone-china jug with lustre decoration; a Wedgwood earthenware plate transfer-printed in underglaze blue; a hybrid body egg-cup of *c*.1800, probably Spode; a Minton porcelain tea-cup in the 'Bute' shape, coffee can and saucer with rounded 'bat' printing; and a Masons 'ironstone' inkstand and miniature watering can for sand. Diameter of Wedgwood plate 24.8 cm. The Bowes Museum, Barnard Castle, Co. Durham.

bone ash, in the manner of the products of the old factory at Bow, with a warm-white body. But whereas the products of Bow contained only about 25 per cent bone ash by weight, added to the ingredients of soft-paste porcelain, the new bone china contained as much as 40 or 50 per cent bone ash by weight, mixed with equal quantities of the traditional ingredients of true hard-paste porcelain, kaolin and pentunse.[14] Spode began the production of a wide range of elegant tea and other wares, mostly decorated within the factory by the firm of Henry Daniel in an elegant neo-classical style.

The success of bone china was immediate, leading to a large number of imitators in Staffordshire, such as John Davenport (1765–1848) and Thomas Minton (1765–1836), founders of the factories of the same name (fig. 264). Even the great pottery firm of Wedgwood was to produce its own version in 1812.[15] All these products were developed without State assistance, though the manufacturers were always seeking royal and aristocratic approval with which to market their products.[16]

The other major development in Staffordshire was 'stone china', a kind of tough high-fired pottery that was developed by the Turners of Lane End, who had obtained a patent in January 1800, and by Josiah Spode as 'New Stone' from about 1813, as well as the firm of Davenport of Longport,[17] and Charles James Mason, son of the china dealer and porcelain maker Miles Mason, who patented 'Ironstone China' in 1813.[18] The ingredients of this body comprised Cornish stone (growan), flint, and a certain kind of hard rock or iron-stone found in Staffordshire. Though items of stone china are not normally considered as porcelain, some do show signs of translucency. They were often decorated with enamelling over a printed underglaze outline, usually in Eastern styles; best-known is perhaps Spode's *Tumbledown Dick* pattern, featuring a bird on the branch of a tree in the manner of Chinese *famille rose* porcelain. Such attractive and durable wares could not fail to be an immediate success, especially with the middle classes who wanted something for everyday use. In 1817 even Queen Charlotte visited the Spode showroom in Lincoln's Inn Fields and bought a service.[20]

The techniques of decoration were now much improved, especially that of transfer-

265 A dinner table laid out at the Bowes Museum in imitation of a watercolour by Mary Ellen Best, 1838, showing the arrangement of dishes *à la française*. The dinner service courtesy of Sion Hill Hall, Yorkshire.

printing. The key to success here was a new machine for making strong tissue paper, invented by the Fourdrinier family, which began producing the paper in 1803 in Frogmore in Berkshire and moved its business to Hanley in Staffordshire in 1827.[21] This paper allowed first-rate impressions from a copper-plate to be taken, enabling ceramic manufacturers to produce transfer-printing on pottery and porcelain as fine as that in book illustration. For finer work, 'bat' printing remained in use from the eighteenth century, whereby the design was printed in an adhesive oil and powdered colour dusted over it. The most popular styles continued to be Chinese or Eastern inspired, and soon 'Willow pattern' and other underglaze-blue printed earthenwares were to put the Chinese export porcelain market out of business.[22] The most popular colour was blue, made from cobalt oxide, which withstood the heat of the firing so well, but underglaze red, green and black were also developed. An enormous export market developed, the potteries serving countries as far afield as the United States.[23]

Most of these cheaper wares were intended not for elegant tea-time use, but for daily meals, where durability was more important than display. A dinner service of what appears to be Staffordshire-blue tableware can be seen in a watercolour of a table laid out for dinner in 1838 by Mary Ellen Best,[24] where it was laid out in an English version of *service à la française* (fig. 265), as described in the letters of the German Prince Pückler-Muskau:

Since you have never been in England, I should like to describe to you, in a few words, the course of an English dinner which, as I have said, is almost the same everywhere . . . in the French style you find, when you go in, the whole first course of the meal set out on the table. After the soup is removed, and as soon as the covers have been taken off, every man helps himself from the dish in front of him, and offers it to his neighbour. If he wants something extra, he must either ask across the table for it or send a servant in search of it . . . when the second course is finished, as well as an intermediate dessert of cheese, salad, raw celery and the like, they bring in ale that is sometimes twenty or thirty years old, and so strong that if it is thrown on the fire it flares up like spirit. The tablecloth is removed and, in the best houses on a still finer tablecloth lying beneath it, in others on the bare, polished table, the dessert is set out. This consists of all possible hothouse fruits, which here are of the finest quality: Indian and English preserves, stomach-strengthening ginger, ice and so on. Before each guest fresh glasses are placed, and under the dessert plates and cutlery small, fringed napkins are set. Before the hosts three bottles of wine are laid – usually claret (wine of Bordeaux), port and madeira. The host now pushes these, either on their mats or on a small silver trolley, to his neighbour on the left. Everyone serves himself, and if there is a lady sitting beside him serves her too with whatever she wants, and so it goes on until it has come back to the starting-point, and from there it sets forth again. Several crystal jugs of iced water allow the foreigner, fortunately, to mix an antidote to the spirit which strongly predominates in English wines. All the servants leave the room, when the dessert has been served, and if fresh wine is needed the butler is summoned, and he alone brings it in [25] (figs. 266, 267 and 268).

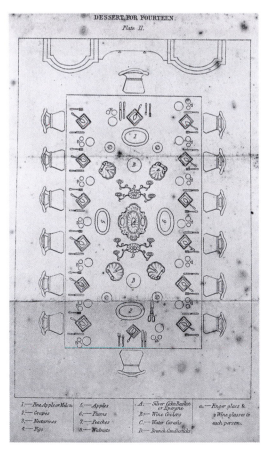

266   Diagram of the first course of dinner, from T. Cosnett, *The Footman's Director*, 1823.

267   Diagram of the layout of dessert, from T. Cosnett, *The Footman's Director*, 1823.

268 J. B. Papworth (1775–1847), illustration of a dessert, from Peter Coxe, *The Social Day*, 1823.

Dinner was followed by a very late supper at about ten o'clock, consisting of cold foods such as sandwiches, or occasionally, covered dishes of hot foods. Special supper-sets were made in pottery, in which a number of segmental dishes surround a central covered pot to serve the different foods.

However, such a way of dining was beginning to be found increasingly unsatisfactory, both from the point of view of ease of service, and the variety of dishes served.[26] By the 1850s most households had adopted the new fashion of *service à la russe*, imported from Russia, whereby each dish was carved or jointed and served individually in succession,[27] although it required more servants and cutlery.[28]

The stylistic variety of ceramics in Britain was not repeated on the Continent. A certain uniformity of taste became apparent again, with the rise of Napoleon Bonaparte in France, who declared himself Emperor in 1804,[39] and his insistence on the development of a suitable Imperial style of decoration based on Roman prototypes. His designers in this field were the architects Charles Percier (1764–1838) and Pierre-François-Léonard Fontaine (1762–1853). They were both trained in the elegant neo-classical style of the late eighteenth century, but made it more austere by stripping it of much of its lighter decoration, such as flowers, and concentrating instead on military symbolism, and emphasising the heavy architectural elements of the design. The general effect was to overwhelm and impress by size and weight, providing a rather showy background to the life of the court. 'Beauty according to him resides only in grandeur' Fontaine wrote of Napoleon in March 1808.[30]

Napoleon attempted to impose French taste on the rest of Europe much as Louis XIV had done. From 1798 a series of exhibitions of *The Products of French Industry* were held in order to stimulate industry. They were at first organised by François de Neufchâteau, later Napoleon's Minister of the Interior,[31] and continued after the fall of Napoleon in 1814; they showed a wide range of lavish, and often rather over-elaborate, French products.[32] They provided the basis of the great International Exhibitions of the mid-nineteenth century.

The great factory at Sèvres came under this cultural domination. The factory regained State support in 1802, and its products were carefully regimented into this system of direction. The didactic aims of the new regime were demonstrated when the architect Alexandre Brongniart was appointed director in 1800. His first task was to remedy the precarious financial situation of the factory; he sacked many workers and ceased to make soft-paste porcelain in favour of purely hard-paste. The workshops were now organised into two sections: manufacture and decoration. Brongniart made use of the great designers, Percier and Fontaine, and the products of this period all tend to be characterised by massiveness of form, with much use of overall gilding and painted *réserves* of figurative or landscape scenes.

Brongniart attempted a twin policy of creating massive pieces intended as decoration or gifts for the new regime, at the same time as trying to produce a smaller and lighter range of goods for the public.[33] Many of the grandest and most ambitious pieces were made for the Bonaparte family, or to commemorate successes of the regime. As in the eighteenth century, these often took the form of presentation vases. The *vase à bandeau* was designed by Bergeret on strict Greek lines, and painted with a scene of an allegorical representation of the Battle of Austerlitz. Similarly the *vase étrusque à rouleaux* was designed in 1808 by the court architect Charles Percier, and a specimen of 1813 is painted with ten cameos and a frieze representing the arrival of plundered works of art into the new Musée Napoleon (fig. 269).[34] The most ambitious pieces from the factory are perhaps the two porcelain tables painted with cameo portraits of Napoleon's marshals and Alexander the Great's captains, dating from 1806–12; one, the *Table des Maréchaux*, remains in France; the other, the *Table des Grands*

Capitaines, with mounts by the great ormolu-maker Pierre-Philippe Thomire, was given to George IV by a grateful Louis XVIII after the defeat of Napoleon, and then included in all official portraits of the English king.[35]

One of the more interesting developments of early nineteenth-century taste was the Egyptian style. Its origin lay in Napoleon's campaigns in Egypt in 1798. Its great monument in ceramics is the dessert service made for the Emperor of Russia in Moscow, based on the drawings of Baron Vivant-Denon, who had attended the campaign, which were published in his *Voyage dans la Basse et la Haute Egypte* in 1802.[36] The architectural surtout was designed by the architect Jean-Baptiste Le Peyre, and the plates were painted by Jacques-François-Joseph Swebach-Desfontaines, each bearing a different scene in Egypt copied from Denon, and painted in sepia monochrome. The borders of *beau bleu*;

269　Vase *étrusque à rouleaux*. Hard-paste porcelain, painted in enamel colours and gilt. Sèvres, 1813. Musée National de la Céramique, Sèvres.

with gold decorations, were designed by Théodore Brongniart, father of the Sèvres director. The service was given to Alexander I of Russia after the Treaty of Tilsit in 1807 and is now in the Ceramic Museum at Kuskovo outside Moscow, while another version, made for Empress Joséphine, was rejected by her and later given to the Duke of Wellington by Louis XVIII in 1818. It now resides with other great gifts of Continental porcelain at his old home of Apsley House, London (fig. 270).[37]

Much of the lesser production of Sèvres was still intensely ambitious by present-day standards, comprising elaborately decorated *déjeuners*, often fitted into a presentation or travelling case, and complete dinner services, often intended as official gifts (fig. 271). Such wares were of very high quality, painted in the rich style made popular in the eighteenth century, but with details derived from Roman ornament, and

270 Ice pail. Hard-paste porcelain, painted in enamel colours and gilt. Sèvres, *c.*1810. Wellington Museum, Apsley House, London.

271 Plate painted by J. H. C. Develly with a *Patisserie* from the *Service des arts industriels*. Hard-paste porcelain, painted in enamel colours and gilt. Diameter 24 cm. Sèvres, 1823. Courtesy Christie's, London.

a range of shapes based on Greek prototypes, particularly cups with the handles raised above the rim. It was also in this period that the porcelain factories of Paris came into their own as competitors for the lesser end of the market for porcelain in a lighter taste, with less emphasis on overall gilding, and much use of the 'arabesque' style of the reign of Louis XVI. As we have seen, the factories were largely based in the north and the north-east of Paris, but in the early nineteenth century there was a large number of decorating workshops as well. The most famous factories were those of Dihl and Guérhard, Dagoty and Nast.[38] They made an enormous number of tea wares, toilet wares, chocolate cups and saucers, and general items which we today would class as 'gift wares' for the fashionable lady. Some of these were presented in leather cases in order to make their luxury status clear (fig. 272).[39]

By this time the *faïence* industry in France had died out as a result of the commercial treaty with England of 1786 (with much support from Wedgwood) which allowed the import of English earthenware on payment of a purely nominal duty.[40] However, by the early nineteenth century the French had devised a rival to the English creamware centred on the factory at Creil on the outskirts of Paris, founded in 1795. It followed the classical forms of Wedgwood, but was decorated with elegant transfer prints, usually in black, of mythological scenes or landscapes, some apparently applied by the firm of Stone, Coquerel and Legros d'Anisy of Paris. The shapes are extremely refined, and the overglaze printing restrained, the whole providing a suitable utilitarian rival to French porcelain of the period.

The French Empire style of Percier and Fontaine became dominant throughout the rest of mainland Europe in the period 1800–20. The central role in the formation of taste that France had developed from the seventeenth century onwards was reinforced by Napoleon's victories and enforced alliances with other powers, including his marriage to the Austrian emperor's daughter Marie-Louise in 1810, and his penchant for setting up his relations and marshals as kings in their own right, all of whom carried the Empire style across the Continent.

The great German and Austrian State porcelain factories fell into this pattern. They continued to use the finest sculptors and designers in their service, although by now all trace of rococo frivolity had gone. Figures were still made in these factories, but they were now almost exclusively white and left in the biscuit stage, and intended to resemble small-scale sculpture as much as possible. There was now little demand for the fanciful porcelain figures of the eighteenth century for dessert decoration, and by 1835 the German writer Eichendorff records a last sight of them on display during the preparations for a country birthday party, in a garden room.[41] The leading porcelain factories continued to be the state-subsidised ones at Meissen, Berlin, Nymphenburg and Vienna, though again they were subject to the vagaries of their country's economic climate and problems caused by the Napoleonic wars. Some of the distinguished factories of the eighteenth century, such as Frankenthal, had to close, and lesser porcelain and pottery factories had to withstand the Napoleonic wars followed by the cold blast of commercial competition from Staffordshire in England.

At Meissen the courtier Marcolini continued in his post until 1814, when he was replaced as director by the Inspector of Mines, von Oppel. Von Oppel developed as a speciality porcelain in relief tinted to resemble Wedgwood's jasperware, based on specially bought-in specimens. With the coming of peace and the return of the monarchy in 1814 the new technical head, Heinrich Gottlieb Kühn, set about developing a much wider range of colours to compete with the factory at Sèvres, which is specifi-

272 Teaset (*déjeuner*), originally in a leather case, taken from the coach of Joseph Bonaparte after the Battle of Vittoria in 1813. Hard-paste porcelain, painted in enamel colours and gilt. Paris (Dihl and Guérhard), *c.*1810. Wellington Museum, Apsley House, London.

cally mentioned in a document of 1824.[42] The chief breakthrough at this time was the development of an underglaze green, which was used in some very attractive and simple laurel border decoration.

The factory at Berlin suffered the indignity of French occupation and control during the Napoleonic wars, although many of its products, such as high-handled *Campana*-form cups and saucers, were in imitation of French taste in any case. The sculptor Johann Gottfried Schadow (1764–1850) continued to provide models for biscuit porcelain, often executed by the talented modeller Johann Karl Friedrich Riese. The most beautiful designs were prepared after the Napoleonic wars by the great Prussian architect Karl Friedrich Schinkel (1781–1841), who devised a range of chaste neo-classical shapes, based on such models as the *Medici* vase, for the factory. However, his most remarkable work is probably the *Persian* vase, a curvaceous work intended to evoke the forms and elaborate decoration of the East (figs. 273 and 274). It is one of a number of vase-forms that were created to act as diplomatic gifts throughout the world.[43]

A similar stylistic pattern can be seen at the factories at Nymphenburg, whose most notable products were large ceremonial vases and gilded and painted Grecian cups and saucers intended more for decoration or souvenirs rather than for use. A whole series of two-handled vases based on amphora-type forms were designed by Frederick von Gärtner (1787–1847) and heavily gilt by the gilder Joseph Hammerl (1793– 1842) with tight miniature-type painting by Christian Adler (1787–1850); many of these survive in the former royal collections at Munich today (fig. 275), together with vases from the factories at Sèvres and Naples.[44] Cups and saucers based on Parisian models were also made, but painted with portraits of the royal family or local events, such as the great *Oktoberfest*.[45]

At Vienna, the factory came under the direction of Matthias Niedermayer after the death of von Sorgenthal in 1805. He continued the tradition of white biscuit figures and lavishly decorated pieces in the French style, influenced by his personal friendship with Brongniart of the Sèvres factory. Particularly notable was the quality of painting, from the flowers executed by Joseph Nigg to good quality landscape views from a

273 Group of Berlin porcelain exhibited at the Great Exhibition of 1851, including (back) a 'Schinkel' vase.

274 Vases of Berlin porcelain exhibited at the Great Exhibition of 1851, including (front) a 'Persian' vase.

275 Vases from the 'Onyx' service. Hard-paste porcelain, painted in enamel colours and gilt. Height 33 cm. Nymphenburg, *c*.1830. Residenzmuseum, Munich.

276 Cup and saucer inscribed with the name of the English painter Sir Thomas Lawrence. Hard-paste porcelain, painted in enamel colours and gilt. Height of cup 9.3 cm. Vienna, *c*.1825. Royal Museum of Scotland, Edinburgh.

wide-angle executed by the painters Jacob Schuhfried (worked 1798–1857), Franz Sartory (worked 1799–1841), and Anton Kothgasser (worked 1784–1840), who is also famous for his enamelled work on glass goblets. Such wares were used as display and presentation pieces (fig. 276).

The severe outlines and gilded surfaces of early nineteenth-century continental porcelain found little following in Britain, which had no reason, artistic or political, to follow the Empire style of Napoleon. The most influential ceramics were the wares of the eighteenth-century factory at Sèvres – especially those in the florid rococo taste – which became widely collected in this period[46] and set in train a whole movement of faking, copying and stylistic imitation that came to dominate ceramic design in Britain in the period after the Napoleonic wars. It was all part of a revived interest in the products of the French eighteenth century, which was stimulated by the sale of the furnishings of the French royal palaces. These came on the market immediate-

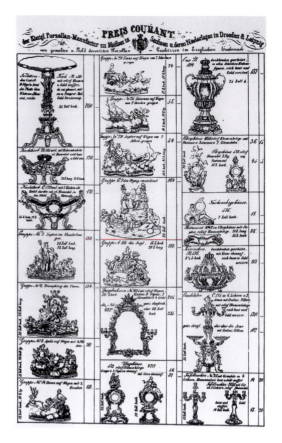

ly after the fall of the monarchy and were exported in bulk to the vastly wealthy aristocracy in Britain.[47] This taste was centred on the Prince of Wales, later the Prince Regent,[48] and his immediate circle, including the 3rd Marquess of Hertford, who formed the nucleus of what is today the Wallace Collection in London, the finest collection of eighteenth-century French art and *objets d'art* outside France.

This taste for the French rococo led to wholesale copying and faking of Sèvres porcelain. The fashion was aided by the decision of the director of Sèvres, Brongniart, to sell off undecorated or lightly decorated soft-paste items from 1804 onwards, which were imported into England and decorated in the appropriate style. Dinner services decorated with simple sprigs of flowers on a white ground, which were unsaleable in Paris, were sent to England where the decoration was removed with hydrofluoric acid and refired with rich ground-colours, gilding and painting in reserves.[49] Soft-paste porcelain in the manner of Sèvres was made at Nantgarw and Swansea in Wales[50] and bone-china at Coalport in Shropshire.[51] Some was sent to the china-dealer Mortlock's for decoration in the Sèvres manner, to the extent that the potters of these factories protested to the government in 1814 about the amount of undecorated porcelain being imported from Sèvres itself.[52] The most deceptive seems to have been a soft-paste factory set up at Madeley in Shropshire by Thomas Martin Randall (1786–1859), who also appears to have made a speciality of redecorating old Sèvres porcelain in a more lavish manner. He ran an enamelling business, Robins and Randall, in Barnsbury Street, Islington, which seems to have continued until 1825, and sold his wares to the antique-dealer Edward Holmes Baldock.[53]

The taste for lavish porcelain in the rococo style of Sèvres also extended to the products of other factories, such as the mid-eighteenth-century productions of Meissen.[54] Indeed, the demand from the London dealers for the wares of Meissen of this period was

277 Page from the Meissen illustrated price-list of 1846, showing pieces in the revived rococo taste for the English market.

278 Vase in the rococo revival taste. Hard-paste porcelain, painted in enamel colours and gilt. Meissen *c.*1830. Royal Museum of Scotland, Edinburgh.

279 'Rhinoceros' vase. Bone china, painted in enamel colours with a scene from *Don Quixote* and gilt. Height 1 m 14 cm. Rockingham, 1826. Clifton Park Museum, Rotherham, courtesy of Rotherham Museums & Arts Service.

sufficient to prevent the factory going bankrupt in the difficult days after the Napoleonic wars, when the factory started making reproductions after using up their existing stocks of undecorated porcelain. The factory owners, steeped in the neo-classical style, perceived the taste for the rococo as *scurril* (crazy or eccentric), but allowed it to dominate production to encourage visits from London dealers.[55] The catalogue of 1846 shows a wide range of these mid-eighteenth-century models, including many of the large vases and pieces made for Louis XV, as well as the famous 'monkey band', describing them 'im Englischen Geschmack' (in the English taste) (figs. 277, 278).

Thus it was that the rococo style became generally accepted as *the* style throughout Britain in the 1820s; it was at first accepted as an aristocratic taste and eventually worked its way down to the middle-classes, and then to the rest of Europe. There came into being in England a whole group of porcelain-makers of the finest quality who made their fortune from producing ordinary tea and dinner wares in the rococo taste. The most famous is that of Rockingham. This was a short-lived factory, founded by the pottery-makers Brameld, which was unique among British factories in that it gained the direct patronage of an aristocrat, the Marquess of Rockingham, in 1827. Most of its wares were in the most extravagant rococo style, usually lavishly painted and encrusted with a multitude of applied flowers in the style of eighteenth-century Meissen. In 1826 it produced what is its masterpiece in this style, the pair of 'Rhinoceros' vases (so-called from their finials), probably designed by the manager, Thomas Brameld, himself (fig. 279).[56] However the obvious design deficiencies in this technical *tour de force* have led this to be called 'possibly the most hideous object in the universe'.[57]

Standards of design had in fact reached such a low level that the British government was beginning to show concern, not for any reason of taste, but from fear that Britain would lose the ability to compete in world markets, with a consequent lack of employment and unrest among the masses. A government committee was set up in 1835 'to inquire into the best means of extending a knowledge of the ARTS, and of the PRINCIPLES OF DESIGN, among the People (especially the Manufacturing Population) of the Country'. The committee took evidence from all the leading designers and interested parties in Britain, who were united in their condemnation of the reproduction of 'Louis Quartorze' and 'Louis Quinze', since, according to the architect J. B. Papworth, 'twist it about as much as they like, it is only copying and copying'.[58] Papworth himself favoured a rich Roman or Grecian style, but the general feeling of the time was that designers and makers should be thoroughly familiar with the styles of the past in order to produce items which maintained a consistent stylistic unity – the regressive taste dominant in nineteenth-century Europe termed today 'Historicism'. As a result, government schools of design were set up, and official interest in industrial design culminated in the Great Exhibition of 1851, which led in turn to the setting up of the South Kensington (now Victoria and Albert) Museum, at first in the government school of design at Marlborough House in 1853.[59] From then on, developments in the history of ceramic design were no longer the prerogative of a wealthy aristocracy or landed class, but the result of officially directed social and economic policies given expression in international exhibitions. The great age of nineteenth-century design had begun.

Detail of fig. 276. Cup and saucer inscribed with the name of the English painter Sir Thomas Lawrence.

Overleaf. Detail of fig. 89. Posset pot and salver

Notes

Introduction

1. *The Complete Works of Sir Joshua Reynolds, first President of the Royal Academy*, London, 1824, p.XCIX.

2. See H. Coutts, 'Josephine Bowes and the Craze for Collecting Ceramics in the 19th century', *The International Ceramics Fair and Seminar* [Handbook] (1992), pp.16–23.

3. 'Ceramics, as well as other forms of material culture, become historical documents which supplement the written sources, and, provided that some information is available as to place, maker, or cultural context, they are of value [in solving historical or cultural problems] – whether accumulated by antiquarians, by ethnologic or artists collection, or by archaeological excavation', R. W. Ehrich, 'Ceramics and Man. A Cultural Perspective' in F. R. Matson (ed.), *Ceramics and Man*, London, 1966, p.11. See also O. Shepherd, *Ceramics for the Archaeologist*, 1956, and D. Gaimster, 'The Archaeology of Post-Medieval Society, c.1450–1750: Material Culture Studies in Britain Since the War', in *Building on the Past: Papers Celebrating 150 Years of the Royal Archaeological Institute*, London, 1994, pp.283–312.

4. R. Weinhold, *The Many Faces of Clay*, Leipzig, 1983.

5. H. Brigstocke, *Italian and Spanish Paintings in the National Gallery of Scotland*, Edinburgh, 1978, p.176.

6. 'Un vaso per bever o per sol belvedere'. J. Hayward, *Virtuoso Goldsmiths and the Triumph of Mannerism*, London, 1976, p.45.

7. 'La porcelaine un peu décorée est bien souvent plus objet de décoration que d'usage journalier'. R. Savill, *The Wallace Collection: Catalogue of Sèvres Porcelain*, London, 1988, p.489.

8. In 1787 the king's 'chef du gobelet du roi' wrote to him that 'Sa Majesté a bien ordonné un riche Service, mais joint a ce qu'il ne sera complet que dans bien des années, son extrême beauté ne permettra pas qu'on s'en serve habituellement'. G. de Bellaigue, *Sèvres Porcelain in the Collection of Her Majesty the Queen: The Louis XVI Service*, Cambridge, 1986, p.12.

9. Quoted by G. Jackson-Stops in *Courts and Colonies: The William and Mary Style in Holland, England, and America*, New York/Pittsburgh, 1988, p.36.

10. See W. David Kingery (ed.), *Learning from Things: Method and Theory in Material Culture Studies*, Washington, Smithsonian Institute, 1996.

11. T. Veblen (ed.), *The Theory of the Leisure Class: A Study of Institutions*, London, 1949.

12. A guest 'consumes vicariously for his host at the same time that he is a witness to the consumption of that excess of good things which his host is unable to dispose of single-handed, and he is also made to witness his host's facility in etiquette'. Veblen, op.cit., p.74. c.f. also Pierre Bourdieu, *Distinction: A Social Critique of the Judgment of Taste*, London, 1986.

13. 'Use value is *also* a fetishized social relation . . . it is an abstraction of the system of needs cloaked in the false evidence of a concrete destination and purpose, an intrinsic finality of goods and products'. J. Baudrillard, *For a Critique of the Political Economy of the Sign*, St Louis, 1981, p.131.

14. 'An excellent and well-arranged dinner is a most pleasing occurrence, and a great triumph of civilised life. It is not only the descending morsel, and the enveloping sauce – but the rank, wealth, wit and beauty which surround the meats – the learned management of light and heat – the smiling and sedulous host, proffering gusts and relishes – the exotic bottles – the embossed plate – the pleasant remarks – the handsome dresses – the cunning artifices in flour and farina! The hour of dinner, in short, includes every thing of sensual and intellectual gratification which a great nation glories in producing'. Sydney Smith, quoted in J. Green, *Consuming Passions*, London, 1985, p.32.

15. A. Adburgham, *Silver Fork Society: Fashionable Life and Literature from 1814 to 1840*, London, 1983, p.50.

16. 'Wealthy, inordinate and immense as the dinner may be, it cannot give the *tact*, the manner of doing things. In the midst of the golden dishes and golden vases, there is always some mistake at such dinners, some little blunder which neither the master nor mistress of the house can hope to rectify on any future occasions, not being conscious of anything wrong . . . in short, there is always some drawback, some terrible qualifier in the affair, which it would be difficult to define, but which invariably gives the *air bourgeoise* to all the attempts of upstart wealth to imitate the tone and manner of the aristocracy of our country', quoted in Adburgham, op.cit., p.49.

17. As recounted in an interview on the programme *Face to Face* (1959), repeated on BBC2, 13 November 1988. The point is developed by M.Visser, *The Rituals of Dinner*, London, 1992, p.19.

18. The Victorian humourist Richard Harris Barham, writer of *The Ingoldsby Legends*, asked 'How our ancestors managed to do without tea/I must fairly confess is a mystery to me/Yet your Lydgates and Chaucers/Had no cups and saucers'. R. H. Barham, *The Ingoldsby Legends*, 1840, quoted in J. Green, op.cit., p.232.

19. See, for instance, L. Weatherill, *Consumer Behaviour and Material Culture in Britain 1660–1760*, London, 1988.

20. B. Hillier, *Pottery and Porcelain 1700–1914*, London, 1968, p.77.

21. J. Steegman, *The Rule of Taste from George I to George IV*, London, 1936, p.191.

22. K. E. Farrer, *Letters of Josiah Wedgwood 1762–1770*, Manchester, 1903 [reprint], p.141.

23. But c.f. A. Adburgham, *Shops and Shopping, 1800–1914*, and Hoh-Cheung Mui and H. Lorna, *Shops and Shopkeeping in 18th century England*, 1989; Claire Walsh, 'Shop Design and the Display of Goods in Eighteenth-Century London', *Journal of Design History* (1995), vol.8, no.3, pp.157–76.

24. Summaries included in the appendix of J. Twitchett, *Derby Porcelain*, London, 1980.

25. Although John Mallet points out to me that both Solon and the Staffordshire potters were using liquid clay or 'slip' as decoration.

26. L. Solon, *The Ancient Art of Stoneware in the Low Countries and Germany*, London, 1892, vol.1, p.26.

27. 'However simple an ornamental earthen pot, it is seldom the product of the ingenuity and talent of a single individual. Without taking into account the accumulated experience handed down to their followers by the preceding generation – of which any work we are trying to analyze is partly the result – many hands have assisted in the completion of this single object. The potter's art is eminently a collective one'. Solon, op.cit., p.20.

28. E.g. the potter 'is absorbed first and foremost with the technical mysteries of his craft, and is prepared to accept as incidentals whatever forms and decoration are proposed by his teacher, who may live at the opposite end of the world'. A. Lane, *Style in Pottery*, London, 1948, p.12.

29. This was noted by the Italian Bernardino Ramazzini in his *De Morbis Artificum* of 1700: 'There's scarce any City in which there are not other Workmen, besides those mention'd above, who receive great Prejudice from the Metallick Plagues. Among such we reckon the Potters; for what City, what Town is without such a practice that is the Ancientest of all Arts? Now, the Potters make use of burnt and calcin'd Lead for glazing their Ware; and for that end grind their Lead in

Marble Vessels, by turning about a long Piece of Wood hung from the Roof, with a square Stone fasten'd to it at the other end. While they do this, as well as when with a pair of Tongs they daub their Vessels over with melted Lead before they put 'em into the Furnace; they receive by the Mouth and Nostrils and all the Pores of the Body all the virulent Parts of the Lead thus melted in Water & dissolv'd, and thereupon are siez'd with heavy Disorders. For first of all their Hands begin to shake and tremble, soon after they become Paralytick, Lethargick, Splenetick, Cachectick and Toothless, and in fine, you'll scarce see a Potter that has not a Leaden Death-like Complexion'. B. Hillier, op.cit., pp.19–20.

30. He then goes on to say that other qualities matter more, and that 'a right mind, and generous affection, had more beauty and charm, than all other symmetries in the world besides'. Quoted in D. Irwin, *Winckelmann: Writings on Art*, London, 1972, p.39.

CHAPTER 1
Pottery-Making in Medieval Europe

1. D. E. Arnold, *Ceramic Theory and Cultural Process*, Cambridge, 1985.

2. M. R. McCarthy and C. M. Brooks, *Medieval Pottery in Britain* AD *900–1600*, London, 1988, p.15.

3. I. Freestone, D. Gaimster *et al.*, *Pottery in the Making*, British Museum, London, 1997, p.33.

4. *See* D. M. Billington, *The Technique of Pottery*, London, 1974.

5. *See* J. D. Beazley, 'Potter and Painter in Ancient Athens', *Proceedings of the British Academy*, 30 (1944), republished in *Greek Vases, Lectures by J. D. Beazley*, D. C. Kurtz, (ed.), Oxford, 1989, pp.39–59. I owe this reference to J.V. G. Mallet.

6. McCarthy and Brooks (1988), op.cit., p.27; Freestone and Gaimster (1997) op.cit., p.95.

7. Freestone and Gaimster (1997), op.cit., p.94.

8. J. Musty, 'Medieval Pottery Kilns' in V. I. Evison (ed.), *Medieval Pottery from Excavations*, London, 1974, pp.41–67.

9. McCarthy and Brooks (1988), op.cit., p.13.

10. C. Wickham, 'Problems of comparing rural societies in early medieval Europe', *Transactions of the Royal Historical Society*, 6 (second series) (1992), pp.221–46.

11. For a general discussion of the use of metal, wooden and ceramics items in early Medieval England, *see* C. Earwood, *Domestic Wooden Artefacts in Britain and Ireland from Neolithic to Viking Times*, Exeter, 1993, and J. Hatcher and T. C. Barker, *A History of British Pewter*, London, 1974, p.40. For a discussion of wooden vessels found in Ribe in Denmark, see H. Stiesdal, 'An Excavation in the town of Ribe, Denmark', *Rotterdam Papers, A contribution to Medieval Archaeology*, Rotterdam, 1968, p.159.

12. *See* H. Hodges, 'The medieval potter: artisan or artist' in Vera I. Evison, (ed.), *Medieval Pottery from Excavations*, London, 1974, pp.33–41.

13. Freestone and Gaimster, 1997, pp.92–3.

14. For a survey of simple cooking and eating utensils, see A. Ruempol and A. van Dongen, *Pre-Industrial Utensils 1150–1800*, Museum Boymans-van Beuningen, Rotterdam, 1990.

15. See C. Dyer, 'The Social and Economic Changes of the Later Middle Ages and the Pottery of the Period', *Medieval Ceramics*, 6 (1982), pp.33–42.

16. J. D. Frierman, *Medieval Ceramics: VI to XIII Centuries*, University of California, 1975, p.17.

17. K. J. Barton, 'The Medieval Blackwares of Northern France', in V. I. Evison (ed.), (1974), op.cit.

18. Frierman, op.cit., p.18.

19. J. Chapellot, *Potiers de Saintonge: huit siècles d'artisanal rural*, Paris, 1975.

20. G. C. Dunning, 'Polychrome pottery found in Britain', *Archaeologia*, LXXXIII (1933), pp.109–38; 'The Trade in Medieval Pottery around the North Sea', *Rotterdam Papers*, Rotterdam, 1968, pp.35–58.

21. P. Kristian Madsen 'A Survey of the Research of Danish Medieval Pottery', *Medieval Ceramics*, 10 (1986), pp.57–84.

22. U. Lobbedey, 'Untersuchungen Mittelatericher Keramik', *Arbeiten zur Frühmittelalterforschungen*, 3 (Berlin 1968).

23. Dunning (1968), op.cit., p.35.

24. See F. Verhaeghe, 'La Céramique en Flandres (XIIIe–XVe siècle): quelques aspects de l'évolution et la concurrence' in J. Chapelot, H. Galinie and J. Pilet-Lemière, *La Céramique (Ve–XXe s): Fabrication – Commercialisation – Utilisation. Actes du premier colloque international d'archéologie médiévale (Paris 4–6 Octobre 1985)* Caen, 1985, pp.203–25.

25. M. Biddle and K. Barclay, 'Winchester Ware', in V. I. Evison (ed.), (1974), op.cit., pp.137–66.

26. J. Pearce and A. Vince, *Surrey Whitewares*, London, 1988.

27. McCarthy and Brooks, 1988, op.cit., p.97.

28. K. J. Barton, 'Ceramics Changes in Western European littoral at the end of the Middle Ages: a personal view' in David Gaimster and Mark Redknap (eds), *Everyday and Exotic Pottery from Europe: Studies in honour of John G. Hurst*, London, 1992, pp.246–55.

29. See note 2; see also *A Guide to the Classification of Medieval Ceramic Forms*, Occasional Papers from the Medieval Pottery Research Group, no.1, London, 1988.

30. Freestone and Gaimster (1997), op.cit., p.94.

31. S. Jennings, *Medieval Pottery in the Yorkshire Museum*, York, 1992, p.10.

32. See P. G. Farmer, *An Introduction to Scarborough Ware and a Re-Assessment of the Knight Jug*, Hove, 1979.

33. M. R. McCarthy and Brooks (1988), op.cit., p.128.

34. Ibid., p.128.

35. Dunning (1968), op.cit. p.35; Dennis Hazelgrove, 'Imported Pottery in the "Book of Rates": English Customs Categories in the 16th and 17th centuries', in Gaimster and Redknap (1992), op.cit.

36. For the export of Spanish pottery to Northern Europe, see W. Childs, 'Documentary Evidence for the Import of Spanish Pottery to England in the later Middle Ages' and J. G. Hurst, 'Spanish Medieval Ceramics in North-West Europe', in C. M. Gerrard, A. Gutiérrez and A. G. Vince, *Spanish Medieval Ceramics in Spain and the British Isles*, Oxford, 1995, pp.25–31 and pp.367–9.

37. P. Davey (ed.), and R. Hodges, *Ceramics and Trade*, Sheffield, 1983, pp.3–4.

38. J. le Patourel, 'Documentary evidence for the pottery trade in north-west Europe' in Davey and Hodges (1983), op.cit., pp.27–35.

39. Davey and Hodges (1983), op.cit., pp.19–21.

40. McCarthy and Brooks (1988), op.cit., p.17.

41. E. Eames, *English Medieval Tiles*, London, British Museum, 1985, p.7.

42. Ibid., pp.20–1.

43. O. Van Os, 'Meditation on some Tiles in a Country Church', *English Ceramic Circle Transactions*, vol.7, part 3 (1970), pp.155–9.

44. Frierman (1975), op.cit., p.18.

CHAPTER 2
The Spread of Tin-Glazed Earthenware: Italian Maiolica

1. A. Caiger-Smith, *Tin-glaze Pottery in Europe and the Islamic World*, London, 1973, p.83.

2. J. D. Frierman, *Medieval Ceramics: VI to XIII Centuries*, California, 1975, p.17.

3. T. Wilson, *Ceramic Art of the Italian Renaissance*, London, 1987, p.24.

4. Frierman, op.cit., p.84.

5. D. Whitehouse, 'Medieval pottery in Italy: the present state of research', in *La Céramique Médiévale en Méditerranée Occidentale Xe–XVe siècles*, Colloques Internationaux du Centre National de la Recherche Scientifique no.584, Valbonne, 1978, pp.65–83.

6. Caiger-Smith, op.cit., p.84.

7. Wilson (1987), op.cit., p.28.

8. T. Wilson, 'The Beginnings of Lustreware in Renaissance Italy', *The International Ceramics Fair and Seminar [Handbook]*, London, 1996, pp.35–43.

9. Wilson (1987), op.cit., nos.15 and 16.

10. B. Rackham, *Italian Maiolica*, London, 1952, fig. 10a.

11. Caiger-Smith, op.cit., p.85.

12. The origin of blue is discussed by Anna Moore Valeri, 'Il Campanile di Giotto e le Origini della Maiolica Blu in Toscana', *Faenza*, LXXII (1986), pp.281–9, although the earliest uses of blue appear to be derived from copper rather than cobalt.

13. Wilson (1987), op.cit., p.32. Another possible workshop is that of Maso and Miniato di Domenico; *see* G. Conti *et al.*, *Zaffera et Similia nella Maiolica Italiana*, Viterbo, 1991, p.52.

14. Caiger-Smith, op.cit., p.86.

15. For a Florentine version of a Hispano-Moresque jug see T. Wilson, *Maiolica: Italian Renaissance Ceramics in the Ashmolean Museum*, Oxford, 1989, pp.12–13.

16. See F. Ames-Lewis and J. Wright, *Drawing in the Italian Renaissance Workshop*, Nottingham and London, 1983, pp.95–101.

17. J. Pope-Hennessy, *Luca della Robbia*, Oxford, 1980, p.241. Della Robbia in fact used a higher degree of tin-oxide in the glaze, without the addition of sand, producing a whiter body than in ordinary maiolica; see Julia Poole, *Italian Maiolica and Incised Slipware in the Fitzwilliam Museum, Cambridge*, Cambridge, 1995, p.110, no.165.

18. S. Nepoti, *Ceramiche Graffite della donazione Donini Baer*, Faenza, 1991.

19. P. Berardi, *L'Antica Maiolica di Pesaro*, Florence, 1984, pp.18–19, n.21, and Carmen Ravanelli Guidotti, *Il Pavimento della Capella Vaselli in S. Petronio a Bologna*, Bologna, 1988.

20. A. Bettini, 'Sul servizio di Mattia Corvino e sulla maiolica pesarese della second metà del XV secolo', *Faenza* (1997), pp.169–175.

21. G. Donatone, *Maioliche napoletane della speziera aragonese di Castelnuovo*, Naples, 1970.

22. There were two distinct manners or ways of engraving: the 'fine' manner, with narrow grooves in the plates, which was developed by Baccio Baldini in Florence, but had the disadvantage of wearing away quickly, and the 'broad' or coarser manner, developed by Francesco Roselli, which could produce many more impressions. J. A. Levenson *et al.*, *Early Italian Engravings from the National Gallery of Art*, Washington, 1972.

23. F. Lippmann, *The Art of Wood-Engravings in Italy in the 15th Century*, London, 1888, pp.4–9.

24. B. Rackham, 'The Sources of Design of Italian Maiolica', *The Burlington Magazine*, XXIII (1913), pp.193–203.

25. G. Szabo, *The Robert Lehman Collection*, New York, 1975, figs 144–6; T. Wilson 'Pollaiulo's Lost "Hercules and the Lion" Recorded on Maiolica?', *Journal of the Warburg and Courtauld Institutes*, 53, 1990, pp.299–303.

26. B. Jestaz, 'Les Modèles de la Maiolique Historiée', *Gazette des Beaux-Arts*, LXXIX (1972), pp.215–40, LXXXI (1973), pp.109–28; Carmen Ravanelli Guidotti, 'Medaglie, Placchette, Incisioni e Ceramiche, un Itinerario Iconografico Attraverso Materiali del Rinascimento' in *Piccoli Bronzi e Placchette del Museo Nazionale di Ravenna*; Grazia Biscontini Ugolini and Jacqueline Petruzzellis Scherer, *Maiolica e Incisione*, Milan, Castello Sforzesco, 1992.

27. 'Acquisitions in the Victoria and Albert Museum Department of Ceramics and Glass 1987–9', *The Burlington Magazine*, CXXXII, May, 1990, p.384, no.II.

28. G. Cora and A. Fanfani, *La maiolica di Cafaggiolo*, Florence, 1982, no.6.

29. W. Watson, *Italian Renaissance Maiolica from the William A. Clark Collection*, London, 1986, p.29.

30. Cora and Fanfani (1982), op.cit., nos.7 and 5.

31. J. Schulz, 'Pintoricchio and the Revival of Antiquity', *Journal of the Warburg and Courtauld Institutes*, 25, 1962, pp.47–55.

32. Vitruvius wrote that 'On the stucco are monsters rather than definite representations taken from definite things. Instead of columns there rise up stalks; instead of gables, striped panels with curled leaves and volutes. Candelabra uphold picture shrines, and above the summit of these, clusters of thin stalks with heads of men and animals attached to half the body . . . Such things neither are, nor can be, nor have been'. E. H. Gombrich, *The Sense of Order*, London, 1979, p.20.

33. Wilson (1987), op.cit., no.134.

34. Ibid., no.184.

35. C. W. Talbot (ed.), *Dürer in America: His Graphic Work*, New York, 1971.

36. L. Moszaros, 'Italianisches Majoliken und ihre Beziehung zur deutschen Druckgrafik des 16. Jahrhunderts', *Kunstspiegel*, Nuremberg, 1 (1979), pp.47–58.

37. Wilson (1987), op.cit., no.40.

38. P. Collins, 'Prints and the Development of *istoriato* Painting on Italian Renaissance Maiolica', *Print Quarterly*, IV, 3, pp.223–35.

39. Wilson (1987), op.cit., p.91.

40. B. Rackham, 'A New Chapter in the History of Italian Maiolica', *The Burlington Magazine*, XXVII (April 1915), pp.28–35.

41. The work is commented on by Leandro Alberti in his *Description of the Whole of Italy*, published in 1550: 'The earthenwares made here are renowned for being made to look as if they were gilt. It is such an ingenious technique that up to now no other workman in Italy has been found to equal them, although attempts and experiments have often been made. They are called *Majorica* wares'. Wilson (1987), op.cit., p.91.

42. 'Possibly no other printmaker has had as great an influence upon the development of the arts as Marcantonio. His prints were circulated far and wide; they were eagerly sought after for generations because they carried the attitudes and ideals of the High Renaissance, especially of Raphael and the members of his circle, to all parts of the civilized world'. I. H. Shoemaker and E. Brown, *The Engravings of Marcantonio Raimondi*, exhn. cat., Lawrence (Kansas) and Chapel Hill (N.C.), 1981, p.xi.

43. J.V. G. Mallet, 'In Botega di Maestro Guido Durantino', *The Burlington Magazine*, CXXIX (June 1987), p.285.

44. Wilson (1987), op.cit., nos.66 and 67.

45. At one time he was thought to be identical to Guido's father, Nicolo Pellipario (or Pellipario), who, however, was dead by 1511. Mallet (1987), op.cit., p.284.

46. Ibid., p.286.

47. H. Wallis, *XVII Plates by Nicola Fontana da Urbino at the Correr Museum Venice A Study in Early XVIth Cent[ur]y Maiolica*, London, 1905.

48. Wallis (1905), op.cit., figs 2, 3, 14, 15.

49. B. Rackham, 'Nicola Pellipario and Bramante', *The Burlington Magazine*, LXXXVII (June 1945), pp.144–8.

50. In the end Trotti ordered two sets, one from Faenza and one from Venice. T. Wilson, 'Maiolica in Renaissance Venice', *Apollo*, 125 (1987), pp.184–9.

51. J.V. G. Mallet, 'Mantua and Urbino: Gonzaga Patronage of Maiolica', *Apollo*, 114 (1981), pp.162–9.

52. The subject of Isaac and Rebecca is copied from the scene in Raphael's Loggia of 1517–19. It had not been engraved, and moreover shows knowledge of the colouring of the fresco, suggesting that possibly Nicola benefited from the advice of Raphael's pupil Giulio Romano, who was employed by the Court of Mantua from 1524 onwards. Mallet (1981), op.cit., p.164.

53. F. Ames-Lewis, ' Nicola da Urbino and Raphael', *The Burlington Magazine*, CXXX (September 1988), pp.691–2.

54. After Marcantonio, Bartsch XIV.331.441. See Burr Wallen, 'A Majolica Panel in the Widener Collection', *Report and Studies in the History of Art*, 1968, National Gallery of Art, Washington, D. C., pp.95–105.

55. Mallet (1981), op.cit., pp.284–95.

56. Ibid., p.286.

57. Wilson (1987), op.cit., p.52.

58. These enable us to put his birth-date back to *c.*1486–7, making him a contemporary of Nicola rather than a follower. J.V. G. Mallet, 'La Biografia di Francesco Xanto Avelli alla Luce dei Suoi Sonetti', *Faenza*, 70 (1984), pp.398–402.

59. J. Triolo, 'L'Urbs e l'Imperatore: a proposal for the interpretation of the Pucci Service by Xanto Avelli' in T. Wilson, (ed.), *Italian Renaissance Pottery*, London, 1991, pp.36–43. *See also* F. Cioci, 'Xanto e il Duca di Urbino: Il servizio pucci e il suo titolare: un omaggio all'impero', *Faenza* (1997), pp.205–29.

60. Wilson (1987), op.cit., no.75. A painter heavily influenced by Fra Xanto was Giulio da Urbino: *see* Dora Thornton, 'An allegory of the Sack of Rome by Giulio da Urbino', *Apollo*, 48 (June 1999), pp.11–18.

61. A.V. B. Norman, 'Sources for the design on a majolica dish', *Apollo*, 81 (June 1965), pp.460–2.

62. See, for instance, the three figures on a plate in the British Museum depicting *the Expulsion of Adam and Eve* are dependent on three separate prints by Marcantonio, all adapted in such a way as to hide their original subject. P. Collins, 1987, pp.230–1.

63. See J.V. G. Mallet, 'Francesco Urbini in Gubbio and Urbino', *Faenza*, 6 (1979), pp.279–91.

64. 'An excellent master without rival in the art of *maiolica* [i.e. lustreware], whose work brings honour to the city, lord and people of Gubbio in all the nations to which this pottery of his workshop is exported, as well as the great income it brings in customs dues'. In 1536 the kiln was made over to his sons Vincenzo and Ubaldo, who established a branch in Urbino itself. Wilson (1987), op.cit., p.103.

65. T. Clifford and J.V. G. Mallet, 'Battista Franco as a Designer of Maiolica', *The Burlington Magazine*, CXVIII (June 1976), pp.387–410.

66. Vasari tells us that 'before he left, he made all the drawings for a service which the Duke had carried out in earthenware at Castel Durante, as a present for King Philip of Spain'. The service was recorded as complete on 17 December, 1562, and described as bearing scenes from the life of Julius Caesar. The programme had been laid down by Muzio Giustino Politano. J. Gere, 'Taddeo Zuccaro as a Designer for Maiolica', *The Burlington Magazine*, 105 (1963), pp.3, 6, 315.

67. C. Piccolpasso, *The Three Books of the Potter's Art*, trans. by R. Lightbown and A. Caiger-Smith, London, 1980.

68. T. Wilson, 'Maiolica in Renaissance Venice', *Apollo*, 125 (March 1987), pp.184–9.

69. This was observed by Montaigne on a journey to Italy in 1581: 'Considering the fineness of this earthenware which is so white and clean it seems like porcelain, I found it so cheap that it seems to me really pleasanter for the table than the pewter of France – particularly what one finds in inns, which is squalid.' Wilson (1987), op.cit., p.148.

70. A service made for the Elector Johann Georg I of Saxony, painted with his coat-of-arms and slight decorations in blue, survives in Dresden. G. Reinheckel, *Prächtvolle Service*, Leipzig, 1989, p.13.

71. A contract of 1543 reveals that he agreed to supply 5,000 drug-jars to the apothecary Pierre Dubosc, some of which are thought to be identifiable with surviving items, painted with profile heads and a leaf and scroll background. J. Chompret, *Répertoire de la Faïence Française*, Paris, 1935, pp.210–12; *Faïences Françaises XVIe–XVIIIe Siècle*, Paris, Grand Palais des Champs-Elysées, 1980, p.193.

72. The British Museum owns a plate painted with Aaron's rod inscribed on the back in Italian 'lla verga di farao in serpentte' and signed and dated *1582 GTVF leon*. Wilson (1987), op.cit., no.257.

73. Caiger-Smith, op.cit., p.106.

74. See J. McNab, *Seventeenth-Century French Ceramic Art*, New York, Metropolitan Museum, 1987, pp.12–21.

75. A. Frothingham, *Talavera Pottery*, New York, 1944; A. Ray, 'Renaissance Pottery in Seville', *The Burlington Magazine*, CXXXII (May 1990), pp.343–4; 'Sixteenth-century pottery in Castile: a documentary study', *The Burlington Magazine*, CXXIII (May 1991), pp.298–305.

76. H. Coutts, 'Castelli Maiolica: The collection of Sir Brinsley Ford', *Apollo*, CXXII (October 1990), pp.250–5.

77. H. Coutts, 'Francesco Bedeschini: Designer of Maiolica', *Apollo*, CXXX (June 1987), pp. 401–3.

78. L. Arbace, *Maiolica di Castelli. La raccolta Acerbo*, Ferrara, 1993.

79. E. Pelizzoni and G. Zanchi, *La Maiolica dei Terchi*, Florence, 1982, p.125. Fine plates painted with architectural backgrounds were made in Pavia in the eighteenth century: *see* Elena Pelizzoni and Marica Forni, *La Maiolica di Pavia tra Seicento e Settecento*, Milan, 1997.

CHAPTER 3
'Court Styles' of the Renaissance: Urbino Maiolica, Saint-Porchaire and Palissy Ware

1. Marco Spallanzani, *Ceramiche alla Corte dei Medici nel Cinquecento*, Modena, 1994, p.129. I owe this reference to Timothy Wilson.

2. Mark Girouard, *Life in the English Country House*,

London, 1978, plate 1, p.41.

3. S. Bursche, *Tafelzier des Barock*, Munich, 1974, fig. 2.

4. A dinner given by Gaston de Foix in 1458 comprised seven courses, the fifth of which was given to custards and tarts, and the last to sweet things and confections. W. E. Head, *The English Medieval Feast*, London, 1931, p.160.

5. M. Girouard (1978), op.cit. pp.47–50. The best introduction to the subject of table-layout through the ages perhaps remains G. Brett, *Dinner is Served*, London, 1968.

6. P. Thornton, *The Italian Renaissance Interior 1400–1600*, London, 1991.

7. R. Tannahill, *Food in History*, London, 1973, revised edition 1988, pp.231–3.

8. M. Visser, *The Rituals of Dinner*, London, 1992, p.196.

9. See Christoforo Messibugo, *Banchetti*, Ferrara, 1549; G. Brunetti, *Cucino Mantovano*, Castel Gadolfi; M. Alberini, *4000 Anni a Tavola*, Milan, 1972; G. Maffiioli and G. Bellini, *Il Romanzo della Grande Cucina*, Rome, 1965; for the general setting, see M. Fagiolo (ed.), *La Festa a Roma: Dal Rinascimento al 1870*, Turin, 1997, and M. Fagiolo dell'Arco, *Corpus delle feste a Roma: la festa barocca*, Rome, 1997.

10. A reconstruction of a fifteenth-century place-setting is shown in D. Hartley, *Food in England*, London, 1954, p.222.

11. S. Bursche, *Tafelzier des Barock*, Munich, 1974, fig. 1.

12. For an English sixteenth-century set of plates, *see* D. Thornton and M. Cowell, 'The "Armada Service": A Set of Late Tudor Dining Silver', *The Antiquaries Journal*, vol.76 (1996), pp.153–80.

13. J. Hatcher and T. C. Barker, *A History of Pewter*, London, 1974, p.44.

14. M. Spallanzani, 'Un "Fornimento" di Maioliche di Montelupo per Clarice Strozzi de'Medici', *Faenza*, 70, 1984, pp.381–7.

15. Ianfrancesco, El Poeta, wrote to Duke Federico of Ferrara's secretary in August 1530 that 'I have been in Urbino and have seen really excellent ware painted with landscapes, fables and histories, to my eyes of surpassing beauty, and have explained to them about the service of which you wrote to me. The answer has been that they can't tell me the price unless they know the quality and quantity, but they say two gold ducats, and two and a half for one of those big dishes, and for some others one scudo, and two for a scudo, that is half a scudo for one, and *scudelli* and *tondi* at three and four pieces a scudo, according to the workmanship, because they are worth more or less depending on the greater or lesser amount of work, but I didn't tell them why I wanted the said service.' By 25 August he had 25 scudi for buying maiolica, 'and because these large dishes are not used any more I would like to omit them as they would not please, your Excellence will advise me by the bearer of this letter how many little plates you want, and of what kind, and also 'tondi', 'scutelle' and 'scutellini' . . . and whether you want candlesticks, basins and ewers. . . . as soon as I can, I shall set off and will arrange for the said maiolica, and I believe I shall have nearly a hundred pieces for the 25 scudi, leaving out the large dishes which cost one scudo each'. Quoted and translated in J.V. G. Mallet, 'Mantua and Urbino: Gonzaga Patronage of Maiolica', *Apollo*, CXIII (September 1981), pp.162–9.

16. The list includes drinking cups (*coppette*), footed bowls (*ongaresche, piadene*), plates with or without rims (*piatti strati*), trenchers (*tondi*), porringer or broth bowls in two sizes (*schudelle, schudellini*), covered cups (*tazze*) for women in childbed, and smaller ones (*tazzine, ciotelette*). He also lists wares by size, for the better setting of the kiln. These include among the *baconi* plates with rims or without (*piatti co' fondo e senza*), so-called meat plates (*piatti detti da carne*), baskets for fruit (*canestrelle da frutti*), raised salvers (*aborchiati*). Smaller plates included plates for salad and soup, in the silver manner (*piatti da insalata, piatti canati dallo argento [per?] minestre*), and for napkins and sauces (*piatti da saluiette e da samore*). C. Piccolpasso, *The Three Books of the Potter's Art*, translated and introduced by Ronald Lightbown and Alan Caiger-Smith, London, 1980, vol.II, pp.30–3.

17. C.f. a bill from Pino Bettisi of Florence of 1568: '2 catini grandi e 2 brocche per acqua per lavare mane'. A. V. B. Norman, *The Wallace Collection: Catalogue of Ceramics 1: Pottery, Maiolica, Faience, Stoneware*, London, 1976, p.19.

18. G. Pontano, *I trattati delle virtu sociali*, Naples, 1498, discusses dining as one of five social virtues, including conviviality, splendour and magnificence. See R. A. Goldthwaite, *Wealth and the Demand for Art in Italy 1300–1600*, Baltimore, 1993, p.245.

19. At a dinner given by Cardinal Pietro Riario in honour of Eleanor of Aragon on 7 June, 1483, there were 'Sugar confections in the shapes of castles, ships, and mythological figures, including the tasks of Hercules, artfully contrived' M. Baur-Heinhold, *Baroque Theatre*, London, 1967, p.13.

20. A description of one is given by the chronicler Pierre de l'Estoile of a dinner given to Henri III by Cardinal de Birague in 1580: after the dinner '*there were two large tables covered with 1,100 or 1,200 pieces of faience, full of dried fruits, sugar-plums, and confects of all kinds, built up into castles, pyramids, platforms, and other magnificent fashions, most of which were thrown down and broken in pieces by the pages and servants of the Court, who were of a wanton and insolent nature. And great was the loss, for all the service was excellently beautiful.*' P. Burty (ed.), W. Chaffers, *Chefs-D'oeuvres of the Industrial Arts*, London, 1869, pp.51–2. Gervase Markham gives a full description of preparation in *The English Hus-wife* of 1615 'having showed you how to preserve, conserve, candy and make pastes of all kinds, in which four heads(?) courses the whole Art of banqueting dishes, I will now proceed to the ordering of setting forth of a banquet, wherein you shall observe that March-panes [marzipan] have the first place, the middle places and the last place, your preserved fruits shall be dished up first, your pastes next, your wet suckets [syllabubs or creams], then your dried suckets [tarts or biscuits], then your marmalades and continiates [fruit pastes] then your comfets of all kinds . . . Thus you shall order them in the closet, but when they go to the table, you shall first send forth a dish made for show only, as Beast, Bird, Fish, Fowl according to invention, then your Marchpane'. E. Ayrton, *The Cookery of England*, London, 1954, p.461.

21. Raphael designed bronze salvers for Agostino Chigi in 1510, and a bronze perfume-burner for François I of France, and Michelangelo a salt-cellar for Francesco Maria della Rovere, Duke of Urbino, in 1537. J. F. Hayward, *Virtuoso Goldsmiths and the Triumph of Mannerism 1540–1620*, London, 1976, pp.83, 133.

22. B. L. Holman, exh. cat., *Disegno: Italian Renaissnace Designs for the Decorative Arts*, New York, 1997.

23. In a letter of 24 February, 1542, to Ferrante Gonzaga, Giulio refers to a pitcher and ewer (*boccale e bacino*) in the form of a ewer dripping water into a basin in the form of a whirlpool below. The latter specifies 'a variety of fish which are hard to distinguish from real ones' (*quella varieta de'pesci quale bisogneria vederli dalli veri*). J. T. Martineau, 'Giulio Romano's Designs for Silversmiths' in *Splendours of the Gonzaga*, London, 1981, pp.195–6.

24. Hayward, op.cit., p.82.

25. It was the son who seems to have specialised in the making of this luxury ware; according to the terms of the agreement, the father took responsibility for the white wares (*Lavori bianchi*), wares in the Venetian style (*Lavori alla Venezian*) and unfinished wares by the dozen (*Lavori dozzinali cotti e da cuocere*). J.V. G. Mallet, 'In Botega di Maestro Guido Durantino in Urbino', *The Burlington Magazine*, 129 (June 1987), p.286.

26. T. Wilson, *Ceramic Art of the Italian Renaissance*, London, 1987, no.90.

27. Ibid., no.208.

28. See R. Lightbown, *Mantegna*, Oxford, 1986, p.186 for an outline of the early history of *studioli*; also W. Liebenwein, *Studiolo: die Entstehung eines Raumtyps und seine Entwicklung bis um 1600*, 1977; D. Thornton, *The Scholar in His Study. Ownership and Experience in Renaissance Italy*, New Haven and London, 1997.

29. Hayward, op.cit., p.151.

30. Interest in porcelain was already apparent in the court of the Medici in Florence, where several hundred pieces of porcelain are recorded in inventories made between 1456 and 1555. In 1545 Jacopo Capponi was sent to Alexandria to buy porcelain and carpets for Cosimo I. M. Spallanzani, *Ceramiche orientalia a Firenze nel Rinascimento*, Florence, 1978, pp.176–93.

31. A recent scientific analysis of Francesco's porcelain has revealed it to be composed of a mixture of white clay, fine white sand and the glazemaker's sintered *marzacotto* made from sand, salt and calcined wine-lees. This use of silica rather than clay is Levantine in origin. The glaze was made from a mixture of sand, salt, lead oxide and calcined wine-lees in the manner of Italian maiolica. The low clay content made the items difficult to form, and the high firing temperature of 1,100°C led to warping and losses in the kiln. W. D. Kingery and P. B.Vandiver, 'Medici Porcelain', *Faenza*, 70 (1984), pp.441–51.

32. From 1573 to 1578 the maiolica expert Flaminio Fontana, nephew of Orazio, supervised firings. In 1573 he was paid by the Medici for ten earthenware vases, and inventory records of the Medici guardaroba list more than three dozen pieces by him, including oil- and vinegar-cruets and grotesque ornamented pieces. G. Cora and A. Fanfani, *La Porcellana dei Medici*, Milan, 1986, pp.41–3.

33. *Grand Duke Francesco has found the way of making 'Indian' porcelain and in his experiments has equalled the quality – its transparency, hardness, lightness and delicacy; it has taken him ten years to discover the secret, but a Levantine showed him the way to success.* Wilson, (1987), op.cit., p.157.

34. Two pieces of Medici porcelain are exceptional in that they are painted in enamel colours: a vase with handles in the collection at Brunswick, painted with a landscape in the manner of Italian maiolica, and a similarly shaped vase (now cut down) in the British Museum painted with a frieze of figures after B. Beham. The decoration on both pieces has been attributed to Flaminio Fontana himself. T. Wilson, (1987), op.cit., no.248, and J. Lessmann, 'Polychromes

35. C. Le Corbeiller, 'A Medici Porcelain Pilgrim Flask', *The J. Paul Getty Museum Journal*, 16 (1988), pp.119–26.

36. Cora and Fanfani, op.cit., pp.100–13.

37. Ibid., pp.140–3.

38. Ibid., p.79.

39. Ibid., p.125.

40. Y. Hackenbroch, 'Some Florentine Jewels: Bountalenti and the dragon theme', *The Connoisseur*, 169 (1968), pp.137–43.

41. Cora and Fanfani, op.cit., p.132.

42. Ibid., p.99.

43. Ibid., p.152.

44. See H. Zerner, *The School of Fontainebleau*, London, 1969.

45. E. Chami, 'L'Art Céramique de Beauvais au XVe et au XVIe Siècle', *Cahiers de la Céramique du Verre et des Arts du Feu*, 30 (1963), pp.79–116; [with H. P. Fourest] 'La Poterie Vernissée au XVIe Siècle' *Cahiers de la Céramique du Verre et des Arts du Feu*, 53 (1973), pp.28–36.

46. J. Giacometti, 'Renaissance Pottery – France' in *World Ceramics*, R. J. Charleston (ed.), London, 1977, p.118.

47. For a review of literature, see M. Brunet, *The Frick Collection: An Illustrated Catalogue. Vol. VII: Porcelains*, New York, 1974, pp.161–73.

48. On a flagon in the Louvre and two pieces in the Hermitage, Leningrad, and missing item found in 1890 at the Château de Lude. See B. Jestaz, 'Poteries de Saint Porchaire', *La Revue du Louvre*, 25 (1975), pp.384–95.

49. T. Crépin-Leblond *et al.*, *Une Orfèvrerie de Terre: Bernard Palissy et la céramique de Saint Porchaire*, Ecouen, Musée national de la Renaissance, 1997–8.

50. P. Ward-Jackson, 'Some main streams and tributaries in European ornament 1500–1700; Part 2: The Arabesque', *Victoria and Albert Museum Bulletin*, III, no.3 (July 1967), pp.90–103.

51. Jestaz, op.cit., p.388.

52. D. Barbour and S. Sturman (eds), *Saint-Porchaire Ceramics*, Washington, 1994.

53. Crépin-Leblond (1997), op.cit., p.52.

54. See M. Kemp. 'Wrought by No Artist's Hand', in *Reframing the Renaissance*, C. Farrago (ed.), New Haven and London, 1995.

55. From the *Discours admirables*, translated by C. C. Dauterman, 'Snakes, snails and creatures with tails: Palissy ware in the Metropolitan Museum', *The Connoisseur*, 169 (1968), pp.185–93.

56. A. M. Massinelli, Filippo Tuena, *Treasures of the Medici*, London, 1992.

57. 'At last I found means to make several vessels of different enamels intermixed in the manner of Jasper. That sustained me for several years, but, while making a living from these things, I sought always to make further progress, thus incurring expenses and disbursements – as you know that I am doing still. When I had discovered how to make my rustic pieces, I was in greater trouble and vexation than before; for having made a certain number of rustic basins and having fired them, my enamels turned out some beautiful and well fused, other ill fused; others were scorched, because they were composed of different materials that were fusible at different temperatures – the green of the lizards was overfired before the colour of the serpents was even melted; and the colour of the serpents, lobsters, tortoises, and crabs was melted before the white had attained any beauty.' Dauterman, op.cit., p.187.

58. P. Ward-Jackson, op.cit., p.122.

59. L. Amico, *Bernard Palissy: In Search of Earthly Paradise*, Paris and New York, 1996, p.18.

60. Ibid., p.71.

61. L. Amico, 'Les Céramiques rustiques authentiques de Bernard Palissy, *Revue de l'Art*, 78 (1987), pp.61–9.

62. E. Kris, 'Der Stil "rustique" ', *Jahrbuch der Kunsthistorischen Sammlungen in Wien*, N.F.1, 1926, pp.137–208; N. Gramaccini, 'Das genaue Abbild der Natur – Riccios Tiere und die Theorie des Naturabgusses seit Cennino Cennini', *Natur und Antike in der Renaissance*, Frankfurt am Main, 1985, pp.198–225.

63. In his *Recepte Véritable* of 1563 he describes an ideal garden which would be a refuge of the day (surely a reference to the Wars of Religion of 1562–3). The garden was to be situated in the mountains in accordance with Psalm 104, where Christians could take refuge in times of persecution. He discusses the origins of materials, such as crystal being 'congealed water and salt', or that metals are created by sulphur of quick silver; and the need for a fountain or stream to pass through the garden. Above all, he would divide the garden up into sections marked by eight *cabinets* or small pavilions, one of which would be similar to Montmorency's grotto, 'sculpted and enamelled' like a *rocher tortu*, decorated with frogs, tortoises, lobsters and snails, 'all the aforesaid animals will be sculpted and enamelled so close to nature that other real lizards and serpent will often come and admire them. [tous lesdits animaux seront insculpez et esmaillez si pres de la nature que les autres lizars naturels et serpents les viendront souvent admirer]. *Les Oeuvres de Bernard Palissy*, Paris, 1880, p.85.

64. J. McNab, *Seventeenth-Century French Ceramic Art*, New York, 1987, pp.6–7.

CHAPTER 4
The Stoneware Tradition

1. See H.-G. Stephan, *Die bemalte Irdenware der Renaissance in Mitteleuropa*, Munich, 1987.

2. A maiolica dish from Faenza in the British Museum (T. Wilson, *Ceramic Art of the Italian Renaissance*, London, 1987, no.183) is copied from Dürer's print of *Christ Washing the Feet of his Disciples* or the copy by Raimondi.

3. See catalogues *Heinrich Aldegrever: die Kleinmeister und das Kunsthandwerk der Renaissance*, Unna, Ev. Stadtkirche, 1986, and *The World in Miniature: Engravings by the German Little Masters, 1500–1550*, S. H. Goddard (ed.), Spencer Museum of Art, University of Kansas, 1988.

4. B. Lipperheide, *Das Rheinische Steinzeug und die Graphik der Renaissance*, Berlin, 1961, p.22.

5. W. Watson, *Italian Renaissance Maiolica from the William A. Clark Collection*, London, 1986, no.58.

6. A. V. B. Norman, *The Wallace Collection: Catalogue of Ceramics 1: Pottery, Maiolica, Faience, Stoneware*, London, 1976, no.C.113.

7. H.-G. Stephan, *Die bemalte Irdenware der Renaissance in Mitteleuropa*, Munich, 1987, p.264.

8. R. L. Wyss, 'Swiss Majolica from Winterthur', *The Connoisseur* (August 1965), pp.222–6.

9. For the best discussion in English of the German guild system in relation to the production of works of art, see M. Baxandall, *The Limewood Sculptors of Renaissance Germany*, Yale, 1980, pp.106–16.

10. J. F. Hayward, *Virtuoso Goldsmiths and the Triumph of Mannerism*, London, 1976, pp.38–40.

11. L. Solon, *The Ancient Art of Stoneware in the Low Countries and Germany*, London, 1892, p.61.

12. I. Unger, *Kölner Ofenkacheln. Die Bestände des Museums für Angewandte Kunst und des Kölnischen Stadtmuseums*, Cologne, 1988.

13. H. P. Mielke, 'Ein hessicher Hafner und sein Werk: Hans Bermain', *Kunst in Hessen am Mittelrhein*, 21 (1982), pp.23–52.

14. Hayward, (1976), op.cit., p.38.

15. See catalogue *Nürnberg 1300–1550: Kunst der Gotik und Renaissance*, Nuremberg, Germanischen Nationalmuseum, 1986, no.242–3.

16. E. Hannover, *Pottery and Porcelain: A Handbook for Collectors. Volume 1: Europe and the Near East: Earthenware and Stoneware*, London, 1925, p.193, fig. 205.

17. D. R. Gaimster (ed.), *Zur Keramik des Mittelalters und der beginnender Neuzeit im Rhein (Medieval and Later Pottery from the Rheinland and its Markets)*, Oxford, 1988.

18. H.-G. Stephan, 'The Development and Production of medieval stoneware in Germany' in P. Davey (ed.), and R. Hodges, *Ceramics and Trade*, Sheffield, 1983, pp.95–120.

19. K. Goebels, *Rheinisches Töpferhandwerk*, Frechen, 1971.

20. Lipperheide, op. cit., p.10.

21. M. R. Holmes, 'The So-Called "Bellarmine" Mask on Imported Rhenish Stoneware', *Antiquaries Journal*, 31 (1951), pp.173–9.

22. D. Gaimster, *German Stoneware 1200–1900*, London, 1997, pp.191–3.

23. Lipperheide, op. cit., p.19.

24. Gaimster (1997), op.cit., p.193.

25. Ibid., p.48.

26. L. Solon, *The Ancient Art of Stoneware in the Low Countries and Germany*, London, 1892, pp.56–65.

27. Gaimster (1997), op.cit., p.164.

28. Solon, op.cit., p.68.

29. Gaimster (1997), op.cit., p.48.

30. Lipperheide, op. cit., p.21.

31. Gaimster (1997), op.cit., pp.39–40.

32. G. Reinheckel, *Masterepieces of Western and Near Eastern Ceramics: Vol. VIII: German and Austrian Ceramics*, Tokyo, 1978, no.30.

33. Solon, op.cit., p.69.

34. Lipperheide, op.cit., p.24.

35. Ekkart Klinge, *Deutsches Steinzeug der Renaissance- und Barockzeit*, Düsseldorf, Hetjens-Museum, 1979, nos.29–32.

36. A. Ohm and M. Bauer, *Steinzeug und Zinn*, Frankfurt-am-Main, ill.56.

37. Gaimster (1997), op.cit., p.165.

38. The regulations were renewed in 1760. Solon, op.cit., p.140.

39. Solon, op.cit., p.80; Lipperheide, op.cit., p.47.

40. Klinge, op.cit., p.65.

41. However, in 1726 restrictive regulations were introduced, allowing only one child to take up his father's work, and forbidding new designs, suggesting that the trade was in difficulties. Further attempts at regulation occurred in 1775, suggesting that the trade was still declining. Solon, op.cit., p.89.

42. Lipperheide, op.cit., p.47.

43. Solon, op.cit., vol.2, p.32.

44. Klinge, op.cit., p.86.

45. Gaimster (1997), op.cit., pp.105–10.

46. M. Biddle, 'Imports of Medieval Stoneware from the Rhineland', *Medieval Archaeology*, 6–7, 1962–3, pp.298–300.

47. D. Gaimster, 'The supply of Rhenish stoneware to London 1350–1600', *The London Archaeologist*, vol.5, no.13, 1987, pp.339–47.

48. They are apparently mentioned in a scene of drunkenness by Ben Johnson in *Bartholomew Fair* where he describes a man who has 'wrashled so long with the bottle here, that the man with the beard hash almost streek up hish heelsh' Holmes, op.cit., p.177.

49. Gaimster (1997), op.cit., pp.133–4, 210.

50. A. Henstock, 'The Monopoly in Rhenish Stoneware Imports in Late Elizabethan England', *Post-Medieval Archaeology*, 9 (1975), pp.219–25.

51. J. Allan, 'Some post-medieval documentary evidence for the trade in ceramics', in P. Davey (ed.), and R. Hodges, *Ceramics and Trade*, Sheffield, 1983, p.43.

52. Some Bellarmines dated 1672 and inscribed 'WK' are thought to be the product of this pottery. D. Haselgrove, *London Archaeologist*, 6, no.6 (1990), pp.154–6.

53. R. Hildyard in Gaimster (1997), op.cit., p.311.

54. A. Oswald, R. J. C. Hildyard and R. C. Hughes, *English Brown Stoneware 1670–1900*, London, 1982, p.24.

55. Dr Plot, in his *Natural History of Oxfordshire* (1676), calls Bellarmines 'D'Alva' bottles, presumably after the Spanish Duke of Alva, and that 'heretofore made only in England, and by the Dutch brought over into England in great quantities,' but now John Dwight discovered the secret and was sole supplier to the Glass Sellers Company. Holmes, op.cit., p.178.

56. J. Horne, 'John Dwight: The Master Potter of Fulham', *The Art Quarterly* (Autumn 1992). See also C. Green, *Excavations at John Dwight's Fulham Pottery 1971–9*, London, 1993.

57. For an illustration of a bust of Charles II by John Bushnell, showing the closeness of modelling to Dwight's figures, see D. Sutton, 'London as an Art Centre', *Apollo* (November 1981), p.298.

58. M. Bimson, 'John Dwight', *Transactions of the English Ceramic Circle*, 5, part 2, 1961, pp.101–2.

59. R. Tyler, *Francis Place 1647–1728*, City Art Gallery, York, and Kenwood House, London, 1971, pp.42–3.

60. Oswald, Hildyard and Hughes, op.cit., p.39.

61. Ibid., p.35.

CHAPTER 5
The Influence of the East

1. These substances are closely related, both being silicates of alumina; the china clay being composed of decomposing granite, the china stone being a harder version. The china clay was mined from river beds; both materials required sieving and purifying before being used to mould objects, or else the objects would be cracked in the kiln. The proportions of these substances can be varied, but the ideal balance would be half and half. The glaze was composed mostly of *baidunzi*, which was mixed with water and some vegetables ashes (for instance, those from ferns) in order to strengthen it.

2. Y. Hackenbroch, 'Chinese Porcelain in European Silver Mounts', *The Connoisseur* (June 1955), pp.22–9.

3. For example inventories of the Duke of Normandy (1363) or the Duc de Berry (1416). *See* S. Bursche, *Tafelzier des Barock*, Munich, 1974, p.18.

4. Arthur Lane, 'The "Gaignières-Fonthill" vase', *The Burlington Magazine*, CIII (1961), pp.124–37. The best surviving piece from this period is perhaps a mounted Chinese celadon bowl in Cassel bearing the arms of Count Philip von Katzenelnbogen (before 1453) on the mounts. L. Klein, 'Princely Porcelain at Kassel', *Apollo* (September 1990), p.181.

5. J. Graca, 'The Portuguese Trade with China', *Arts of Asia*, November–December (1977), pp.45–51.

6. D. F. Lunsingh Scheurleer, *Chinese Export Porcelain*, London, 1974, p.22. The best short introduction to the subject of imports of Eastern porcelain to Europe is perhaps still Soame Jenyns, 'Exports from the Orient', *Apollo* (June 1975), pp.490–2.

7. Lunsingh Scheurleer, op.cit., p.48.

8. C. L. van der Pijl-Ketel (ed.), *The Ceramic Load of the Witte Leeuw (1613)*, Amsterdam, 1982.

9. T. Volker, 'Porcelain and the Dutch East India Company as recorded in the dagh-registers of Batavia Castle, those of Hirado and other contemporary papers, 1602–1682', *Mededelingen van het Rijksmuseum voor Volkenkunde, Leiden*, 11, Leiden, 1954.

10. Lunsingh Scheurleer, op.cit., p.55.

11. C. H. de Jonge, *Delft Ceramics*, London, 1970, pp.22–3.

12. The best modern summary of the tin-glazed earthenware industry in seventeenth-century Holland is perhaps J. D. van Dam, 'Geleyersgoet en Hollants Porceleyn; ontwikkelingen in de Nederlandse aardewerk-industrie 1560–1660', *Mededelingenblad nederlandse vereniging van vrienden van de ceramiek*, 108, 1982 pp.6–80.

13. H. P. Fourest, *Delftware: Faience Production at Delft*, London, 1980, pp.19–20.

14. De Jonge (1970), op.cit., p.34.

15. Fourest, (1980), op.cit., no.47.

16. De Jonge (1970), op.cit., p.40.

17. C. H. de Jonge, *Dutch Tiles*, London, 1971, pp.104–8.

18. See Christie's catalogue, *The Vung Tau Cargo*, Amsterdam, 7–8 April, 1992.

19. See, for instance, an illustration of a Dutch interior by Gonzales Coques of about 1630 in P. Thornton, *Authentic Decor: The Domestic Interior 1620–1920*, London, 1984, no.16.

20. T. Volker (1954), op.cit., p.3.

21. Daniel Defoe wrote later: 'The Queen brought in the Custom or Humour, as I may call it, of furnishing Houses with Chinaware, which increased to a strange degree afterwards, piling their China upon the tops of Cabinets, Scritoires (writing-desks), and every Chymney-Piece, to the tops of the Ceilings, and even setting up Shelves for their China-ware, where they are wanted for such Places, till it became a grievance in the Expense of it, and even injurious to their Families and Estates.' Daniel Defoe, *A Tour thro' the Whole Island of Great Britain* (1724–27), G. D. H. Cole and D. C. Browning (eds), London and New York, 1962, i, p.166.

22. A. Lane, 'Queen Mary II's Porcelain Collection at Hampton Court', *Transactions of the Oriental Ceramic Society*, 1949–50, pp.21–31; J. Wilson, 'A Phenomenon of Taste: The China Ware of Queen Mary II' *Apollo* 126, (August 1972), pp.116–24; L. Rosenfeld Shulsky, 'The Arrangement of the Porcelain and Delftware Collection of Queen Mary in Kensington Palace', *American Ceramic Circle Journal*, vol.VII, 1990, pp.51–74.

23. Volker (1954), op.cit., p.48.

24. T. H. Lunsingh Scheurleer, 'The Dutch at the Teatable', *The Connoisseur*, October, 1976, pp.85–93.

25. Lunsingh Scheurleer (1974), op.cit., p.167.

26. Our first record of this is an advertisement by the potter Lambert Cleffius in the *Haarlemse Courant* on 18 August 1678, who asserts that he has 'achieved such perfection in the manufacturing of red teapots that they are in no way inferior in colour, purity and durability to the Indian teapots 'maecken van roode Theepotten . . . tot sodanighe perfectie heeft gebracht, dat dezelve in couleur, netheyt, sterckte em gebruyck de Indische niet behoeven te wijcken.' De Jonge (1970), op.cit., p.64.

27. Ibid., pp.65–9.

28. The company wrote from Deshima to Batavia: 'If this lot had not been in stock, we should not have been able to fill the order for Surat before next year, as it consists mainly of various kinds of bowls, large, deep dishes, coffee-cups and the like which the Japanese do not stock of their own accord.' T. Volker, 'The Japanese porcelain trade of the Dutch East India Company after 1683', *Mededelingen van het Rijksmuseum voor Volkenkunde, Leiden*, 13, Leiden, 1959, p.135.

29. The trade with Japan was short-lived and unprofitable, due to the problems made by the Japanese ruler (*Shogun*) and the higher wages of the Japanese potters. In 1734 the Dutch East India Company complained about the difficulty of having European designs executed in China, and lamented that: 'if this work will not succeed in China, how then shall it succeed in Japan where the wages of the porcelain bakers come much dearer.' Volker (1959), op.cit., p.80.

30. See O. Impey, *The Early Porcelain Kilns of Japan: Arita in the First Half of the Seventeenth Century*, Oxford, 1998.

31. F. Scholten, 'Vroege Japonaiserie in Delft, 1660–1680', *Mededelingenblad Nederlandse Vereniging van vrienden van de ceramiek*, 1987, 3, p.17.

32. *Kakiemon* porcelain was rarely copied in Holland, as tin-glazed earthenware does not always succeed in reproducing the sheen of porcelain. However, there did flourish a market in decorating undecorated Japanese porcelain of *Kakiemon* type by outside workshops in the early eighteenth century. There also existed in Holland workshops which decorated porcelain in Eastern styles, such as that of Gerrit van der Kade, who was working in Delft and Amsterdam in 1705. The rage for *Kakiemon* porcelain persisted into Europe to the mid-eighteenth century, especially in France, where it was christened 'premier qualité de Japon'. Eastern porcelain decorated in Holland seems to have remained fashionable well in to the eighteenth century, and is listed in French inventories of the Duke of Bourbon in 1740 ('Deux pots à tabac de porcelaine de la Chine repeinte en Hollande'; Lunsingh Scheurleer, (1974) op.cit.) p.179) and the sale of the dealer Gersaint in Paris in 1747. F. Reichel, *Early Japanese Porcelain*, London, 1981, p.127.

33. 'Coloured jars of six square'.

34. Lunsingh Scheurleer, (1974) op.cit., p.34.

35. 'We had intended to send you some samples of well-baked porcelains to have the same imitated in China, which to make ready we have done what we could, but we heard from the porcelain-bakers at Delft, that this could indeed be done for blue and white but not for coloured wares, because their kilns are not appointed for this. Since then we have been informed that if the Chinese had some well-painted designs before them, they would be able to copy them. Several amateurs here who had sent drawings to China have shown us their sample pieces which when sold have yielded an extraordinary profit, which we have decided to try also . . . the work shall have to be not only blue and white as abovesaid, but

also coloured in two ways, that is enamelled and also, smooth and even glazed as shown by the coloured Japanese porcelain, because the enamelled work looks beautiful indeed, but has the fault that it is sometimes apt to come off, from which the evenly and smoothly coloured work like the Japanese does not suffer.' Volker (1959), op.cit., p.38.

36. Ibid., pp.78–81.

37. C. J. A. Jörg, *The Geldermalsen: History and Porcelain*, Groningen, 1986 and C. Sheaf, and R. Kilburn, *The Hatcher Porcelain Cargoes: The Complete Record*, Oxford, 1988.

38. Their aim was stated in a letter to the Graf of Hanau in 1675: 'Wir wollen diese Manufaktur noch um ein Merkliches zu versta[e]rken, und mit einer ganz neuen Invention, wodurch das feineste dem chinesischen nicht viel nachgebende Porzellan verfertigt wird.' ('We want to strengthen this manufacture into a notable one, to make it equal to the finest Chinese porcelain through a new invention'). They obtained a twenty-five year monopoly within Hanau, as well as exemption from customs duties and certain *Beschwerden*. By 1675 the factory employed seventy-five people, mostly Dutch and was directed by a Dutchman, Johannes Bally. For most of the eighteenth century it was run by the van Alphen family, who brought the factory to its highest point. The factory survived until 1806. A. Merk, 'Hanauer Fayencen', *Weltkunst*, 59, 21, (1 November 1989), pp.3294–9.

39. It is very difficult to precisely identify its products, and recently it has been the subject of much dispute as to the precise origin of the more finely painted blue-and-white wares, which some Dutch scholars attribute to Delft. See exh. cat. *Frankfurter Fayencen des Barock*, Frankfurt, 1988/9.

40. R. J. Charleston in L. Lipski and M. Archer, *Dated English Delftware*, London, 1984, p.9.

41. F. Britton, *London Delftware*, London, 1987, p.84.

42. W. M. Beaumont, 'The Pedigree of Blue-dash chargers', *The Connoisseur* (September 1925), pp.3–6.

43. R. Hildyard, 'A group of dated Southwark delftwares', *The Burlington Magazine*, CXXXII (May, 1990), pp.354–5.

44. M. Archer, *Delftware: The Tin-glazed Earthenware of the British Isles: A Catalogue of the Collection of the Victoria and Albert Museum*, London, 1997, p.30.

45. F. Britton, 'Bernard Palissy and London Delftware', *English Ceramic Society Transactions*, 14, 2 (1991), pp.1 69–76.

46. C.f. James Orton, *Memoirs of the late Reverend Dr. Philip Doddridge*, 1802 (I, p.180: 'I have heard him relate, that his mother taught him the history of the Old and New Testament, before he could read, by the assistance of some Dutch tiles in the chimney of the Room, where they commonly sat' quoted in B. Hillier, *Pottery and Porcelain 1700–1914*, London, 1968, pp.124–5.

47. An important but uncharacteristic product is a group of twelve delftware plates painted with allegories of the signs of the Zodiac in The British Museum. On their back they each carry the inscription 'J. Thornhill fecit. Delph Aug: 1711', indicating their attribution to the English painter James Thornhill and their execution in Delft itself. However, it is not clear whether they were actually painted by him, or by a painter in Delft working to his designs under his supervision. H. P. Fourest (1980) op.cit., pp.124–5.

48. F. H. Garner, *English Delftware*, London, 1958, p.14.

49. For a recent study, see P. Burke, *The Fabrication of Louis XIV*, London, 1992.

50. D. Watkin, 'Louis XIV', *Antique* (Winter 1988), pp.53–8.

51. T. Hutchinson, *Before Adam Smith: The Emergence of Political Economy 1662–1776*, Oxford, 1988, pp.88–9.

52. F. Buckland, 'Silver Furnishings at the Court of France 1643–70', *The Burlington Magazine*, CXXXI (May, 1989), pp.328–36.

53. See catalogue *Courts and Colonies: The William and Mary Style in Holland, England, and America*, New York, Cooper-Hewitt Museum, 1988.

54. A. Lane, 'Daniel Marot, Designer of Delft', *The Connoisseur*, CXXIII (1949), pp.19–24; A. M. L. E. Erkelens's 'Koninginnes Gonst. Delftse vazen van Mary Stuart (1662–1695)', *Antiek*, 23, no.2, (Aug/Sept. 1988), pp.88–93.

55. A. M. L. E. Erkelens, '*Delffs Porcelijn' van koningin Mary II/Queen Mary's 'Delft porcelain*, Apeldoorn, Paleis Het Loo, 1996.

56. M. Archer, 'Delft at Dyrham', *The National Trust Year Book*, 1975–6, pp.12–19; 'Pyramids and Pagodas for Flowers', *Country Life* (22 January 1976), pp.166–9.

57. An enraged character in a comedy by Dancourt of 1688 enters a friend's house and breaks 'toutes ces porcelaines d'Hollande' for the lack of the 'finer' (i.e. true Eastern porcelain). A. Lane, *French Faïence*, London, 1948, p.16.

58. They brought Chinese porcelain in Japanese cases, including 'Douze autres assiettes du Japon de diverses couleurs, 6 assiettes à huit côtés, du Japon, 1 plat ouvrage à jour, du Japon, 1 oiseau de proye et 2 canards du Japon, and 6 vases, some Chinese, some Japanese. E. Auscher, *La Céramique au Château de Versailles Sous Louis XIV*, Versailles, 1903, pp.23–30. For his son's collection, see F. Watson and J. Whitehead, 'An Inventory dated 1688 of the Chinese porcelain in the collection of the Grand Dauphin, son of Louis XIV, at Versailles', *Journal of the History of Collections*, 3,1 (1991), pp.13–52.

59. Our best contemporary witness is the English writer Giles Rose, who in 1681 published a translation of a French textbook on etiquette which accurately reflects contemporary usage in France: he specifies various household officers in attendance, amongst whom we can recognise the descendants of the medieval butler, carver and sewer: the Master of the Household, the Master Carver, the Master Butler (who deals with the plate, including the 'Bason and Ewer, the Essay Cup and Cadnet [a personal cutlery and napkin tray for the Lord], Flagons, Salts, Plates, Spoons, Forkes, Knives, Riders for Places [under-dishes?], Table-cloths, Napkins),' the Master Cook, the Master Confectioner and the Master Pastryman. These latter two were responsible for the cold confection at the end of the meal that is based on the sixteenth-century *banquet* and was soon to be called the *dessert*. Rose goes on to describe the preparations for a grand dinner in some detail, giving precise instructions as to the behaviour of the servants: 'The hour of Meals being come, and all things are now in a readiness, le *Maistre Hostel* takes a clean Napkin, folded at length, but narrow, and throws it over his Shoulder . . . and being come into the Hall, where the Company are to eat, he pulls off his Hat, but immediately puts it on again upon his Head, and so proceeds to the covering of the Table with Dishes and Plates, beginning at the upper end and continuing till he comes at the lower end . . . he should begin . . . at the upper end of the Table, but set on the first Dish at the right side of the Cadnet or Cover (which is always set if any great person is to

be treated) and the next on the left side of the Cover, with a Plate upon a Rider between the two Dishes against the Salt-seller [sic], doing this all a long till he come to the lower end with the last dish.' He then goes on to explain that all the guests wipe their hands on a towel, and that the second course is followed by a banquet. Giles Rose, *A School of Instructions* (1681), (a translation of the French *Escole Parfaite des Officers de Bouche*), p.4.

60. The inventory of 1653 for Cardinal Mazarin, for instance, lists '15 assiettes creusés "à l'italienne" '; by 1680 we find 'assiettes à la mazarine' listed, and the inventory of 1687 differentiates between 'assiettes potagères' and 'assiettes à mouchettes'. E. Auscher, op.cit., p.47. The inventory of the French Crown on 20 February 1673, a 'service complet de vermeil doré' for twelve people is listed. It comprised 231 pieces, including 'douze plats, huit assiettes de fonds, huit moyen plats, quarante-huit assiettes ordinaires, deux bassins ovales, un bassin rond, quatre esguières, quatre sous-couppes, quatre colliers, huit flambeaux, quatre sallières rondes, vingt-quatre cuilliers, vingt-quatre fourchettes, dix-huit manches de couteaux, un sucrier, un vinaigner, une assiette à mouchette, douze cuillères, douze fourchettes, douze cousteaux (à dessert), dix plats, douze assiettes potagères, un poivrier.' H. Havard, *Dictionnaire de l'Ameublement de la Décoration*, Paris, 1889–90, vol.4, p.1055.

61. N. Butcher, *Spanish Cookery*, London, 1990, pp.129–31. A description of 1765 describes it as a 'ragoût des Espagnols qui consiste dans un mélange de toutes sortes de viandes et de légumes, et qu'on fait cuire dans une large marmite . . . il n'y a guère de grande table en France ou ce mets ne soit pas connu.' R. Savill, *The Wallace Collection: Catalogue of Sèvres Porcelain*, London, 1988, p.737.

62. A Parisian silver *écuelle* of 1672–3 is in the Victoria and Albert Museum; see R. Lightbown, *Victoria and Albert Museum Catalogues: French Silver*, London, 1978, no.39. An anonymous French engraving of about 1750 in the National Gallery, Scotland, shows a woman reading at a table by the fireside with an *écuelle* in front of her, demonstrating its use outside the dining room.

63. Specific evidence for table-layout at the French court is seen in a drawing from the royal palace at Marly, dated 1702, in Stockholm, one of a vast body of drawings sent from the French court by the Swedish ambassador to show the Swedish court what was fashionable in France. The drawing depicts the two courses of dinner on each half of the sheet, the other half forming a mirror image, all carefully annotated with the names of the different dishes. It shows various plates and tureens for soups and *olio* laid out symmetrically around a centrepiece, described as a 'device for holding the sugar, vinegar etc. pepper and candlesticks in the evening', (la machine ou l'on met le sucrier, vinaigner etc. le poivre et les bougets en soir). This central feature was what came to be known as a *surtout de table* in eighteenth-century France (called in Germany a *plat de ménage* and in England an *epergne*) which was usually a silver centrepiece with holders for the appropriate condiments and spices, which apparently remained on the table until the dessert. It is surrounded by the side-dishes called the *entrées*, with the *hors d'oeuvre* fitted between. The second course shows a roast, salads in a bowl (*en jatte*), and the side-dishes called *entremets*, to be eaten between the roast and the dessert. In F. Massialot's *Le Cuisinier royal et bourgeois* (first published 1691; extensively revised and repub-

lished as *Le Nouveau cuisinier royal et bourgeois* in 1712) a *surtout de table* is illustrated with the caption that it remains on the table 'pendant tous les services' (during all the courses). *See* catalogue *Versailles et les tables royales en Europe XVIIeme-XIXeme siècles*, Versailles, 1993–4.

64. Besongne, in the *Etat de la France pour 1694* gives two descriptions of a dessert, according to whether it is for the *Grand Couvert*, the dinner that the king took in public, or for the *Petit Couvert*, when he dined in private: for the *Grand Couvert* 'the *fruit* is composed of two large basins containing raw fruit, in porcelain, and two other plates with all sorts of dry jams made in cups, also in porcelain . . . at the *petit Couvert*, two small plates of raw fruit, and four compotes or liquid jams in porcelain.' (Fruit est composé de 2 grand bassins de fruits crus dans de porcelaines, et 2 autres plats de toutes sortes de confitures sèches faites au goblet, aussi en porcelaine . . . Au petit couvert, 2 petits plats de fruit crus, de confitures sèches dressés dans des porcelaines, et de 4 compotes ou confitures liquides en porcelaine). E. Auscher (1903), op.cit., p.23.

65. The descriptions of the festivities at the court of Versailles give some kind of flavour of their usage and appropriateness, where the skills of the *Office*, and the *Menus Plaisirs* (the organisation that catered for royal entertainments) were paramount. A description of a festival called *Pleasures of the Enchanted Isle*, held at Versailles in May, 1664, shows their inventiveness. The theme was taken from the courtly sixteenth-century Italian poet Ariosto, who had celebrated knightly chivalry in his poem *Orlando Furioso*: Versailles was to be an island, inhabited by Roger and his knights who had been put under a three-day spell by the sorceress Alcina, which is eventually broken by the use of a magic ring given to Roger by Melissa disguised as Atlas. On the first day, the king attended a feast, on the second day a collation was prepared by the *office*, '[composed of] all kinds of fruits ingeniously arranged in one hundred dozen little porcelain dishes, which served as the solid body of the agreeable building. It was divided by sixteen arcades, and each arcade had two pairs of serpentine columns which carried the cornice. These columns were gilded and garnished with flowers, as were the bases and capitals. In the middle of the arcade hung double garlands, and above the columns were chandeliers illuminated with candles. One hundred little vases of tuberoses and orange flowers were set on the cornice, completing the decoration of the upper part of the building. But the almost incredible quantity of porcelain basins and dishes filled with fruit, and the large number of crystal vases used for the ice and liqueurs, made this table a sumptuous one, on which the foods were served with extraordinary magnificence.' A. Félibien, *Les Plaisirs de l'Isle Enchantée*, quoted in B. K. Wheaton, *Savouring the Past: The French Kitchen and Table from 1300 to 1789*, London, 1983, p.133. Such festivities often ended in the destruction of the confections by the populace, in contrast to the polite behaviour of the court: 'the destruction of so handsome an arrangement served to give another agreeable entertainment to all the court, by the alacrity and disorder of those who demolished these castles of marzipan, and these mountains of preserved fruit'. Similarly at a fête organized by Colbert in the park at Versailles in July, 1678 fifteen tables arranged as buffets contained one 'filled with pyramids of preserved fruits, and another with an infinity of glasses filled with all kinds of liqueurs, and the last was composed of caramels.

Between the tables were orange trees bearing preserved fruit; on either side stood two other trees with similar fruit of different species.' B. K. Wheaton (1983), op.cit., pp.134–5.

66. An illustration of such a device being brought into a dance at the court of Louis XIV can be seen in P. Thornton, *Authentic Decor: The Domestic Interior 1620–1920*, London, 1984, fig. 74. They were somewhat precarious; Madame de Sévigné refers to a disaster when the pyramid of fruit was much too high and 'with twenty porcelains, was completely overturned at the door, the noise of which silenced the violins, oboes, and trumpets'. Wheaton (1983), op.cit., p.188.

67. The Comte de Préhac commented in 1698 that 'Everybody thought of this palace as an enchantment, as it had only been begun at the end of winter, and was discovered ready in the spring, as if it had sprung from the ground with the flowers of the garden.' quoted in J. Rykwert, *The First Moderns: The Architects of the Eighteenth Century*, Cambridge, 1986, p.54. Eleanor P. Delorme, *Gardens, Pavilions and the 18th Century French Court*, Woodbridge, 1996, p.51, gives the foods prepared there as *confitures, entremets, potages* and the *buffet*.

68. The destruction of 1709 was recorded by the courtier Saint-Simon in his memoirs, who describes how Madame de Gramont tried to persuade the courtiers to present their silver to the king, but 'Some people clung to their silver plates as a last resource, and dreading parting with them; others feared the dirtiness of pewter and earthenware'. But eventually even the king himself set an example: 'Everyone of rank furnished themselves in eight days with faïence, exhausting the shops . . . the King began to obtain faïence, sending his gold plate to the Mint, and his brother the Duc d'Orléans the little that he had . . . the King and the royal family itself used silver plate, while Prince and Princesses of the Blood used *faïence* (the name for tinglazed earthenware in France and Germany)' (les uns la gardaient pour une dernière ressource, dont il les fachoit fort de se priver; d'autres cragnoient la malproprieté de l'étain et de la terre, Tout ce qu'il y eut de grand et de considerable se mit en huit jours en faïence, en épuiserent les boutiques . . . le Roi agita de se mettre à la faïence, il envoya sa vaisselle d'or a la Monnaie, et M. le duc d'Orléans le peu qu'il avait . . . Le Roi et la famille royale se servirent de vaisselle de vermeil et d'argent; les princes et les princesses du Sang, de faïence. Pour d'Antin, qui en avait (de la vaisselle d'or) en grande quantité et de la plus achevée, il courut a Paris choisir force porcelaine admirable, qu'il eut a grand enlever, et enlever deux boutiques de faïences qu'il fit porter pompeusement a Versailles.) L. Norton (ed.), *Historical Memoirs of the Duc de Saint-Simon*, vol.1, London, 1967, pp.438, 440.

69. Auscher, op.cit., p.22.

70. See P. Thornton, *Baroque and Rococo Silks*, London, 1955.

71. *Il faut qu'il y ait de la jeunesse mêlé dans ce que l'on fera*. F. Kimball, *The Creation of the Rococo*, 1943, p.58.

CHAPTER 6
The Discovery of True Porcelain in Europe

1. H. Tait, *Porcelain*, London, 1972, p.16.

2. An attempt at making porcelain in England was made at Fulham in London by the stoneware-maker John Dwight of Fulham, who obtained in 1671 a patent for the manufacture of 'transparent earthenware commonly known by the name of Porcelaine China or Persian Ware'. Recently excavated wasters from his pottery suggest that he got very close to producing the real thing, and include small Chinesestyle baluster and fluted vases painted (unsuccessfully) in underglaze blue. The reason for his failure seems to have lain in his inability to create a paste which would not warp in the firing, due to his lack of knowledge of the essential ingredient, china clay (*kaolin*). C. Green, *Excavations at John Dwight's Fulham Pottery 1971–9*, London, 1993.

3. 'Perclus de ses membres par les ingrédients qui entrent dans la composition de la porcelaine.' In 1694 it was said that 'the secret was very little used, the petitioners devoting themselves rather to faiencemaking'. A few specimens of soft-paste porcelain painted in underglaze blue are known which could be of Rouen manufacture, including some vases and a mustard-pot bearing the arms of Asselin de Villequier family of Rouen in the Musée at Sèvres. Cte X. de Chavagnac and Mis de Grollier, *Histoire des Manufactures Françaises de Porcelaine*, Paris, 1906, p.4.

4. In the patent of 1702 it was stated that he had produced 'works almost as perfect as those made in China and the East' (ouvrages presque aussi parfaits que les porcelaines de la Chine et des Indes.) Cte X. de Chavagnac, op.cit., p.10. *See also* C. Lahaussois, *Porcelaines de Saint-Cloud, la Collection du Musée des Arts Décoratifs*, Paris, 1997.

5. The factory was seen and described by an Englishman, Dr Martin Lister (1638?–1712), when he visited Paris with the British Ambassador William Bentinck in 1698: 'I saw the "Potterie of St Clou [sic]", with which I was marvellously well pleased, for I confess I could not distinguish betwixts the Pots made there, and the finest China Ware I ever saw. It will, I know, be easily granted me, that the Painting may be better designed and finisht, (as indeed it was), because our Men are far better Masters in that Art, than the Chinese; but the Glazing came not in the least behind theirs, not for whiteness, nor the smoothness of running without bubles [sic]; again, the inward Substance and Matter of the Pots was, to me, the very same, hard and firm as Marble, and the self same grain, on this side vitrification. Farther the transparency of the Pots the very same. . . . They sold these Pots at St Clou at excessive Rates; and for their ordinary Chocolate Cups askt Crowns a-piece. They had arrived at the Burning on Gold in neat Chequer Works. He had sold some Furnitures of Tea Tables at 400 Livres a Sett . . . There was no Molding or Model of China Wares, which they had not imitated; and had added many Fancies of their own, which had their good effects, and appeared very beautiful.' G. Wills, 'Dr Martin Lister and Early French Porcelain', *Connoisseur*, CXLI, 1958, pp.74–6.

6. S. Jenyns, *Later Chinese Porcelain*, London, 1971, pp.6–16; D. Langford, *The Letters of Père d'Entrecolles*, Canterbury Ceramic Circle, 1995.

7. See U. Heise, *Kaffee und Kaffee in Kulturgeschichte*, Leipzig, 1987.

8. In 1717 the Dresden court specifically bought in Paris 'a service of Japanese porcelain for the dessert' ('un service de Porcellaine du Jappon pour le dessert'). S. Bursche, *Tafelzier des Barock*, Munich, 1974, p.19.

9. In 1717 the third prize in a Viennese archery competition was 'a complete table or dessert service consisting of 21 pieces of Japanese porcelain of various types, namely, four large and five small bowls (cups?)

and twelve similar plates'. J. F. Hayward, *Viennese Porcelain of the Dupaquier Period*, London, 1952, p.48.

10. Its main proponent was Johann Joachim Becker (1635–82), who stressed the importance of consumption and spending, rather than saving, as a means of keeping the economy moving, but thought that imports should be kept to a minimum. His maxim was that 'One must always see that money is kept in the country and that still more is brought in from abroad.' His follower, the Austrian Philipp von Hoernigk (1640–1714) advocated the banning of all imports which duplicated goods made locally, even if these were of inferior quality, probably an attempt to restrict imports from France. T. Hutchison, *Before Adam Smith: The Emergence of Political Economy 1662–1776*, Oxford, 1988, pp.90–3.

11. J. Menzhausen *et al.*, exh.cat., *The Splendor of Saxony: Five Centuries of Art Collecting*, Washington, New York, San Francisco, 1978–9.

12. Menzhausen (1978–9), op.cit., nos.356 and 357.

13. He is supposed to have criticised the import of china, with consequent loss of silver to Saxony, as 'the bleeding bowl of Saxony'. W. B. Honey, *Dresden China*, London, 1954, p.41.

14. The origins of alchemy can be traced back to Islamic or Chinese teaching, with the addition of classical thought, particularly Aristotle's division of the world into the four elements: Earth, Fire, Air and Water. In its broadest form, it was a branch of 'philosophy', as scientific research was called in the eighteenth century, in that it purported to examine the mystery of life itself, and the way in which things below the human level – in particular metals – could be raised or transmuted into higher states. This was of course particularly applicable to the ceramic arts, which rested on making something of beauty and value from 'ignoble' clays dug from the ground. J. Read, *Prelude to Chemistry: An Outline of Alchemy, its Literature and Relationships*, London, 1939, pp.2–17.

15. O. Walcha, *Meissen Porcelain*, London, 1981, pp.16–17; Janet Gleeson, *The Arcanum: The Extraordinary True Story of the Invention of European Porcelain*, London, 1998.

16. By 1711 there were thirteen workers under the direction of Peter Eggebrecht, working as compounders, modellers, throwers, glaziers, kiln-masters or general hands, much in the manner of the Dutch tin-glaze factories. In charge of the factory was Christoph Rühle, who was paid twenty-four talers a month, while his son-in-law, Gerhard van Malcem, earned sixteen as a *Schilderer* or decorator. Walcha (1981), op.cit, p.20.

17. He visited the factory on 29 October 1711, and was allowed to take back three tons of *allerfeinsten rothen Massa* (finest red clay) for modelling. Further orders came in 1712. By 1719 he was owed 1,261 talers by the factory. Walcha, op.cit., p.34.

18. Ibid., p.23.

19. W. Honey, *Dresden Porcelain*, London, 1954, p.47.

20. Walcha, op.cit., p.50.

21. Ibid., p.43.

22. H. Jedding, *Meissener Porzellan des 18. Jahrhunderts*, Munich, 1979, p.32; Hans Sonntag. 'Der Meissener "Neue Willkommen, Der Schüssel Genannt" – Ein Symbol des Erfolges der Alchemie?', *Keramos*, 159 (1998), pp.3–11.

23. The earliest known piece painted in enamel colours is a cup and saucer decorated with the arms of Sophia, Electress of Hanover (d. 1714) in the British Museum. Tait, op.cit., plate 7.

24. S. Ducret, *German Porcelain and Faïence*, London, 1967, pp.371–2. See also Pazaurek, *Deutsche Fayence- und Porzellan-Hausmaler*, 1925; Meredith Chilton, 'Hausmaler decorated porcelain', *The International Ceramics Fair and Seminar [Handbook]*, London, 1987, pp.20–9.

25. Walcha, op.cit., p.40.

26. M. Cassidy-Geiger, 'Two Pieces of Porcelain Decorated by Ignaz Preissler in the J. Paul Getty Museum', *The J. Paul Getty Museum Journal*, 15 (1987), pp.35–53.

27. M. Cassidy-Geiger, 'The Porcelain Decoration of Ignaz Bottengruber', *Metropolitan Museum Journal*, 33 (1998), pp.245–62.

28. A large tankard with this style of decoration in the British Museum bears silver mounts by the goldsmith Paul Solanier (d. 1725), suggesting that this kind of work is found fairly early in the history of European porcelain. Tait, op.cit., p.24.

29. A report in a Dutch newspaper said 'that the porcelain which was manufactured at Vienna was strong and of exceptional beauty, but that its price was so high that hardly anyone was willing to buy it, with the result that it was already expected that the supporters of this factory would be obliged to abandon it'. J. F. Hayward, *Viennese Porcelain of the Dupaquier Period*, London, 1952, p.64. See also E. Sturm-Bednarezyk, *Claudius Innocentius du Paquier: Wiener Porzellan der Frühzeit 1718–1744*, Vienna, 1994.

30. Hayward, op.cit., p.38.

31. In 1726, for instance, the *Wiener Diarium*, advertised 'a fairly large stand or table centre of solid silver . . . upon which are set six valuable covered Olio-cups of white porcelain finely decorated with gilding and artistic painting from the Imperial factory'. In 1729, they speak of 'two large wine-coolers of white porcelain with decorative painting in gold and black enamel, together with two long-necked flasks or bottles for Tokay wine'. Hayward, op.cit., pp.66–7.

32. It was recorded as a prize in the *Wienier Diarium* for 1725. Hayward, op.cit., p.15.

33. A tall enamelled beaker decorated with portraits of three Habsburg emperors attributed to Hunger exists in the Metropolitan Museum, New York. R. Berges, 'C. K. Hunger: Itinerant enameller extraordinary', *Connoisseur*, CLXIII (1966), pp.202–5.

34. Hayward, op.cit, p.172.

35. *See* W. Baer and H. Walter Lack, *Pflanzen auf Porzellan*, Charlottenburg, Berlin, 1979.

36. A. Lane, *Italian Porcelain*, London, 1954, pp.8–13.

37. By 1737, 178,000 blue-and-white pieces out of a total production of 260,000 white pieces had been made. K. P. Arnold, *Weltkunst*, 59, 21 (1 November 1989), p.3303.

38. *See* Ulrich Pietsch, *Johann Gregorius Höroldt und die Meissener Porzellanmalerei*, Dresden, 1996.

39. It would thus appear that the factory at Vienna had a slight pre-eminence in developing the art of painting on porcelain in coloured enamels, and the disgruntled Hunger commented later that 'these godless and dishonourable men' had taken his colours because 'no one at Meissen before this time knew how to use blue, green and red enamels on porcelain'. Berges, op.cit., p.204.

40. The report of 1723 comments on the 'new colours smoothly embedded in the glazing [that] had been invented to suit the taste of the buyers'. Walcha, op.cit., p.57.

41. From the mid-1720s painters were no longer divided into 'blue' and 'colour' painters, but according to their

42. Ibid., p.71.

43. For Höröld see R. Wark, 'Meissner Chinoiserien der Heroldzeit', *Keramik Freunde der Schweiz*, 30/31 (March 1955), pp.29–31.

44. In 1724 Höroldt must have decorated a tankard painted in colours with a Chinese figure in the British Museum inscribed 'George Ernst Keil [his future father-in-law] Meissen den 6 Juli 1724', H. Tait, *Porcelain*, London, 1972, p.15.

45. M. Cassidy-Geiger, 'Gestochene Quellen für frühe Höroldt-Malereien', *Keramos*, 161/98, (1998), pp.3–38.

46. R. Behrends, *Das Meissener Musterbuch für Höroldt-Chinoiserien*, Munich, 1978.

47. One reproduced in R. Schmidt, *Porcelain as an Art and a Mirror of Fashion*. London, 1932, p.77.

48. M. D. Gutter, 'Meissen Chinoiseries and Harbour Scenes', *Antique Collector*, May 1988, pp.70–7.

49. G. Reinheckel, *Prächtvolle Service aus Meissner Porzellan*, Leipzig, 1989, p.44.

50. Other early marks include KPM (*Königliche Porcellan Manufaktur*), KPF (*Königliche Porcellain Fabrique*) and MPM (*Meissner Porzellan Manufaktur*), that were in use from 1723 to 1725. Walcha, op.cit., p.54.

51. Walcha, op.cit., p.61.

52. 'Let not the Europeans any longer Flatter themselves with the empty notions of having surpassed all the world beside in stately Palaces, Costly Temples, and sumptuous fabrics; Ancient and Modern Rome must now give place. The glory of one Country, Japan alone, has exceeded in beauty and magnificence all the pride of the Vatican at this time, and the Pantheon heretofore . . . Japan can please you with a more noble prospect, not only whole Towns, but Cities too are adorned with as rich a covering, so bright and radiant are their buildings that when the sun casts forth his lustre upon their Golden roofs they enjoy a double day', quoted in Hayward, op.cit., p.172.

53. See F. Reichel, *Early Japanese Porcelain*, London, 1981; Ulrich Pietsch, *Meissener Porzellan und seine ostasiatischen Vorbilder*, Leipzig, 1996.

54. Honey, 1934, op.cit., p.75.

55. Geneviève Le Duc, 'Rodolphe Lemaire de la manufacture de porcelaine de Meissen. Style extrême-oriental ou goût français?', *Revue de l'Art*, 116 (1997–2), pp.54–60.

56. Two signed pieces, a tureen and a lantern, survive in the Dresden collection and show his style distinguished by white faces with iron-red outlines and figures holding umbrellas. Walcha, op.cit., p.67.

57. The Eastern theme was paramount, and the king himself specified that the porcelain was to 'decorate the walls against a background of wall coverings, of Eastern splendour, great Indian figures painted onto silk or golden dragons embroidered on silk, or Indian gilded paper onto which various Chinese pagodas would be painted, clearly and neatly'. M. Chilton, 'Rooms of Porcelain', *The International Ceramics Fair [Handbook]*, London, 1992, p.30.

58. Chilton, (1992), op.cit., p.30.

59. The resulting ensemble was one of the great wonders of the age for visitors to Dresden; the Englishman, Jonas Hanway, wrote that 'Here are a great number of porcelain figures of dogs, squirrels, monkeys, wolves, bears, leopards, &c., some of them as big as life; also elephants and rhinoceroses of the size of a large dog;

a prodigious variety of birds, as cocks, hens, turkeys, peacocks, pheasants, hawks, eagles, besides parrots and other foreign birds, and a curious collection of different flowers. The Apostles, here three feet high, are in white porcelain. There is a representation of the Crucifixion, four or five feet high, with numerous other curious pieces; these last are intended for the Romish chapel, which is to be finished with these rare materials. A clock is preparing for the gallery in this palace, whose bells are to be also of porcelain. I heard one of them proved, and they are sufficient to form any music, but the hammer must be of wood.' Quoted in J. Marryat, *A History of Pottery and Porcelain*, London, 1857, p.250. The 'clock' in Hanway's description is presumably the organ and carved wooden case of 1736–7 which still survives in the Dresden collection. *Porzellansammlung im Zwinger*, Dresden, 1980, fig. 44.

60. Honey, op.cit., p.90.

61. Honey, op.cit, p.88.

62. K. Berling, *Das Meissner Porzellan und seine Geschichte*, Leipzig, 1900, p.180.

63. A service made in 1735 for Count Brühl's friend the Count von Hennicke was decorated with rich applied decoration of leaves and flowers described a 'japanische Belege'. Honey, op.cit, p.106.

64. Kaendler also modelled the centrepieces for the service for the Count von Sulkowski of 1736, although the tureens are copied from one made in Augsburg before 1730 by J. Biller. G. Reinheckel, *Prächtvolle Service*, Leipzig, 1989, p.86.

65. It comprises a wide range of tureens, soup plates, dinner plates of different sizes, candelabra, butter dishes, and condiment sets, painted in the centre with figures of animals copied from engravings by J. E. Ridinger. The borders of this service are adorned not with Eastern flowers, but with sprays of rather stiffly drawn European cut-flowers taken from Weinmann's *Phytanthoza-Iconographia* of 1738–40. T. H. Clarke, 'Das Northumberland-Service aus Meissner Porzellan', *Keramos*, 70 (1975), pp.1–75; an English eighteenth-century list of its contents is published in the Earl of Ilchester, 'A Notable Service of Meissen Porcelain', *The Burlington Magazine*, LV (1929), pp.188–90.

66. As late as 1743, Frederick the Great of Prussia, who was an enthusiast for porcelain, used a new service made out of gold. Meissen porcelain appeared only at the dessert (Konfekt) course. S. Bursche, *Tafelzier der Barock*, Munich, 1974, p.19.

67. Honey, op.cit., p.105.

68. Cf. the example sold at Sotheby's, 22/3-2-1988, lot 358: '1 Confect Schaale in Gestalt einer Sonnen-Rose von Thon bausirt'.

69. Reinheckel, op.cit. p.198, n.113.

70. S. Bursche, op.cit., fig. 93, for a print of a 'Schwanen-Pastet, mit natürlichen kopff und flügel, oder gantz von Teig gemacht', from Conrad Hagger, *Neues Saltzburgisches Kochbuch*, Augsburg, 1719.

71. A reversed copy of the engraving was published in Germany by Johann Leonhard Buggel in Nuremberg in 1700 in a collection of prints *Neu-vollstaendiges Reissbuch . . . von einem dieser Preiss-wur-dingen Kunst eyfrigst Ergeben* G.H. M. Cassidy-Geiger, 'From Barlow to Buggel: A New Source for the Swan Service', *Keramos*, 119 (1988), pp.64–8.

72. *See* M. Kunze-Koellensperger, *Idylle in Porzellan. Kostbare Tischdekorationen aus Meissen*, Leipzig, 1996.

73. J. Montagu, *Roman Baroque Sculpture: the Industry of Art*, London, 1989, pp.192–7. Our best record seems to be

the drawings that P. Sevin (1650–1710) made of a feast laid out for Queen Christina (converted to Catholicism in 1656) by Pope Clement IX. P. Bjurström, *Feast and Theatre in Queen Christina's Rome*, Stockholm, 1966, p.55.

74. A. Bruning, 'Schauessen und Porzellanplastik', *Kunst- und Kunsthandwerk*, Vienna, 1 (1904), pp.130–1. Some figures from the Royal Palace are actually marked *K.H.C.* ('Königliche Hof-Conditorei' or Court Pantry) in red. Honey, op.cit., p.172.

75. The sale catalogue of the Frenchman Roussel of 1769 lists '*Vingt & un Plateaux de cuivre argenté, garnis de glaces, à l'usage des Desserts, avec plusieurs petites figures de porce-laine, & autres ornemens assortissans*'. R. Savill, *The Wallace Collection: Catalogue of Sèvres Porcelain*, London, 1988, p.820.

76. R. Schimdt, *Porcelain as an Art and a Mirror of Fashion*, London, 1932, p.299.

77. E. Pauls-Eisenbeiss, *German Porcelain of the 18th centu-ry: the Pauls-Eisenbeiss Collection*, London, 1972, p.24.

78. For the most recent history of the *commedia dell'arte*, see K. and L. Richards, *The Commedia dell'Arte*, Oxford, 1990.

79. J. Watson and G. McKernie, *A Cultural History of Theatre*, New York and London, 1993, p.102.

80. As it is difficult tracing specific instances of humour at the court of Augustus the Strong, an example from the court of Russia must suffice. In 1740 the Empress Anne forced the weak-willed Prince Galitzin, still only a court page although in his for-ties, to marry the hideous Avdotaya Ivanovna (nick-named *Bujenina* or pork stew) in a special ceremony in the winter of 1739–40. The wedding procession consisted of members of the 'Barbarous' races of Lapps, Kirghiz, Tunguses, Tartars and Finns, seated in sleighs drawn by goats, pigs, cows, camel, dogs and reindeer. After a wedding feast consisting of crude national dishes – where the unfortunate pair were read an ode 'Greetings to the Bridal Pair of Fools' – the happy couple were led to a palace constructed completely of ice, where they consummated their marriage on a bed of ice. L. Kelly, *St Petersburg: a traveller's companion*, London, 1981.

81. See R. Rückert, *Der Hofnarr Joseph Fröhlich 1694–1757: Taschenspieler und Spassmacher am Hofe Augusts des Starken*, Offenbach, 1998.

82. H. E. Backer, 'Komödienfiguren in der Sammlung Dr Ernst Schneider', *Keramik Freunde der Schweiz*, 50, pp.59–66.

83. We are fortunate in having an eye-witness account of its use at dessert from the British ambassador to Poland, who saw it in 1748: 'I was once at a Dinner where we sat down at one table two hundred and six People ('twas Count Bruhl's). When the Dessert was set on, I thought it was the most wonderful thing I ever beheld. In the middle of the Table was the Fountain of the Piazza Navona at Rome [Hanbury-Williams is here confusing the two foun-tains], at least eight foot high, which ran all the while with Rose-water, and, 'tis said that Piece alone cost six thousand Dollars.' R. J. Charleston, *The James A. De Rothschild Collection at Waddesdon Manor: Meissen and Oriental Porcelain*, Fribourg, 1971, p.17.

84. Reinheckel, 1989, op.cit. p.47.

85. Quoted in T. Friedman, T. Clifford *et al.*, *The Man at Hyde Park Corner; Sculpture by John Cheere 1709–1787*, Leeds, 1974, p.18.

86. C. Boltz, 'Ein Beitrag zum grünen Watteau-Service für Neapel', *Keramos*, 79 (1978), pp.5–24.

87. R. Rückert, *Meissener Porzellan* (1966), nos.948–50.

1. E. Dacier and A. Vauflart, *Jean de Julienne et les Graveurs de Watteau au XVIII siècle*, Paris, 1929.

2. See F. Kimball, *The Creation of the Rococo*, Philadelphia, 1943 (reprinted 1964).

3. C.f. Sir Christopher Wren's comment after a visit to Versailles in 1665: 'The Palace, or if you please, the *Cabinet of Versailles* call'd me twice to view it; the Mixture of Brick, Stone, blue Tile and Gold makes it look like a rich Livery: Not an Inch with in but is crowded with little Curiosities of Ornaments: the Women, as they make here the Language and Fashions, and meddle with Politicks and Philosophy, so they sway also in Architecture; Works of Filgrand, and little Knacks are in great Vogue; but Building ought to have the Attribute of eternal, and therefore the only Things uncapable of New Fashions. The masculine Furniture of the *Palais Mazarin* pleas'd me much better where is a great and noble Collection of antique Statues and Bustos'. Quoted in E. H. Gombrich, *The Sense of Order*, London, 1979, p.23.

4. 'Faiseurs de rien et marchands de tout.' F. J. B. Watson, 'The Paris marchands-merciers and French 18th century taste', *Antiques*, LXXXVIII, 3 (September 1965), pp.347–51.

5. L. Courajod (ed.), *Livre-Journal de Lazare Duvaux, Marchand-Bijoutier, 1748–1758*, Paris, 1873.

6. 'Deux singes de Japon remuant la tête'. Watson, op.cit., pp.15, 48, 50.

7. Cte X. de Chavagnac and Mis de Grollier, *Histoire des Manufactures Françaises de Porcelaine*, Paris, 1906, p.61.

8. G. Le Duc, *Porcelaine tendre de Chantilly au XVIIIe siè-cle* , Paris, 1996.

9. Chavagnac, op.cit., p.96.

10. P. Verlet, *Les Bronzes Dorés Français du XVIIIe siecle*, Paris, 1987, p.268.

11. F. J. B. Watson, in C. Dauterman, *The Wrightsman Collection: Porcelain*, New York, 1970, p.389.

12. The design for a *surtout de table* is one of a series of designs that were published together in 1734; the first true rococo design is one for a candlestick therein published in 1728. M. Snodin (ed.), *Rococo: Art and Design in Hogarth's England*, London, Victoria and Albert Museum, 1984, no.A12.

13. See P. Jean-Richard, *L'Oeuvre Gravé de François Boucher*, Paris, 1978.

14. 'Façon Saxe peinte et dorée à figure humaine'. S. Eriksen and G. de Bellaigue, *Sèvres Porcelain*, London, 1987, p.30.

15. Eriksen and De Bellaigue (1987), op.cit. p.36.

16. R. Savill, *The Wallace Collection: Catalogue of Sèvres Porcelain*, London, 1988, p.24.

17. Eriksen and De Bellaigue (1987), op.cit., pp.190–206.

18. B. L. Grandjean, *Louis Antoine Fournier*, Copenhagen, 1969.

19. The factory's sales records show that between two and twenty-one sculptures of children after Boucher were delivered with prestigious services ranging from the Empress's Maria Theresa in 1758, through to the Duke of Bedford's in 1763, Madame du Barry's in 1769 and the Prince de Rohan in 1771. As late as 1792, the Prince of Wales (later George IV) had four Sèvres dessert services and about forty biscuit figures in the 'Confectionary' at his London palace at Carlton House (G. de Bellaigue, *Sèvres: Porcelain from the Royal Collection*, London, 1979, p.7).

20. The number of models after Boucher rose eventually to over seventy; a number were bought by *L'Office du*

Roi, the king's pantry, in December, 1767, and again in December, 1769, presumably for use as decoration for the dessert table. C. C. Dauterman, 'Sèvres Figure Painting in the Anna Thompson Dodge Collection', *The Burlington Magazine*, CXVIII (November 1976), p.754.

21. 'Les morceaux exécutés à la manufacture royale de porcelaine de Sèvres sont la plupart dignes de subsister plus longtemps que ne le permet la fragilité de cette matière. On vient donc d'en former une suite de planches qui feront survivre ces pièces a elles-mêmes; elles sont toutes la composition de M. Boucher'. R. Savill, 'François Boucher and the Porcelains of Vincennes and Sèvres, *Apollo*, 115 (1982), pp.162–70.

22. Eriksen and De Bellaigue (1987), op.cit., p.236.

23. In 1781, during the highpoint of the neo-classical movement, the factory director Bachelier was to write of Duplessis: 'it is he who through his passion for precision has trained throwers and repairers who are to be esteemed on account of the exactness of their work. He might be criticized for baroque shapes, overloaded with detail; but, being Meissonnier's pupil, he had his faults and those of Oppenord and Pineau, who forty years ago gave us the taste for contrast and tortuous shapes.' Eriksen and De Bellaigue, op.cit., p.82.

24. Savill (1988), op.cit., p.492.

25. This often appear unduly small for the set, but it would appear that it contained a concentrated brew of tea to which hot water was added separately to dilute it, which would avoid cracking the body. Savill (1988), op.cit., pp.490–1.

26. The stocklist of 1752 records 1105 prints and drawings, including putti after Boucher, landscapes, battle scenes and marine subjects, and even three boxes of dead insects. G. de Bellaigue, 'Sèvres Artists and their Sources', *The Burlington Magazine* (1980), 122, pp.667–78.

27. A.-M. Belfort, 'L'Oeuvre de Vieilliard d'après Boucher', *Cahiers de la Céramique du Verre et des Arts du Feu*, 58 (1976), pp.6–35.

28. De Bellaigue (1987), op.cit., pp.49–53.

29. A blue-and-green *vaisseau à mat* of 1758 decorated with a central panel of two rustics in the Royal Collection is probably identical to '1 pot pory Vaisseau saffre et Verd Teniere' sold to Madame de Pompadour for 960 livres in December, 1759, along with two companion 'pots pourri fontaine' in the collection of the Duke of Buccleuch. *The Treasure Houses of Britain: Five Hundred Years of Private Patronage and Art Collecting*, Washington, 1985, no.397.

30. In September 1769 the newspaper *Mercure de France* carried an advertisement from one Niquet for Teniers engravings for use for painters and decorators. De Bellaigue (1980), op.cit., p.752.

31. '1 pendule petit verd [432 ll]; 2 pots pouris à feuillages verds chinois [864 ll]; and [2 pots pouris] bobèches [verds chinois] [672 ll]'. They are listed in the inventory of the Château de Ménars taken after her death in 1764. P. Ennès, 'Essai de reconstitution d'une garniture de Madame de Pompadour', *The Journal of the Walters Art Gallery*, 42/43 (1984/1985), pp.70–82.

32. The borders of this service were decorated with *bleu céleste* and the centres painted with bunches of flowers. Little survives of this service as the king apparently tired of it and sold portions of it to Lazare Duvaux in 1757. See P. Gregory, 'Le service bleu céleste de Louis XV à Versailles', *La Revue du Louvre* 1 (February 1982), pp.40–6.

33. Savill (1988), op.cit., p.736.

34. Eriksen and De Bellaigue (1987), op.cit., p.240.

35. S. Bursche, *Tafelzier des Barock*, Munich, 1974, figs 139 and 140.

36. Vincent La Chappelle's *The Modern Cook* (London, 1733, The Hague, 1742) supplies recipes for only the first courses of the meal, since the third, the dessert, was the responsibility of the 'office', the section of the kitchen which was responsible for the preparation of pastries and cold foods. The meal opens with a pair of soups in the tureens, flanking a quarter of veal; these were 'removed' (i.e. replaced) by fish; a turbot and a salmon. There were four side-dishes or entrees of poultry and hors d'oeuvres of such delicacies as mutton chops with chicory, glazed eels with an Italian sauce, or a dish of chicken breasts. The second course repeated this pattern, but included a ham in the centre and cakes to replace the turbot and salmon. The new hors d'oeuvres included sweetbreads, artichokes, duck tongues and eggs with a meat sauce. B. K. Wheaton, *Savouring the Past: The French Kitchen and Table from 1300 to 1789*, London, 1983, p.140.

37. Savill (1988), op.cit., pp.744–5.

38. A depiction of all four lined up together to show the difference in sizes is shown in G. de Bellaigue, *The Louis XVI Service*, Cambridge, 1986, plate XVI.

39. S. Macdonald, *Porcelain from Europe*, Manchester, 1986, p.8. It would appear that the innovations in the production of dinner services made at Meissen had had only limited influence, and most Frenchman still used plate when possible, c.f., Rouquet's surprise on seeing the lack of plate in use in England in *L'Etat des Arts en Angleterre*, Paris, 1755, pp.134–39. But for the grandest occasions of the rich, items of gold and silver were still used, as in the service sent to the Court of Denmark in the eighteenth century; surviving table plans have allowed fairly precise reconstructions of the settings, using the items themselves. *La table d'un roi: l'orfèvrerie du XVIIIe siècle à la Cour de Danemark*, Paris, Musée des Arts Décoratifs, 1987.

40. In 1763 the service given by the king to the Duchess of Bedford, wife of the English ambassador, comprised '1 pot a oglio et platteau, 2 terrines et platteau, 72 assiettes, 4 sallières à 3 parties, 4 sallières doubles, 8 sallières simples, 4 moutardiers et platteaux, 2 beurriers, 14 pots à jus, 2 platteaux, 2 saussières, 2 platteaux, 2 saladiers 1re grandeur, 2 saladiers 2re grandeur, 16 compotiers, 2 sucriers de M. le Premier, 16 tasses à glaces, 4 platteaux Bouret, 4 soucoupes à pieds doubles, 2 platteaux à 3 pots à confitures, 2 seaux à bouteilles, 2 seaux à demi bouteilles, 2 seaux crennelés, 2 seaux ovales à liqueurs, 4 seaux du Roy à liqueurs, 1 jatte a ponche et mortier'. The total cost 18,374 livres. *Les Grands Services de Sèvres*, Musée National de Céramique, Sèvres, 1951, pp.26–7.

41. C. Dauguet and D. Guilleme-Brulon, 'Le Décor de la Table au XVIIIe Siècle', *L'Estampille* (January 1975), pp.5–15.

42. M. Brunet and T. Préaud, *Sèvres: des origines à nos jours*, Fribourg, 1978, p.174, no.149.

43. A 'seau à glaces' (ice-pail) appears in the factory records for 1759. M. Brunet and T. Préaud, op.cit., p.174, no.151.

44. They are described in the *Encyclopédie* as 'un nom moderne donné à des liqueurs agréables au goût, preparées avec art & glacées en forme de tendres congelations'. Savill (1988), op.cit., p.773.

45. Sèvres porcelain is even mentioned in one of the amorous encounters of Casanova, dating from the 1750s: 'The service was made of Sèvres porcelain. Eight made [specially prepared] dishes composed the supper; they were set on silver boxes filled with hot water which kept the food always hot. It was a choice and delicious supper. I exclaimed the cook must be French, and she said that I was right. We drank only Burgundy, and we emptied a bottle of 'oeil de perdrix' champagne and another of some sparkling wine for gaiety. It was she who dressed the salad; her appetite was equal to mine. She rang only to have the dessert brought, together with all the ingredients for making punch. In everything she did I could not but admire her knowledge, her skill and her grace.' G. Casanova, *History of My Life*, 4, 39, quoted in B. K. Wheaton, op.cit., p.159.

46. An advertisement by one Germain-Despargnes which appeared on 22 June 1758, gives an idea of what the factories aimed at: 'Le sieur Germain-Despargnes fait fabriquer une très belle faïence japonné [enamelled] façon Saxone, dans les goûts les plus nouveaux, rue de Boulets, faubourg St Antoine, à la Croix-Faubin, no.3 Cette faïence imite singulièrement la porcelaine et a, d'ailleurs, l'avantage d'être plus solide et de coûter beaucoup moins. L'émail en est très brillant; les formes sont très agréables. On a même trouvé moyen d'y faire briller l'or, comme sur la porcelaine.' J. Térrasson, *Les Hannong et leurs Manufactures Strasbourg Frankenthal*, Paris, 1971, p.46.

47. '*Mêlées avec cette terre ignoble, connue sous le nom de fayence*'. Rouquet, *L'Etat des Arts en Angleterre*, Paris, 1755, p.134.

48. A. Lane, *French Faïence*, London, 1948, p.17. See also G. Le Duc, 'Paris, rue de Charenton: Une Maufacture royale de "terre d'Angleterre" 1743–1747', *Revue de la Société des Amis du Musée National de Céramique* (1993), no.2, pp.20–8.

49. In 1771 the factory issued a price-list of the *Prix Marchand des Fayances de la Manufacture de JOSEPH HANNONG, A Strasbourg. 1771*. This lists *assiettes, plats rond* and *plats ovales, façon d'argent* in different sizes and priced according to their size and the quality of decoration. H. Haug, *Les Faïences et Porcelaines de Strasbourg*, 1922, [reprint Heppenheim, 1979], p.17.

50. J. Giacomotti, *French Faïence*, Fribourg, 1963, p.153.

51. The products of the factory were advertised in the newspapers in 1754, advertising 'nouvelles terres et faïences japonnées' at the Paris shop address, 'on y trouve tout ce qu'on peut désirer en bijoux et services de table. La couleur et la dorure appliquées sur ces nouvelles faïences n'en cédent guère pour le dessin et pour la nouveauté à celle des porcelaines de Saxe. Térrasson, op.cit., p.44.

52. H.-P. Fourest, 'The Sceaux Faïence Factory', *The Connoisseur* (October 1961), pp.107–12.

CHAPTER 8
The Spread of Porcelain Factories Throughout Europe

1. A. Fauchier-Magnan, *The Small German Courts in the 18th Century*, London, 1958, p.18.

2. Fauchier-Magnan, op.cit., p.57.

3. Ibid., pp.26–7.

4. The French writer and philosopher Voltaire, who sought German patronage and for a time was employed by Frederick II of Prussia, wrote to his favourite niece, Mme Denis, that 'the majority of the German Courts today are like those of the ancient Paladins. They are old castles where one seeks amuse-

ments. One finds there pretty ladies-in-waiting, handsome bachelors; they engage mountebanks.' Ibid., p.11.

5. In Germany hunting was a privilege reserved exclusively for the nobility, but was really more akin to butchery, since the animals were herded into closed spaces or enclosures to be the target of pot-shots by the courtiers, and then left to run around until they died: 'I went on Thursday to see the Chasse which was not far from hence. It was, I think, nothing but a kind of massacre of two or three hundred poor beasts, & had something in it quite shocking, especially when some of them ran about, as they did for some time, excessively wounded & mangl'd before they died.' Sir Charles Hanbury-Williams from Leipzig in 1751. T. H. Clarke, 'Porcelain for a Pack of Hounds; A Meissen Service at Blenheim', *Country Life* (29 January 1987), p.78.

6. Fauchier-Magnan, op.cit., pp.199–211.

7. A decree stated that 'Now that porcelain [sic] is available, made here in the noble factory, of such quality and refinement that everyone recognizes it to be better and stronger than the wares of Frankfurt, it should be made known to the other towns and councils so that those who do business will come here. No foreign ware may be bought and sold, and must be confiscated if it appears.' D. Imber, *Collecting Delft*, London, 1968, p.91.

8. Ibid., p.92.

9. The French Duchesse d'Orléans had already observed in 1721 that 'Germany not only imitates France but always does double what is done here.' G. Beard, *Stucco and Decorative Plasterwork in Europe*, London, 1983, p.113.

10. Identical prints by Nilson and Amiconi were used by porcelain factories as widespread as Frankenthal, Kloster Veilsdorf, and Zürich; see S. Ducret, *Keramik und Graphik des 18. Jahrhunderts*, Brunswick, 1973.

11. 'It is disgusting to note the increase in the quantity of coffee used by my subjects and the amount of money that goes out of the country in consequence. Everybody is using coffee . . . My people must drink beer. His Majesty was brought up on beer, and so were his officers. Many battles have been fought and won by soldiers nourished on beer; and the King does not believe that coffee-drinking soldiers can be depended upon to endure hardships or to beat his enemies in the case of the occurrence of another war.' Quoted in J. Green, *Consuming Passions*, London, 1985, p.235.

12. *Zur Geschichte von Kaffee, Tee, Schokolade und Tabak. Der bitter-süsse Wohlgeschmack*, Göttingen, Städtisches Museum, 1994. I owe this reference to Charlotte Jacob-Hanson.

13. K. Berling, *Meissen China: An Illustrated History*, London, 1910, reprint 1972, pp.54–6.

14. W. B. Honey, *Dresden China*, London, 1934, p.130.

15. Meissen archive, V.9.55.

16. M. Oppenheim. 'Das Porzellan' in *Frankenthaler Porzellan*, Frankenthal, 1955, p.10.

17. In Saxony and Vienna it took the form of a festival in which the court imitated a village wedding at a country inn; it was held on Shrove Tuesday, or for the benefit of visiting dignitaries and was carefully enacted in the manner of a stage production. It included sleigh rides, amateur theatricals and ballets, and the courtiers put on national dress, or dressed as tradesmen, farmers, gardeners, millers, shepherds, cobblers, acrobats or peddlers. A vivid description of a court festivity is given by Catherine II of Russia,

herself a princess of German extraction. It occurred in 1758 at the palace of the Oranienbaum in Russia, and was designed to titillate the jaded senses of her husband. She described in her memoirs thus: 'I therefore instructed my architect, Antonio Rinaldi, to build, in a distant corner of the wood, a great float which would hold an orchestra of sixty people, musicians and singers. I had verses written by the Italian court poet and music by the court musician Araja. In the garden, the main avenue was decorated with lights and a curtain was hung, facing the supper table . . . After the first course the curtain concealing the avenue was raised and we could see approaching from a distance the orchestra on its carriage pulled by a score of oxen, adorned with garlands, and escorted by as many dancers as I had been able to find. The avenue was so well lit that we could see everything clearly. When the float halted, by a happy chance, the light of the moon fell exactly upon it with such exquisite effect that the whole company was amazed . . . After [the music] had finished we heard fanfares and drumrolls, and a showman made his appearance, crying "Ladies and Gentlemen, roll up, roll up, you will find free lottery tickets in my booths!" On either side of the curtains two little curtains were raised and we saw two brightly lit stalls, in one of which they were giving away lottery tickets for the porcelain that it held, and in the other for flowers, ribbons, fans, combs, brushes, gloves, swordknobs, and other knick-knacks of that kind. When the stalls were empty we sat down to dessert, and then danced till six in the morning'. Catherine II, *Mémoires de l'Impératrice Catherine II, écrits par elle-même*, London, 1859, pp. 292–3, quoted in M. Baur-Heinhold, *Baroque Theatre*, London, 1967, pp.13–14.

18. P. Stahl and S. Ohlig, *Höchster Porzellan 1746–1796*, Mainz, 1994.

19. T. H. Clarke, 'Johann Jacob Wolrab's engravings of characters from the *commedia dell'arte*, Nuremberg, c.1720', *Keramik-Freunde der Schweiz*, 104 (October 1989), pp.11–15.

20. M. Newman, *Die deutschen Porzellanmanufakturen im 18. Jahrhundert*, Brunswick, 1977, 1, p.288.

21. H. Reber, 'Johann Peter Melchior und die Kurmainzische Plastik seiner Zeit', *Keramos*, 119, 1988, pp. 103–144; *Johann Peter Melchior, 1747–1825. Bildhauer und Modellmeister in Höchst, Frankenthal und Nymphenburg*, Gelsenkirchen, 1997.

22. Newman, op.cit., 1, p.294.

23. See catalogue by K. H. Esser and H. Reber, *Höchster Fayencen und Porzellane*, Mainz, 1964, no.152.

24. G. Zick, *Berliner Porzellan der Manufaktur von Wilhelm Caspar Wegely 1751–1757*, Berlin, 1978.

25. W. O. Henderson, *Studies in the Economic Policy of Frederick the Great*, London, 1963, pp.20–30.

26. The salaries paid at the Berlin factory in the eighteenth century: Modellmeister [head of modelling] – 2000 taler; Malereivorsteher [head of painting] – 2000 taler; Manufakturdirektor [Director] – 1400 taler; Arkanist [first chemist] – 1200 taler; Malereivorsteher [deputy head of painting] – 1100 taler; Figurenmaler [figure painter] – 1000 taler; Rechnungsfuehrer [accountant] – 800 taler; Hauptkassierer [head cashier] – 500 taler; Güldermeister [gilder] – 500 taler; Revisor [auditor] – 500 taler; Ofenmeister [kiln master] – 480 taler; Verwaltungsinspektor [head of administration] – 400 taler; Geschirrschreiber [tablewware painter] – 180 taler. The original list gives 'Gurtelmeister' for

'Güldermestier', but this is probably misspelling (information from Charlotte Jacob-Hanson). G. Schade, *Berliner Porzellan*, Leipzig, 1978, pp.109–10.

27. G. Schade, *Berliner Porzellan*, Leipzig, 1978.

28. There survives in the Berlin archives a drawing of the figures set out on mirror trays for the dessert, surrounded by baskets for fruit and leaf-shaped dishes; this appears to be one of our best surviving records of the layout of an eighteenth-century dessert service. Schmidt, *Porcelain as an Art and a Mirror of Fashion*, London, 1932, p.298.

29. E. Köllmann and M. Jarchow, *Berliner Porzellan*, Munich, 1987, figs. 144–7.

30. The courtier and factory manager von Langen commented that 'Glaser is a miserable painter; everything else he had produced is useless, and whatever he still plans to do is a lie. We are as far removed from true porcelain as brass is from gold.' S. Ducret, *German Porcelain and Faience*, Fribourg, 1962, p.47.

31. T. H. Clarke, 'Johann Jacob Wolrab's engravings of characters from the *commedia dell'arte*, Nuremberg, c.1720', *Keramik-Freunde der Schweiz*, 104 (October 1989), pp. 11–15.

32. S. Ducret, *The Colour Treasury of Eighteenth Century Porcelain*, Oxford, 1976, p.70.

33. R. Rückert, 'The Nymphenburg Commedia dell'Arte by Franz Anton Bustelli', *Christies Review of the Season 1977*, pp.370–3; Michael Newman, *The Comedians of Franz Antony Bustelly [sic]*, Swanage, 1998.

34. M. Newman, *Die deutschen Porzellan-Manufakturen im 18. Jahrhundert*, Brunswick, 1977, vol.2, p.97, fig. 50.

35. For Gessner's overall achievement, see J. Hibberd, *Salomon Gessner: His creative achievement and influence*, Cambridge, 1976.

36. B. Zehmisch, 'Eighteenth-century Zürich: Aspects of intellectual and artistic life', *Apollo* (October 1974), pp.39–50.

37. R. Schnyder, 'Eighteenth-Century Swiss Faïence', *The Connoisseur* (November 1963), pp.156–60.

38. S. Ducret, *German Porcelain and Faience*, London, 1967, pp.362–70.

39. 'Schleswig-holsteninsche Fayence', *Weltkunst*, I (October 1984), pp.2636–40.

40. 'Tafelgeschirr', *Weltkunst*, I (March 1985), pp.540–4.

41. R. J. Charleston, 'Transfer-Printing on Swedish Faïence', *The Connoisseur* (October 1960), pp.91–5.

42. A. Lane, 'Giacomo Boselli: An Italian Potter from Savona', *The Connoisseur* (November 1955), pp.161–4.

43. See K. Lankheit, *Die Modellsammlung der Porzellanmanufaktur Doccia: Ein Dokument italienischer Barockplastik*, Munich, 1982.

44. V. de Martini in *The Golden Age of Naples*, Detroit and Chicago, 1981, pp.382–3.

45. H. Honour, 'G. D. Tiepolo and the Aranjuez Porcelain Room', *The Connoisseur* (November 1960), pp.183–4.

46. A. Ray, 'Julian Lopez and Figure Models at Alcora', *Apollo* (June 1990), pp.405–9.

47. B. F. de Tavares e Tavora, 'Portuguese Faïence of the Eighteenth Century', *Apollo* (April 1973), pp.388–95.

48. Jose Meco, 'Fliesenkultur in Portugal', *Keramos*, 124 (1989), pp.5–99; Rioletta Sabo and Jorge Nuno Falcato, *Portuguese Decorative Tiles*, New York, 1998.

49. K. Rueff, 'The Lively Forms of Brussels Faïence' in P. Atterbury (ed.), *European Pottery and Porcelain*, New York, 1979, pp.43–7.

50. E. J. Soil de Moriame and L. Deplace de Formaoir, *La Manufacture Impériale et Royale de Porcelaine de Tournay*, Paris, 1937, fig. 590.

51. T. Clifford, 'Nicolas Gauron – a Virtuoso Modeller at Tournai and Chelsea', in *The Rococo in England – a Symposium*, C. Hind (ed.), London, 1986, pp.161–74.

CHAPTER 9
Porcelain in Eighteenth-Century Britain

1. 'For a tiny minority of peers and landed magnates this expansion meant unprecedented wealth; but the middling classes and some of the more fortunate artisans and workers may also have enjoyed a higher standard of living and more spare cash in this period than ever before'. L. Colley in M. Snodin (ed.), *Rococo: Art and Design in Hogarth's England*, London, 1984, p.10.

2. Snodin (1984), op.cit., p.10.

3. 'The later eighteenth century saw such a convulsion of getting and spending, such an eruption of new prosperity, that a greater proportion of the population than in any previous society in human history was able to enjoy the pleasures of buying consumer goods'. N. McKendrick in *The Birth of a Consumer Society*, London, 1982, p.9. For a contrary opinion, see J. Brewer and R. Porter (eds), *Consumption and the World of Goods*, London, 1993.

4. See L. Weatherill, *Consumer Behaviour and Material Culture in Britain 1660–1760*, London, 1988.

5. D. G. Callan, *William Shipley: Founder of the Royal Society of Arts*, London, 1968.

6. The subject of this chapter has been most recently reviewed by S. Richards, *Eighteenth-Century Ceramics. Products for a Civilised Society*, Manchester, 1999, and H. Young, *English Porcelain, 1745–95: Its Making, Design, Marketing and Consumption*, London, 1999.

7. T. H. Clarke, 'Das Northumberland-Service aus Meissener Porzellan', *Keramos*, 70 (October 1975), pp. 9–92.

8. Another service given to William Eden after the Treaty of Navigation and Commerce between France and Britain in 1787; see Aileen Dawson in G. Jackson-Stops (ed.), *The Treasure Houses of Britain: Five Hundred Years of Private Patronage and Art Collecting*, Washington, 1985, No.399.

9. Lord Bolingbroke bought a Sèvres *surtout de table* from the dealer Lazare Duvaux just before the Seven Years War in 1756. S. Eriksen 'Rare Pieces of Vincennes and Sèvres Porcelain' *Apollo*, LXXXVII (January 1968), pp.34–8; The Duke of Richmond bought a garniture of three very expensive vases in the latest neo-classical taste on his visit to the factory on 12 November 1765, and ordered a dinner service costing five hundred pounds. R. Savill in G. Jackson-Stops, op.cit., No.409. The Reverend William Cole recorded in his travel diary that his friend Horace Walpole, son of the former prime minister and an important arbiter of taste in his own right, spent the enormous sum of ten Louis or guineas on a single Sèvres coffee cup and saucer in Paris in 1765. Cole himself could only afford six cups and saucers at '9 livres each cup & Saucer, the whole 54 livres . . . for the Seat, with a neat Sugar Dish & Cover at 12 Livres' or 'a single Coffee Cup & Saucer of the enamelled Chantilly manufactured China for which I gave 12 Livres, or about half a Guinea'. W. Cole, *A Journal of my Journey to Paris in the year 1765*, London, 1931, pp.232–3, 245. A less wealthy traveller in France, Philip Thicknesse, visited the factory at Saint Cloud (probably meaning Sèvres) in 1766, where 'the cheapest thing I could find was a small salladbowl [sic], which, however, cost me a guinea; here I was

shewn three small pieces of ornamental china for a chimney piece, that came to a thousand livres', quoted in B. Hillier, *Pottery and Porcelain 1700–1914*, London, 1968, p.202. It was also possible to order Sèvres porcelain in London via a Parisian dealer, as when the fashionable hostess Lady Melbourne ordered a dessert service after her marriage in 1769. It comprised eighty pieces at a cost of 5,197 livres 19 sous and was delivered to Lord Melbourne's Paris agent on 20 March 1771. R. Savill in Jackson-Stops (1985), op.cit., No.411.

10. One of the first to be hit seems to have been Horace Walpole, who returned to England in that year with some French porcelain and complained that he had to pay '7 1/2 guineas for a common set of coffee things that had cost me but five.' B. McLeod, 'Horace Walpole and Sèvres Porcelain: The Collection at Strawberry Hill', *Apollo* (January 1998), pp.42–7.

11. R. Savill in G. Jackson-Stops, op.cit., No.402, and R. Savill, *The Wallace Collection: Catalogue of Sèvres Porcelain*, London, 1988, p.825.

12. 'China vessels are playthings for women of all ages' wrote Addison in 1714. B. Hillier, *Pottery and Porcelain 1700–1914*, London, 1968, p.267.

13. Hillier (1968), op.cit., p.270.

14. According to Walpole, she 'inherited the Passion of her Family for Collecting. At first her Taste was chiefly confined to Shells, Japan & Old China, particularly of the blue & white with a brown Edge, of which she formed a large closet at Bulstrode; but contenting herself with one specimen of every pattern she could get, it was a collection of old pieces.' A blue-and-white Japanese dish in the collection of the Earl of Ilchester, bears the following label; 'Plate bid for at a sale and obtained by Elisabeth Countess of Ilchester, for £100 against the Duchess of Portland, which was carefully put away when the Duchess visited her for fear of recalling the fact'. Hillier (1968), op.cit., p.281.

15. As early as 1710 Jonathan Swift 'sauntered at China-shops' with the antiquary and collector Sir Andrew Fountaine. Hillier (1968), op.cit., p.202.

16. Benjamin Goodison was paid for '4 carved and gilt ornaments over the chimney with branches to d[itt]o to hold china – between 1734 and 1740'. R. J. Charleston 'Porcelain as room decoration in eighteenth-century England', *Antiques* (December 1969), pp.894–8.

17. G. Lang, *European Ceramics from Burghley House*, 1991, p.30–1.

18. As early as 1694 the ship the *Dorothy* imported a wide range of Eastern goods, including lacquer, china, tea and fans 'china ware of all the variety that can be got in the Country, both fine and coarse, particularly a quantity of fine teapots, blew and white, purple and white, red and white, a grate to be made before the spout within the side. Lacquer ware the finest that can be made. . . . Fans of all the variety that the country affords . . Hand skreens for ladys, tea fine and good quality, all well packed in tutenage {a zinc-like metal} as close as can be and then wrapt round in leaves of the country, and then put into tubs. . . . Bring the tea in no small pots, in sweetwood chests not in any pots till well assured that they are cleared from all scents, especially from the smells of the soldering oyl'. G. Godden, *Oriental Export Market Porcelain and its Influence on European Wares*, London, 1979, p.28.

19. John Thomas, *The Rise of the Staffordshire Potteries*,

Bath, 1971, op.cit., p.103. A selection of inventories from the London Orphans' Court in the period 1675–1725 shows that the percentage listing utensils for 'hot drinks' (tea, coffee or chocolate) rose from 2% to 96% in this period, and those owning china from 4 to 80%. L. Weatherill (1988), op.cit., pp.27–8.

20. P. Brown, *In Praise of Hot Liquors: The Study of Chocolate, Coffee and Tea-Drinking 1600–1850*, York, 1995, p.58; *see also* R. Emmerson, *British Teapots and Tea Drinking*, London, 1992.

21. H. C. and L. Mui, *Shops and Shopkeeping in 18th Century England*, London, 1989, p.178.

22. The Frenchman François De La Rochefoucauld, who visited England in 1784, wrote that 'Through the whole of England the drinking of tea is general. You have it twice a day, and though the expense is considerable, the humblest peasant has his tea twice a day just like the rich man; the total consumption is immense. The high cost of sugar or molasses, of which large quantities are required, does not prevent this custom being a universal one, to which there are no exceptions.' F. De La Rochefoucauld, *A Frenchman in England 1784*. Cambridge, 1933, p.23.

23. By 1777–8 England was importing 348 tons of chinaware, in contrast to Holland (111 tons), France (100 tons), Sweden (99 tons), and Denmark (39 tons). G. Godden (1979), op.cit., p.47.

24. 'Plate in England is less of real use than parade, porcelain being all the fashion; this custom is of long standing.' Mons. Grosley's Tour to London [in 1763], London, 1772, vol.II, p.76, quoted in J. Marryat, *A History of Pottery and Porcelain*, London, 1857, p.279.

25. This is born out by Lady Shelburne's description of a dinner with the Duke of Northumberland: 'the dinner was very magnificent being all served on gilt plate and the Desert on the finest Dresden china I had seen. The Plates of which had cost near thirty Guineas a dozen'. These were possibly pieces from the Hanbury–Williams service. Jackson-Stops (1985), op.cit., no.389, p.455. Similarly the German Count Frederick Kielmansegge observed at a dinner at the Duke of Newcastle's in 1761 that there was as much gold and silver plate as could be found at a German prince's: 'the quantity of gold and silver plate, and vessels on the sideboards, was such that it would be hard to find the like in the houses of many German princes. At one time we have silver, at another gold, and at another china plates, according to the different course. At least ten to twelve servants out of livery waited upon us, all these people . . . expect tips when you leave.' Count F. Kielmansegge, *Diary of a Journey to England in the Years 1761–2*, London, 1902, p.53.

26. By about 1740 the English had begun to stipulate conditions: 'Observe that the colour of the blue in No.3 [a sample piece] will do for the blue and white china throughout, for most people like a pale blue and the china thin.' In 1749–50 they were instructed: 'You must not buy any coloured dishes or plates and of the rest of the china-ware not above one-tenth part of the coloured sort.' G. Godden, *English China*, London, 1985, ch. 3.

27. Snodin (1984), op.cit., no.1, 2.

28. G. A. Godden, *Oriental Export Market Porcelain and its influence on European wares*, London, 1979, p.18, fig. 2.

29. The best introduction to 18th English porcelain perhaps remains R. J. Charleston (ed.), *English Porcelain 1745–1850*, London, 1965.

30. The petition of the Vincennes factory of that year refers to 'un nouvel etablissement qui vient de se former en Angleterre, d'une manufacture de porcelaine

qui paraît plus belle que celle de Saxe.' A. Lane, *English Porcelain Figures of the 18th Century*, London, 1961, p.3.

31. Snodin (1984), op.cit., nos.G.19, O.8.

32. B. Dragesco, *English Ceramics in French Archives*, London, 1993.

33. Some pieces are decorated with beautifully painted pieces with landscapes close to those of Vincennes, reinforcing the French influence. T. H. Clarke, 'French Influences at Chelsea', *English Ceramic Circle Transactions*, 4, part 5, pp.45–57.

34. J.V. G. Mallet, 'Chelsea' in R. J. Charleston (ed.), op.cit., p.31.

35. The transaction is recorded in a letter from Sir Charles himself to him friend Henry Fox of 9 June 1751: 'I received a letter of about ten days ago from Sr. Everard Fawkener, who is, I believe, concerned in the manufacture of China at Chelsea. He desir'd me to send over models for different Pieces from hence, in order to furnish the Undertakers with good designs; and would have had me send over fifty or threescore pounds' worth. But I thought it better and cheaper for the Manufacturers to give them leave to take away any of my China from Holland House [London], and to copy what they like. I have therefore told Sr. Everard, that, If he will go to your house, you will permit him, and anybody He brings with him, to see my China, & to take away such pieces as they may have a mind to Copy. I find also that the Duke is a great encourager of the Chelsea China, and has bespoke a set for his own Table.' Sir Everard wrote expressing thanks on the 12th August, 1751: 'I found on my return to Town that many imitations are made, as well in some forms as in paintings. This is of the greatest consequence to this new manufacture, as that of Dresden has not only the advantage of a longer Establishment, & of all the support of a Royal expense, by wh[ich] a number of the best artists in the way they want are drawn thither, but there exists at Dresden the greatest collection of old china in Europe, from whence many excellent patterns are to be had. . . . I have been desired to move you for a further favor in the behalf of this new manufactur, when I should return thanks for that advantage let them know the prices at the Whare houses of the Royal Manufacture of the several things you have indulged them with the sight & use of . . . they would have such a price for their ware as to re-imburse them & leave some advantage . . . they met with good encouragement last spring, tho' they had little but separate Pieces to sell, except Tea and Coffee services. They propose opening a Whare house in town by the King's birthday, when there will be a large quantity of dishes, plates, etc. for table & desert services.' Earl of Ilchester, 'A Notable Service of Meissen Porcelain', *The Burlington Magazine*, LV (1929), p.189.

36. T. H. Clarke, 'Sir Charles Hanbury Williams and the Chelsea Factory', *English Ceramic Circle Transactions*, 13, 2, 1988, pp.110–21.

37. Two terracotta figures by him of a shepherd and shepherdess in the Ashmolean Museum, Oxford, are dated 1749 and show a slightly ponderous style of modelling which can be traced in some of the Chelsea figures. A. Lane, 'Chelsea Porcelain Figures and the modeller Joseph Willems', *Connoisseur*, CXLV (1960), pp.245–51.

38. B. M. Watney, 'Origins of Designs for English Ceramics of the Eighteenth Century', *The Burlington Magazine*, CXIV (December 1972), pp.818–26.

39. Horace Walpole, who saw it on 3 March 1763, wrote to his friend Sir Horace Mann with much justified criticism: 'There are dishes and plates without number, an epergne, candlesticks, salt-cellars, sauce-boats, tea and coffee equipages – in short, it is complete – and cost twelve hundred pounds! I cannot boast of our taste; the forms are neither new, beautiful nor various. Yet Sprimont, the manufacturer, is a Frenchman: it seems their taste will not bear transplanting.' E. Adams, *Chelsea Porcelain*, London, 1987, p.156.

40. The *olio* or mixed meat and vegetable stew was almost unknown in Britain and referred to with derision in contemporary accounts cf. Mrs Elizabeth Fay, *Letters from India*, London, 1925, pp.189–90 on a Burdwan stew 'composed of everthing at table, fish, flesh and fowl; somewhat like the Spanish 'Olla Podrida' '.

41. This was noticed by a French visitor, La Rochefoucauld, in 1784, who remarked on their custom of dining at four o'clock, and the great joints of meat eaten: 'The courses are much the same as in France except that the use of sauce is unknown in the English kitchen and that one seldom sees a "ragout". All the dishes consist of various meats either boiled or roasted and of joints weighing about twenty or thirty pounds.' F. De La Rochefoucauld, *A Frenchman in England 1784*, Cambridge, 1933, pp.29–30. The comment on the absence of stews in England is interesting, as it explains why the Earl of Bristol commissioned two round tureens to match two existing oval tureens by Charles Kandler during his embassy to Turin in 1755–8; presumably he was following the continental fashion for *olio* pots in a hunting region that even today serves *bollito misto* (mixed boiled meats). See G. Jackson-Stops op.cit., no.454. Thomas Bentley, Wedgwood's partner, commented with surprise on 'a great many broth dishes and saucers' on a visit to the Sèvres factory in 1776, and the dealer Daguerre brought some to London in the 1780s and 1790s, but could only sell dinner services. Savill (1988), op.cit., p.643.

42. 'Giving direction for a grand dessert would be needless, for those persons who could give such grand desserts, either keep a proper person, or have the use of a confectioner . . . but for county ladies it is a pretty amusement both to make the sweetmeats and dress out a dessert, as it depends wholly on fancy and but little expense.' E. Ayrton, *The Cookery of England*, London, 1975, p.403. Over twenty years later De La Rochefoucauld was to comment that 'after the removal of the cloth, the table is covered with all kinds of wine, for gentlemen of modest means always keep a large stock of good wine. On the middle of the table there is a small quantity of fruit, a few biscuits (to stimulate thirst), and some butter, for many English people take it at dessert.' F. De La Rochefoucauld (1933), op.cit., pp.29–30.

43. The latter set up by Edward Heyleyn and the engraver Thomas Frye, which they claimed would 'save large sums of money that were yearly paid to the Chinese and the Saxons'. A. Lane, *English Porcelain Figures*, London, 1961, p.3.

44. A visitor to the factory in 1748 wrote that 'They have already made large quantities of tea-cups, saucers etc, which by some skilful persons are said to be little inferior to those brought from China.' G. Godden, *English China*, London, 1985, ch. 4.

45. Hillier (1968), op.cit., p.203.

46. A good idea of the wide range of their products can be found in the sale catalogue of the most prominent member of their number, the London dealer Thomas Morgan, whose sale catalogue of March 1772 lists a 'Great Variety of the most beautiful SEVE, CHANTILLY, TOURNAY, and SAXON Porcelain . . . A Superb Collection of the very rare old blue and coloured Japan with the Brown Edge . . Roman Earthenware . . Together his large Stock of India and Japan China, both useful and Ornamental.' It is only at the end of the description that we encounter 'Great choice of Chelsea, Derby and Worcester Porcelaine' along with 'lacquered ware, Pearl Beads, Fish and Counters, India Mats and Prints, with many Oriental and other Curiosities'. Preface to his sale at Christie's, 10 February and five following days, 1772.

47. The *Norwich Chronicle* for July 1783, ran the following advertisement from William Beloe, Chinaman, Market Place, Norwich: 'Has just received from the India Company's sale a large and regular assortment of useful and ornamental china. . . . . He has also a large parcel of useful china from Commodore Johnstone's Prize Goods taken from the Dutch [a reference to goods taken in sea-battle]'. G. Godden (1979), op.cit., p.53.

48. In that year it advertised for sale at auction 'A curious collection of fine figures, jars, sauceboats, services for deserts [sic], and a great variety of other useful and ornamental porcelains after the finest Dresden models, all exquisitely painted and enamelled with flowers, insects, India plants, & c.' It again advertised 'Derby, or the second Dresden' in 1757. G. Savage, *English Ceramics*, London, 1961 (reprinted 1983), p.168.

49. The original models have recently been rediscovered, and suggest the work of a number of different artists. P. Rowan, 'Derby Models Rediscovered', *The Antique Dealers and Collectors Guide* (May 1988), pp.56–7.

50. A commentator in the *Gentleman's Magazine*, 1763, wrote that although its products did not discolour or crack, 'this excellence is confined to comparatively few articles. The tea-table indeed it completely furnishes, and some of it so well enamelled as to resemble the finest foreign china, so that it makes up costly sets that are broken, without a perceptible difference. But, from whatever cause, this manufacture has never yet found its way to the dining table except in sauce-boats, toys for pickles, and hors d'oeuvres'. Quoted in E. Meteyard *Life and Works of Wedgwood*, London, 1865 (reprint 1980), pp.170–1.

51. C. Cook, *The Life and work of Robert Hancock*, London, 1948, p.3.

52. Snodin (1984), op.cit., No.18.

53. D. Drakard, 'Early On-glaze Transfer Printing', *Transactions of the English Ceramics Circle*, vol.15, part 3, 1995, pp.331–40; Colin Wyman, 'A Review of Early Transfer Printing Techniques', *Transactions of the English Ceramics Circle*, vol.16, part 3, 1998, pp.307–17.

54. M. Snodin *Rococo; Art and Design in Hogarth's England*, London, 1984, p.27.

55. M. Girouard, 'English Art and the Rococo', *Country Life* (13 January 1966), pp.58–61, (27 January 1966), pp.188–90, (3 February 1966), pp.224–7.

56. Reprinted in 1966 by the Ceramic Book Company, Newport, England. For a full (?) list of Sayer's productions, see *Sayer & Bennett's Enlarged Catalogue of New and Valuable Prints* of 1775 republished London, 1970.

57. An advertisement in the Leeds Intelligencer, 25

October 1760, reads; 'Robinson and Rhodes, opposite the George in Briggate, enamel and burn in gold and colour foreign and English china and tea-ware and make them complete to any pattern required – either Indian [i.e. Eastern] or Dresden. They also enamel coats of arms etc, and sell a good assortment of foreign china'. Similarly, in Aris's Birmingham Gazette, 23 September 1751, we read: 'Abraham Seaman, enamel painter, at Mrs. Weston's in Freeman, St. Birmingham, makes and sells all sorts of enamelling colours, especially the rose colours [presumably for 'famille rose'], likewise all sorts for China painters.' G. Godden (1979), op.cit., pp.372–4.

58. His ledger survives for the period 1771–6, and records purchases by the nobility and gentry. G. Coke, *In Search of James Giles*, Wingham, 1983.

59. J. V. G. Mallet in Snodin (1984), op.cit., No.O.37.

60. D. Barker and S. Cole, *Digging for Early Porcelain: The Archaeology of Six British Porcelain Factories*, Stoke-on-Trent, City Museum, 1998.

61. Godden (1979), op.cit., p.128.

62. As the century progressed, the desire to have items all of one pattern increased, and in 1782 the directors in London were complaining that 'goods have come of a variety of patterns, where they should all have been alike, particularly in Table and other sets – in some cases there have been so many patterns and so very different from each other that they could not possibly be put up to Sale in Sets, but have been obliged to be sold as odd pieces'. G. Godden (1979), op.cit., p.48. G. Coke (1983), op.cit., p.42, observes that at the Worcester sale of December, 1769, 'complete services nearly always sold and quite a few of them went to private purchasers'.

63. G. Godden, *English China*, London, 1985, ch. 10.

64. See R. Copeland, *Spode's Willow Pattern and Other Designs after the Chinese*, London, 1980, pp.33–9.

65. In July 1794 the following dinner service was sold by Caughley: 'A fine oval Nankin table service of the fine Willow landscape, and dagger border, containing 18 long dishes in 6 sizes, 72 table plates, 24 soup plates, 24 dessert plates, 2 large tureens and dishes, 2 small ditto, 4 sauce boats, 4 stands, 2 large salad vessels and 6 pudding dishes. £33.12.0d.' G. A. Godden, *Caughley and Worcester Porcelains 1775–1800*, London, 1969, p.13.

66. In August 1790 Joseph Lygo, the London Derby representative, wrote to William Duesbury observing that 'chamber pots they have none, they have not made any for some time and the reason is foreign Nankin ones are so much cheaper than theirs'. Godden (1969), op.cit., p.13.

67. On 21 January of that year the Council of Supracargoes in Canton wrote to the directors in London that 'the order this year received from the Honble. Court give us reason to suppose that China ware is not now an article in so high demand as some past'; no new china was ordered in 1779–80, though new designs were ordered in for the 1781–2 season. Godden (1979), op.cit., p.47.

68. Godden (1979), op.cit., p.50.

CHAPTER 10
The Rise of Staffordshire

1. In 1681 Thomas Malkin of Sneyd, potter, was ordered to 'fill up the pit he hath made in lane near to the Dale Hall before 14 Oct.' A. Mountford, *The Illustrated Guide to Staffordshire Salt-Glazed Stoneware*, London, 1971, p.10.

2. J. Thomas, *The Rise of the Staffordshire Potteries*, Bath, 1971, p.4.

3. Mountford, op.cit., p.18.

4. See R. G. Cooper, *English Slipware Dishes*, London, 1968.

5. D. Gaimster, 'Regional Decorative Traditions in English Post-Medieval Slipware' in I. Freestone and D. Gaimster (ed.) *Pottery in the Making*, London, 1997, pp.128–33.

6. Cooper, op.cit., p.101.

7. D. Towner in *World Ceramics*, London, 1968, fig. 738.

8. B. Rackham, *Early Staffordshire Pottery*, London, 1951, p.7.

9. In 1697 Dwight similarly prosecuted Moses Middleton of Shelton, Cornelius Hamersley of Howle Ley and Joshua Astbury of Shelton for the same offence. Mountford, op.cit., pp.5–10.

10. They are presumably the 'Dutchmen' recorded by Dr Martin Lister with such praise: 'As for the Red Ware of China, that has been, and is done in England, to a far greater perfection than China, we having as good materials, viz. the soft Haematites, and far better artists in Pottery, but in this particular we are beholden to two Dutchmen [sic] brothers who wrought in Staffordshire.' W. B. Honey, 'Elers Ware', *Transactions of the English Ceramic Circle*, 1, no.2 p.15. See also G. Elliot, *John and David Elers and their Contemporaries*, London, 1998.

11. An advertisement in the *Daily Advertiser* of 24 August 1747 says that 'To be sold . . . during the Welch fair. All sorts of Welch ware, Derby and Staffordshire fine stoneware, amongst which are great varieties of curious teapots of all sizes, that far excel either silver or china, both for drawing and pouring, and not inferior in make or beauty.' L. Weatherill, *Consumer Behaviour and Material Culture in Britain 1660–1760*, London, 1988, p.85.

12. Ibid., p.30.

13. D. Barker in *The Wedgwood Society of New York [Newsletter]*, March 1994, p.4.

14. Mountford, op.cit., p.37.

15. Ibid., fig. 106.

16. H. Tait, 'Blocks for Spouts' *The British Museum Quarterly*, Vol.XXVI, nos.3–4 (Spring 1963), pp.103–9.

17. Documented examples of his work are a block for a 'spitting pot' in the British Museum and a plate with a barleycorn and basketwork moulding with an inscription on the back by Enoch Wood saying it was moulded by his father in 1760. Mountford, op.cit., pl.152. His son Enoch was to write of him he 'was modeller to all the potters in Staffordshire at the latter end of the time that white ware or white stoneware was made'. quoted by J. Mallet in *Rococo: Art and Design in Hogarth's England*, London, 1984, p.241.

18. Thomas (1971), op.cit., p.7.

19. L. Weatherill, *The Pottery Trade and North Staffordshire 1600–1760*, Manchester, 1971, p.43.

20. Weatherill, op.cit., pp.61, 73.

21. Ibid., p.52.

22. Thomas, op.cit., p.13.

23. Ibid., p.11.

24. D. Barker, 'Discovering Staffordshire Ceramics' in *The International Ceramics Fair and Seminar (Handbook)*, 1991, pp.12–18.

25. The process is recorded by Simeon Shaw: 'The Flowerers now scratched the jugs and tea ware, with a sharp pointed nail, and filled the interstices with ground zaffre [cobalt oxide mixed with sand], in rude imitation of the unmeaning scenery on foreign porcelain; and in this art women were instructed, as a constant demand was made on the men for plastic branches.' Mountford, op.cit., p.48.

26. Ibid., p.56.

27. '[Enamelling] was first practiced by some Dutchmen, in Hot Lane who, to preserve their operation secret, had their muffle in a garden at Bagnall . . . Mr. Daniel, of Cobridge, was the first native who practised enamelling. Workmen were soon employed, from Bristol, Chelsea, Worcester and Liverpool . . . For some years the branch of Enamelling was conducted by persons wholly unconnected with the manufacture of the Pottery; in some instances altogether for the manufacturers; in others on the private account of the Enamellers; but when there was a great demand for these ornamented productions, a few of the more opulent manufacturers necessarily connected this branch with the others. At first, the enamellers embellished merely the tasteful productions, figures, jugs, cornucopiae, &c., and the rich carved work on the vessels; then they painted groups of flowers, figures and birds; and at length they copied their breakfast and dessert sets, the designs of the richest oriental porcelain.' Mountford, op.cit., p.56.

28. P. Halfpenny, 'Creamware: Its Origins and Development', *The International Ceramics Fair and Seminar (Handbook)*, London, 1993, pp.19–27.

29. Thomas (1971), op.cit., p.88.

30. 'In Burslem, and its neighbourhood, are near 150 separate Potteries, for making various kinds of Stone and Earthen Ware; which together, find constant Employment and Support for near 7,000 People. The Ware of these potteries is exported in vast Quantities from London, Bristol, Liverpool, Hull, and other Sea Ports, to our several Colonies in America and the West Indies, as well as to almost every Port in Europe. Great Quantities of Flint Stones are used in making some of the Ware, which are brought by Sea from different Parts of the Coast to Liverpool and Hull; and the clay for making the White Ware, is brought from Devonshire or Cornwall, chiefly to Liverpool; the Materials from whence are brought by Water up the Rivers Mersey and Weaver, to Winsford in Cheshire; those from Hull up the Trent to Wellington and from Winsford and Wellington, the Whole are brought up by Land Carriage to Burslem. The Ware when made, is conveyed to Liverpool and Hull, in the same Manner the Materials are brought from those Places.' Mountford, op.cit., p.12.

31. D. Towner, *Transactions of the English Ceramic Circle*, V, part IV, p.814.

32. Wedgwood himself summed up the situation in his *Experiment Book*: 'This suite of Experiments was begun at Fenton hall, in the parish of Stoke upon Trent, about the beginning of the year 1759, in my partnership with Mr. Whieldon, for the improvement of our manufacture of earthenware, which at that time stood in great need of it, the demand for our goods decreasing daily, and the trade universally complained of as being bad & in a declining condition. White stone ware (viz with salt glaze) was the principal article of our manufacture; but this had been made a long time, and the prices were now reduced so low that the potters could not now afford to bestow much expence [sic] upon it, or make it so good in any respect as the ware would otherwise admit of. And with regard to Elegance of form, that was an object very little attended to. The article next in consequence to Stoneware was an imitation of Tortoiseshell. But as no improve-

ment had been made in this branch for several years, the country was grown weary of it; and though the prices had been lowered from time to time, in order to increase the sale, the expedient did not answer, and something new was wanted, to give a little spirit to the business. I had already made an imitation of Agate; which was esteemed beautiful & a considerable improvement; but people were surfeited with wares of these variegated colours. These considerations induced me to try for some more solid improvement, as well in the *Body* as the Glazes, the *Colours*, the *Forms*, of the articles of our manufacture. I saw the field was spacious, and the soil so good, as to promise an ample recompence to any one who should labour diligently in its cultivation.' A. Dawson, *Masterpieces of Wedgwood in the British Museum*, London, 1984, pp.10–11.

33. J. V. G. Mallet, 'John Baddeley of Shelton, An Early Staffordshire Maker of Pottery and Porcelain', *Transactions of the English Ceramic Circle*, VI, III, 1967, pp.208–9.

34. In May 1764 Greatbatch wrote to Wedgwood that 'There are now ready two of the Crates of the Pine Apple ware, and a large quantity of Plates – about a gross & 1–2 of Light Couler teapots & a good quantity of China tpts the same as Mr. Whieldon & other sorts . . . Should be glad to have your advice in the shape of the Squirrel & Bird tpt Block, & whether you would have a ground work upon it or not, the work will be Compleated to Day or to Morrow to lay on – There is one size ready of the fruit dish and stand & will make a few for your approbation'. Mallet (1967), op.cit., p.43.

35. Ibid., p.43.

CHAPTER 11
The Classical Revival

1. See, for instance, the letters page of *Apollo* (January 1968), pp.66–7, and April, 1968 pp.310–11.

2. As early as 1737 the French architect J. F. Blondel, in his influential book *De la Distribution des Maisons de Plaisance*, criticised 'the ridiculous jumble of shells, dragons, reeds, palm-trees, and plants which is the be-all and end-all of modern interior decoration.' Quoted in S. Eriksen, *Early Neo-Classicism in France*, London, 1974, p.25.

3. The architect Isaac Ware complained that we aped the taste of the French, 'a frivolous people whom we are too apt to imitate' and that the rococo style 'consists of crooked lines like C's and S's'. Quoted in M. Snodin, 'English Rococo and its Continental Origins' in *Rococo: Art and Design in Hogarth's England*, London, 1984, p.33.

4. Even before the Seven Years War of 1757–63 an Anti-Gallican league was formed, headed by Lord Blakeney, to whom the furniture carver Thomas Johnson dedicated his *One Hundred and Fifty New Designs* in 1758. The title page shows the figure of Britannia, who holds a shield bearing the arms of the association, while, above her, flies a putto labelled 'Genius' who sets fire to a strip of linked scrolls labelled 'French Paper Machee.' Snodin (1984), op.cit., p.176, no.L.44.

5. The French draughtsman Cochin was to write of him that the time of a return to a better taste can be dated to the arrival of Legeay 'on peut donner pour première époque du retour d'un meilleur goust, l'arrivée de Legeay'. Eriksen, op.cit., p.30.

6. Soufflot made a point of taking him to see the rococo palace at Stupinigi in Turin 'in the frivolous style

of Meissonnier'. The party was shocked by the degeneracy that they saw in architecture and design, finding buildings to admire only in Florence. Everywhere followed the French taste for extravagance; 'the most extravagant caprices have become the fashion and the most applauded', *les caprices les plus extravagans y sont devenus l'architecture à la mode, & la plus applaudie*. Eriksen op.cit., p.35.

7. Cochin, though himself in origin an accomplished rococo draughtsman, wrote a series of articles in the French paper *Mercure de France* criticising the rococo style for its irrationality. For instance, in the *Mercure de France* for December 1754 he wrote an ironic petition to goldsmiths that 'whenever they execute a life-size artichoke or celery stalk on an olio pot or some other piece of plate, to be good enough not to set beside a hare as big as a finger, a lark as large as life and a pheasant about a quarter or a fifth of its real size'. Eriksen, op.cit., p.27, pp.233–5.

8. Augustus III of Saxony acquired three statues excavated at Herculaneum with the collection of Prince Eugen of Vienna in 1736. *The Splendor of Dresden*, Washington, New York and San Francisco, 1978–9, p.25.

9. A. Fauchier-Magnan, *The Small German Courts in the 18th Century*, London, 1958, p.179.

10. For a survey of seventeenth and eighteenth-century prints of Antiquity, see *L'Immagine dell'Antico fra Settecento e Ottocento: Libri di archeologia nella Biblioteca Comunale dell'Archiginnasio*, Bologna, 1983–4.

11. The Long Gallery at Syon House, Middlesex, retains a collection deriving from Hamilton himself; it was built in about 1763–8 to designs by Robert Adam. On 7 June 1765, the 1st Duke of Northumberland wrote to William Hamilton in Naples to see if he could procure him vases or urns for the circular recesses, and 'Statues, Vases, Tripods or other Pieces of Vertu' for the round-headed arches that now contain books. G. Beard, *Craftsmen and Interior Decoration in England 1660–1820*, London, 1981, p.151.

12. D. Irwin, *Winckelmann: Writings on Art*, London, 1972, p.84.

13. Eriksen, op.cit., p.44.

14. D. Watkin, *Athenian Stuart*, London, 1982, pp.35–7.

15. C.f. his letter from Paris in 1764: [the French] 'believe they make discoveries when they adopt what we have had these twenty years. For instance, they begin to see beauties in the antique, every thing must be "à la grecque".' Quoted by P. Thornton, *Apollo* (April 1968), pp.311.

16. The Baron de Grimm, a German visitor to Paris, wrote in May, 1763, that 'for some years now the ornaments and forms of the Antique have been sought after, taste has gained considerably thereby and the fashion for them has become so general that today everything is made in the Greek manner. The exterior and interior decoration of buildings, furniture, stuffs, jewellery of all kinds, everything in Paris is in the Greek manner'. Baron de Grimm, *Corréspondance litteraire*, 1 May 1763, quoted in Eriksen, op.cit., pp.264–5.

17. Cochin himself was later to write 'At last everybody turned or attempted to turn back to the path of the good taste of the previous century, and since everything has to be twisted into a nickname in Paris it was called architecture in the Greek manner. Soon even braids and ribbons were made in the Greek manner; it remained as good taste only in the hands of a small number of people and became extravagance in the hands of all the rest.' C. N. Cochin,

Mémoires Inédits (written about 1780–90), Charles Henry (ed.), Paris, 1880, pp.142–3, quoted in Eriksen, op.cit., p.50. For a comprehensive discussion of the ever-changing fashions for trimmings in eighteenth-century France, see P. A. Parmal, 'Fashion and the Growing Importance of the Marchand des Modes in Mid-Eighteenth-Century France', *Costume*, 31 (1997), pp.68–77. The goldsmith Germain supplied tureens to the court of Russia in the form of 'antique oval vases, intended for sacrifices' as early as 1761 (H. Havard, *Dictionnaire de l'Ameublement et la Décoration*, Paris, 1889–90, vol.IV, 1383).

18. See C. Gilbert and A. Wells-Cole, *The Fashionable Fire Place 1660–1840*, Leeds, 1985.

19. Small vases in the classical style had been made before, for instance in biscuit porcelain at Mennecy for the service delivered to Louis XV. However, these were for the dessert course at the dinner table, where neo-classical vases would have been peculiarly appropriate, since they imitated the vases to be found in gardens. P. Gregory, 'Le Service bleu céleste de Louis XV à Versailles', *La Revue du Louvre* (1982), 1, figs 5, 6.

20. R. Savill, *The Wallace Collection: Catalogue of Sèvres Porcelain*, London, 1988, p.148.

21. S. Eriksen, *The James A. De Rothschild Collection at Waddesdon Manor: Sèvres Porcelain*, Fribourg, 1966, pp.140–1. Another early model was a pair of wildly rococo *pots-pourris feuilles de mirte* with a Greek key pattern base, probably modelled by the great sculptor Duplessis. Savill, op.cit., p.198.

22. Savill, op.cit., no.C.261–6.

23. Ibid., no.C.259. A version was possibly bought by the English collector Horace Walpole on a visit to Sèvres with the Duke of Richmond in 1765; the decoration consists solely of a blue colour (*bleu nouveau*), with some gilding. Savill, op.cit., no.C.259.

24. Ibid., nos.C.272–5.

25. Ibid., nos.C.284–5.

26. A set from the collection of Queen Marie Leczinska, wife of Louis XV, has recently been acquired by the Louvre. P. Ennès, 'Un vase avec des cygnes et deux vases à jets d'eau', *La Revue du Louvre* (1987), no. 3, pp. 201–6.

27. G. Levitine, *The Sculpture of Falconet*, Greenwich (CT.), 1972.

28. S. Eriksen and G. de Bellaigue, *Sèvres Porcelain*, London, 1987, p.113.

29. The most famous examples are the garnitures painted on both sides which were sold from the factory with a *vase a ruban* on 12 November 1765; these appear to correspond to a garniture in the collection of the Duke of Richmond at Goodwood, who visited the factory on that day. R. Savill in G. Jackson-Stops *The Treasure Houses of Britain*, Washington, 1984, no.409.

30. Savill, op.cit., nos.C.297–302 and C.310.

31. See G. Levitine, *The Sculpture of Falconet*, Greenwich (CT.), 1972.

32. See chapter 12.

33. Eriksen, op.cit., p.374.

34. C. C. Dauterman, *Sèvres Porcelain: Makers and Marks of the Eighteenth Century*, New York, 1986, pp.18–19.

35. 'Sans aucun chantournement sur des modèles antiques avec des reproductions de camées'. A document was prepared to explain how the commission was to be tackled, which explicitly rejected the style of Meissonnier and La Joue: 'Ce service ne pouvait être exécuté sur les formes actuellement usitées à la manufacture de Sèvres, quelque agréables qu'elles paraissent à des yeux accoutumés au prestige des contours que Meissonier et La Joue introduisirent, il y a environ

quarante ans, dans les ornemens de notre architecture et qui successivement passèrent dans notre ameublement et notre vaisselle. Le gout sévère des anciens artistes de la Grèce et de Rome bannit bientôt ces formes irregulières et baroque de notre architecture; mais l'orphèvrerie y est restée assujetie pour le service de nos tables'. With this in mind the designers did careful research: 'On a rassemblé parmi les originaux de l'antiquité qui ont echappé au temps ce que les artistes de la Grèce et de Rome ont produisait d'élégant dans les formes et dans les dessins; c'est dans ces receuils qu'on a fit un choix pour composer les pièces de ce service'. R. Savill, 'Cameo Fever': Six Pieces from the Sèvres Porcelain Dinner Service made for Catherine II of Russia', *Apollo*, 116 (1982), p.304.

36. Wedgwood wrote to his partner, Thomas Bentley, in April, 1772, that: 'I make no doubt of our friend Mr. Boultons things being very excellent, in contrivance & execution, & wish him every encouragement his ingenuity, spirit & industry deserve, but Mr. Cox [the jeweller, and maker of gaudy ornaments] has so far outshone him that I am afraid that he will be under some little bit of an eclipse in that respect, this season; & I am not without some little pain for our Nobility & Gentry themselves, for what with the fine things in Gold, Silver & Steel from Soho, the almost miraculous magnificence of Mr. Coxes Exhibition, & the Glare of the Derby & other China shews – What heads or Eyes could stand all this dazzling profusion of riches & ornament if something was not provided for their relief, to give them at proper intervals a little relaxation, & repose. Under this humble idea then, I have some hope for our black, Etruscan, & Grecian Vases still, & as I expect the golden surfeit will rage with higher than ever this spring, I shall almost tremble even for a gilt listel amongst your Vases, & would advise you by all means to provide a curtain immediately for your Pebble ware shelves, which you may open or shut, inlarge or diminish the shew of gilding as you find customers affected'. D. Buten, *18th Century Wedgwood; a Guide for Collectors & Connoisseurs*, New York, 1980, p.88.

37. H. Coutts, 'A Chelsea-Derby vase and Its Sources', *Derby Porcelain International Society Newsletter*, 18 (May 1990), pp.22–30.

38. The Chelsea and Derby sale catalogue of March 1773 lists a large number of new shapes, including 'an Extensive Variety of Ornamental and Useful Articles./Those for Ornament are principally Designs after the Antique, representing Tripods, Altars, Urns, Jars, &c., embellished with beautiful Devices, elegantly enriched, and particularly adapted for the Decoration of Chimney Pieces, Cabinets, Toilets, &c.' The development of the range of types can be traced from the advertisement on the title page of the sales held at Christies: whereas the 1770 sale of Chelsea porcelain, as left by Nicholas Sprimont, lists 'Beautiful Vases, Antique Urns, Perfume-Pots, Table and Desert Services. . . .', the 1771 catalogue lists rather more firmly 'A Variety of Superb and Elegant Antique-Shaped VASES, URNS, ESSENCE-POTS, JARS, and BEAKERS. . . .' J. Nightingale, *Contributions towards the History of Early English Porcelain from Contemporary Sources*, Salisbury, 1881, pp.1, 15, 42.

39. T. Clifford, 'Polidoro and English Design', *The Connoisseur* (August 1976), pp.282–97.

40. Bouchardon's vase designs date to before 1737, when they were advertised in the *Mercure de France*. M. Jordan, 'Edmé Bouchardon', *Apollo* (June 1985), pp.388–90.

41. In the 1773 auction the Derby factory sold 'a large antique jar and pedestal, decorated with cupids, dolphins, &c. a fine crimson ground and superbly finished with gold (£17.17)'. This is clearly copied from an engraving of *Première suite de vases antiques* after the French artist Jacques-François-Joseph Saly (1717–76). It appears to be number 2 in Duesbury's trade catalogue of 1773–4, bearing out its early date. C. B. Lippert, *Eighteenth-Century English Porcelain in the Collection of the Indianapolis Museum of Art*, Indianapolis, 1987, No.30.

42. He probably modelled some of the charming biscuit groups with putti, such as two groups of the *Elements*, or *Four Cupids as Sportsmen*. His work for the firm seems to have terminated in about 1774. T. Clifford, 'Nicolas Gauron – a Virtuoso Modeller at Tournai and Chelsea', in C. Hind (ed.), *The Rococo in England: A Symposium*, London, 1986, pp.161–74.

43. Timothy Clifford, 'Vulliamy clocks and British Sculpture', *Apollo* (October 1990), pp.226–37. Lygo wrote to William Duesbury II on 31 May 1784, that he had seen both 'French figures' (presumably from Sèvres) and 'your figures' laid out on a dessert at a Grand Ball in London, and the French were decidedly superior: Savill (1988), op.cit., p.820.

44. M. Savage, 'An Important Clock by Benjamin Vulliamy', *Derby Porcelain International Society Newsletter*, 17 (December 1989), pp.7–10.

45. T. Clifford, 'J. J. Spaengler, a virtuoso Swiss modeller at Derby', *The Connoisseur*, 198 (1978), pp.145–55.

46. R. J. Charleston, 'A Decorator of Porcelain and Glass – James Giles in a New Light', *English Ceramic Circle: Transactions*, 6, part 3, p.292.

47. The Frenchman François de La Rochefoucauld commented on the English habit of tea drinking in 1785, adding that 'it provides the rich with an opportunity to display their magnificence in the matter of tea-pots, cups and so on, which are always of the most elegant design based upon Etruscan and other models of antiquity. It is also the custom for the youngest lady of the household to make the tea.' F. de La Rochefoucauld, *A Frenchman in England 1784*, Cambridge, 1933, p.24.

48. 'All these figures to be about 10 inches high, after having seen the Derby Figures, I did not recommend Ease and Elegance in the Shaped drops, but the latter I shall just mention as the Antique robes are very easy and have a Propriety which is not to be met with in foreign Drapes.' He specifies the figure of *Fire* as 'A Vulcan forging a Thunderbolt in the Attitude of striking with his Anvil & Hammer, some pieces of Iron or Coals or anything peculiar to a Blacksmith's Shop to be Scatter'd about'. From a letter reproduced in facsimile in H. Owen, *Two Centuries of the Ceramic Art in Bristol*, London, 1873.

49. David Holgate in G. Godden (ed.), *Staffordshire Porcelain*, St Albans, 1983, p.62, and D. Holgate, *New Hall and its Imitators*, London, 1971.

50. In August, 1772, Wedgwood was writing to Bentley that 'The Great People have had these Vases in their Palaces long enough for them to be seen and admired by the Middling Class of People, which class we know are vastly, I had almost said, infinitely superior in number to the Great, and though *a great price* was, I believe, at first necessary to make the vases esteemed *Ornament for Palaces*, that reason no longer exists. Their character is established, and the middling People would probably by [sic] quantitys of them at a reduced price.' N. McKendrick, *The Birth of a Consumer Society*, London, 1982, p.131.

51. They had first met in about 1762, when Wedgwood was laid up in Liverpool owing to a riding accident. G. Blake Roberts, 'Wedgwood and Bentley – a unique alliance' *The International Ceramics Fair and Seminar [Handbook]*, London, 1993, pp.28–35.

52. Blake Roberts (1993), op.cit., p.29.

53. R. Reilly, *Wedgwood*, London, 1989, pp.50, 62.

54. 'That W & B do enter into Partnership in making ornamental Earthenware or Porcelain viz Vases, Figures, Flowerpots, Toilet Furniture and such other Articles as they shall from Time to Time agree upon.' A. Dawson, *Masterpieces of Wedgwood in the British Museum*, London, 1984, p.25.

55. T. Clifford, 'Some English Ceramic Vases and their Sources', Part I, *English Ceramic Circle Transactions*, 10, 3, 1978, pp.159–74.

56. However, by January 1771, Wedgwood was sufficently ashamed of 'two middle size Chetwynd Vases and 2 Orfords Cream-colour, Engine-lathed and gilt' to write to Matthew Boulton, offering to replace them with 'Etruscan painted ones'. J.V. G. Mallet, 'Wedgwood's Early Vases', *Country Life* (9 June 1966), pp.1480–2.

57. David Buten, *Eighteenth-century Wedgwood: A Guide for Collector and Connoisseurs*, Pittstown, New Jersey, p.57.

58. Farrer, *The Letters of Josiah Wedgwood*, 1903 (reprinted) 1, p.233.

59. Blake Roberts (1993), op.cit., pp.31.

60. For d'Harcanville see F. Haskell, 'The Baron d'Harcanville: An Adventurer and Art Historian in 18th century Europe', *Past and Present in Art and Taste*, London, 1987.

61. A garniture of five black basalt vases bought by Lord George Sackville from Wedgwood and Bentley in 1774 is still in place on the chimney piece of the dining-room of Drayton House, Northamptonshire. M. Pick, 'Ever Ascending Circles', *Traditional Interior Decoration* (March/April 1987), p.31–2.

62. However, as Wedgwood knew, this was not the true Greek manner (which was dependent on allowing air into the kiln during the firing to affect differently coloured slips), but a decoration in matt colours, where the red colour was painted directly onto the surface of the black basalt, allowed to dry, then shaded, and then fired again. Buten, op.cit., p.88.

63. 'The character of Urns is simplicity, to have covers, but no handles, nor spouts, they are monumental, they may be either high or low, but sho[ul]d not seem to be Vessels for culinary, or sacred uses. – Vases are such as might be used for libations, & other sacrificial festive & culinary uses, such as Ewers, open Vessels & c.' Clifford (1978), op.cit., p.161.

64. E.g. letters of August 1765, and February 1767, Farrer, op.cit., pp.51, 113.

65. T. Friedman et al., *The Man at Hyde Park Corner: Sculpture by John Cheere 1709–1787*, Leeds, 1974.

66. N. Goodison, *Ormolu: The work of Matthew Boulton*, London, 1974.

67. In 1768 he had the carver John Coward make drawings of 'Vauzes, baskets, Dishes after the Duke of Richmond's', presumably the Sèvres porcelain mentioned above. E. Meteyard, *The Life of Josiah Wedgwood from the Private Correspondence and Family Papers*, 1865 (reprint 1980), II, p.91.

68. 'Mr. Boulton tells me I sho.d be surprised to know w.t a trade has lateley been made out of Vases at Paris. The Artists have even come over to London, picked up all the old whimsical ugly things they could meet with, carried them to Paris where they have mounted & ornamented them with metal &

sold them to the Virtuosi of every Nation, & particularly to Millords d'Anglaise, for the greatest rar023 & if you remebr we saw many such things at L.d. Bolingbrokes which he bro.t over with him from France. Of this sort I have seen two or three old China bowles, for want of better things, stuck rim to rim which have had not bad effect but look whimsical & droll enough.' KE Farrer, *Letters of Josiah Wedgwood 1762–1772*, 1903, pp.20–9.

69. In September, 1769, he wrote: 'And do you really think we may make a *complete conquest* of France? Conquer France in Burslem? – My blood moves quicker, I feel my strength increase for the contest. Assist me my friend & the victorie is our own. . . . Are you certain the French Nation will be pleased with simplicity in the Vessells? Either I have been greatly deceiv'd, or a wonderfull reformation has taken place amongst them. *French & Frippery* have jingled together so long in my ideas, that I scarcely know how to separate them, & much of their work I have seen *cover'd over with ornament*, had confirmed me in the opinion'. Farrer, op.cit., pp.301–2, quoted in J.V. G. Mallet, 'Wedgwood and the Rococo', *Apollo* (May 1974), pp.320–31.

70. Farrer, op.cit., p.311.

71. 'They have an *immense* number of ornamental vases, highly enriched with enamel and burnished gold; and among *several hundreds* there may be about *half a dozen* very elegant forms. All the rest are neither antique nor gothic, but barbarous beyond conception.' G. Blake Roberts, 'Ceramics' Unsung Hero – Thomas Bentley', *English Ceramic Circle Transactions*, 15, 1 (1993), p.33.

72. Buten, op.cit., p.181.

73. Ibid., p.173.

74. It was much in demand in the early nineteenth century when restrictions on the use of flour led to a shortage of pastry in cooking and the immediate development of a pottery substitute. 'The scarcity two years after Brummell's retirement (July 1800) was so great that the consumption of flour for pastry was prohibited in the Royal Household, rice being used instead: the distiller left off malting; hackney-coach fares were raised twenty five per cent. and Wedgwood made dishes to represent pie-crust.' Captain Jeffs, *The Life of George Brummell, Esq*, 1814, quoted in B. Hillier, *Master Potters of the Industrial Revolution: The Turners of Lane End*, London, 1965, p.19.

75. Blake Roberts (1993), op.cit., p.31.

76. Dawson, op.cit., p.18.

77. Ibid., p.15. A description of the pattern is contained in a letter from Wedgwood to Erasmus Darwin, sold at Phillips, London, on 13 June 1991, and published in the *Wedgwood Society of New York News*, October 1991, p.5: 'The commission I am honour'd with is for a Tea & Coffee service ornamented with sprigs to my own fancy, in alto relievo, the ground to be gold, & the sprigs green, & besides these I am to send patterns of my manufacture of everything that I think will be acceptable & as a farther inducement to my industry I am told that if the samples are agreeable I may depend on serving the Court, & the Ladys [sic] who attend it with these articles . . .'

78. Farrer, op.cit., pp.39, 91, 97.

79. Dawson, op.cit., p.19.

80. In October 1765 he took moulds from 'a set of french china at the Duke of Bedford's worth at least £1,500, the most elegant things I ever saw.' Farrer, op.cit., p.60.

81. In September, 1769, that he wrote of the need to

'simplify', and that 'as a first essay I have discarded the twiggen and flower'd handles from the Terrines, & everything except the baskets, where I think their *apparent lightness & real strength* will induce me to retain them', and was comparing his [dessert] baskets advantageously to those from Chelsea. Farrer, op.cit., pp.301–2, quoted in Mallet, op.cit., p.327.

82. It was especially suitable for wares in everyday use and in 1783 Mrs Papendieck, wife of a minor court official, wrote on her marriage that 'our tea and coffee set were of common Indian China, our dinner service of earthenware [the new creamware], to which, for our rank, there was nothing superior, Chelsea porcelain and fine India China being only for the wealthy. Pewter and delft ware could also be had but were inferior.' P. Walton, *Creamware and other English Pottery at Temple Newsam House, Leeds*, Leeds, 1976, p.69. The composition of a dinner service, as described in the illustrated sale catalogue of 1773/4, comprised 'A service of Queen's Ware, of a middling size', consisted of 2 oval dishes, 2 smaller, 2 round dishes, 2 smaller, 4 oval dishes, 4 [smaller], 4 [smaller still], 4 round dishes, 4 covered dishes, 2 terrine for Soup, 2 sauce terrine, 4 sauce boats, 2 salad dishes, 6 salts, 2 mustard pots, 4 pickle, 6 dozen flat plates, 2 dozen soup plates. W. Mankowitz, *Wedgwood*, London, 1953, p.63.

83. J. Woodforde, *The Diary of a Country Parson 1758–1802*, London, 1978, p.130.

84. Ibid., p.465.

85. On 2 March 1765 he wrote to Sir William Meredith that 'The bulk of our particular manufacture you know is exported to foreign markets . . . & the principal of these markets are the Continent & islands of N. America. To the Continent we send an amazing qu[anti]ty of white stone ware & some of the finer kinds, but for the Islands we cannot make anything too rich & costly.' K. E. Farrer, *Letters of Josiah Wedgwood 1762–1770*, Manchester, 1903 [reprint], p.31.

86. G. Blake Roberts 'The London Decorating Studio' in H. Young (ed.), *The Genius of Wedgwood*, London (Victoria and Albert Museum), 1995, pp.92–101.

87. A. Kelly, 'Wedgwood's Catherine Service', *The Burlington Magazine*, 122 (1980), pp.554–61; M. Raeburn et al., *The Green Frog Service*, London, 1995.

88. The illustrations feature everything for the dinner table, centrepieces, candlesticks, vases, as well as more utilitarian items such as a 'water closet pot' and 'stool pot', as well as a 'cross, with Holy Water Cup', clearly intended for the export market to Catholic countries. D. Towner, *The Leeds Pottery*, London, 1963, pp.56–140.

89. A dessert service sent by the Worcester factory to the Prince of Orange at Hampton Court in 1796 consisted of: '2 Ice pails complete, 2 Fruit baskets and stands, 2 Cream tureens and covers, 2 stand to do. and spoons, 1 centre dish and stand, 4 triangular [shaped] dishes, 4 mellon [shaped] dishes, 4 shell [shaped] dishes, 2 heart [shaped] dishes, 36 dessert plates'. The whole was 'all Blue & gold with different figures'. G. A. Godden, *Chamberlain-Worcester Porcelain 1788–1852*, London, 1982, p.31.

90. P. Halfpenny, 'Creamware: Its Origins and Development', *The International Ceramics Fair and Seminar [Handbook]*, London, 1993, p.27.

91. J. Leonard Benson, 'Dutch Decorated English Creamware: fiction and fact', *Mededelingenblad nederlandse vereniging van vriendren van de ceramiek*, 137 (1990/1), pp.3–29.

92. D. MacPherson, *Annals of Commerce*, (1805 edition),

iii, p.430, quoted in B. Hillier, *Master Potters of the Industrial Revolution: The Turners of Lane End*, London, 1965, p.20. His views were echoed by Arthur Young on a visit to the fair at Falaise in France in 1788 'I found the quantity of English goods considerable, hard and queen's ware; cloths and cottons. A dozen of common plain plates, 3 livres and 4 livres for a French imitation, but much worse . . . a dozen with blue or green edges; English, 5 livres 5 sous' quoted in B. Hillier, *Pottery and Porcelain 1700–1914*, London, 1968, p.207.

93. J. and G. Lewis, *Pratt Ware: English and Scottish relief decorated and underglaze coloured earthenwares 1780–1840*, London, 1993.

94. Buten, op.cit., p.73.

95. D. Eyles, *'Good Sir Toby': The Story of Toby Jugs and Character Jugs through the Ages*, London, 1955.

96. P. Halfpenny, 'The Wood family', *Ceramics*, III (May/June 1986), pp.118–26.

97. He issued a catalogue in 1775. J. Holloway, *James Tassie 1735–1799*, Edinburgh, National Galleries of Scotland, 1986.

98. Wedgwood was well aware of the rivalry with him and wrote in February, 1776, to Bentley that about competition with Tassie and Voyez: 'The former by making them more beautifull [sic], the latter by selling them cheaper, and carrying them to market himself.' Farrer, op.cit., pp.272–3.

99. By 1775 he was able to announce in his sale catalogue of that year that 'The Cameos will be made of a new Composition as fine as Parian marble, but infinitely more durable, with burnt-in Grounds of various Colours', Buten, op.cit., p.140.

100. A. Kelly, *Decorative Wedgwood in Architecture and Furniture*, London, 1965.

101. B. Tattersall, *Stubbs and Wedgwood: Unique Allliance between Artist and Pottery*, London, Tate Gallery, 1974.

102. He was aware of the need to maintain high standards of modelling and employed the sculptor Henry Webber (1754–1826) to 'undertake a Tour or Journey into Italy for the purpose of making Models Drawings and other Improvements in the Arts of Modelling and Designing for the Benefit and Advantage of the said Josiah Wedgwood.' Webber himself supplied few designs, but delegated work to a whole school of Italian modellers such as Angelo Dalmazzoni, Camillo Pacetti (1758–1826) and Giuseppe Angelini, all of whom supplied fine models in the classical taste. On his return to England in 1788, Webber acted as head of the modelling studio at Etruria and was later to supply models such as the figure of *Britannia Triumphant* of 1802, very much in the taste of the late eighteenth century. B. Tattersall, 'Henry Webber: Art at the Service of Industry', *Apollo* (July 1985), pp.36–42.

103. Bentley wrote to Hamilton in 1779 that 'Having modelled a large Tablet from one of the unpublished Designs in your Excellency's Collection at the British Museum which we copied from a drawing lent us by Mr. D'Harcarville, and which we consider as one of the most perfect Specimens of the present State of our Ornamental Manufactory, we could not resist the desire of presenting you with a Coppy [sic] of this Work, which has come very happily thro' the fiery Trial, and which we hope you will do us the Honour to place in your Cabinet, or in some of your Apartments.' Dawson, op.cit., p.107.

104. The firm also made pearlware and creamware, and was big enough to employ a London agent, Andrew Abbott, with premises in Fleet Street, opened about

1783, and by 1784 they were styling themselves *Potters to the Prince of Wales*. Hillier (1965), op.cit., pp.58–9.

105. See Diana Edwards and Rodney Hampson, *English Dry-Bodied Stoneware: Wedgwood and Contemporary Manufacturers 1774–1830*, Woodbridge, 1998.

CHAPTER 12
The Spread of Neo-Classicism in Europe

1. GK I 5312. I assume the frame is contemporary with the picture, but do not know when it reached Germany.

2. Illustrated in *Kunst und Antiquäten*, 3 (1976), p.82.

3. J. Hibberd, *Salomon Gessner: His creative achievement and influence*, Cambridge, 1976, figs 5, 6.

4. B. von Roda, 'Adam Friedrich von Seinsheim. Auftraggeber zwischen Rokoko und Klassizismus. Zur Würzburger und Bamberger Hofkunst anhand der Privatkorrespondenz des Furstbischofs (1755–1779)', *Veröffenlichungen der Gesellschaft für Frankische Geschichte. R.8. Quellen und Darstellungen zur Frankische Kunstgeschichte 6*, Neustadt, 1980, pp.168–70.

5. For an introduction to the social and intellectual life of this period, see H. Rosenberg, *Bureaucracy, Aristocracy and Autocracy: The Prussian Experience (1660–1815)*, Cambridge, Mass., 1958; W. H. Bruford, *Germany in the Eighteenth Century: the Social Background of the Literary Revival*, Cambridge, Mass., 1959; E. Sagarra, *A Social History of Germany 1648–1914*, London, 1977, and N. Boyle, *Goethe: the Poet and the Age*, Oxford, 1991.

6. D. Irwin, *Winckelmann: Writings on Art*, London, 1972, p.25.

7. 'The decline of good taste in various arts among several of our neighbours is coupled with a decline in the decency of manners', which was clearly a criticism of the French, and his editor makes the point clear when he writes 'At this point the author touches on the true sources of these strange decorations. It is not Germany but France, the mistress of so many absurd fashions, which is the inventor of this corrupt taste. The dislocated and lopsided curvature of these decorations is also a French whim, which is rightly abhorred by several great artists in Germany, for instance by Herr Giese in Berlin'. Yet dominance of the rococo style is so strong that it would appear that Herr Giese is none other than the sculptor Giese who contributed to the flamboyant rococo decoration of Frederick the Great's palace at Sanssouci, Berlin. In 1759 a more considered attack appeared, when Friedrich August Krubsacius published anonymously a pamphlet entitled *Thoughts on the Origins, Growth and Decline of Decoration in the Fine Arts*. Here he heavily criticised the rococo style, with a satirical plate of a rococo cartouche, composed of venomous animals and rubbish. E. H. Gombrich, *The Sense of Order*, Oxford, 1979, pp.24–5.

8. *Von kindischem Geschmack* and *Lächerliche Puppen*; J. J. Winkelmann, *Geschichte der Kunst des Altertums*, 1763–8, Donaueschingen, 1825, p.119.

9. In it, an apothecary of a small German town complains about the new taste which has deprived him of all the pleasure that he once took in his garden pavilion, in which he was wont to take coffee. The poem is essentially a lament for the rococo, with all its conceits of scale and decoration:

'Every traveller paused to look through the red-coloured trellis
At the beggars of stone and the painted dwarfs in the garden.

But, when coffee I served to my guests in the wonderful grotto
-Covered with dust it is now, and nearly a ruin in my life-time-
Dear, how much they enjoyed the colourful sparkle of shell-work
Beautifully set out – and even the expert was dazzled
By the gleam of the lead and by intricate corals,
Nor did they fail to admire the painted walls of the parlour
Where such elegant men and ladies were seen promenading
Daintily holding or handing a flower with delicate fingers.
True – but who would now but give it a glance; yes, I rarely
Go there myself, for they want it different now, only 'tasteful'
As they describe it, the trellis should be white and so
should the benches.
All must be simple and flush without any carving or gilding
– Now it is the wood from abroad that is the most costly.

quoted in E. H. Gombrich, *The Sense of Order*, London, 1979, p.30.

10. T. H. Clarke, 'Johann Joachim Friedrich Elsasser's Engravings of the "Academic" and Marcolini Periods 1785–1792', *Keramik Freunde der Schweiz*, 103 (January 1988), p.10; Rainer Richter, 'Die Kunst in Sachsen unter Einfluss des Ministers Camillo Graf Marcolini', *Keramos*, 124 (1989), pp.7–26.

11. *The Splendor of Dresden: Five Centuries of Art Collecting*, Washington, 1978, pp.26, 169.

12. 'The return to Antiquity was seen not so much as an end in itself, so much as a means to a higher end – the true imitation of Nature.' H. Honour, 'Neo-Classicism' in *The Age of Neo-Classicism*, London, Royal Academy, 1972.

13. This naturally led to a diminution of the role of the aristocrat: 'In our era it has come about that the nobleman who is nothing else than that will be tolerated in the circle of the reputable burgher estate, the scholars, the merchants, and the artists, only by making an effort to display extraordinary humility' wrote the philosopher Fichte, co-founder of German idealism, in 1793. H. Rosenberg, *Bureaucracy, Aristocracy and Autocracy: The Prussian Experience 1660–1815*, Cambridge (Mass.), 1958, p.183.

14. A. Fauchier-Magnan, *The Small German Courts of the Eighteenth Century*, London, 1958, p.211.

15. He had appointed a factor, Georg Michel Helbig, who was responsible for the production of a number of dinner services, some apparently designed by the king himself, including one decorated with 'Vestuns' (festoons) in the antique manner, with a centrepiece in 'the form of a beautiful antique vase on which two genii are to appear', designed by the great modeller Kaendler. However, this appearance of neo-classical motifs seems to have been an isolated instance, and was not immediately followed. K. Berling, *Meissen China: An Illustrated History*, London, 1910, reprint 1972, pp.54–6.

16. In Paris the modeller David Erlasser observed that 'the so-called Greek style henceforth has the upper hand', and at Sèvres they particularly admired the rose, green and 'bleu de roi' colours ('*der so genannte Gout grec annoch die Oberhand hat*'). Clarke, op.cit., p.4.

17. A neo-classical *pot-pourri* supported by two putti by Kaendler's assistant Johann Carl Schönheit is dateable to about 1765. Berling, op.cit., p.66.

18. The Paris *Metamorphoses* was used on a tea set at Meissen by 1775, when Richard Champion of Bristol records copying a Meissen tea set so decorated in that year. H. Owen, *Two Centuries of Ceramic Art in Bristol*, London, 1873, p.124.

19. Berling, op.cit., p.68.

20. G. Reinheckel, *Prächtvolle Service aus Meissner Porzellan*, Leipzig, 1989, figs 109, 112.

21. This trend is typified by the large centrepiece that Acier and Schönheit, working after Kaendler's retirement in 1775, produced for a royal dinner service, glorifying the reign of Frederick Augustus III. This consisted of a pyramid ornamented with portraits of Augustus II, Augustus III and Frederick Christian, with personifications of Virtue, Knowledge, Peace and Mercy and the Nine Muses; another group represented an allegorical figure of Saxonia, accompanied by Fertility and Abundance, presiding over the china- and textile industries of the state, including lace-making. A third group represented Commerce, Agriculture and Mining, with two temples in the Doric (with a figure of Victory) and Corinthian styles (with a figure of Virtue). Berling, op.cit., p.74.

22. 'At the great ceremonial dinners the dessert is often used to display allegorical and figural representations, in the proper arrangement of which considerable knowledge of History, Poetry and Mythology, likewise of Architecture and Perspective is called for. The easiest representations at great desserts are pleasure-gardens, with promenades, buildings, fountains, parterres, vases and statues, of which last the porcelain factories at Meissen, Berlin, Vienna etc, make the prettiest and most decorative pieces and ensembles imaginable, thus saving the confectioner much work.' R. J. Charleston, *The James A. De Rothschild Collection at Waddesdon Manor: Mounted and other European Porcelain*, Fribourg, 1971, p.17.

23. 'Gästen notorisch mehr Kenntnisse zu gewähren und diese zu Unterhaltungen über die ältesten Denkmale und andere Gegenstände der Kunst zu ermuntern.' Quoted in U. Erichsen-Firle, *Kunstgewerbemuseum der Stadt Köln: Figürliches Porzellan*, Cologne, 1975, p.20.

24. Illustrated in R. Schmidt, *Porcelain as an Art and a Mirror of Fashion*, London, 1932, p.249.

25. See catalogue *Weisses Gold aus Fürstenberg*, Münster and Brunswick, 1988–9, p.97, fig. 5.

26. A *déjeuner* from the Fürstenberg is listed in their pricelist for 1779 as follows: 'In the 'déjeuner' coffee set are included: one coffee-tray, one coffee-pot, one cream-jug, one sugar-basin, two pairs of coffee-cups with handles, and two spoons. In the 'dejeuner' tea set are included: one tea-tray, one teapot, one cream-jug, one sugar-basin, one pair of cups, and one spoon' R. Schmidt, *Porcelain as an Art and a Mirror of Fashion*, London, 1932, p.138.

27. M. Newman, *Die Deutschen Porzellan-Manufakturen*, Brunswick, 1977, colour plate III.

28. G. Coke, *In Search of James Giles*, Wingham, 1983, pp.134–5.

29. K. H. Esser and W. Reber, *Höchster Fayencen and Porzellane*, Mainz, 1964, pp.212–19.

30. G. Lenz, *Berliner Porzellan*, 1913, p.92.

31. E. Köllmann and M. Jarchow, *Berliner Porzellan*, Munich, 1987, p.118.

32. Ibid., p.98.

33. 'La Nature est grande dans son principe, incompréhensible dans ses opérations; ses productions invitent les humaines à des jouissances continuelles et les âmes sensibles en sont toujours reconnaissantes'. Quoted by J.V. G. Mallet in *The Age of Neo-Classicism*, London, Royal Academy and the Victoria and Albert Museum, 1972, no.1421.

34. An idea of their efficiency may be gauged from the fact that Volkstedt paid its workers only around 4–15 Gulden a month, when the cost of a tea set (*déjeuner*)

or pot-pourri vase painted in enamel colours was 10–15 Gulden. H. Scherf, *Thüringer Porzellan*, Wiesbaden, 1980, p.26.

35. J. Sattler, 'Beiträge zur Thüringischen Porzellanmanufaktur Ilmenau', *Keramos*, 120, 88, pp.39–64.

36. M. C. Cross, *Russian Porcelains*, Oklahoma, 1968, pp. 37–41.

37. A. K. Lansere, *Russian Porcelain: The Art of the First Russian Porcelain Works*, Leningrad, 1968.

38. B. L. Grandjean, *The Royal Copenhagen Porcelain Manufactory*, Copenhagen, 1975.

39. See *Flora Danica and the Danish Royal Court*, exh. cat., Copenhagen, 1990, pp.178–86.

40. B. Hillier, *Pottery and Porcelain 1700–1914*, London, 1968, p.133.

41. His general work on antiquities in Naples led to him being entitled 'General Superintendent of the antiquities of the Kingdom, of the excavations, both public and private, and president of the council for the royal museums'. A. González-Palacios in *The Golden Age of Naples: Art and Civilization Under the Bourbons 1734–1805*, Detroit and Chicago, 1981, p.337.

42. The 'Herculaneum' service included centrepieces comprising busts of Scipio, Seneca, Pallas, Jupiter Ammon and others, and a biscuit group of 'Charles II exhorting his son Ferdinand to pursue the excavations'. An explanatory book of engravings was published by Venuti to accompany the service. The 'Etruscan Service' of 282 pieces was sent to George III of England in 1787. Like the 'Herculaneum' Service, it was described by Venuti in a separate publication. The soup-dishes, tureens, compotiers and so on are adapted from ancient Greek vases in the red-figure or black-figure styles, and the plates painted on a tin-glazed ground with depictions of actual vases found at Nola and elsewhere in the Kingdom of Naples. The aim of the gift of the service was to obtain English naval know-how to rebuild the Neapolitan fleet; most of the service survives today at Windsor Castle, but not the centrepiece of Tarchon, King of the Etruscans, presiding over gladiatorial contests. For lesser markets the factory also made a large variety of tablewares painted with scenes from antiquity, and of local customs and dress. Straight copies of antique statues were also made by the engraver Giovanni Volpato at his factory in the via Pudenziana, Rome (founded 1785). In a letter written in 1786 he stated that 'its main object is to reproduce in biscuit the most beautiful antiquities – statues, low reliefs and ornaments – that are found in such great numbers in this realm, to replace the ridiculous dolls which are used on dining- and side-tables'. A pricelist of his work in the Victoria and Albert Museum includes copies after the Apollo Belvedere and the Sleeping Faun. H. Honour, 'Statuettes after the Antique: Volpato's Roman Porcelain Factory', *Apollo* (May 1967), LXXXV, pp.371–4.

43. A. González-Palacios, *Lo scultore Filippo Tagliolini e la porcellane di Napoli, Archivi d'Arte Antica*, c.1988.

44. J. Whitehead, 'The Marchand-Merciers and Sèvres', *The International Ceramics Fair and Seminar [Handbook]*, London, 1993, pp.36–43; Carolyn Sargentson, *Merchants and Luxury Markets*, London, 1996.

45. R. Savill, *The Wallace Collection: Catalogue of Sèvres Porcelain*, London, 1988, p.838.

46. J. Parker, *Decorative Art from the Samuel H. Kress Collection at the Metropolitan Museum of Art*, London, 1964, pp.105–16.

47. Savill (1988), op.cit., p.840.

48. W. Cole, *A Journal of my Journey to Paris in the Year 1765*, London, 1931, pp.232–3.

49. Louis XVI's aunts displayed eighteen cups and saucers with different decoration on two tables between the windows of their winter drawing-room at their Château de Bellevue. Savill (1988), op.cit., p.489.

50. 'His Majesty wishes to favour private privileges, small factories will henceforth be able to produce ordinary porcelain in white and painted in blue, Chinese style only.' The production of separate flowers and items moulded in relief was banned in 1763. R. de Plinval de Guillebon, *Paris Porcelain 1770–1850*, London, 1972, p.14.

51. Ibid., p.30.

52. G. de Bellaigue, *Sèvres: Porcelain from the Royal Collection*, London, 1979, nos.28, 38, 40.

53. G. de Bellaigue, 'Sèvres Artists and their Sources, II', *The Burlington Magazine* (1980), 122, pp.748–59.

54. R. Pulver, 'Nyon Neo-classic', *The Antique Dealers and Collector Guide*, September, 1989, pp.30–4. See also E. Pelichet, *Merveilleuse Porcelaine de Nyon*, Paris, 1973.

55. I. Ceballos-Escalera, 'Porcelain from a Garden Factory', *Apollo* (May 1968), pp.363–9.

56. K. Tasnadi-Marik, *Viennese Porcelain*, Corvina, 1971.

57. This collection had been put on loan at Sèvres in 1786 by the Comte d'Angiviller, having been bought in the king's name 'to serve as models for simple forms and change, by example, the false direction given by the form of the preceding reign' ('pour servir comme modèles de formes simples pures et changer, par ces exemples, la mauvaise direction donnée aux porcelaines sous le règne précèdent'). P. Verlet, *Sèvres*, Paris, 1953, pp.38, 220.

58. S. Schwartz, *The Sèvres Porcelain Service for Marie-Antoinette's dairy at Rambouillet: An Exercise in Archaeological Classicism*, London, The French Porcelain Society, 1992.

59. See G. De Bellaigue, *Sèvres Porcelain in the Collection of Her Majesty the Queen: the Louis XVI Service*, Cambridge, 1986.

CHAPTER 13
Ceramics in the Period 1790–1830

1. The fashion seems to have reached Derby by 1791, when a *Botanical Magazine* was purchased (presumably Curtis's *The Botanical Magazine*, published in 1790). A. Ledger in *The Derby Porcelain International Society: Newsletter* No.17 (December 1989), p.3.

2. H. Sandon, *Flight and Barr Worcester Porcelain 1783–1840*, Woodbridge, 1978.

3. G. A. Godden, *Chamberlain-Worcester Porcelain 1788–1852*, London, 1982, pp.39–57.

4. It comprised: '2 Ice pails complete, 2 Fruit baskets and stands, 2 Cream tureens and covers, 2 stand (sic) to do. and spoons, 1 centre dish and stand, 4 triangular (shaped) dishes, 4 mellon (sic) (shaped) dishes, 4 shell (shaped) dishes, 2 heart (shaped) dishes, 36 dessert plates.' G. A. Godden (1982), op.cit., p.31.

5. Since this was before the development of afternoon tea, they would presumably have been used at breakfast, where bread and butter were eaten, or for the tea and coffee that was drunk after dinner at about 7 o'clock c.f. the comment of the Swiss C. P. Moritz on an English breakfast in 1780: 'The slices of bread and butter they give you with your tea are as thin as poppy leaves. But there is another kind of bread usually eaten with tea, which is toasted by the fire and incomparably good. This is called toast.' Quoted in A. Palmer, *Movable Feasts Changes in English Eating Habits*, Oxford, 1952, reprint 1984.

6. Godden (1982), op.cit., p.77.

7. Palmer, op.cit., pp.54–5. The development is often credited to the Duchesses of Rutland or Devonshire, and an official five o'clock afternoon tea had developed in country houses by 1849–50. J. Lees-Milne, *The Country House*, Oxford, 1982, p.62. See also Fanny Kemble's description of afternoon tea at Belvoir Castle in 1842 in her *Later Records*, and Georgina Caroline Sitwell's introduction to five o'clock tea through Lord Alexander Russell, son of the 5th Duchess of Bedford, in 1849–50, in O. Sitwell, *Two Generations*, London, 1940. I owe these references to Anne Stevens.

8. See N. D. Gent, *The Patterns and Shapes of the Pinxton China Factory 1796–1813*, Pinxton, 1996; C. Barry Sheppard, *Pinxton Porcelain 1795–1813*, Alfreton, 1996.

9. See J. O. Wilstead and B. Morris, *Thomas Baxter: The Swansea Years 1816–1819*, Ceredigion, 1997.

10. This taste put paid to factories which had depended on a more restrained and classical taste, such as Wedgwood, which in this period suffered a serious decline. 'The public taste has been led to expect such a dazzling mixture of colour with gold in broad shades covering the whole area that their eyes are spoilt, for delicate & elegant borders, which are not dazzling & do not produce a striking effect' wrote Wedgwood's agent Josiah Byerly in 1813. R. Reilly, *Wedgwood*, London, 1989, p.597.

11. 'The elegance of the breakfast set forced itself upon Catherine's notice . . . [the General, her host] was enchanted by her approbation of his taste, confessed it to be neat and simple; and for his part, to his uncritical palate, the tea was as well flavoured from the clay of Staffordshire, as from that of Dresden or Seve', Jane Austen, *Northanger Abbey*, (1818), quoted in N. J. Pearce, 'Chinese Export Porcelain for the European Market: The Years of Decline 1770–1820', *Transactions of the Oriental Ceramic Society*, 1987–8, p.35.

12. W. Little, *Staffordshire Blue*, London, 1969, p.16.

13. R. Copeland, *Spode and Copeland Marks and other Relevant Intelligence*, London, 1993, p.12.

14. L. Whiter, *Spode*, London, 1970, p.174. C.f. some commemorative items of bone china, made by Copeland and Garrett (the former Spode factory) in 1834 and inscribed 'MANUFACTURED from the BONES collected after Entertainments given by MESSRS COPELAND & GARRETT Stoke on Trent To their Workpeople on the 13th and 14th Nov. 1834 in Commemoration of their taking the ESTABLISH-MENT 1st MARCH 1833'. V. Wilkinson, *The Copeland China Collection at Treslissick Mansion, Cornwall*, 1989, p.19.

15. The threat to creamware is first mentioned in the Wedgwood correspondence in 1810. However, creamware continued to be made in the nineteenth century, the factory even producing a catalogue of shapes in 1817. R. Reilly, *Wedgwood*, London, 1989, pp.285, 591.

16. After a visit from the Prince of Wales in 1806, Spode was allowed to use the term 'Potter and English Porcelain manufacturer to His Royal Highness', and the *Staffordshire Advertiser* commented that 'We cannot but remark that in France the porcelain manufactory always possessed the high sanction and patronage of the Princes of the Blood, and we doubt not but that, under the auspices of our Princes and Nobility, English china will rival the most finished productions

of foreign countries, and give to our own manufacturers the whole of this important and valuable trade'. Quoted in R. Reilly, *Wedgwood*, London, 1989, p.590.

17. Whiter, op.cit., p.191. See also G. A. Godden, *The Illustrated Guide to Mason's Patent Ironstone China*, London, 1971, pp.7–8.

18. G. A. Godden, *Mason's China and the Ironstone Wares*, Woodbridge, 1980, p.102.

19. Josiah Byerley wrote to Josiah Wedgwood II in March 1814 that 'Everyone enquires for the stone china, made by Spode and Mason and it has a very great run – I presume you know what it is – it is a thick coarse china body, not transparent.' Quoted in Reilly, op.cit., p.583.

20. Reilly, op.cit., p.584.

21. W. L. Little, *Staffordshire Blue*, London, 1969, p.19.

22. See N. J. Pearce, 'Chinese Export Porcelain for the European Market: The Years of Decline 1770–1820', *Transactions of the Oriental Ceramic Society*, 1987–88, pp.21–38.

23. Simeon Shaw observed that 'for novelty and elegance of the Pottery secured the demand, which has continued to increase; and in this day, 1829, few manufacturers do not practice the art; and many have several presses constantly employed in Blue Printing'. S. Shaw, *History of the Staffordshire Potteries*, 1829, p.215, quoted in W. Little, *Staffordshire Blue*, London, 1969, pp.16–17.

24. Reproduced in P. Thornton, *Authentic Decor*, London, 1984, fig. 332.

25. *Pückler's Progress; the Adventures of Prince Pückler-Muskau in England, Wales and Ireland as told in letters to his former wife, 1826–9*, translated by Flora Brennan, London, 1987, pp.37–9.

26. 'The menu of a good dinner was thus composed: Mulligatawny and turtle soups were the first dishes placed before you; a little lower, the eye met with the familiar salmon at one end of the table, and the turbot surrounded by smelts, at the other. The first course was sure to be followed by a saddle of mutton or a piece of roast beef; and then you would take your oath that fowls, tongue and ham would assuredly succeed as darkness after day. Whilst the never-ending pièces de resistance were occupying the table, what were called French dishes were, for custom's sake, added to the solid abundance. The French, or side dishes, consisted of very mild but very abortive attempts at Continental cooking, and I have always observed that they met with the neglect and contempt that they merited. The universally adored and ever-popular boiled potato, produced at the very earliest period of dinner, up to the moment when the sweets appeared. Our vegetables, the best in the world, were never honoured by an accompanying sauce, and generally came to the table cold. A prime difficulty to overcome was the placing on your fork, and finally in your mouth, some half-dozen different eatables which occupied your plates at the same time. For example your plate would contain, say, a slice of turkey, a piece of stuffing, a sausage, pickles, a slice of tongue, cauliflower, and potatoes. According to habit and custom, a judicious and careful selection from this little bazaar of good things was to be made, with an endeavour to place a portion of each in your mouth at the same moment. In fact, it appeared to me that we used to do all our compound cookery between our jaws.' He then goes on to describe the dessert wines. *The Reminiscences and Recollections of Captain Gronow*, London, 1889, vol.1, p.36. The writer and politician Thomas Creevey found that, when he attempted to partake of the fish when

dining with Lord Lambton in 1825, he could not engage his lordship's attention. T. Creevey, *Papers*, vol.II, 24 October 1825, quoted in J. Lees-Milne, *The Country House*, Oxford, 1982, p.60.

27. However, the writer Thomas Walker observed in the 1850s that 'The present system I consider thoroughly tainted with barbarism and vulgarity and far removed from real and refined enjoyment. As tables are now arranged, one is never at peace from an arm continually taking off and setting on a side dish, or reaching over to a wine-cooler in the centre. Then comes the more laborious changing of courses with leanings right and left, to admit a host of dishes, that are set on, only to be taken off again, after being declined in succession by each of the guests, to whom they are handed around.' T. Walker, *The Original*, quoted in Philippa Pullar, *Consuming Passions*, London, 1970, p.196.

28. Mrs Beeton commented on its greater convenience, but observed that 'Dinners à la Russe are scarcely suitable for small establishments; a large number of servants being required to carve, and to help the guests; besides there being a necessity for more plates, dishes, knives, forks, and spoons, than are usually to be found in any other than a very large establishment. Where, however, a service à la Russe is practicable, there is, perhaps, no mode of serving a dinner as enjoyable as this.' I. Beeton, *The Book of Household Management*, London, 1861, pp.954–5.

29. P. Mansel, *The Eagle in Splendour: Napoleon I and his Court*, London, 1987, p.17.

30. Quoted in P. Mansel, *The Court of France 1789–1830*, Cambridge, 1985, p.70.

31. R. de Plinval de Guillebon, *Paris Porcelain 1701–1850*, London, 1972, pp.103–6.

32. D. Alcouffe *et al.*, *Un Âge d'Or des Arts Décoratifs 1814–1848*, Paris, Grand Palais, 1991.

33. 'Ce tableau vous donnera aussi une idée du genre des travaux de la manufacture. J'espère que vous pourrez déjà y voir que je les divise vers deux buts différents autant que j'ai peuvent me le permettre . . . D'un côté je cherche à faire des objets qui par le choix des sujets, la grandeur des pièces, la perfection des peintures, la richesse et la pureté d'exécution des ornements, maintiennent l'art dans sa perfection, lui fasse faire encore de nouveaux progrès, conserve et augmente la réputation de cet ancien établissement et assortissant ses magasins d'objets dignes des personnes augustes auquel il appartient soit qu'elles veulent consacrer ces objets à leur usage, soit qu'elles les destinent à en faire des présents . . . D'un autre côté, je fais exécuter des objets plus ordinaires, d'un prix qui soit à la portée de toutes les classes de consommateurs mais tout en fesant faire ces objets de commerce, j'ai soin que le bon goût et tous les principes d'une bonne et solide fabrication soient scrupuleusement conservés.' M. Brunet and T. Préaud, *Sèvres: Des origines à nos jours*, Fribourg, 1978, p.242. See also Derek E. Ostergard (ed.), *The Porcelain Manufactory at Sèvres 1800–1847. Alexandre Brongniart and the Triumph of Art and Innovation*, New Haven and London, 1997.

34. Brongniart had to intervene to prevent this vase's destruction in 1815, which he considered, 'the finest piece made by the factory', ('le plus beau qui soit sorti des ateliers de la Manufacture'). M. Brunet and T. Préaud, *Sèvres: Des origines à nos jours*, Fribourg, 1978, p.250.

35. G. de Bellaigue, *Carlton House: The Past Glories of George IV's Palace*, London, The Queen's Gallery, 1991–2, no.52.

36. He acted as artistic adviser to the Sèvres factory from as early as 1805, and wrote later that 'Il m'est venu dans la tête un charmant grouppe (sic) egyptien d'une facile exécution pour porter des fruits crus, glacés ou sec et qui, tout à la fois, entrerait dans le service et la décoration du surtout. Dîtes-moi si vous pouvez avec quelque pureté faire de l'architecture . . . Avec un succès assuré dans cette partie, nous obtiendrons un surtout tout à fait monumental'. C. Truman, 'Emperor, King and Duke: the Sèvres Egyptian Service acquired for the Nation', *The Connoisseur*, 202 (1979), pp.148–56.

37. C. Truman, *The Sèvres Egyptian Service 1810–1812*, London, Victoria and Albert Museum, 1982.

38. R. de Plinval de Guillebon, *Paris Porcelain 1770–1850*, London, 1972, pp.200ff; see also R. de Plinval de Guillebon, *Faïence, Porcelaine de Paris. 18e & 19e Siècles*, Paris, 1995.

39. The *Gazette de France* for 21 December 1804, observed: 'The taste for the forms of the Antique now extends to the most fragile belongings of a fashionable woman: her water jug and sugar bowl must have the shape of a roman vase; her soup bowl must be in the Greek taste, and she would give up taking salt at dinner, if the pot that holds it is neither in the Etruscan nor the Attic fashion.' (Le goût des formes antiques s'est étendu jusqu'aux meubles les plus fragiles de l'appartement d'une élégante, son pot à l'eau, son sucrier doivent avoir la forme d'un vase romain; sa soupière doit être grecque; et elle renoncerait à prendre du sel à table, si la coupe qui le contient n'était ni étrusque, ni attique'.) quoted in R. de Plinval de Guillebon, 'La Porcelaine à Paris sous le Consulat et l'Empire', *Bibliothèque de la Société Française d'Archéologie*, 18, Paris, 1985, p.38.

40. The *faïence* makers, led by Richard Glot, mayor of Sceaux and owner of the factory there, wrote a letter of protest saying that about 230–240 factories would have to close down, and 32,500 people would lose their jobs. A. Lane, *French Faïence*, London, 1958, p.17.

41. 'War eine lange Tafel schon festlich gedeckt, buntes Naschwerk schimmerte zwischen den künstlich gefalteten Servietten, in der Mitte ein prächtiger, altmodischer Aufsatz mit Pomeranzenbäumchen von Wachs und porzellananemen Götterfiguren, die sich in dem Spiegelboden, wie in einem Weiher verdoppleten'. Eichendorff, *Dichter und ihre Gesellen*, vol.1, ch. 12, quoted in U. Erichsen-Firle, *Kunstgewerbemuseum der Stadt Köln: Figürliches Porzellan*, Cologne, 1975, p.20.

42. J. Kunze, 'Zur Dekorationsbranche der Meissner Porzellanmanufaktur nach 1814 bis zum Jahre 1860' *Keramos*, 135 (1992), pp.3–36.

43. W. and I. Baer, *Auf Allerhöchster Befehl: Königgeschenke aus der Königlichen Porzellan-Manufaktur Berlin KPM*, Berlin, 1983; I. Baer, *Along the Royal Road: Berlin and Potsdam in KPM Porcelain and Painting 1815–1848*, New York, 1998.

44. H. Glaser (ed.), *Wittelsbach und Bayern: Krone und Verfassung: König Max I. Joseph und der neue Staat*, Munich, 1980, nos.1232–1236.

45. R. Rückert, 'Wittelsbacher Porzellan: Tassen und Vasen des frühen 19. Jahrhunderts', *Kunst und Antiquäten*, I–III, 1980, pp.30–9, 24–31, 20–35.

46. J. V. G. Mallet, 'Rococo English Porcelain: a study in style', *Apollo*, 90 (1969), p.113, fig. 19.

47. This was despite the economic blockade of the Napoleonic wars (the goods were exported via Hamburg).

48. In 1809 he acquired a magnificent rococo garniture

of 1757 of a *pot-pourri gondole* and two *vases héberts* in rose from the dealer Robert Fogg. G. de Bellaigue, *Sèvres Porcelain from the Royal Collection*, Queen's Gallery, London, 1979, nos.59,60.

49. Savill, *The Wallace Collection; Sèvres Porcelain*, London, 1988, p.1167.

50. E. M. Nance, *The Pottery and Porcelain of Swansea and Nantgarw*, 1942.

51. In 1816 an announcement in *The Courier* stated that 'The Sevre China Manufacture has now Competitors which bid fair to excel in the Article of China. The Manufactories at Coalbrook-Dale and at Swansea having just completed some beautiful specimens.' quoted in F. A. Barrett, 'Caughley and Coalport, in R. J. Charleston (ed.), *English Porcelain 1745–1850*, London, 1965, p.110.

52. P. Hughes, 'The French Influence on Swansea and Nantgarw', *The Connoisseur*, CLXXXVIII (1975), pp.260–7.

53. His nephew, John Randall (1810–1910) wrote that he succeeded 'in producing a fret body with a rich glaze which bore so close a resemblance to old Sèvres china that connoisseurs and famous judges failed to distinguish them. He refused, however, from conscientious motives, to put the Sèvres mark, the initials of Louis Louis, crossed at the bottom'. However, 'Mr. Robins had less hesitation however in putting the Sèvres mark on what was known to be Sèvres; and he did very much for Mortlock, Jarman and Baldock, who had agents in Paris, attending all sales where Sèvres was to be sold, in redecorating it in the most elaborate and costly manner. The less scrupulous London agents however did not hesitate to pass it off as being really the work of Sèvres artists. Indeed they have been known to have boxes of china going up from Madeley, sent on to Dover, to be redirected as coming from France, inviting connoisseurs to come and witness them being unpacked on their arrival, as they represented, from Paris. A little entertainment would be got up and supposing themselves to be the first whose eyes looked on the rich goods after they left the French capital, where it would be represented, perhaps, that they had been bought of the Duc-de . . . or of Madame some-one, after having been in the possession of royalty, they would buy freely'. J. Randall, *History of Madeley*, pp.207–8.

54. See H. Coutts, 'Josephine Bowes and the Craze for Collecting Ceramics in the 19th Century', *The International Ceramics Fair* Handbook, 1992, pp.16–23.

55. In 1828 the Inspector of the factory, Heinrich Gottlieb Kühn, wrote that *the first important foreign business connection definitely developed in 1815 when the chiefs of the London firm Rittner and Saxby came here in person, bought a quantity of old-fashioned wares in the contemporary English taste, and kept an uninterrupted connection with the manufactory from this time on. From the year 1825 onwards, however, this connection became more important and spread to other London firms, among whom Enthoven of London (and later the London dealer Elias Bearkley) did by far the greatest business, and now became so important for the manufactory that in 1825 the sale to England, almost without exception in objects of the dominant taste of 70 years earlier, realised a sum of 26,261 taler* 'Die erste bedeutende auswartige Geschaftsverbindung entspann sich nämlich im Jahre 1815, wo die Chefs des Londoner Hauses Rittner & Saxby in Person hierherkamen; eine Parthie veralteter Waren in jetzige englischen Geschmacke kauften, und von dieser Zeit an in ununterbrochener Verbindung mit der Manufaktur blieben. Erst vom Jahre 1825 an wurde diese aber bedeutender und auch auf mehrere Londoner Handlungshauser, unter denen Enthoven aus London bei weitem die grössten Geschafte machte (später noch der Handler Elias Bearkley aus London, d. Verf.) ausgedehnt und nun fur die Manufaktur so wichtig, dass im Jahre 1825 der Debit nach England, fast durchgangig in Gegenstanden des vor 70 Jahren herrschenden Geschmacks, eine Summe von 26 261 Talern ausmachte.' quoted in J. Kunze, 'Die Bedeutung des 'Englischen Handels' mit Porzellanen im 'Altfranzösischen Geschmack' der Meissner Manufaktur in der ersten Hälfte des 19. Jahrhunderts', *Keramos*, 95, 1982, p.37.

56. A. and A. Cox, 'New Light on large Rockingham vases', *Connoisseur*, 173, 1970, pp.238–243.

57. G. Reitlinger, *The Economics of Taste: Volume II: The rise and fall of objets d'art prices since 1750*, London, 1963, p.53.

58. S. Bury, 'The lengthening shadow of Rundell's', *The Connoisseur*, February, 1966, pp.79–80.

59. J. Physick, *The Victoria and Albert Museum*, London, 1982, p.16; see also Malcom Baker and Brenda Richardson (ed.), *A Grand Design: The Art of the Victoria and Albert Museum*, London and Baltimore, 1997.

Index